THE CONCEPT OF

OXFORD MONOGRAPHS ON LABOUR LAW

General Editors: Paul Davies, Senior Research Fellow of Harris Manchester College, Oxford; Keith Ewing, Professor of Public Law at King's College, London; and Mark Freedland, Emeritus Research Fellow of St John's College, Oxford.

This series has come to represent a significant contribution to the literature of British, European, and international labour law. The series recognizes the arrival not only of a renewed interest in labour law generally, but also the need for fresh approaches to the study of labour law following a period of momentous change in the UK and Europe. The series is concerned with all aspects of labour law, including traditional subjects of study such as collective labour law and individual employment law. It also includes works that concentrate on the growing role of human rights and the combating od discrimination in employment, and others that examine the law and economics of the labour market and the impact of social security law and of national and supranational employment policies upon patterns of employment and the employment contract. Two of the contributing authors to the series, Lucy Vickers and Diamond Ashiagbor, have received awards from the Society of Legal Scholars in respect of their books.

Titles published in the series

A Purposive Approach to Labour Law
Guy Davidov

Bullying and Behavioural Conflict at Work
The Duality of Individual Rights
Lizzie Barmes

The Labour Constitution
The Enduring Idea of Labour Law
Ruth Dukes

The Legal Construction of Personal Work Relations
Mark Freedland FBA and Nicola Kountouris

A Right to Care?
Unpaid Work in European Employment Law
Nicole Busby

Regulating Flexible Work
Deirdre McCann

Welfare to Work
Conditional Rights in Social Policy
Amir Paz-Fuchs

EU Intervention in Domestic Labour Law
Phil Syrpis

Towards a Flexible Labour Market
Labour Legislation and Regulation since the 1990s
Paul Davies and Mark Freedland

The European Employment Strategy
Labour Market Regulation and New Governance
Diamond Ashiagbor

The Law of the Labour Market
Industrialization, Employment, and Legal Evolution
Simon Deakin and Frank Wilkinson

The Personal Employment Contract
Mark Freedland

International and European Protection of the Right to Strike
A Comparative Study of Standards Set by the International Labour Organization, the Council of Europe and the European Union
Tonia Novitz

Freedom of Speech and Employment
Lucy Vickers

Women and the Law
Sandra Fredman

Just Wages for Women
Aileen McColgan

The Concept of the Employer

JEREMIAS PRASSL

OXFORD
UNIVERSITY PRESS

OXFORD
UNIVERSITY PRESS

Great Clarendon Street, Oxford, OX2 6DP,
United Kingdom

Oxford University Press is a department of the University of Oxford.
It furthers the University's objective of excellence in research, scholarship,
and education by publishing worldwide. Oxford is a registered trade mark of
Oxford University Press in the UK and in certain other countries

First published 2015
Reprinted with corrections 2015
First published in paperback 2016

Published in the United States of America by Oxford University Press
198 Madison Avenue, New York, NY 10016, United States of America

British Library Cataloguing in Publication Data
Data available

Library of Congress Cataloging in Publication Data
Data available

ISBN 978–0–19–873553–3 (Hbk.)
ISBN 978–0–19–879614–5 (Pbk.)

To my
Mother and Father

. . . nihil tantum repugnat ne verbis illustretur, at nihil adeo necesse est ante hominum oculos proponere ut certas quasdam res, quas esse neque demonstrari neque probari potest, quae contra eo ipso, quod pii diligentesque viri illas quasi ut entia tractant, enti nascendique facultati paululum appropinquant.

H.H.

General Editors' Preface

Almost exactly fifty years ago Lord Wedderburn introduced his new 'simple account of the relationship between British workers and the law' with the words, which became famous, 'Most workers want nothing more of the law than that it should leave them alone' (*The Worker and the Law,* 1965, p 9). In a very changed environment, it could now be said with equal force that most employers want nothing more of the law than that it should leave *them* alone. In its treatment of relations between workers and employers, both individual and collective, English law does not 'leave employers alone' and nor should it do so, but there are some serious shortcomings in the way that it understands and deals with the concept of the employer. This book focuses on those shortcomings and tries to suggest some ways of repairing them.

As the Series Editors, we are very pleased to include this volume in the Labour Law Monographs Series. The volume builds on the author's doctoral thesis and article writings, and we are sure that it will come to be regarded as having made an authoritative contribution to this somewhat neglected and under-theorised aspect of the law of the employment relation. Its claims to that authoritative status will, we think, be reinforced by the ways in which it explores the corporate law dimension of the concept of the employer, especially in the context of Private Equity, and also develops a comparative perspective upon the concept by means of a careful study of the notion of the *Konzern* in German law—both of those being methodologies of which Lord Wedderburn, among others, would have approved as offering crucial insights to English labour law.

Moreover, it seems to us that this highly original work is timely in a practical as well as a theoretical sense. There is a great deal of policy debate about the extension of moral and legal responsibility for exploitative employment practices 'further back up the supply chain' both nationally and internationally, and this book offers much in the way of finely textured technical argumentation to those discussions. In recent years we have been in the fortunate position of being able to commend new additions to our series on the basis that they will maintain and add to the cumulatively high standing of the previously published volumes. We confidently make that assertion with regard to this engaging and innovative new book.

PLD
KDE
MRF
1 December 2014

Preface to the Paperback Edition

The central theme of this book is how the law should grapple with multilateral employment relationships. The proposed functional concept of the employer ascribes responsibilities to the entity, or combination of entities, exercising the functions regulated in a particular domain of employment law. This approach, I suggest, allows us accurately to ascribe responsibility regardless of how complex the underlying work arrangements might be.

The functional concept is developed in the following chapters with particular emphasis on outsourced or agency work and in the context of Private Equity portfolio companies. Since completion of the original manuscript nearly two years ago, the emergence of digital labour markets has presented employment lawyers with a further set of related challenges. A wide range of applications and online platforms have sprung up to connect workers with customers seeking help in the completion of tasks from transportation and domestic work to data processing. Perhaps as a result of their rapid ascent, these digital marketplaces for work are often discussed as novel phenomena. From a legal perspective, however, 'crowdwork' is but the most recent instantiation of the difficulties at the heart of subsequent discussion: the exercise of core employer functions, from hiring and directing workers to paying and firing them, has become fragmented across multiple entities. Whilst a detailed application of the functional concept in this context was beyond the scope of minor revisions for this edition, I hope that the approach proposed might nonetheless prove useful in on-going discussions surrounding the legal status of workers and employers in emerging forms of multilateral work organisation.

J.F.B.B.P.
1 June 2016

Preface

Commenting on his series of paintings depicting faceless men in bowler hats, René Magritte (1898–1967) once noted that:

Everything we see hides another thing; we always want to see what is hidden by what we see. There is an interest in that which is hidden and which the visible does not show us. This interest can take the form of a quite intense feeling, a sort of conflict, one might say, between the visible that is hidden and the visible that is present.

The present work hopes to look behind one such visible that is nearly always present in employment law—the concept of the employee—in order to explore that which is often hidden and which the visible does not show us: the concept of the employer as counterparty to the contract of employment. It is an adaptation of my doctoral thesis, and its completion gives me the opportunity to acknowledge the help which I have had in writing not only this book but the thesis which preceded it. This, above all, is to acknowledge the intellectual example, generosity, and kindness of my *Doktorvater*, Mark Freedland, without whose wise counsel and encouragement neither project would have found fruition.

My two years of doctoral research were funded by the Arts and Humanities Research Council (Studentship *AH/I012826/1*), as well as smaller grants from the Foundation of the Swiss National Bank, the Faculty of Law, University of Oxford, and Magdalen College, Oxford. Columbia Law School, New York, and the Max Planck Institute of Comparative and International Private Law, Hamburg, kindly supported extended research visits. Officials at the European Commission (DG MARKET) provided helpful guidance and discussion of the design and impact of the AIFMD on the Private Equity industry. Tim Jenkinson at the Said Business School, Sean Rainey at Magdalen, and my former colleagues at UBS Investment Bank provided many an important lead into the world of PE; I am deeply grateful to all those fund managers, CEOs, bankers, professional advisers, and industry representatives who agreed to be interviewed, albeit on the condition of strict anonymity.

My examiners, Paul Davies and Simon Deakin, subjected the completed thesis to extensive scrutiny and provided many helpful suggestions for the further development of its enquiries in a stimulating viva and many conversations since. Anne Davies's comments at earlier stages were equally important in shaping and refining its arguments. Eli Ball, Hugh Collins, Joshua Getzler, Gregor Hogan, Franck Lirzin, and Ben Spagnolo commented extensively on the draft manuscript for the present book, and saved me from many an infelicity. I have attempted to state the law as of 1 October 2014; the responsibility for all remaining errors is, of course, entirely mine.

It would not have been possible to complete this work without the support, comments and criticisms of my teachers, colleagues, and friends. I am grateful, in particular, to George Adams, Einat Albin, John Armour, Diamond Ashiagbor, Sue Ashtiany, Dan Awrey, Roderick Bagshaw, Lizzie Barmes, Catherine Barnard, Ulf Bernitz, Michal Bobek, Leon Brittan, Nicola Countouris, Paul Linton Cowie, Richard Ekins, Judy Fudge, Rob George, Sir Roy Goode, Tamás Gyulavári, Angus Johnston, Jeff King, Dorota Leczykiewicz, Sylvaine Laulom, Antonio Lo Faro, Piera Loi, Amy Ludlow, Antoine Lyon-Caen, Luke Mason, Sonia McKay, Hans Peter Meister, Sandy Meredith, Jenny Payne, Amir Paz-Fuchs, Francis Reynolds, Christopher Roeder, Roger Smith, Jane Stapleton, Alain Supiot, Stefan Vogenauer, and Steve Weatherill. As regards comparative matters, I am in the debt of Paula Aschauer, Leopold Bauer, Reinhard Bork, Horst Call, Martin Flohr, Andreas von Goldbeck, Klaus Hopt, Elisabeth Kohlbacher, Laurenz Liedermann, Robert Rebhahn, Martin Voelker, Bernd Waas, Christine Windbichler, and Reinhard Zimmermann for guiding my first steps in German law. In the United States, I benefitted greatly from discussions with Mark Barenberg, Jack Coffee, Cindy Estlund, Ron Gilson, Lynn Rhinehart, and Katherine Stone. Cathy Ruckelshaus and her colleagues at NELP kindly invited me on several occasions to present my ideas to policy makers and practitioners in Washington, DC.

I am grateful to the series editors of the *Oxford Monographs on Labour Law* and my anonymous reviewers for agreeing to publish this work, as well as Alex Flach, Natasha Flemming, and their team at OUP for help at each stage of the publishing process. Thomson Reuters and Hart Publishing, an imprint of Bloomsbury Publishing plc, kindly granted permission to draw on material first published in the *Law Quarterly Review* ('The Notion of the Employer' (2013) 129 LQR 380) and in *The Autonomy of Labour Law* (Hart 2015), a collection edited with A Bogg, C Costello, and A Davies.

I submit this manuscript ten years to the day after I first came up to Oxford. Writing on the eve of becoming an Official Fellow of Magdalen College, I am deeply aware of how tremendously lucky I have been to have the love and support of my entire family, as well as enjoying terrific institutional support and personal guidance throughout the years. In addition to those already mentioned, special thanks are due to Geoffrey Tindyebwa at the Lester B Pearson United World College of the Pacific for introducing me to the joys of writing. As a student in Oxford, I greatly benefited from the teaching and guidance of Liz Fisher, Lucia Zedner, Eloise Scotford, and Simon Douglas at Corpus and Katharine Grevling, my graduate advisor at Magdalen. Gráinne de Búrca, Ben Sachs, and Cass Sunstein supervised my early research efforts at Harvard. Peter Mirfield and Rob George led me through my first teaching steps whilst a Stipendiary Lecturer at Jesus College, and during my subsequent years as a Supernumerary Fellow of St John's, I could not have had better pupil masters than Paul Craig and Simon Whittaker.

Beyond the library, many friends were there with me throughout the research years: Sebastian Butschek, Ben Gardner, Hannah Glover, Ben Jones, Liz Lindesay, Aidan Reay, and Johannes Terwitte always lent a kind ear. Joe Abdalla, Clare Bucknell, Anna Cairns, Hannah Davison, James Hillis, Jess Howley, Kate Mitchell, Marius Ostrowski, the Rev'd Michael Piret, Olivia Reilly, Jaani

Riordan, and Sam Thelin made Magdalen a marvellous place to live, as did James Anderson, Graham Barrett, Maria Bruna, Peter Fifield, Antonia Fitzpatrick, the Rev'd Elizabeth Macfarlane and Emma Smith, Sir Michael Scholar, Edmund Sprott, Abi Stone, Matthew Walker, Tim Webber, and Hannah Williams at St John's. Ehud and Cecile Barak, Jeremiah and Pierre Evarts-Amariglio, and Shai Schmidt welcomed me in New York during the final thesis write-up, most of which took place in Dina and Paul Stukanow-Paterson's living room; Charles Rufus 'Cookie' and Tilly Adams provided much-needed distraction whilst completing the book manuscript at Ivy Farm. Above all, however, I have been sustained every day by the joy, love, and encouragement of life with Abi Adams.

Last, but by no means least, two Hertford labour lawyers deserve special mention: Alan Bogg and Ben Ogden. I first studied labour law primarily on the basis that tutorials were going to be given by Alan, and was richly rewarded: not only by some of the very best teaching I have ever experienced, but also insofar as the very idea for my thesis, and thus this book, was first conceived on a Tuesday evening walk home from Alan's lecture on *The Composition of the Workforce*. A further attraction in taking labour law was the opportunity to share those weekly discussions with Ben, whose sharp intellect and cheeky grin I had come deeply to admire during our Erasmus adventures on the Continent. The joy and elation of putting the finishing touches to my doctoral thesis were overshadowed by the news of Ben's tragic death in September 2012, shortly after his qualification into A&O's employment law team. He is missed every day.

J.F.B.B.P.
Michaelmas Day 2014
Magdalen College, Oxford

Contents

PART II. THE IMPLICATIONS OF A CONCEPT
UNDER PRESSURE

PART III. TOWARDS A FUNCTIONAL CONCEPT OF THE EMPLOYER

Table of Abbreviations

AG	*Aktiengesellschaft*
AIF	Alternative Investment Fund
AIFM Directive	Directive (EU) 61/2011 of the European Parliament and of the Council on Alternative Investment Fund Managers and amending Directives 2003/41/EC and 2009/65/EC and Regulations (EC) No 1060/2009 and (EU) No 1095/2010 [2011] OJ L174/1
AIV	Alternative Investment Vehicle
AktG 1965	*Aktiengesetz 1965*
ARD	Acquired Rights Directive (Council Directive (EC) 23/2001 on the approximation of the laws of the Member States relating to the safeguarding of employees' rights in the event of transfers of undertakings, businesses or parts of undertakings or businesses [2001] OJ L82/16)
ASPV	Acquisition Special Purpose Vehicle
AÜG 2003	*Arbeitnehmerüberlassungsgesetz 2003*
BAG	*Bundesarbeitsgericht*
BetrVG 1972	*Betriebsverfassungsgesetz 1972*
BGB	*Bürgerliches Gesetzbuch*
BGH	*Bundesgerichtshof*
BVCA	British Venture Capital and Private Equity Association
BVG	*Bundesverfassungsgericht*
CA	Court of Appeal
CEO	Chief Executive Officer
CJEU	Court of Justice of the European Union
Collective Redundancies Directive	Council Directive (EC) 59/1998 on the approximation of the laws of the Member States relating to collective redundancies [1998] OJ L225/16
DDA 1995	Disability Discrimination Act 1995
DrittelBG 2004	*Drittelbeteiligungsgesetz 2004*
EASI	Employment Agencies Standards Inspectorate
EAT	Employment Appeals Tribunal
EBITDA	Earnings Before Interest, Taxes, Depreciation, and Amortization
ECSR	European Committee on Social Rights
EHRC	Equality and Human Rights Commission
ERA 1996	Employment Rights Act 1996
ET	Employment Tribunal
EU	European Union

EVCA	European Private Equity and Venture Capital Association
GLA	Gangmasters Licensing Authority
GmbHG 1892	*Gesetz betreffend die Gesellschaften mit beschränkter Haftung 1892*
GP	General Partner
HC	High Court
HR	Human Resources
HSWA 1974	Health and Safety at Work Act 1974
ICFC	Industrial and Commercial Finance Corporation
IDREC	Inter-Divisional Research Ethics Committee
ILO	International Labour Organization
KSchG 1969	*Kündigungsschutzgesetz 1969*
Information and Consultation Directive	Directive (EC) 14/2002 of the Council and the European Parliament of 11 March 2002 establishing a general framework for informing and consulting employees in the European Community [2002] OJ L80/29
KWC	*Konzern* Works Council
LBO	Leveraged Buy-Out
LP	Limited Partner
MBI	Management Buy-In
MBO	Management Buy-Out
MitbestG 1976	*Mitbestimmungsgesetz 1976*
MontanMitbestG 1951	*Montanmitbestimmungsgesetz 1951*
P2P	Public to Private
PE	Private Equity
RRA 1976	Race Relations Act 1976
SDA 1975	Sex Discrimination Act 1975
SER	Standard Employment Relationship
SPV	Special Purpose Vehicle
TFEU	Consolidated Version of the Treaty on the Functioning of the European Union
TUC	Trades Union Congress
TULRCA 1992	Trade Union and Labour Relations (Consolidation) Act 1992
TUPE 2006	Transfer of Undertakings (Protection of Employment) Regulations 2006
UKSC	United Kingdom Supreme Court

Table of Cases

Court of Justice of the European Union

European Court of Human Righs

Germany

Table of Cases

United States of America

Australia

Table of Legislation

United Kingdom Statutes

United Kingdom Statutory Instruments

European Union Directives

Germany

International Labour Organization

United States

Introduction

The Concept of the Employer and the Personal Scope of Employment Law

The contract of employment is the central gateway to employment rights in English law.[1] Only individuals privy to that relationship are classified as employees, and can thus come within the full scope of employment protective norms. Those labouring in work arrangements outside that narrow paradigm, on the other hand, find themselves labelled as non-employee workers or independent contractors, and thus without recourse to the highest levels of protection. The question as to an individual's employment status has therefore become a crucial issue in determining the application of employment law norms.[2] In developing the concept of the employer as counterparty to the contract of employment instead of pursuing the more traditional enquiries surrounding definitions of the employee, the present work adopts an 'unfamiliar perspective, indeed initially a counterintuitive one'.[3] It argues that the received unitary concept of a single-entity employer is an increasingly salient factor in workers' falling outside the personal scope of employment law, as individuals employed in multilateral work arrangements can no longer satisfactorily identify the relevant counterparty to bear employment law obligations. A move towards a functional concept, which identifies the employer—or indeed a group of employers—through the exercise of a particular set of functions (such as, for example, the provision of pay), on the other hand, represents an important step towards restoring coherence in the personal scope of labour law.

The present introduction briefly charts the conceptual problems resulting from employment law's near-exclusive focus on the classification of employees as party to a bilateral contract of employment in determining the personal scope of employment law, and suggests that the enquiry should be widened also to include

---

[1] In the context of employment regulation, the terms English law and United Kingdom law will be used interchangeably. See A Bradley and K Ewing, *Constitutional and Administrative Law* (15th edn Pearson 2010) 40; Trade Union and Labour Relations (Consolidation) Act 1992 (hereinafter, 'TULRCA 1992') s 301(1).

[2] The terms 'employment law' and 'labour law' are used interchangeably throughout this work.

[3] P Davies and M Freedland, 'The Complexities of the Employing Enterprise' in G Davidov and B Langile (eds), *Boundaries and Frontiers of Labour Law* (Hart 2006) 273.

the concept of the employer. Subsequent sections then set out the central argument and overall structure of the work, and outline its scope and methodological approach. A final section sketches the broader implications of a reconceptualized definition of the employer for the scope of employment protective norms in English law.

Broadening the Enquiry

In their exploration of the 'Complexities of the Employing Enterprise', Freedland and Davies note that:

> The normal course of debate about the personal scope of employment law takes place primarily within a paradigm of bilateral . . . contracts between a worker and an employer. The problem about personal scope is perceived primarily or even solely as one of designating the appropriate category of workers to be included within the scope of legislation governing the employment relation. The primarily and traditionally appropriate category is that of dependent employees, in English law those with contracts of employment.[4]

How did employment law come to consider the employment relationship, whether in its individual or collective dimension, primarily from the perspective of the employee? The early normative focus of the discipline was of course directly related to the individual worker,[5] in the sense of rebalancing the employee's inequality of bargaining power inherent in the employment relationship.[6] What started out as the purpose of employment law, however, soon began to have an equally significant impact on the conceptual question as to which apparatus could best achieve that aim. The individual's status as an employee, self-employed contractor or later worker thus became one of, if not indeed the, key enquiry of employment law.

The present work unequivocally accepts the worker's perspective as the appropriate analytical and normative focus for employment law's fundamental concerns.[7] It does set out to question, however, the extent to which a *conceptual* focus on the worker may have come to hamper that larger enterprise by neglecting complex issues and difficult questions surrounding the concept of the employer.

Over more than a century, a considerable amount of case law and scholarship has built up to develop, adapt, and refine a series of common law tests such as control, economic reality, and mutuality of obligation to 'draw a fundamental distinction between employment which is categorized as "dependent" or "subordinate" and that which is "independent" or "autonomous"'.[8] This binary divide distinguishes between individuals who work under a contract of employment or service and therefore 'come under the scope of employment protection and social

---

[4] Davies and Freedland, 'Complexities of the Employing Enterprise' (n 3) 273–4.
[5] K Wedderburn, *The Worker and the Law* (3rd edn Penguin 1986).
[6] P Davies and M Freedland, *Kahn-Freund's Labour and the Law* (Stevens 1983) 14, 69.
[7] For recent discussion, see M Freedland and N Kountouris, *The Legal Construction of Personal Work Relations* (OUP 2011) 364 ff (The Personal Work Profile).
[8] S Deakin and G Morris, *Labour Law* (6th edn Hart 2012) 145.

security legislation' on the one hand, and those who work under a contract for services, which attracts 'fewer of the burdens or benefits of dependent status' on the other.[9]

The resulting model of employment regulation, based on the assumption of a binary—or more recently tripartite—composition of the labour market,[10] has fundamentally been challenged by economic and social developments, particularly as regards the scope and application of employment law norms in increasingly complex organizational settings. A 'tectonic shift in employment relations over the past 20 years', Fudge notes, 'has shaken the foundations of the legal architecture of the employment relationship'.[11] Examples can be drawn from a wide range of extensively analysed circumstances, from the explosive growth of so-called 'atypical' forms of work[12] to new models of business organization resulting from the vertical disintegration of enterprise.[13] A classic illustration combining both elements is the supply of workers by a temporary work agency to end-user clients. There, the definition of the employee as party to a bilateral contract of employment will usually classify the individual worker as an independent or autonomous contractor, without recourse to some of the most significant employment rights. The long-diagnosed crisis in the fundamental concepts of labour law[14] has therefore become 'if anything more serious, so far as employment contracts are concerned'.[15]

Employment law is of course not alone in its difficulty in grappling with new multilateral organizational models[16] and the resulting complex relationships across legally distinct entities.[17] Their negative impact, however, can be particularly harsh in employment law, as the individual worker may be left without recourse to even the most basic employment protection.[18] A near-exclusive focus on the concept of the employee and regulatory questions surrounding its definition has played a significant part in precipitating this crisis, by allowing a conceptual vacuum to

---

[9] Deakin and Morris, *Labour Law* (n 8) 145.

[10] The more recent development of additional categories such as the 'worker' concept do not fundamentally alter the binary approach, in so far as they assume similar characteristics for, and thus a high degree of homogeneity within, each category of workers. See *Byrne Bros Ltd v Baird* [2002] ICR 667 (EAT); *Redrow Homes Ltd v Wright* [2004] EWCA Civ 469, [2004] 3 All ER 98; *Jivraj v Hashawani* [2011] UKSC 40, [2011] 1 WLR 1872; though cf now *Clyde & Co LLP v Bates van Winkelhof* [2014] UKSC 32, [2014] 1 WLR 2047.

[11] J Fudge, 'The Legal Boundaries of the Employer, Precarious Workers, and Labour Protection' in G Davidov and B Langile (eds), *Boundaries and Frontiers of Labour Law* (Hart 2006) 296.

[12] S Fredman, 'Labour Law in Flux: The Changing Composition of the Workforce' (1997) 26 ILJ 337, 339.

[13] H Collins, 'Independent Contractors and the Challenge of Vertical Disintegration to Employment Protection Laws' (1990) 10 OJLS 353, 356.

[14] K Wedderburn, R Lewis, and J Clark (eds), *Labour Law and Industrial Relations: Building on Kahn-Freund* (Clarendon Press 1983) vi.

[15] M Freedland, *The Personal Employment Contract* (OUP 2003) 26.

[16] G Teubner and H Collins, *Networks as Connected Contracts* (Hart 2011) 98ff.

[17] R Gilson, C Sabel, and R Scott, 'Braiding: the Interaction of Formal and Informal Contracting in Theory, Practice and Doctrine' (2010) 110 Columbia Law Review 1377, 1389.

[18] L Benería 'Shifting the Risk: New Employment Patterns, Informalization, and Women's Work' (2001) 15 International Journal of Politics, Culture and Society 272, 348.

develop on the non-worker side of the employment relationship, filled by nothing more than a vague notion reminiscent of old concepts such as the servant's master. This impact was dramatically exacerbated by developments in the structure and organization of the modern enterprise. Just as workers have become a very heterogeneous group, so have the firms employing them: as a result of the facility with which corporate group structures can be set up and controlled and the wide availability of a labour force which can be sourced from external providers, modern work arrangements frequently involve more than one entity with control over when, where, and how work is done. As Weil concludes, '[l]ike a rock with a fracture that deepens and spreads with time, the workplace over the past three decades has fissured'.[19]

Given the traditional focus on defining the employee and the concomitant neglect of the concept of the employer, however, the regulatory responses to increasingly complex work relationships were once again primarily focused on the definition and position of the worker in specific subsets of the labour market.[20] The crucial problem with this approach is its assumption of a high degree of homogeneity in employment scenarios generally, and the problems faced by particular groups of employees in particular. It ignores the considerable degree of 'heterogeneity of [such] work',[21] as reflected in 'a growing nomenclature of "atypical" and "non-standard" work, apart from commonly used categories such as temporary, part-time and self employed work [and including terms such as] "reservist"; "on-call," and "as and when" contracts; "regular casuals"; "key-time" workers; "min-max" and "zero hours" contracts'.[22] The various categories of 'atypical' work will furthermore frequently overlap, for example where agency work incorporates a 'zero-hours contract dimension'.[23]

Even a very preliminary sketch of factual situations can therefore show that current approaches to labour market regulation will continue to fail in their attempts to grapple with the ever-increasing fragmentation or fissure of work arrangements. As long as attention remains focused on the employee category and related secondary conceptions alone, it will be very difficult to address the relevant questions at all. As Freedland and Davies have noted, there may well be a link between this limited focus on defining particular groups of employees and the increasing inefficiencies of the current situation, as technicalities arising from the

---

[19] D Weil, *The Fissured Workplace—Why Work Became so Bad for so Many, and What Can be Done to Improve It* (Harvard University Press 2014) 7.

[20] In domestic law, see eg the extension of anti-discrimination rights to 'contract workers': *Harrods Ltd v Remick* [1998] ICR 156 (CA). At EU level, see eg the equality duty with comparative workers: Directive (EC) 2008/104 of the European Parliament and of the Council of 19 November 2008 on temporary agency work [2008] OJ L327/9. For contrasting examples in US law, see the Fair Labor Standards Act 1938; C Ruckelshaus, R Smith, S Leberstein, and E Cho, *Who's the Boss: Resoring Accountability for Labor Standardas in Outsourced Work* (NELP 2014) 32ff.

[21] D McCann, *Regulating Flexible Work* (OUP 2008) 102.

[22] L Dickens, 'Exploring the Atypical: Zero Hours Contracts' (1997) 26 ILJ 262, 263.

[23] J O'Connor, 'Precarious Employment and EU Employment Regulation' in G Ramia, K Farnsworth, and Z Irving, *Social Policy Review 25: Analysis and Debate in Social Policy* (OUP 2013) 238.

current approach create strong avoidance incentives:[24] employers can easily avoid the vast majority of employment law obligations by recourse to relatively low-cost strategies such as corporate reorganization or the outsourcing of labour-intensive processes.

It is true, as Deakin has argued, that '[w]ork relations which fall on the "margins" of the employment category . . . have always posed a problem of classification', even though to 'point to the recurring nature of the problem is in no way to underestimate the problems involved in solving it today'.[25] Indeed, the persistent difficulties identified warrant further enquiry, albeit in different and perhaps initially counterintuitive directions. In their already-cited work, Davies and Freedland argue that:

some of the difficulties which attend the whole debate about the personal scope of employment can best be resolved, or at least understood, by questioning and de-constructing not, as is traditional, the concept of 'the worker' or 'the employee', but rather that of 'the employer', especially in the context of the contract of employment.[26]

It is this path which the current work hopes to pursue. It presents an enquiry into the legal concept of the employer; both as it has been historically received in the common law and as to how it could develop in future within that framework. An extensive discussion of this perspective is long overdue. As previous paragraphs have noted, numerous detailed conceptual accounts of the specific legal issues facing different types of atypical workers have been developed in recent years. This has yet to be matched by a similarly extensive body of scholarly thought on the employer side: there might be just as many variations on the other side of personal employment relationships. From a regulatory perspective, furthermore, the vast majority of measures regarding employers continue to be framed in terms of a unitary paradigm, thus often imposing liability at a single level even if key decisions in the work arrangement are taken by multiple entities. A 'deepening and reinforcement of the understanding of the employing organization may [therefore be amongst the most promising avenues to] optimise the personal scope of employment laws'.[27]

Argument and Structure in Outline

The central argument put forward in this work is the idea that the current concept of the employer is riddled with internal contradictions, as a result of which employment law coverage will quickly become incoherent or incomplete in complex, multilateral settings. These problems can only be addressed by a careful

---

[24] M Freedland and P Davies, 'Labour Markets, Welfare and the Personal Scope of Employment Law' (1999–2000) 21 CLLPJ 231, 235, 238.

[25] S Deakin, 'The Comparative Evolution of the Employment Relationship' in G Davidov and B Langile (eds), *Boundaries and Frontiers of Labour Law* (Hart 2006) 104.

[26] Davies and Freedland, 'Complexities of the Employing Enterprise' (n 3) 273.

[27] Davies and Freedland, 'Complexities of the Employing Enterprise' (n 3) 293.

reconceptualization and the development of a more openly functional concept, defining the employer as:

the entity, or combination of entities, playing a decisive role in the exercise of relational employing functions, and regulated or controlled as such in each particular domain of employment law.

The work is loosely divided into three parts, each reflecting a particular step in that endeavour. Part I focuses on the traditional concept of the employer, and explains how it has increasingly come under pressure. A first chapter explores two potentially contradictory strands of the received common law concept: the employer has come to be characterized as both a unitary and a multi-functional concept. The resulting tension does not readily become apparent in the traditional paradigm model of single-entity employment. Chapter 2, however, sets out a range of multilateral situations where employer functions are shared across or parcelled out between multiple entities. The two specific contexts to be explored are temporary agency work, where functions are divided between an employment agency and an end-user business, and complex corporate groups, in particular the structures created by Private Equity (PE) investments, where the PE shareholders become closely involved in their portfolio companies' day-to-day decision-making.

Part II then explores the implications of the concept under pressure, in order to demonstrate the significant practical impact of the tension inherent in the current concept of the employer, and to lay the groundwork for the final part. Chapter 3 demonstrates the fragile scope of employment law coverage, beginning with the near-complete inapplicability of protective provisions in the triangular agency work context. Discussion then turns to the incomplete and incoherent coverage that results from an inability to identify the relevant employer in complex corporate structures, as illustrated in the context of employee consultation in collective redundancies and transfers of undertakings. Chapter 4 presents a comparative excursion, analysing the conceptual apparatus developed in German employment and company law in response to the prevalence of large corporate groups. Put together, these chapters provide some of the fundamental criteria against which subsequent developments can be evaluated. Any reconceptualization, first, has to avoid an assumption of excessive homogeneity and thus be capable of accommodating a differentiated view of different domains of employment law. The changes proposed, second, need to remain anchored within existing regulatory frameworks, and represent a careful overall evolution of both the unitary and functional strand of the received concept of the employer. The functional concept to be developed, finally, will have to prove resilient to fast-paced changes in legal structures and commercial operations, focusing on the exercise of specific functions over considerations of legal structures.

The third part turns to that task of reconceptualizing the employer. Building on the specific deficiencies identified in previous parts, it proposes a careful modification of the existing concept. To this end, Chapter 5 explores the multi-functional strand: it develops the very idea of a functional concept, and shows different avenues in existing law through which that approach could be implemented.

Chapter 6, finally, returns to the need for a single concept to ensure coherence across different domains of employment law. It re-examines each of the aspects of the unitary concept as set out in Chapter 1 to demonstrate how the law has developed in those respects, and sets out a subtle reconfiguration in response. A brief overall conclusion tests whether the reconceptualization has been successful, both in practical terms and by addressing the fundamental tension head-on, and returns to the broader implications of a functional concept of the employer in English employment law.

Scope and Methodology

In order to facilitate analytical clarity within the space available, two limitations of scope are necessary. The first of these is as to the range of relationships under examination: the focus of the present work will be firmly on the employing entity as a counterparty to the contract of employment in English Law. This is not to suggest that the concept of the employer is analytically distinct in other personal work relations as a matter of logical necessity—in fact, many aspects are likely to be shared across all contracts personally to execute work. As the paradigm of employment relationships in the common law, the contract of service provides the most appropriate core model in embarking on an analysis of the concept of the employer.

The enquiry to follow will therefore be focused on the contract of employment and the parties to it. It is nonetheless important briefly to look beyond this subset, noting especially that none of the conclusions drawn should be read as a suggestion that opposite concepts apply automatically in other contracts for the personal execution of work. To the contrary, several observations apply directly to *all* personal work contracts. As regards the *unitary* perception of the employer, for example, this will be shown to be influenced by a range of factors, most of which are common to the vast majority of personal work relations—any conclusions drawn therefore extending by definition beyond the contract of service. The most prominent example here is the key role played by the contractual nature of the relationship: this framework has had a major influence, in both form and substance, in shaping the concept of the employer as unitary.[28] As nearly all work relationships have become perceived through this prism today, the unitary view of the parties to it is an essential feature of any personal work contract.

A significant proportion of the case law at the heart of the enquiry in Part I, on the other hand, has traditionally been used to draw a line between different categories of dependent labour, by determining whether the contractual relationship could be classified as one of employment.[29] Conclusions drawn from its analysis

---

[28] M Freedland, *The Contract of Employment* (OUP 1976).

[29] The case law on the definition of the more recent category of the worker is in that sense equally relevant, as the courts have found the distinction between workers and employees to be one of degree rather than kind: see n 10.

are therefore undoubtedly most relevant to the concept of the employer as counterparty to a contract of employment. Whether there are differences in the concepts of the employer in different forms of the employment relationship is beyond the immediate scope of this work; there is nothing however that would exclude the possibility of similar conclusions in other contexts. First, the focus on a subset of personal work relations does not suggest that it is in all regards analytically distinct from other arrangements for the personal execution of labour. Second, while the conceptualization of the contract of employment is built up in the case law through a juxtaposition of employees and those working under a contract for services or other personal work contracts, instructions on how to divide a category (such as personal work contracts) into subsets (including contracts of service and contracts for services) nonetheless reveal interesting aspects about the larger pool. It is, finally, not the practical application of the various tests that is of immediate interest but rather the inherent concepts underpinning each. Whilst the illustrations to be developed in subsequent parts of this work are carefully designed to show how a functional concept of the employer could be put into practice within existing structures, the functional approach developed could therefore equally encompass broader concepts, such as the personal employment contract or even personal work relations.[30]

A second, and similarly non-exclusive, limitation of scope arises from this focus on the contract of employment: for present purposes the collective dimension of relationships between workers and multiple employers cannot be discussed in great detail. Whilst the links between workers' collective voice and the common law in general,[31] and the contract of employment (and therefore the parties to it) in particular, have been the subject of detailed enquiry,[32] the overall domain remains heavily regulated by statutory intervention, and its impact on the concept of the employer might therefore appear somewhat limited.[33] This, however, is again not to be taken as a suggestion that the functional concept of the employer to be developed could not have an equally significant impact in that dimension of labour law, whether in the field of collective bargaining or in the course of industrial disputes. The correct identification of the employer, for example, is an important criterion when determining the lawfulness of a strike. Under what is known colloquially as the 'Golden Formula',[34] any such action will only be protected if it is done 'in contemplation or furtherance of a trade dispute'.[35] This notably means that any strike can only be directed by workers against their immediate employer[36]—a

---

[30] M Freedland, *The Personal Employment Contract* (OUP 2003); Freedland and Kountouris, *Legal Construction of Personal Work Relations* (n 7).

[31] M Freedland and N Kountouris, 'Common Law and Voice' in A Bogg and T Novitz, *Voices At Work—Continuity and Change in the Common Law World* (OUP 2014).

[32] D Brodie, 'Voice and the Employment Contract' in A Bogg and T Novitz, *Voices At Work—Continuity and Change in the Common Law World* (OUP 2014).

[33] With the notable exception, for present purposes, of discussion surrounding the information and consultation of employee representatives, as discussed in-depth in Chapter 3.2.

[34] Wedderburn, *The Worker and the Law* (n 5) 520; B Simpson, 'A Not So Golden Formula: In Contemplation or Furtherance of a Trade Dispute After 1982' (1983) 46 MLR 463, 476.

[35] TULRCA 1992, s 219(1).   [36] TULRCA 1992, s 244(1).

provision which the courts have continuously interpreted in a narrow fashion clearly reminiscent of the received unitary concept of the employer.[37]

This potential significance of the concept of the employer is also evident in the European Court of Human Rights' recent scrutiny of the United Kingdom's ban on secondary action,[38] where the Strasbourg Court explicitly referred to the fact that the narrow single-entity focus embodied in current legislation:

> could make it easy for employers to exploit the law to their advantage through resort to various legal stratagems, such as de-localising work-centres, outsourcing work to other companies and adopting complex corporate structures in order to transfer work to separate legal entities or to hive off companies . . . [as a result of which] trade unions could find themselves severely hampered in the performance of their legitimate, normal activities in protecting their members' interests.[39]

This, together with an earlier citation of the European Committee on Social Rights (ECSR)'s concern that English law could prevent 'a union from taking action against the *de facto* employer if this was not the immediate employer',[40] provides a stark reminder that the focus of subsequent parts on the individual dimension of labour should not be taken as a suggestion that the concept of the employer could not be an equally important question in the discipline's collective dimension.

A final preliminary point to be addressed is the change in methodology to be deployed at different points of the work. As Harlow, building on Dicey, has noted, the:

> possible weakness [of traditional common law methods of reasoning and analysis] as applied to the growth of institutions, is that it may induce men to think so much of the way in which an institution has come to be what it is, that they cease to consider with sufficient care what it is that an institution has [—and here the verbs 'should' and 'could' must be added—] become.[41]

The structure of this work is designed to overcome this weakness, echoed in Roben's observation that the 'greatest obstacle [to the changes proposed] will be not so much the intrinsic complexities of the subject as the fact that many of the arrangements under review are long established',[42] by consciously moving through the three steps implicit in Harlow's analysis and looking at what the institution or concept of the employer is at the moment ('has become'), what it *could* be and in the light thereof what it *should* be. Parts I and II operate within

---

[37] *Dimbleby v NUJ* [1984] IRLR 161; *UCL NHS Trust v UNISON* [1999] IRLR 31 (CA).

[38] *National Union of Rail, Maritime and Transport Workers v United Kingdom* (Application No 31045/10) [2014] IRLR 467; for convincing criticism see A Bogg and K Ewing, 'The Implications of the *RMT* Case' (2014) 43 ILJ 221, 235ff.

[39] *RMT v UK* (n 38) [98].   [40] *RMT v UK* (n 38) [37].

[41] A Dicey, *Introduction to the Study of the Law of the Constitution* (Macmillan 1885) Preface to the First Edition vii, as cited by C Harlow, 'Changing the Mindset: The Place of Theory in English Administrative Law' (1994) 14 OJLS 419, 426.

[42] A Robens, *Report of the Committee on Health and Safety at Work*, Cmnd 5043 (London 1972) 3 [41]: 'In the words of Bagehot (*Physics and Politics*) "one of the greatest pains to human nature is the pain of a new idea".'

the realm of positive law, applying a descriptive-analytical framework to tease out the *is*. They identify the underlying tension between two distinct strands of reasoning in the received common law concept, and demonstrate its implications across a wide range of potential factual scenarios. Part II simultaneously serves as a starting point for the analysis of what the concept *could* be, by looking at a range of potential solutions. The chapters of Part III continue with this analytical-descriptive approach, insofar as they draw on existing techniques and emphasize the feasibility of different models within current frameworks. At the same time, they mark a break with the previous chapters' limitations, turning to an openly normative approach to suggest that the concept of the employer *should* become a more overtly functional one, by proposing specific reforms to each of the two strands identified at the outset.

This shift from the analytical-descriptive to the normative in Part III is not a radical one, however. In eschewing a complete departure from the descriptive, the *should* carefully builds on the *could*: the functional approach advocated will go no further than necessary to resolve existing tensions, and remains as close as possible to the existing framework to address the fundamental challenge posed by complex work arrangements on its own terms, seeking 'to apply established legal principles to [multilateral organizational settings], and then gradually to adapt these principles'.[43]

A particularly important illustration of this approach can be found in the very concept of the employer to be analysed: Part I demonstrates the difficulties arising from the received unitary concept of the employer,[44] where the employer has come to be defined as a single entity, substantively identical in all circumstances and domains of employment law and beyond. Whether the issue at stake relates to unfair dismissal, collective redundancy consultation, or vicarious liability, the only employer identified will be a singular entity, privy to the contract of employment. Part III, on the other hand, advocates the abandonment of this narrow unitary approach, in favour of a functional concept of the employer, which identifies the party, or indeed parties, exercising the relevant employer functions as regulated in each particular domain or subset of employment law: the actual payment of wages (or a duty so to do), for example, will determine which entity will come under the obligation to ensure that national minimum wage levels have been met.

At first glance, this change suggests a rather radical departure from the existing concept, as different and sometimes even multiple entities could be designated as employers. Upon closer inspection, however, abandoning the unitary concept does

---

[43] D Marsden, ' "The Network Economy" and Models of the Employment Contract' (2004) 42 BJIR 659, 671.

[44] The present use of the word 'unitary' is not the only one seen in the literature. In Deakin's work on the evolution of the contract of employment, for example, 'unitary' denotes the single status that has emerged for all employees, distinct from that of independent contractors. See eg S Deakin, 'The Evolution of the Contract of Employment, 1900 to 1950—the Influence of the Welfare State' in N Whiteside and R Salais (eds), *Governance, Industry and Labour Markets in Britain and France—The Modernising State in the Mid-Twentieth Century* (Routledge 1998) 225.

not simultaneously imply that English law has to abandon its reliance on a single underlying concept of the employer. That overall framework, deeply ingrained in statutory provisions and the common law, is easily maintained throughout the proposed development away from a unitary and towards a functional concept of the employer. Indeed, as Chapter 6 explains in detail, the very existence of a single definition of the employer can be maintained only by adopting a functional concept, thus ensuring conceptual unity irrespective of factual complexity.

Restoring the Scope of Employment Law

In concluding this introduction, the final question to be raised is that as to the broader implications of a reconceptualized definition of the employer for the scope of employment protective norms in English law. The preceding discussion has already suggested that the work's focus on the concept of the employer is less of a rejection of existing frameworks rather than an attempt to view the perennial problem of personal scope from a different perspective.

As a result, the development of a functional concept of the employer does not represent a rejection of the concept of the employee or even of the contract of employment as key regulatory tools in employment law. The contract conundrum identified in Chapter 1 notes that the definition of an individual's employment status traditionally takes place in a rather circular line of enquiry, where two analytically distinct questions become intertwined: that as to the existence and definition of a contract of service and that as to the definition of its parties. On the one hand, both employee and employer could be seen as parties to a contract of service. On the other, a contract of service can only come into existence if both parties to it show the necessary features of employer and employee. Whilst puzzling in some analytical contexts, the resulting conundrum suggests that, for present purposes, the concept of the employer is closely tied in with both the identification of the employee and the contract of employment.

The functional concept of the employer proposed will therefore be designed to fit into the larger edifice of the contract of employment: Part III extensively analyses a series of different avenues through which it could be put into operation with surprisingly few changes in existing legal structures. The practical impact of the functional concept, on the other hand, could herald significant change from the status quo. English law's rigid adherence to a unitary concept of the employer has meant that the personal scope of protective norms has become vastly under-inclusive. As Weil explains, '[l]aws that protect workers have not kept pace with the new boundaries of the fissured workplace. [For example, legislator's] commitment to providing safety and health and decent conditions at the workplace has not changed. But relentless subcontracting can blur responsibility for safety and put workers in harm's way'.[45]

---

[45] Weil, *The Fissured Workplace* (n 19) 9.

The key practical implication of the present work is a reversal of that very phenomenon: a functional concept of the employer restores coherence to the personal scope question in multilateral work arrangements. By ascribing responsibility to whichever entity—or combination of entities—exercising the relevant employer function, liability can no longer be blurred by complex organizational structures; laws that protect workers can yet again keep pace with the new boundaries of the workplace. 'Here', as Davies and Freedland suggest, 'is where the future may lie for the personal scope debate.'[46]

[46] Davies and Freedland, 'Complexities of the Employing Enterprise' (n 3) 293.

PART I

A CONCEPT UNDER PRESSURE

Introduction

The contract of employment is the central gateway to employment rights in English law.[1] In determining whether a work relationship falls within its scope, the courts have traditionally focused on analysing whether an individual can be classified as an employee. As a result, the concept of the employer has been neglected in both judicial and academic discussions,[2] leaving it inchoate and built on unquestioned or even unstated assumptions. The first part of this work sets out to elucidate the received concept of the employer by identifying two contradictory strands inherent in the current approach; and to show how the resulting tension increasingly leaves workers without recourse to legal protection.

A unitary strand, first, assumes that the employer must always be a single entity: the counterparty to the employee in the contract of employment. A multifunctional strand, by contrast, defines the employer by reference to the exercise of various functions or roles. A particular 'function' of being an employer in this sense is one of the actions employers are entitled or obliged to take within the open-ended scope of the contract of employment. With the advent of multilateral work settings, from employment agencies to complex corporate group structures, the exercise of such functions is increasingly shared between multiple entities.

---

[1] Employment Rights Act 1996 ('ERA 1996') s 230.
[2] With the notable exception of H Collins, 'Ascription of Legal Responsibility to Groups in Complex Patterns of Economic Integration' (1990) 53 MLR 731; S Deakin, 'Commentary. The Changing Concept of the 'Employer' in Labour Law' (2001) 30 ILJ 72; J Fudge, 'The Legal Boundaries of the Employer, Precarious Workers, and Labour Protection' in G Davidov and B Langile (eds), *Boundaries and Frontiers of Labour Law* (Hart 2006), and P Davies and M Freedland, 'The Complexities of the Employing Enterprise' in G Davidov and B Langile (eds), *Boundaries and Frontiers of Labour Law* (Hart 2006).

Structure

Part I is structured as follows. Chapter 1 explores the received concept of the employer in English law. Chapter 2 then turns to address the resulting tensions in the concept of the employer. Its unitary, yet multi-functional conception is not merely a doctrinal problem for employment law scholarship, but has far-reaching implications for the scope of employment regulation. Once several parties jointly exercise employer functions the rival strands suggest conflicting outcomes, as the unitary concept grapples unsuccessfully with the complex arrangement. This leads to regulatory obligations being placed on inappropriate entities, or even a complete breakdown of employment law coverage in situations where no single employer can be identified.

1

The Received Concept of the Employer

Introduction

The concept of the employer is surprisingly uncharted territory in English law.[1] The present chapter is therefore aimed at an exploration of the received concept, surveying a series of factors which have shaped its composite strands. Section 1 describes the development of a unitary concept, showing how the employer has come to be understood as a single entity in all circumstances. As will be seen, this is rooted to some extent in the anthropomorphic notion of the master, a logical extension of the very origins of the employer–employee relationship in the law of master and servant.[2] A single entity definition is furthermore intrinsic to the law's perception of the employment relationship as a bilateral contractual one, between two parties conceptualized in personal and individual terms.[3] The unitary concept also accords with prevailing economic theories of the firm as an internal marketplace, where traditionally bargained-for transactions are subsumed into a single enterprise.[4] As a result, limited liability companies have taken on the mantle of the master in employment law, becoming a modern example of the unitary paradigm. As a matter of company law, an incorporated company is a separate legal entity, distinct from its directors and shareholders, and represented as a single unit towards the outside world.[5] This unitary corporate personality has been readily identified with the personal master or employer.

Section 2 addresses the apparent absence of case law defining the concept of the employer, and suggests how decisions on the classification of workers may be used instead for that purpose, given the close contractual link between the parties. It then re-examines the traditional tests for employee status, including control, economic reality, and business integration, to show that a unitary concept is not a necessary consequence of the current approach to identifying the scope of employment rights: the test for employment status would work equally well in a multilateral setting. Seen from this perspective, a competing multi-functional

---

[1] J Prassl, 'The Notion of the Employer' (2013) 129 LQR 380.
[2] S Deakin and F Wilkinson, *The Law of the Labour Market* (OUP 2005) 43.
[3] M Freedland, *The Personal Employment Contract* (OUP 2003) 40.
[4] R Coase, 'The Nature of the Firm' (1937) 4 Economica 386.
[5] P Davies and M Freedland, 'The Complexities of the Employing Enterprise' in G Davidov and B Langile (eds), *Boundaries and Frontiers of Labour Law* (Hart 2006) 276.

concept emerges: the employer is defined as the entity exercising various specific functions. Five such functions can be identified, from control over the inception and termination of the employment relationship to the management of market risk. A brief conclusion shows how the resulting tension between unitary and multi-functional conceptions comes to the fore in situations where more than one entity becomes involved in the exercise of employer functions.

Section 1: A Unitary Concept of the Employer

With discipline and hierarchy embodied in the very idea of *the master*, to be found in the common law long before a contract of service evolved,[6] a personified unitary concept of the employer is undoubtedly a historically accurate starting point. The present section proceeds in three parts to show key elements from the range of factors that have shaped a unitary concept. A first subsection will look at external unifying factors, especially the language and fact patterns of the various decisions. Discussion then turns to the crucial influence of contract law doctrine, before concluding with economic theory as reflected in company law.

A. Language and Fact Patterns

An analysis of the language and fact patterns through which early cases developed quickly shows how a unitary concept of the employer came to be shaped and reinforced by the singular and traditionally male language used, even when referring to abstract bodies; how the traditional unitary fact patterns were soon extended to increasingly complex structures; and how this unitary thinking soon framed even multilateral scenarios in singular terms.

The use of terms such as *the* master and *the* employer is a clear expression of the unitary nature of the common law's perception of the employer. This strong attachment to singular language is apparent even in rather curious circumstances: the Conference of the Methodist Church, a body with a variety of structures and committees regulating matters both spiritual and secular, for example, has explicitly been referred to as 'the master'.[7] The context for such analyses was originally created by the fact patterns of early cases, quickly hardening into an established concept, which in turn became self-perpetuating in the way future fact patterns were framed. Many of the early leading cases involved individual employers. *Sadler v Henlock*, where the owner of a ditch was held liable for an accident occurring on an adjacent road following shoddy work by his servant, Pearson, is a clear-cut example.[8] A similar understanding, albeit of distinct doctrinal origins, was soon

---

[6] A Merritt, 'Control v Economic Reality: Defining the Contract of Employment' (1982) 10 *Australian Business Law Review* 105.

[7] *President of the Methodist Conference v Parfitt* [1984] QB 368 (CA) 373. Though cf now *President of the Methodist Conference v Preston* [2013] UKSC 29, [2013] 2 AC 163.

[8] *Sadler v Henlock* (1855) 4 El&Bl 570, 119 ER 209 (HC).

applied to companies,[9] who were equally seen as a unitary master.[10] In the public sector, statutory interventions paved the way for a unification of the employing entity, yet again on different conceptual and policy grounds: when Mr Cassidy sued the Liverpool Corporation for vicarious liability following negligent medical care, the Ministry of Health was substituted as a defendant.[11] Despite these widely different backgrounds, the fact pattern was always seen as a unitary one, with the enquiry directed at the relationship with *the* master, or later *the* employer.

In the majority of cases this is not a problem in and of itself: a company or even a government ministry can, after all, still legitimately be conceived of as a single entity, even if not in anthropomorphic terms. There are, however, other fact patterns that could not legitimately be perceived as bilateral or single-employer scenarios, but on which the unitary paradigm nonetheless began to impose its conceptual straitjacket.

An early illustration of this is *Vamplew v Parkgate*.[12] A worker had been killed in the pits, and his dependants brought an action under the Workmen's Compensation Act of 1897. The Court of Appeal, led by Collins MR, affirmed the County Court's decision that the deceased had been an independent contractor, rather than a servant; giving prominent weight to the fact that he had engaged a group of men and boys to work below him.[13] The unitary conception meant that by acting, in part, as an employer, Mr Vamplew could not at the same time also be an employee. This conceptual influence is evident even more explicitly in *Littlejohn v John Brown & Co Ltd*.[14] There, a rivet heater boy had been severely injured after falling into a vessel, due to the shipbuilders' negligent installation of internal scaffolding. Upon an action for compensation, both at common law and under statute,[15] it was held, however, that the shipbuilding company were not the rivet heater's employers, despite a clear relationship with the boy: whilst usually paid and selected by teams of riveters, a strong residual control, up to and including the power to procure dismissal 'if a lad became obnoxious', rested with the company.[16] There were, therefore, clear multilateral relationships between the claimant, the riveter foremen, and the defendant shipbuilders. The challenging nature of these facts was even acknowledged by the court, with Lord Guthrie noting that '[d]ifficult cases may arise where some of the tests point in one direction and some in another'.[17] Nonetheless his Lordship went on to find that on the day of the accident, the boy had not been in the shipbuilders' employment, and

---

[9] For example *Simpson v Ebbw Vale Steel, Iron, and Coal Co* [1905] 1 KB 453 (CA) and *Initial Services v Putterill* [1968] 1 QB 396 (CA). Cf *Hill v Beckett* [1915] 1 KB 578 (HC) where the respondent was one of three partners in a firm of coal dealers, rather than the partnership itself.

[10] In fact, even in growingly complex business structure scenarios, groups were seen as a (potential) single employer. See for example *Ready Mixed Concrete Ltd v Minister of Pensions* [1968] 2 QB 497 (HC), where other group companies such as RM Finance Ltd also interacted with the lorry drivers.

[11] *Cassidy v Ministry of Health* [1951] 2 KB 343 (CA) 360; National Health Service Act 1946, s 6.

[12] *Vamplew v Parkgate Iron & Steel Co Ltd* [1903] 1 KB 851 (CA).

[13] *Vamplew* (n 12) 853.   [14] *Littlejohn v John Brown & Co Ltd* 1909 SC 169 (CS).

[15] Employers Liability Act 1880, s 1.   [16] *Littlejohn* (n 14) 174.

[17] *Littlejohn* (n 14) 174.

could therefore not recover. The existence of one employer (in the form of riveters Gemmell and Lacy) had negated any potential link with further parties.

The understanding of the employer as a singular and unitary concept thus depicted is by no means a thing of the past. It is just as prevalent in modern situations where reliance on the unitary concept can easily lead to 'morally . . . unattractive proposition[s]'[18] being put forward by defendant employers. Even in relatively clear-cut cases, however, the concept is rarely challenged: in *Bolwell v Redcliffe*,[19] the Court of Appeal saw itself bound to choose a relationship of employment with either of two supposedly distinct employers despite their being an economic unit.[20]

B. The Contractual Framework

Language and fact patterns are thus the backdrop for the main driver of unitary conceptual channelling today: the contractual framework in terms of which nearly all employment relationships are cast. In 1967, Lord Wedderburn famously referred to contract as the 'fundamental legal institution' of labour law.[21] Whilst Deakin and Wilkinson have successfully challenged the traditional assumption that a common law system of employment law, based on freedom of contract, pre-dated the welfare state,[22] the institution of the contract and its connected doctrines have nonetheless had a fundamental effect on the perception of the employment relationship in general, and of the employer as a work-taking counterparty to a contract of service in particular. By looking at the vast majority of personal work relationships through a bilateral contractual prism, itself built on notions of a bargaining exchange at the heart of contractual obligations, a unitary view of the employing entity is bound to emerge: if the exchange of wage and work is characterized as a bilateral contractual relationship, emphasis shifts onto a single employing counterparty at the non-employee end. When used as the central category of personal work relationships the contract of employment thus has a strong normative function in shaping our understanding of its parties.

With the exception of very limited categories such as office holding, the paradigm bilateral contract has supplanted all other potential explanations of the employment relationship. It continues to do so in modern contexts, leading to acute problems for employment coverage, most notably in the context of agency workers. There, work is performed in a triangular contractual setup, with workers

---

[18] *McDermid v Nash Dredging & Reclamation Co Ltd* [1987] AC 906 (HL) 912 (Lord Hailsham).

[19] *Bolwell v Redcliffe Homes Ltd* [1999] IRLR 485 (CA). Though cf now developments in cases such as *Viasystems (Tyneside) Ltd v Thermal Transfer (Northern) Ltd* [2005] EWCA Civ 1151, [2006] QB 510 and *Catholic Child Welfare Society v Institute of the Brothers of the Christian Schools* [2012] UKSC 56, [2013] 2 AC 1 (discussed extensively in Chapter 5.2 and 6.1, below).

[20] Though cf the growing literature on enterprise liability: D Brodie, *Enterprise Liability and the Common Law* (CUP 2010); S Deakin, '"Enterprise Risk": The Juridical Nature of the Firm Revisited' (2003) 32 ILJ 97.

[21] K Wedderburn, *Cases and Materials on Labour Law* (CUP 1967) 1.

[22] Deakin and Wilkinson, *The Law of the Labour Market* (n 2).

paid by an agency, which in turn provides their labour to its end-user clients. The bilateral contractual model has been the fundamental impediment to the judicial acceptance of a direct relationship between worker and end-user. The existence of a contractual arrangement with the agency crowds out any rival explanations, be it the judicial implication of a second bilateral contract or a multilateral agreement between the three parties. In *James v Greenwich LBC*,[23] a housing support worker who had been employed through a series of agencies claimed for unfair dismissal. In rejecting her claim for want of a direct relationship with the defendant local authority, the Court of Appeal took up dicta from the earlier decision in *Muscat*.[24] There, the court had explicitly linked the idea that a contract could only be implied where 'necessary'[25] to the business reality test of necessity espoused by Bingham LJ in *The Aramis*,[26] despite the fundamentally different context of that decision concerning a one-off commercial agreement.[27] Given this narrow interpretation of contractual doctrine, the existence of a contract between agency and worker was therefore enough not only to inhibit the use of implied contracts as a solution to the dilemmas inherent in multilateral employment situations,[28] but also to block the possibility of a second contract between end-user and worker.

In substantive terms, the most significant influence of a contractual analysis in the employment context is its inherent emphasis on *bilateral* relationships between two individual parties. The nature of the implied contract under consideration in *James* illustrates this fundamental attachment to the notion of bilateral relationships: even clearly multilateral scenarios are tackled through several bilateral contracts.[29]

C. Economic Theory and Company Law

The factors identified thus far have been of general application to all work-taking counterparties to the contract of employment. Discussion now turns to the single most important form of employing entity in today's labour market: the limited liability company.[30] Despite a multitude of actors, from employees and management to a board of directors and shareholders, it has become a singular focal point for a unitary conception of the corporate entity, with powers and responsibilities

---

[23] *James v London Borough of Greenwich* [2008] EWCA Civ 34, [2008] ICR 577.
[24] *James* (n 23) [23], [48]; citing *Cable & Wireless Plc v Muscat* [2006] EWCA Civ 220, [2006] ICR 975.
[25] *Dacas v Brook Street Bureau (UK) Ltd* [2004] EWCA Civ 217, [2004] ICR 1437 [16].
[26] *Cable & Wireless Plc v Muscat* (n 24) [45]. The idea was also taken up by Elias J in *National Grid Electricity v Wood* [2007] UKEAT/0432/07.
[27] *The Aramis* [1989] 1 Lloyd's Rep 213 (CA).
[28] See eg E Brown, 'Protecting Agency Workers: Implied Contract or Legislation?' (2008) 37 ILJ 178; M Wynn and P Leighton, 'Agency Workers, Employment Rights and the Ebb and Flow of Freedom of Contract' (2009) 72 MLR 91.
[29] *James* (n 23) [5] (Mummery LJ). Despite dicta to the contrary in *Stephenson v Delphi Diesel Systems Ltd* [2003] ICR 471 (EAT) [53], the potential for multipartite contracts is not entirely barred: *Dacas v Brook Street Bureau (UK) Ltd* (n 25) [20], [78]; *Cable & Wireless Plc v Muscat* (n 24) [41].
[30] References to company or corporation should be taken as synonyms for this.

perceived in anthropomorphic terms; a concept to which employment relationships then fasten.

In economic theory, the conception of the firm as a singular unit is built on two factors: the firm as internalizing what would otherwise be cost-inefficient market transactions between factors of production, and the firm as concentrating management powers in the hands of a small group, thus taking them away from the shareholders of the company. Two different relationships are at stake here—that between employees and the company; and that between owners and the company. Whilst the precise approaches to these groups differ, the outcome is the same: the conceptualization of the company as a unitary entity.

The former aspect is discussed in Coase's economic analysis of the corporate firm as a central market actor. There, the rationale behind the existence of a firm is said to be the increase in economic efficiency that results from subsuming one set of actors (those dealing in factors of production) under the centralized control of a single 'entrepreneur co-ordinator'.[31] In particular, Coase looks to the contract of employment as evidence for the importance of directional powers, suggesting that 'it is the fact of direction which is the essence of the legal concept of employer and employee'.[32]

Turning next to financial structures and corporate governance,[33] ie the relationship between the company (as represented by the management of the firm) and its shareholders (the owners of the equity in the firm), multiple actors within the realm of the company again do not stand in the way of a perception of the enterprise as a single unit. The economic explanation of governance structures sees them as transaction cost-reducing relationships,[34] 'where owners of various resources are seen as committing to some "contractual governance arrangement" '.[35] In Anglo-American corporate structures, this arrangement has traditionally been described as one of diffuse shareholdings, in contrast to the blockholder model of concentrated equity ownership frequently encountered in jurisdictions inspired by continental European systems.[36]

Berle and Means identify three functions of enterprise: 'having interests in an enterprise, . . . having power over it, and . . . acting with respect to it'.[37] Through the corporate form these functions have become separated—especially the traditional bond between the first pair. This is the second facet of the economically

---

[31] Coase, 'The Nature of the Firm' (n 4) 388. Today, centralized management exercises the entrepreneur's role.

[32] Coase, 'The Nature of the Firm' (n 4) 404.

[33] H Gospel and A Pendleton, 'Corporate Governance and Labour Management: An International Comparison' in H Gospel and A Pendleton (eds), *Corporate Governance and Labour Management: An International Comparison* (OUP 2005).

[34] O Williamson, *The Economic Institutions of Capitalism* (The Free Press 1985).

[35] W Allen, R Kraakman, and G Subramanian, *Commentaries and Cases on the Law of Business Organization* (2nd edn Wolters Kluwer 2007) 10.

[36] P Gourevitch and J Shinn, *Political Power and Corporate Control: The New Global Politics of Corporate Governance* (Princeton University Press 2005) 4–5.

[37] A Berle and G Means, *The Modern Corporation and Private Property* (The Macmillan Company 1939) 119.

unitary view of the corporation, where all actors are kept separate from the commercial entity, either by disappearing within it or being separated from it. Company law developed against this background, setting the legal boundaries of the company not at the economic remit of all those involved, but on a far narrower basis, shaped by two closely related doctrines: separate legal personality, and limited liability.

The attribution of separate legal personality to a validly incorporated limited liability company is of common law origins.[38] In *Salomon v Salomon*,[39] a sole trader had turned his enterprise into a limited liability company, becoming in effect its only director and principal shareholder. The House of Lords held that shareholders' liability could extend no further than their initial contributions, and that the company was 'a distinct legal persona'.[40] *Lee v Lee's Air Farming*[41] confirmed this when finding that Mr Lee had been an employee of a company which he himself had incorporated and solely managed as both director and controlling shareholder. Lord Morris, giving the speech for the Privy Council, held that 'an application of the principles of Salomon's case demonstrates that the company was distinct from the deceased'.[42]

Today, one further consequence flowing from valid incorporation is the potential to limit investors' liability. Through incorporation, shareholders can limit their economic and legal risk exposure to the value of their shares,[43] which is either the amount of money initially paid to the company for an equity subscription, or the market value of the shares if purchased subsequently. This protection of shareholders from claims against their individual assets is often referred to as the corporate veil—hiding the company's members behind it in a manner reminiscent of the earlier economic analysis.

The corporate veil may on occasion be pierced or lifted by the courts,[44] for example in order to impose liability for the company's acts on the shareholders behind it—a process to which the common law has traditionally been very hostile. The orthodox position asserts that the veil may only be lifted (in the sense just outlined) in case of fraud,[45] evasion,[46] or by operation of certain statutory provisions.[47]

---

[38] Though the rules for incorporation are found in statute. The Companies Act 2006, s 3(1)–(3) defines limited liability companies, and Part II of the Act sets out the incorporation process. cf J Getzler and M Macnair, 'The Firm as an Entity Before the Companies Acts' in P Brand, K Costello, and W Osborough (eds), *Adventures of the Law* (Four Courts Press 2005) 267.

[39] *Salomon v Salomon & Co Ltd* [1897] AC 22 (HL).

[40] *Salomon* (n 39) 42 (Lord Herschell). For a different account focused on the role of floating charge security, see J Getzler, 'The Role of Security over Future and Circulating Capital: Evidence from the British Economy circa 1850–1920' in J Getzler and J Payne (eds), *Company Charges: Spectrum and Beyond* (OUP 2006).

[41] *Lee v Lee's Air Farming Ltd* [1961] AC 12 (PC).   [42] *Lee* (n 41) 30.

[43] P Davies and S Worthington, *Gower and Davies' Principles of Modern Company Law* (9th edn Sweet & Maxwell 2012) 8–1. The following paragraphs build on the discussion there.

[44] S Ottolenghi, 'From Peeping Behind the Corporate Veil, to Ignoring It Completely' (1990) 53 MLR 338, 340.

[45] The bar for which is set high: *Adams v Cape Industries Plc* [1990] Ch 433 (CA).

[46] *Petrodel Resources Ltd v Prest* [2013] UKSC 34, [2013] 2 AC 415 [28] (Lord Sumption); see also *VTB Capital plc v Nutritek International Corp* [2013] UKSC 5, [2013] 2 AC 337; R George, 'The Veil of Incorporation and Post-Divorce Financial Remedies' (2014) 130 LQR 373.

[47] For example in the Insolvency Act 1986, ss 213 and 214 (fraudulent and wrongful trading).

A range of potential policy explanations supports this strict line—most nota-bly the idea that limited liability is necessary for the efficient functioning of public securities markets,[48] and the assignment of creditors to relevant economic units.[49] On the other hand, it has been suggested that the 'tyrannical sway' of the 'calamitous decision' in *Salomon* fosters unnecessary artificiality, leading to a capricious lack of clarity and predictability and the potential for fraudulent abuse.[50]

Not all shareholders are individuals, however: businesses are often structured as groups of companies, with parent entities holding the entirety of shares in each subsidiary. In these situations, it is difficult to see how the above-discussed ration-ales for limited liability can justify the law's equal application of the doctrine, given its potentially negative impact on creditors, including wage creditors, of individual subsidiaries[51]—or even on the company itself.[52] For a brief period fol-lowing the decision in *DHN*,[53] where Lord Denning had led the Court of Appeal in holding that three separate companies 'should not be treated separately so as to be defeated on a technical point',[54] it appeared as if a group enterprise or single economic unit exception to the limited liability of each individual group company could develop.[55] Orthodoxy was however quickly reasserted,[56] ignoring manage-ment reality in corporate groups. As Goff LJ put it, the concern of the courts was to be 'not with economics but with law. The distinction [between two group companies] is, in law, fundamental and cannot here be bridged'.[57] Each company, once properly incorporated, is therefore in principle free of the debts and liabilities of any other company in a group structure.[58]

Hansmann and Kraakman suggest that the independent position of each com-pany allows each creditor to be assigned to the relevant economic unit, with poten-tially significant benefits, not least from lower monitoring cost.[59] This approach may be appropriate in the case of voluntary creditors, despite academic commen-tary to the contrary.[60] In commercial negotiations with a company, they will be

---

[48] P Halpern, M Trebilcock, and S Turnbull, 'An Economic Analysis of Limited Liability' (1980) 30 University of Toronto Law Journal 117 (as cited in Davies and Worthington, *Gower and Davies* (n 43)).

[49] The 'asset partitioning rationale' set out in H Hansmann and R Kraakman, 'The Essential Role of Organizational Law' (2000) 110 Yale Law Journal 387 (as cited in Davies and Worthington, *Gower and Davies* (n 43)).

[50] O Kahn-Freund, 'Some Reflections on Company Law Reform' (1944) 7 MLR 54, 56; K Wedderburn, 'Multinationals and the Antiquities of Company Law' (1984) 47 MLR 87, 90.

[51] Davies and Worthington, *Gower and Davies* (n 43) 8–2.

[52] The 'boomerang' hitting 'the man who was trying to use it', as envisaged by Kahn-Freund, 'Some Reflections on Company Law Reform' (n 50) 56.

[53] *DHN Food Distributors v Tower Hamlets LBC* [1976] 1 WLR 852 (CA).

[54] *DHN* (n 53) 860.

[55] A development criticized in F Rixon, 'Lifting the Veil Between Holding and Subsidiary Companies' (1986) 102 LQR 415.

[56] *Woolfson v Strathclyde RC* 1978 SC (HL) 90.

[57] *Bank of Tokyo Ltd v Karoon* [1987] AC 41 (CA) 64.

[58] *Re Southard & Co Ltd* [1979] 1 WLR 1198 (CA).

[59] Hansmann and Kraakman, 'The Essential Role of Organizational Law' (n 49).

[60] Wedderburn, 'Multinationals and the Antiquities of Company Law' (n 50) 90.

able to bargain for appropriate protection through risk pricing mechanisms that account for the legal structure of individual units.

The problem is a different one in the context of involuntary creditors who have no such opportunity to ensure *ex-ante* protection,[61] as is the case most notably with tort victims.[62] In the employment context, Davies and Freedland suggest that limited liability applies within group structures:

> even though the managerial structure of the group (or part of it) itself ignores the division of the group into separate legal entities . . . The fact that the business organisation of the group ignores the separate legal entities of the group companies will not enable the employee to go behind or beyond his or her employing company.[63]

The potential for abuse of the limited liability form in this context is rarely doubted; the courts have nonetheless shown themselves highly unwilling to lift the corporate veil. *Adams v Cape Industries*[64] provides clear affirmation of the 'right . . . inherent in our corporate law'[65] to rely on the principles expounded in *Salomon* in deliberately structuring corporate groups to parcel out liability. Here, two of the leading policy arguments against the corporate veil coincided on the facts: the claimants were involuntary creditors (asbestosis victims), and the defendant one of a large international group of companies forming a single economic unit.[66] Nonetheless, the veil was upheld, subject only to a narrow fraud exception.[67] As Davies and Freedland put it, this confirms that 'ignoring the group structure will rarely be a policy available to the courts'.[68]

The perception of companies as anthropomorphic individual units as a result of separate legal personality is thus a further factor contributing to the historical assumption that the employer must be a singular entity, substantively identical across all different domains of employment law. As the following section will show, however, this is rather different from the conception of the employer borne out in another context: the common law tests through which the notion of the employee as party to the contract of employment has evolved.

Section 2: A Multi-Functional Concept of the Employer

In order to explore the factors which shaped the second, multi-functional strand of the received concept of the employer, this section turns to the well-rehearsed common law tests through which employment status is determined. It will be

---

[61] Most trade creditors, whilst technically voluntary, are in a similar position.

[62] H Hansmann and R Kraakman, 'Towards Unlimited Shareholder Liability for Corporate Torts' (1991) 100 Yale Law Journal 1879 (as cited in Davies and Worthington, *Gower and Davies* (n 43)).

[63] P Davies and M Freedland, 'The Employment Relationship in British Labour Law' in C Barnard, S Deakin, and G Morris (eds), *The Future of Labour Law: Liber Amicorum for Sir Bob Hepple QC* (Hart 2004) 137.

[64] *Adams v Cape Industries plc* (n 45).   [65] *Adams v Cape* (n 45) 544.

[66] Davies and Worthington, *Gower and Davies* (n 43) 8–7.   [67] *Salomon* (n 39) 56–7.

[68] Davies and Freedland, 'The Employment Relationship in British Labour Law' (n 63) 137.

suggested that the traditional concept of the employer is not necessarily inherently unitary. Indeed, the opposite case can be made out: what emerges from the decisions is a fundamentally multi-functional conceptualization.

A. The Contract Conundrum

The absence of case law discussing the concept of the employer has already been noted: it is striking that outside pockets such as triangular employment relationships, there are comparatively few decided cases on the question of the nature of the employer, while there is an abundance of judgments on the definition of employees, workers, and dependent labour more generally. Upon closer inspection, however, a peculiar feature of that case law, which in other contexts frequently presents major problems, means that most decisions are equally relevant to the question at hand: the contract conundrum. The legal institution of the contract is central to English employment law, most obviously as a key notion in the common law of employment. Through the dramatic increase of legislative activity in the labour market from the second half of the twentieth century onwards,[69] contract gained an additional important function, which may well be in the process of eclipsing the former: it is a legal relationship that confers an externally defined status on its parties. This latter function as a gateway to statutory rights and duties is illustrated in the interpretative provisions of the Employment Rights Act 1996, which simply provide that ' "employee" means an individual who has entered into or works under . . . a contract of employment'.[70]

Large parts of the British system of labour market regulation are thus designed to hinge on this status, the definition of which is left to the common law.[71] Cases disposing of questions as diverse as obtaining particulars of employment,[72] health and safety provisions,[73] and collective representation rights[74] thus have to deal with the issue of the claimant's status as an initial hurdle. The definition of an individual's legal position, however, traditionally takes place in a rather circular line of enquiry, where two analytically distinct questions become intertwined: that as to the existence and definition of a contract of service and that as to the definition of its parties. On the one hand, both employee and employer could be seen as parties to a contract of service. On the other, a contract of service can only come into existence if both parties to it show the necessary features of employer and employee. Whilst puzzling in some analytical contexts, the resulting conundrum is a useful basis for the present work: it facilitates deduction of information about the concept of the employer from pronouncements on the concept of the

---

[69] Deakin, 'The Evolution of the Contract of Employment, 1900 to 1950—the Influence of the Welfare State' in N Whiteside and R Salais (eds), *Governance, Industry and Labour Markets in Britain and France—The Modernising State in the Mid-Twentieth Century* (Routledge 1998).

[70] Employment Rights Act 1996 ('ERA 1996') s 230(1).

[71] The same is true for the more recent notion of the worker: ERA 1996 (n 70) s 230(2).

[72] *Carmichael v National Power Plc* [1999] 1 WLR 2042 (HL).

[73] *Ferguson v John Dawson Ltd* [1976] 1 WLR 1213 (CA); Construction (Working Places) Regulations 1966, SI 1966/94, reg 28(1).

[74] *O'Kelly v Trusthouse Forte Plc* [1984] QB 90 (CA).

employee. The decisions are, after all, also on the question of the existence of a contract—and thus in turn on the nature of both, rather than merely one, of the parties to it.

This point is further underscored by the idea of reciprocity which lies at the heart of the bilateral contractual agreement between employer and worker.[75] In *Devonald*,[76] the Court of Appeal implied an obligation on the employer from a contractual duty on the employee. The plaintiff workman had been dismissed following the closure of the employer's tin plant, and claimed for loss arising from the latter's failure to provide him with work during a notice period. The Court made it clear that the contract was a two-sided bargain,[77] and that the employer's duty was a 'necessary implication' of the employee's binding obligation to work.[78] Translated into the present context, the idea of duties implied from obligations means that an analysis of factors that make an individual an employee will equally allow conclusions to be drawn about the concept of the employer.

While the distinction between criteria for the existence of a contract of service and the definition of the parties thereto might thus pose a challenge in some contexts, it is at present an advantage that makes a large body of case law available for detailed analysis. At least three broad categories can be identified: cases concerning employment law per se, cases straddling the boundary of employment law and other, related, areas such as social security, taxation, or health and safety, and cases in entirely different areas of the law that nonetheless turn to some extent on the existence of an employment relationship. It is suggested, however, that for present analytical purposes these are not three distinct sets. Rather, they are on different points of the same spectrum: the question asked remains the same. What differs is its relative importance, and thus prominence, in the context of the overall decision. This can be illustrated with reference to several cases along the spectrum. At one end, the legal question often extends only marginally further than the applicant's status. A good example is the right of an employee to a written statement outlining the particulars of employment,[79] enforceable, if necessary, through recourse to an Employment Tribunal.[80] On several occasions this appears to have been the basis for test cases concerning groups of workers, such as 'regular casual' tour guides[81] or orchestra musicians.[82] This end of the spectrum can also be seen to include cases on the definition of workers, a regulatory tool which saw rapid growth from 1997 onwards.[83] As has already been suggested, the distinction was soon seen as one of degree rather than kind.[84] Academic commentary has

---

[75] Deakin and Wilkinson, *The Law of the Labour Market* (n 2) 43.

[76] *Devonald v Rosser & Sons* [1906] 2 KB 728 (CA).   [77] *Devonald* (n 76) 731 (Jelf J).

[78] *Devonald* (n 76) 742 (Sir Gorrel Barnes).   [79] ERA 1996 (n 70) s 1.

[80] ERA 1996 (n 70) s 11(1).

[81] *Carmichael v National Power Plc* (n 72). The right to particulars of employment at that time was set out in s 1(1) of the Employment Protection (Consolidation) Act 1978, and is in all material aspects identical to the ERA 1996.

[82] *Addison v London Philharmonic Orchestra* [1981] ICR 261 (EAT).

[83] For example in the National Minimum Wage Act 1998, s 54(3) or the Trade Union and Labour Relations (Consolidation) Act 1992 ('TULRCA 1992') ss 145A, 145B, and 146 (as amended).

[84] For example in *Byrne Bros Ltd v Baird* [2002] IRLR 96. Though cf now *Clyde & Co LLP v Bates van Winkelhof* [2014] UKSC 32, [2014] 1 WLR 2047 [26]; J Prassl, 'Members, Partners, Employees, Workers? Partnership Law and Employment Status Revisited' (2014) 43 ILJ 495.

similarly tended to conceptualize the worker as another degree of semi-dependent contractor, rather than an analytically distinct category.[85] While the individual weighing exercise in worker-defining cases might thus be different, the fundamental questions about the *concept* of the dependent labourer (and thus in reflection of the employer) remain the same.

One example of cases in areas adjacent to employment law is occupational health and safety provisions such as construction industry employers' duties to erect and maintain scaffolding and protective rail guards. When this duty is owed only to employees, but not to independent contractors, the question as to the nature of the parties' relationship arises.[86] A similar area is tax law. The amount of cases distinguishing employees and independent subcontractors in this area has however decreased somewhat following changes in taxation practices that mandated PAYE tax deduction at source.[87] Illuminating discussions about the concept of the employer may be found even in areas as seemingly unrelated as Intellectual Property. In *Nora Beloff v Pressdram Ltd*,[88] a journalist sued for copyright infringement following publication of an internal memorandum in *Private Eye*. She could only do so, however, if she was the actual owner of the copyright. This, in turn, was dependent on whether the document had been written whilst she had been an employee of the *Observer* newspaper, in which case statute allocated copyright to the publishing company.[89] On the facts of the case, the High Court found that Ms Beloff's relationship with the Observer Ltd had indeed been a contract of service; her copyright infringement claim failed accordingly. Even though the focal point in the last category may thus not be employment law, the suggestion made above holds true: the question as to the relationship of the parties is essentially the same, even if the cases are found on different points along a spectrum when it comes to the importance of that question in relation to other issues before the court.

B. Revisiting the Unitary Concept

Most of the relevant case law in this context is directed at classifying the status of individual workers, with the result that any pronouncements on the concept of the employer are *obiter* assumptions. On the basis of the close contractual link identified in the first section, the decisions can nonetheless be used in a conceptual enquiry focused on the nature of the employer. The specific question to be asked for each of the major tests is whether its requirements are *inherently* unitary: is it logically workable only if a single counterparty exercises the function under scrutiny; with the test thus necessarily tied to a unitary concept of the employer?

---

[85] Though cf G Davidov, 'Who is a Worker?' (2005) 34 ILJ 57.
[86] *Ferguson v John Dawson Ltd* (n 73).
[87] The first provision of this kind was s 28 of the Finance Act 1972. The facts in *Ferguson* fell on either side of the change: (n 73) 1218.
[88] *Nora Beloff v Pressdram Ltd* [1973] 1 All ER 241 (HC).
[89] Copyright Act 1956, s 4(4).

To illustrate in practical terms, if the regular inspection of worker schedules is a criterion for employee status, this would not point to an inherently unitary concept of the employer: the exercise of such control is not necessarily confined to a single party. It could of course be so limited in practice, for example under a contractual arrangement, but that is not *inherent* in the correlated rights and duties. The enquiry as to whether an individual is part and parcel of an organization is an example in the opposite direction: even when considered in the abstract, it does not allow for anything other than a single entity conceptualization.

Control

Control was historically conceived of as a unitary test, in line with the factual contexts set out earlier. The initial assumption was one of a single party, the master, in exclusive exercise of the control right over the servant.[90] That this is not a logical necessity, however, quickly becomes evident when looking at the different functions cited as evidence of control. Even from a very small cross-section, such as the process of engaging or dismissing workers, their supervision and instructions as to the performance of daily duties and their location, it is clear that the functions could be, and in reality often are, split or shared in their exercise between different parties.

With the emergence and inclusion in protective statutory regimes of professional jobs, the courts began to encounter more and more situations where control was exercised by several parties. At first, the law's reaction to the ascent of such multilateral scenarios was a somewhat awkward search for the party exercising the highest level, or 'most control' over the individual. This approach is evident in the foreman cases discussed earlier: in *Littlejohn*, Lord Guthrie's enquiry focused on the fact that the shipbuilder's control over the boy was more indirect and remote than that exercised by the riveters.[91] Similarly, in *Ready Mixed Concrete* MacKenna J suggested that 'all . . . aspects of control must be considered in deciding whether the right exists in a sufficient degree to make one party the master and the other his servant'.[92] The latter case, incidentally, was one of several turning points away from the control test, for the very reason that it threw into sharp relief the incongruence between the unitary concept and the multilateral results that a strict application of the test would have demanded: each concrete delivery 'owner-driver' was interacting with several entities within the Ready Mixed Concrete group.[93]

Instead, the courts started to substitute other tests, particularly in cases where control was exercised by a range of different parties. In *Morren v Swinton Borough*

---

[90] *Yewens v Noakes* (1880–81) LR 6 QBD 530 (CA); *Sadler v Henlock* (n 8). The idea that 'No man can serve two masters' can be traced back to the New Testament, Matthew 6:24: ' . . . for either he will hate the one, and love the other; or else he will hold to the one, and despise the other.'

[91] *Littlejohn* (n 14) 147.

[92] *Ready Mixed Concrete Ltd* (n 10) 515.

[93] *Ready Mixed Concrete Ltd* (n 10) 500–1.

Council,[94] for example, this shift to an integration test as a move beyond control is clearly visible. The local authority and its consulting engineers had agreed to engage a resident engineer who, in practical terms, was controlled by both parties. Despite earlier explicit statements from the Council that he would be unable to join its superannuation scheme, Morren attempted to do so, arguing that he was in fact a local authority employee. In upholding his claim, the court found that control could not be the decisive test when dealing with a professional man.[95]

There is nothing in the nature of the control test that demands a unitary concept of the employer. If anything, it often instinctively leads to a multilateral analysis of complex work arrangements. The emphasis throughout the judgments is on the employee as the controlled. Notwithstanding a unitary paradigm approach, control exercised by a range of different parties is a realistic option on both a practical and theoretical level without necessarily being lethal to the existence of an employment relationship. Despite, or perhaps because of this, the control test came to be supplanted by other criteria.

Integration

Amongst the four tests under analysis, the integration test is closest to the unitary end of the spectrum. Both in terms of the language and concepts deployed, it points to an underlying conception of the employer as a single entity. As Denning LJ put it, 'the test of being a servant does not rest nowadays on submission to orders. It depends on whether the person is part and parcel of the organization'.[96]

It is not just the language of this approach that is unitary—on a conceptual level, being part of *the*, or even *an*, organization can also be seen as supporting a unitary concept: the individual is only an employee if he or she is integrated into one organization.

This can be illustrated on the facts of *Stevenson Jordan v MacDonald*. MacDonald claimed the copyright to a book published by a former employee. The first of its five parts consisted of a series of lectures given to the public during the author's employment with the claimant. The Court of Appeal, applying a business integration test, found that the lectures had not been given under a contract of service, drawing a stark contrast between 'a man . . . employed as part of the business, and his work . . . done as an integral part of the business'; and one working 'under a contract for services where his work, although done for the business, is not integrated into it but is only accessory to it'.[97] This demonstrates that, under the integration test, the conception of the employer is unitary to the degree that it excludes from the sphere of the company related, even if somewhat extraneous, functions.

The integration test could therefore, to some extent, be characterized as an opposite notion to that inherently underlying control. In contrast to the latter, however, it

---

[94] *Morren v Swinton and Pendlebury BC* [1965] 1 WLR 576 (DC).

[95] *Morren* (n 94) 582.

[96] *Bank voor Handel en Scheepvaart NV v Slatford (No 2)* [1953] 1 QB 248 (CA) 290.

[97] *Stevenson Jordan & Harrison v MacDonald & Evans* [1952] 1 TLR 101 (CA) 111.

never saw a second lease of life, and remains of comparably little significance—possibly because its inherently strong unitary approach sat uneasily with many factual situations.

Economic or Business Reality

In the United States, an enquiry into the economic reality of the relationship between the parties overtook the control test early on. In *United States v Silk*,[98] the Supreme Court emphatically rejected a reliance on 'technical concepts', holding instead that the category of ' "employees" ' included workers who were such as a matter of economic reality'.[99] The courts' focus on economic factors in this test is construed very widely, from the provision of tools, other working materials and general investment in a project to the bearing of overall market risk. If none, or few, of these factors fall upon the individual whose status is to be determined, he or she will in all likelihood be considered an employee. There is nothing in the tests, however, that suggests that the various aspects, from micro- to macroeconomic factors, need to be concentrated in a single party. The conclusion demonstrated in the discussion of the control test rings equally true here: there is nothing in the reference to a party *other than* the worker to say that it could only be *one* other party. The test is workable with single or multiple employing entities.

The first case directly to import the US Supreme Court's language into English law was *Market Investigations Ltd v Minister of Social Security*, affirming the Secretary of State's finding that a part-time interviewer had been employed under a contract of service. Having discussed *Silk* and other authorities, Cooke J formulated the test as follows: 'Is the person who has engaged himself to perform these services performing them as a person in business on his own account?'[100] Through a focus on the employee, this formulation leaves open a variety of potential accounts of the employer, without at any point hinting at a unitary concept as a logical necessity. In fact, a later paragraph explicitly considers, and approves of, the potential plurality of employers, suggesting that there is nothing:

inconsistent with the existence of a contract of service in the fact that [the interviewer] was free to work for others during the relevant period. It is by no means a necessary incident of a contract of service that the servant is prohibited from serving any other employer.[101]

On a narrow interpretation, this only covers an individual's independent service for two distinct employers.[102] Upon further consideration, however, there is little in the present context to distinguish this from other multilateral scenarios: they are all different variations of not being in business on one's own account.[103] While the paradigm underpinning Cooke J's judgment is clearly one of a unitary

---

[98] *United States v Silk* [1947] 331 US 704, 67 S Ct 1463 (SCOTUS).

[99] *United States v Silk* (n 98) 713.

[100] *Market Investigations Ltd v Minister of Social Security* [1969] 2 QB 173 (HC) 184.

[101] *Market Investigations Ltd* (n 100) 186.

[102] On the basis of which submissions seem to have been made before Cooke J.

[103] Though, of course, if this number becomes very large, with resulting short service periods, the contracts will be for services: *Hall (Inspector of Taxes) v Lorimer* [1994] 1 WLR 209 (CA).

relationship between a worker and a single employer, this is so as a matter of fact, rather than due to anything inherent in the test.

Examples from case law on the provision of tools and project investment illustrate the same point from a slightly different angle: the focus here is again on the idea that it is not the worker from whom capital inputs stem. Judicial pronouncements to this effect can be found in cases ranging from major capital investment in a large construction project,[104] to those of much less capital-intensive items, for example the provision of necessary tools on site.[105] As in all variations of the economic reality test, the focus on the employee here means that any other party, or combination of parties, might provide the capital input.

Mutuality of Obligation

The final test to be examined is by far the most prominent in practice today: mutuality of obligation. At first glance, it appears to build on a unitary concept of the employing entity. Both the exchange of work and remuneration and the obligation to offer work and to accept such offers on a long-term basis can be characterized as promises between worker and employer: a bilateral contract, with one party on each side. In *Nethermere v Gardiner*, Dillon LJ summarized earlier case law and held:

that there is one *sine qua non* which can firmly be identified as an essential of the existence of a contract of service and that is that there must be mutual obligations on the employer to provide work for the employee and on the employee to perform work for the employer. If such mutuality is not present, then either there is no contract at all or whatever contract there is must be a contract for services or something else, but not a contract of service.[106]

On the facts of that case, a group of home workers was held to have been employed under contracts of service. More generally, however, the requirement of mutuality of obligation has become a significant hurdle in establishing such a relationship.[107] Regardless of outcome, on the facts of all these cases there was only a single employer under discussion; indeed it would appear that the language of the test makes it clear that it is *the* employer who undertakes to provide future work, and to whom the employee's duties point.

As has already been noted, however, the question here is not how the criterion has been used in practice, but rather what concept of the employer can be gleaned from the test in the abstract. Considered at this level, there is ample evidence that the concept of the employer underpinning the mutuality of obligation test is not as inherently unitary as it initially appeared: it could be readily applied to multilateral situations. This is, first, evident in the very meaning of the word

---

[104] *Lee Ting Sang v Chung Chi-Keung* [1990] 2 AC 374 (PC HK).
[105] *Ferguson v John Dawson Ltd* (n 73).
[106] *Nethermere (St Neots) Ltd v Gardiner* [1984] ICR 612 (CA) 632.
[107] See, for example, the leading cases of *O'Kelly v Trusthouse Forte Plc* (n 74) and *Carmichael v National Power Plc* (n 72). The test itself receives surprisingly little judicial attention in these judgments.

mutual. On a historical understanding, there may be a bilateral connotation to it; modern definitions however make it clear that mutuality can always refer to 'two or more parties'.[108] Upon reflection, this is already manifested in the case law: any employer with more than one employee enters into mutuality of obligation with several counterparties, promising each of them to provide, and pay for the execution of, work on a regular basis. As a matter of logic, there is therefore nothing that would prevent an employee from similarly undertaking to provide his labour to several parties.

A second point arises out of Deakin and Morris's characterization of mutuality of obligation as a 'fresh emphasis on a form of personal control'.[109] In discussing the latter, the conclusion reached was that the control test could often instinctively point to a multilateral understanding of the employing entity in a wide range of situations. If the mutuality of obligation test can thus be seen as a reworking of a form of the personal control test, what has been said above may be imported *mutatis mutandis* into the present discussion. It further corroborates the idea that, in the abstract, there is nothing inherently unitary about the mutuality of obligation requirement, which would stop the contract of employment from imposing obligations on multiple parties.

A complete characterization of mutuality of obligation, and indeed all tests discussed thus far, should not be blind to the reality of most decided cases, where the underlying concept will frequently be unitary, with single employers undertaking the obligation to provide work. This position, however, is *not* due to anything inherent in the tests: the meaning of the word *mutual* itself is broad enough comfortably to include multilateral scenarios, and as a modern-day version of the control test the criterion should be equally susceptible to being shared amongst multiple parties.

In conclusion, apart from the short-lived development of an enterprise integration doctrine,[110] none of the traditional tests could thus be said to necessitate an inherently unitary conception of the employer. Indeed, they pose a potentially significant challenge to the unitary strand developed in Section 2, by painting an intuitively multi-functional concept.

C. A Multi-Functional Concept

A 'function' of being an employer is one of the various actions employers are entitled or obliged to take as part of the bundle of rights and duties falling within the scope of the open-ended contract of service. In trawling the established tests for such employer functions, the possible mutations of different fact scenarios are

---

[108] The Oxford English Dictionary defines *mutual* as '1. experienced or done by each of *two or more* parties towards *the other or others*, 2. (of *two or more* parties) having the same specified relationship to each other, and 3. held in common by *two or more* parties', before also noting the historically bilateral point made in the text (emphasis supplied).

[109] S Deakin and G Morris, *Labour Law* (6th edn Hart 2012) 164.

[110] *Stevenson Jordan & Harrison v McDonnell & Evans* (n 97) 111; *Bank voor Handel en Scheepvaart NV v Slatford (No 2)* (n 96) 290.

nearly endless, rendering categorization purely on the basis of past decisions of limited assistance. As with previous sections, therefore, subsequent paragraphs look at the concepts underlying different fact patterns, rather than the actual results on a case-by-case basis, in order to classify them into functional groups.[111] The result is the following set of functions, with the presence or absence of individual factors becoming less relevant than the specific role they play in any given context. Individual elements can vary from situation to situation, as long as they fulfil the same function when looked at as a whole.[112] Key to this concept of the employer's being a *multi-functional* one is the fact that no one function mentioned above is determinative in and of itself. Rather, it is the *ensemble* of the five functions that matters: each of them covers one of the facets necessary to create, maintain, and commercially exploit employment relationships, thus coming together to make up the legal concept of employing workers or acting as an employer.

The *five main functions* (and their functional underpinning) of the employer are:

[1] **Inception and Termination of the Contract of Employment**

> This category includes all powers of the employer over the very existence of its relationship with the employee.

[2] **Receiving Labour and its Fruits**

> Rights correlative to duties owed by the employee to the employer, specifically to provide his or her labour and the results thereof, as well as rights incidental thereto.

[3] **Providing Work and Pay**

> The employer's obligations towards its employees.

[4] **Managing the Enterprise-Internal Market**

> Coordination through control over all factors of production.

[5] **Managing the Enterprise-External Market**

> Undertaking economic activity in return for potential profit, whilst also being exposed to any losses that may result from the enterprise.

The division of employer functions into discreet categories is not a novel idea. Deakin, for example, has suggested three 'overlapping and complementary' functional criteria in the context of developing a potential definition of employing entities, namely:

coordination, which associates the employment unit (or parts of it) with the presence of centralised managerial control; risk, which treats the employer as a juridical form of absorbing, processing, and spreading social and economic risks which are associated with

---

[111] In line with established methodology: S Deakin, 'Commentary. The Changing Concept of the "Employer" in Labour Law' (2001) 30 ILJ 72, 83. Freedland, *The Personal Employment Contract* (n 3) 40.

[112] The 'equipollency principle' (*Äquivalenzprinzip*): L Nogler, 'Die Typologisch-Funktionale Methode am Beispiel des Arbeitnehmerbegriffs' (2009) 10 ZESAR 459, 463.

the enterprise; and equity, which sees the employment unit as a space within which the equal treatment principle, in its various forms, should be observed.[113]

More recently, Freedland has identified four main categories comprised in the concept of employing workers, or acting as an employer:

(1) engaging workers for employment and terminating their employment; (2) remunerating workers and providing them with other benefits of employment; (3) managing the employment relation and the process of work; and (4) using the worker's services in a process of production or service provision.[114]

Why, then, are employer functions divided into five categories for present purposes? At first glance, the five categories are reasonably similar to the list just set out, subject only to a subdivision of Freedland's category (4) into aspects concerning the specific *enterprise-internal market* of each organization [4], and those relevant to *external markets* more generally [5]. This reflects analytical distinctions present in both economic theory and law—for example different sets of legal rules regulating the two spheres. Furthermore, as the overall purpose of the present work is to look at challenges arising from a split of employer functions between different entities, the additional subdivision will allow for a clearer analysis of the resulting challenges.

Before turning to the categories themselves, finally, it is important to focus for a moment on two aspects of the *multi-functional* concept. The first is its relationship with the main common law tests: while the material in the five categories draws extensively on the same case law, there is no direct overlap with the traditional tests for the classification of an employment relationship. This is primarily due to the fact that any one test can comprise different functional concepts, just as each function can be implicated in different tests. The control test provides a straightforward illustration of this, as the functions expressed through it can include control over the inception of a contractual relationship, management in the course of the employment, and duties owed by the employer to its employees.

A related problem might arise from the fact that some functions appear to fit into multiple categories: the duty to pay employees and provide work for them,[115] for example, could be relevant both to [3] *Providing Work and Pay* and [5] *Managing the Enterprise-External Market*. Upon closer inspection, however, this problem is solved through the use of a typological-functional method, where individual facts matter less than the functions of which they are examples, and according to which they have been characterized. Returning to the payment of wages example, the duty to provide work and pay on an individual transaction basis, will form part of category [3], whereas the 'continuing obligation'[116] to provide work (and thus pay) even if there is no immediate demand for the production output falls within economic risk allocation in [5].

---

[113] Deakin, 'The Changing Concept of the "Employer"' (n 111) 83.
[114] Freedland, *The Personal Employment Contract* (n 3) 40.
[115] eg *Short v J&W Henderson Ltd* 1945 SC 155 (CS).
[116] *Hellyer Brothers Ltd v McLeod* [1987] 1 WLR 728 (CA) 750.

Discussion thus turns to the five functions. In the order set out above, the rationale underpinning each category will be explained, before moving on to illustrative case law examples of the various functions subsumed under it.

[1] Inception and Termination of the Contract of Employment

This category includes the power to hire and fire employees, and accessory processes. In functional terms, the emphasis here is on power over the very existence of the contract. The employer has the power to bring about a personal work relationship with the employee, but also the right to terminate it subject to statutory and common law rules on unfair and wrongful dismissal.[117] The 'power of selection',[118] first, covers a range of actions even before an actual contract is concluded, from advertising a position, interviewing and selecting applicants, and making a formal offer of employment, to appointing the desired candidate.[119] The right to dismiss[120] as an 'ultimate conduct sanction',[121] is the logical counterpart to this, as are powers of suspension and related disciplinary procedures that could lead up to the termination of the contract.[122]

[2] Receiving Labour and its Fruits

This category explains why employers are sometimes referred to as work-takers: the central purpose of being an employer is arguably the power over employees' labour and the resulting products. In cases focused on the employee's position, this has traditionally been framed in terms of 'the principal obligation of an employee: to provide himself to serve'.[123] The duty must be a legal one, as well as exclusive to a reasonable degree.[124] As regards exclusivity, however, suggestions vary from men not being allowed to sign on elsewhere,[125] a rather high threshold, to the case of a skilled artisan working for more than one company, yet always giving priority to his employer.[126] The essence in both cases is the employer's right to demand, and if so to receive, the worker's labour.

The employer not only has a right to receive an employee's own work,[127] but also any goods and materials—including intellectual property—produced as a result of this work.[128] Incidental duties, such as confidentiality, owed by employees to their employers, support this.[129] The main function of these duties is to protect the

---

[117] The statutory regime is found in the ERA 1996 (n 70), as amended by the Employment Acts of 2002 and 2008.

[118] *Short v J&W Henderson Ltd* (n 115).

[119] *Morren v Swinton and Pendlebury BC* (n 94).

[120] *Narich Pty v Commissioner of Payroll Tax* [1984] ICR 286 (EAT) 295.

[121] *Cassidy v Ministry of Health* (n 11) 360 (Denning LJ).

[122] *Collins v Hertfordshire CC* [1947] KB 598 (HC).

[123] *WHPT Housing Association v Secretary of State for Social Services* [1981] ICR 737 (HC).

[124] *United States v Silk* (n 98).   [125] *Hellyer Bros Ltd v McLeod* (n 116) 749.

[126] *Lee Ting Sang v Chung Chi-Keung* (n 104).

[127] *Nethermere (St Neots) Ltd v Gardiner* (n 106).

[128] *Stevenson Jordan & Harrison v McDonnell & Evans* (n 97). Though this might be contingent on the terms of the contract: M Freedland and J Prassl, 'Resolving Ownership Invention Disputes: Limitations of the Contract of Employment' in M Pittard (ed), *Business Innovation—A Legal Balancing Act* (Edward Elgar 2012).

[129] *Initial Services v Putterill* (n 9).

employer's wider economic interests. Finally, there are a range of further common law duties, such as fidelity and obedience, owed to the employer in order to ensure that the overall function can be exercised.[130]

[3] Providing Work and Pay

In return for these obligations the employer similarly owes its employees a range of duties, most notably to provide regular work and pay as contractually agreed. In functional terms, this is the reciprocal element to receiving labour and its fruits, placing employees at the wage-taking end of the relationship.[131] Payment of wages is the most frequently referenced aspect,[132] even if there is a relationship of employment only on an hourly basis.[133] The payment of expenses and other allowances can also be a relevant factor.[134] The functional category is considerably wider than this, however. Intimately related to the remunerative obligation is the duty to provide work to the employee—the '*sine qua non*'[135] of the relationship.[136] The obligation to pay an employee can continue to exist under certain circumstances even if no work is actually being done.[137]

[4] Managing the Enterprise-Internal Market

This function is central to the role of the entrepreneur-coordinator: only through the use of directional powers stemming from the contract of employment can management achieve the necessary control over all factors of production. Initial formulations of this built on the power to require both how and what was to be done,[138] even if the right needed not be unrestricted.[139] More recent examples include moving workers from site to site,[140] requiring their presence during certain hours,[141] choosing employees for specific tasks,[142] or even varying the terms of individual engagements.[143] The functional concept underpinning this category is an open-ended right to direct employees, regardless of the actual level of detail of that instruction.

---

[130] *McMeechan v Secretary of State for Employment* [1997] ICR 549 (CA) 565.

[131] On the role of customers' tips in this context, see E Albin, 'A Worker–Employer–Customer Triangle: The Case of Tips' (2011) 40 ILJ 181 and E Albin, 'The Case of *Quashie*: Between the Legalisation of Sex Work and the Precariousness of Personal Service Work' (2013) 42 ILJ 180.

[132] *Cassidy v Ministry of Health* (n 11) 360.   [133] *Ferguson v John Dawson Ltd* (n 73).

[134] *Morren v Swinton and Pendlebury BC* (n 94).

[135] *Nethermere (St Neots) Ltd v Gardiner* (n 106) 632 (Dillon LJ).

[136] Although it has also been suggested in *Nethermere* (n 106) (Kerr LJ in dissent) that it might not be necessary for the courts to decide if an employer's duty is to provide a reasonable amount of work, or merely to pay an agreed and reasonable sum. See also *William Hill v Tucker* [1999] ICR 291 (CA).

[137] *Clark v Oxfordshire HA* [1998] IRLR 125 (CA).

[138] *Simmons v Heath Laundry Co* [1910] 1 KB 543 (CA).

[139] *Ready Mixed Concrete Ltd v Minister of Pensions* (n 10).

[140] *Ferguson v John Dawson Ltd* (n 73).

[141] *WHPT Housing Association v Secretary of State for Social Services* (n 123).

[142] *Cassidy v Ministry of Health* (n 11) 360.

[143] *Calder v H K Vickers* [1988] ICR 232 (CA) 252.

[5] Managing the Enterprise-External Market

The final function of the employer is to engage with the market at large. This comprises a number of different aspects, all of which centre on the chance of financial profit and the risk of loss.[144] It is on the employer's account that all business activities take place.[145] The frequently cited ownership of tools[146] stands for all investment in projects and facilities.[147] The obligation to keep paying employees even when the enterprise is not profitable has already been discussed,[148] and stands alongside the risk of bad debt and outstanding invoices for employers' financial buffer function.[149]

Conclusion

A careful analysis of the case law defining the scope of employment protective norms through their definition of the employee has thus yielded the observation that there is nothing inherent in the control, economic risk, and mutuality of obligation tests that could work only with the unitary concept of the employer as a singular counterparty to the contract of employment, as identified in Section 1. Indeed, further scrutiny suggested a different, and potentially more realistic, approach to the concept of the employer: the definition which has emerged from Section 2 is highly functional one, driven not by factors such as the bilateral contract of service or separate legal personality, but rather looking to the exercise of five overlapping categories of employer functions. The result is a potential conflict between a unitary strand and a multilateral strand, which together make up the received, composite concept of the employer.

Combining the two conceptions of the employer which have emerged is not necessarily an analytical problem: a single entity could after all exercise all employer functions. There are, however, several different modes of exercising the functions of employing individuals under a contract of service. As a detailed analysis in Chapter 2 will show, at least three scenarios are possible: functions might be bundled into one entity, shared between two or more entities, or parcelled out between different entities. The first of these modes is the paradigm situation: a single individual or entity exercises all employer functions.[150] There is thus no automatic incompatibility between a *unitary* concept of the employer and a *functional* one.

---

[144] *Ready Mixed Concrete Ltd v Minister of Pensions* (n 10) 522.
[145] *Market Investigations Ltd v Minister of Social Security* (n 100).
[146] *Montreal v Montreal Locomotive Works* [1947] 1 DLR 161 (PC).
[147] *United States v Silk* (n 98).   [148] *Clark v Oxfordshire HA* (n 137).
[149] *Hall (Inspector of Taxes) v Lorimer* (n 103) 217.
[150] Such as the franchisee in *Narich Pty v Commissioner of Payroll Tax* (n 120).

An Inherent Tension

The same cannot be said of the other two modes. In *shared exercise*, some functions of the employer are simultaneously vested in more than one party. A classic example of this is the case of *Hill v Becket*,[151] where a coal yard employed a foreman to be in charge of a gang of workers. In practice, the foreman was tasked with engaging and dismissing workers under him and the direction of their day-to-day work. The coal yard, however, also reserved a right of general control, as well as the power to procure the dismissal of individual workers. When individual functions are *parcelled out*, on the other hand, distinct entities fulfil mutually exclusive roles. The best illustrations for this arise in the context of triangular work relationships. In *Dacas*,[152] an agency worker cleaned hostels for a local authority, the end-user. Under the arrangement the agency paid the worker, while day-to-day control over her work was exercised by the authority. Finally, there is the possibility that in the context of a single worker some functions are exercised jointly whilst others are parcelled out—such as in triangular situations where both agency and end-user have the right to procure dismissal.[153] These different distributional models do not sit easily with the paradigm unitary model of the employer.[154]

The problem is further exacerbated by the fact that there is no legal distinction between the potential to fulfil an employer function, and its actual exercise. In *Ready Mixed Concrete*, MacKenna J held that whether or not anyone had ever attempted to instruct the concrete lorry driver was 'irrelevant: it is the right of control that matters, not its exercise'.[155] Put differently, it is of little relevance whether a party had in fact enjoyed control over the worker. What matters is 'ultimate authority over [a] man'.[156] That said, there is a clear limit to this fairly extensive approach to the exercise of employer functions: the power or authority must be a legal one (albeit not necessarily stemming from a contract of employment), rather than being social or commercial.[157]

Viewed thus, the multi-functional conceptualization of the employer poses a direct challenge to the unitary concept, reconcilable only in a small set of paradigm cases. On the other hand, in situations where different functions may be exercised from more than one *locus* of control,[158] the tension quickly comes to the fore. As Chapters 2 and 3 will demonstrate, the practical implications of this

---

[151] *Hill v Beckett* (n 9).   [152] *Dacas v Brook Street Bureau (UK) Ltd* (n 25).

[153] *Construction Industry Training Board v Labour Force Ltd* [1970] 3 All ER 220 (HC).

[154] M Wynn and P Leighton, 'Will the Real Employer Please Stand Up? Agencies, Client Companies and the Employment Status of the Temporary Agency Worker' (2006) 35 ILJ 301, 303.

[155] *Ready Mixed Concrete Ltd v Minister of Pensions* (n 10) 515.

[156] *Humberstone v Northern Timber Mills* (1949) 79 CLR 389 (HCA).

[157] *PA News Ltd v Loveridge* [2003] EAT/0135/03/MAA.

[158] The term *locus* of control is designed to avoid additional complexities arising out of the fact, noted inter alios by Freedland, *The Personal Employment Contract* (n 3) 45–7, that even in traditional companies without external influence management control is often exercised by more than one person amongst a group of relatively senior executives.

conflict are considerable, from regulatory obligations placed on unsuitable entities to a complete breakdown of employment law coverage.

The first chapter of this work set out to identify and challenge the unspoken assumptions surrounding the legal concept of the employer in English law. Historically, the language and fact patterns of early cases quickly became a fixed perspective from which future scenarios were analysed, enforcing a unitary view of the employer even where this led to a highly artificial analysis of the relevant facts. This unitary conceptualization was strengthened by the growing importance of contract as the main framework for personal work relationships, casting the wage-work bargain as a bilateral contract between individual parties. In the subset of corporate employers, the company then became the bearer of this unitary view.

Upon closer investigation, however, it emerged that in the actual cases testing for employment status, a unitary view was rarely *inherent* in the tests used. Instead, the concept builds on a multi-functional classification of employers' rights and duties. There is nothing to suggest that all employer functions ought necessarily to be exercised by the same entity: they can be exercised jointly by several parties, or parcelled out between different *loci* of control. This results in a deep tension between the two conceptions identified.

This inherent tension becomes an acute challenge for regulatory coverage once employment relationships move beyond a narrow bilateral paradigm: as examined in Chapters 2 and 3, the emergence of a second *locus* of control over the worker can render protective obligations inapplicable; in the case of parcelled-out functions it may even place the individual outside the remit of employment law.

2

The Shared Exercise of Employer Functions Across Multiple *Loci* of Control

Introduction

In concluding the last chapter, it was suggested that the tension between a *unitary* and a *multi-functional* strand in the concept of the employing entity would come to the fore in multilateral organizational settings. The present chapter explores such setups with multiple entities or *loci* of employer functions. This forms the necessary backdrop for Chapter 3, where the problematic implications for employment law coverage of such multi-entity scenarios will be spelled out.

From a wide range of potential examples, this chapter will focus on two areas in particular: Private Equity (PE) control over portfolio companies, and the relationships arising from a company's use of temporary work or labour agencies. These are prime examples of the challenges to the paradigm concept of the employer as a single work-taking counterparty in a bilateral relationship, as an additional *locus* of control over the employment relationship emerges: traditional employer functions become exercised by both management and shareholders, or shared between a work agency and its end-user clients.

The two areas are, at first sight, rather different. When a general picture is abstracted from the different fact patterns, several distinctions become apparent: the entities jointly exercising employer functions in the temporary agency worker scenario, for example, are distinct commercial enterprises, usually contracting with each other at arm's length. The economic incentives of Private Equity portfolio companies, on the other hand, are closely aligned with those of the investing fund, as the profitability of the latter depends to a significant degree on the performance of the portfolio company. In the agency context, on the other hand, there will usually be no such alignment, given distinct ownership and management.[1] It is only when looking at the underlying factual cause of the problem in triangular scenarios that important similarities become apparent: in both agency work and Private Equity transactions, traditional employer functions are exercised by more than one entity.

---

[1] Though there are also reports of 'in-house agencies': M Aziz et al, 'Hard Work, Hidden Lives: The Full Report' (TUC Commission on Vulnerable Employment 2008) 188.

Furthermore, whilst both factual scenarios have been the subject of academic scrutiny, different labels have traditionally been applied. On the one hand, agency work can be placed in what Fudge has referred to as the 'commercialization' of employment:

In developed countries, commercialisation takes many forms. Employment is increasingly project-, task-, or term-limited rather than ongoing, and pay has been individualised. Self-employment—often in the form of 'freelancers'—has increased, and the distinction between employment and self-employment is blurring as employment practices rapidly change. Labour-only subcontracting, franchises, joint ventures, and project employment are examples of the commercialisation of employment.[2]

The Private Equity model, on the other hand, can be placed in the context of discussions about the disintegration of the enterprise,[3] where '[t]he boundaries of the firm have proved to be quite porous, "making it difficult to know where the firm ends and where the market or another firm begins"'.[4] Both examples are brought together for present purposes, however, as they are stark illustrations of the fragmented exercise of employer functions.

The problems discovered in labour agencies and Private Equity are furthermore a good *pars pro toto* illustration of their respective larger areas: agency work problems are mirrored in areas such as subcontracting, and the use of personal service companies. PE issues in turn are reflected in corporate groups and in other situations of block shareholders exercising control over a company. They are, finally, both numerically significant in the UK labour market. In 2008, the most recent year for which comparable figures are available, an approximate 1.3 million, or 5 per cent of the UK workforce,[5] worked in a triangular agency setting. Private Equity 'employment' numbers ran to approximately 3 million workers in PE portfolio companies; the equivalent of more than 21 per cent of private sector employees.[6]

In order to explore the shared exercise of employer functions across multiple entities in the agency work and Private Equity contexts respectively, this chapter is structured as follows: the analysis of each area begins with a brief overview of the relevant industry and its regulation, primarily in order to show how the crucial issue of employer status is usually left untouched. A subsequent part then turns to a description of key actors and the relationships between them which condition the emergence of multiple *loci* of control. Drawing on examples from qualitative

---

[2] J Fudge, S McCrystal, and K Sankaran, *Challenging the Legal Boundaries of Work Regulation* (Oñati International Series in Law and Society, Hart 2012) 10 (citations omitted).

[3] H Collins, 'Independent Contractors and the Challenge of Vertical Disintegration to Employment Protection Laws' (1990) 10 OJLS 353.

[4] Fudge, McCrystal, and Sankaran, *Challenging the Legal Boundaries of Work Regulation* (n 2) 11, citing W Powell, 'The Capitalist Firm in the Twenty-First Century: Emerging Patterns in Western Enterprise' in P DiMaggio (ed), *The Twenty-First Century Firm: Changing Economic Organization in International Perspective* (Princeton University Press 2003) 58.

[5] EMAR, 'Agency Working in the UK: A Review of the Evidence' (Employment Relations Research Series No 93, BERR 2008) Table 1.1, drawing on a survey of recruitment agencies in 2007.

[6] IE Consulting, 'The Economic Impact of Private Equity in the UK' (BVCA 2008) 5.

fieldwork, discussion finally returns to each of the five employer functions identified in the previous chapter to demonstrate their shared exercise.

An emphasis on practical detail at this juncture may be surprising. It is however crucial in order to show how multi-entity work settings are a considerably more prevalent phenomenon than is generally assumed; indeed in that sense it could be said that there is little left that is 'atypical' about multiple *loci* of employer functions. The practical examples will furthermore be essential in challenging the traditional assumptions that were seen to underpin much of the unitary concept that emerged in Chapter 1. As Barmes has noted:

[t]he richness of non-legal accounts and analyses starkly contrast with the abstracted, convoluted and, with respect, frequently baffling, reflections of judges in categorising different kinds of workers in order to determine the statutory rights they have (or more typically, especially the more needful of external protection the working person, that they don't have).[7]

In drawing on these practical illustrations, an important factor to keep in mind is the sheer variety of factual scenarios, and therefore, of ways in which the exercise of employer functions can be shared. At least three different scenarios were identified in the previous chapter: employer functions might be bundled into one entity, shared between two or more entities, or parcelled out between different entities. Joint exercise in the multilateral scenarios to be explored will usually involve a combination of all these different modes, with further complexity added by the fact that the courts increasingly refuse to 'ignore practical aspects of control that fall short of direct legal rights'.[8]

Finally, it is important to note that power accrued to investors or end-users is not necessarily power taken away from management. This insight is the key challenge to a unitary concept of the employing entity in the Private Equity and agency work contexts. Only if the power of control within employment, contractual, and corporate governance structures were seen as a zero-sum game would this not be the case: the accrual of power to owners or end-users has to lead to a loss of power for management or the agency only if there is a 'finite amount' of control that is constantly reallocated between different actors. Lukes has convincingly demonstrated, however, that where there is power, control over a situation can be exercised in many ways, 'whether through the operation of social forces and institutional practices or through individuals' decisions'. Thus understood, additional actors' gaining power will increase the overall set of influencing factors and 'can occur [even] in the absence of actual, observable conflict'.[9]

The two-way relationships at the basis of concentrated shareholders' control over corporate management or end-users' detailed contracts for the supply of agency labour fit into Lukes' description of power. They are therefore *additional*

[7] L Barmes, 'Learning from Case Law Accounts of Marginalised Working' in Fudge, McCrystal, and Sankaran, *Challenging the Legal Boundaries of Work Regulation* (n 2) 305.

[8] *Motorola Ltd v Davidson* [2001] IRLR 4 (EAT) [11].

[9] S Lukes, *Power: A Radical View* (Palgrave 2005) 28.

loci of power within the employment structure, rather than a subsumption of another entity's influence. This is the key challenge to the unitary strand of the concept of the employer in sole control over the employment relationship, as it emerged in Chapter 1.

Section 1: Temporary Agency Work

The first illustration of shared employer function exercise is drawn from triangular or agency work settings, where workers are retained by an agency, and then sent out to work for third-party end-users. It stands as a good example of other areas of the 'informalization' of work, where workers are placed outside employment law protection because of the 'externalization' of labour.[10] In labour-only subcontracting or personal service companies, for example, similar issues will arise as there is no direct (contractual) relationship between the worker and the person or entity behind the economic activity. Whilst such situations have traditionally been analysed from the perspective of the insecurity of some of the most vulnerable workers, triangular work settings are by no means limited to those contexts.[11]

A. The Operation of the Agency Work Industry

Whilst the modern form of work agencies has been in existence since the 1950s, there are early reports of labour market intermediaries dating back as far as the 1920s.[12] Indeed, one of the ILO's earliest measures was to call for a legal response to agency work, in the rather radical form of a complete prohibition of employment agencies.[13] In gauging the size of the industry in the United Kingdom today it is rather difficult to obtain accurate data, as agency work is not always distinguished as such in published statistics riddled with curious exceptions,[14] and because issues of classification tend to lead to significant underestimates.[15] In

---

[10] T Teklè, 'Labour Law and Worker Protection in the South: An Evolving Tension Between Models and Reality' in T Teklè (ed), *Labour Law and Worker Protection in Developing Countries* (Hart 2010) 3, 20 (as cited by Fudge, McCrystal, and Sankaran, *Challenging the Legal Boundaries of Work Regulation* (n 2) 2).

[11] A Pollert and A Charlwood, 'The Vulnerable Worker in Britain and Problems at Work' (2009) 23 Work, Employment and Society 343.

[12] C Forde and G Slater, 'The Role of Employment Agencies in Pay Setting' (ACAS Research Paper 05/2011) [2.1], citing C Forde, '"You know we are not an employment agency": Manpower, Government and the Development of the Temporary Employment Agency Industry in Britain' (2008) 9 Enterprise and Society 337.

[13] ILO Unemployment Recommendation 1919 (No 1), Art 1; as noted by E McGaughey, 'Should Agency Workers be Treated Differently?' (LSE Working Papers 07/2010) 8. The ILO has softened its stance since.

[14] EMAR, 'Agency Working in the UK' (n 5) [1.1], for example, excludes entertainment, modelling, writers, and professional sports persons.

[15] E Markova and S McKay, 'Agency and Migrant Workers: Literature Review' (TUC Commission on Vulnerable Employment 2008) 6. The review extensively covers most of the material cited in the first part of this chapter.

2008, the number of agency workers was put at a mid-point of 1.3 million, with other sources reporting figures as high as 1.5 million.[16] The industry has continued to undergo rapid growth in subsequent years,[17] despite brief stagnation in the early period of domestic recession.[18] By 2013, the TUC estimated that the number of temporary agency workers had risen by at least 15 per cent since the onset of the recession, 'faster than any other form of employment'.[19] Indeed, a report commissioned in 2014 by the Recruitment & Employment Confederation, an industry representative body, suggested that '24% of the British population [have] worked as a temporary agency worker at some point in their working life',[20] and an international comparison published in the same year put the number at 1.13 million.[21] Relative to the overall size of the labour market, the agency industry is therefore larger in the UK than anywhere else in the European Union (EU).[22] Industry figures from 2014 suggest that there are approximately 18,000 agencies operating across the UK, employing a workforce of approximately 93,360 internal staff to match agency workers with assignments.[23]

Regulatory Context

There are several layers of industry regulation through domestic and European Union measures. In spite of this, the crucial question for present purposes—the actual status of an entity as the employer of temporary workers—is not defined for employment law purposes; in stark contrast, for example, to taxation.[24] The question is therefore left to the common law, the implications of which will be discussed in the first section of Chapter 3.

In the domestic context, agencies were first regulated by the Employment Agencies Act 1973 under somewhat different terminology.[25] The Act drew a

---

[16] EMAR, 'Agency Working in the UK' (n 5) Table 1.1.

[17] C Forde, G Slater, and F Green, 'Agency Working in Britain: What Do We Know?' (Centre for Employment Relations Innovation and Change Policy Report Number 2, CERIC 2008).

[18] C Forde and G Slater, 'A Survey of Non Regular Work in the UK' (Report prepared for the Japan Institute of Labour Policy and Training 2010).

[19] Press Release, 'TUC Lodges Complaint Against Government For Failing to Give Equal Pay to Agency Workers' (TUC, 2 September 2013).

[20] REC, *Flex Appeal: Why Freelancers, Contractors and Agency Workers Choose to Work This Way* (Recruitment & Employment Confederation 2014) 5.

[21] F van Haasteren, A Muntz, and D Pennel, *Economic Report: 2014 Edition* (CIET 2014) 15, 17.

[22] E Berkhout, C Dustmann, and P Emmder, 'Mind the Gap' (International Database on Employment and Adaptable Labour 2007); van Haasteren, Muntz, and Pennel (n 21) 19.

[23] van Haasteren, Muntz, and Pennel (n 21) 29; D Winchester, 'Thematic Feature: Temporary Agency Work in the UK' (National Report 2007; available through the EIROnline database at <http://www.eurofound.europa.eu> accessed 28 August 2014; J Arrowsmith, 'Temporary Agency Work in an Enlarged European Union' (Office for Official Publications of the European Communities, Luxembourg 2006).

[24] S Deakin and G Morris, *Labour Law* (6th edn Hart 2012) [3.35]: Income Tax (Earnings and Pensions) Act 2003, Pt II Ch 7, and Social Security (Categorisation of Earners) Regulations, SI 1978/1689.

[25] This was at the same time as most other European countries, see eg the *Arbeitnehmerüberlassungsgesetz* 1972 in Germany.

distinction between 'employment agencies', businesses who find employment for workers or search for workers on behalf of companies, and 'employment businesses', enterprises that supply workers to end-users. The latter are, however, commonly understood to be employment agencies today. The legislation set certain minimum standards, for example, as regards payments by workers and accuracy of advertisements, and, crucially, made provisions for a mandatory licensing regime. The latter was however revoked in 1994.[26]

Various regulations introduced under the Act are in operation today, most notably the Conduct of Employment Agencies and Employment Businesses Regulations 2003,[27] placing a series of general obligations on agencies to avoid particular instances of exploitation:[28] an agency cannot, for example, force workers to use additional services or hire and purchase goods from the agency,[29] and it may not withhold payment for a number of reasons, including 'non-receipt of payment from the hirer'.[30] There is also a prohibition on supplying workers to break industrial action,[31] and the requirement that the parties agree on certain terms before any services are provided.[32] A partial licensing system was reintroduced in 2004 by the Gangmasters (Licensing) Act,[33] limited in its application by a sector-specific focus on areas such as agriculture and food processing.[34] Overall, however, the UK remains one of only five EU countries that do not require a licence to operate a temporary work agency.[35]

On the European level, consensus on regulating work agencies proved impossible to achieve over a period of nearly 30 years. A Directive on Temporary Agency Work[36] was eventually enacted in the autumn of 2008, with the primary aim of providing for equality in treatment of temporary agency staff and an end-user's permanent workforce.[37] This is significantly weakened, however, not only because of the way the scope of application of the Directive is defined,[38] but also given the significant number of carve-outs and exceptions, most importantly as to the minimum length of service provision before the equality duty applies.[39] It is

---

[26] Deregulation and Contracting Out Act 1994.

[27] As amended: Conduct of Employment Agencies and Employment Businesses (Amendment) Regulations 2007, SI 2007/3575.

[28] Conduct of Employment Agencies and Employment Businesses Regulations 2003, SI 2003/3319, Pt II.

[29] Conduct of Employment Agencies and Employment Businesses Regulations (n 28) reg 5.

[30] Conduct of Employment Agencies and Employment Businesses Regulations (n 28) reg 12(a).

[31] Conduct of Employment Agencies and Employment Businesses Regulations (n 28) reg 7.

[32] Conduct of Employment Agencies and Employment Businesses Regulations (n 28) Pt III; Markova and McKay, 'Agency and Migrant Workers: Literature Review' (n 15) 33.

[33] Gangmasters (Licensing) Act 2004, s 7.

[34] Gangmasters (Licensing) Act 2004, s 3.

[35] M Wynn, 'Regulating Rogues? Employment Agency Enforcement and Sections 15–18 of the Employment Act 2008' (2009) 38 ILJ 64, 69.

[36] Directive (EC) 104/2008 of the European Parliament and of the Council of 19 November 2008 on temporary agency work [2008] OJ L 327/9 ('Temporary Agency Work Directive').

[37] Temporary Agency Work Directive (n 36) art 5.

[38] N Countouris and R Horton 'The Temporary Agency Work Directive: Another Broken Promise?' (2009) 38 ILJ 329, 330.

[39] Countouris and Horton, 'The Temporary Agency Work Directive: Another Broken Promise?' (n 38) 333.

therefore unsurprising that Countouris and Horton conclude that the Directive 'is a regulatory instrument that seeks to remove any remaining stigma, restriction or prohibition, associated with temporary agency work without providing for a sufficiently protective, equitable and fair regulatory framework'.[40] The United Kingdom's implementation in 2010[41] reluctantly gave effect to the basic rights set out in the Directive, for example as regards the use of joint facilities and the provision of information about job vacancies from the start of the employment'.[42] As already suggested, however, there are significant carve-outs, most notably in the form of a 12-week threshold,[43] which end-users will frequently explicitly contract around by limiting the length of any individual assignment to an 11-week period.[44] Liability for breach of various obligations is apportioned between the agency and its end-user client, subject to the latter's ability to invoke a series of defences.[45]

The overall weakness of the combined domestic and European regulatory efforts is compounded by a glaring lack of enforcement, primarily due to a lack of significant numbers of inspectors and the division of responsibilities between overlapping bodies such as the Employment Agencies Standards Inspectorate (EASI) and the Gangmasters Licensing Authority (GLA).[46] The Employment Act 2008 brought some improvements in this regard,[47] but commentators continue to note a 'disturbing picture of variations in enforcement activity across the UK recruitment industry'[48] as a result of weak enforcement mechanisms.[49] It is not surprising, then, when Markova and McKay conclude that 'in practice it is possible for agencies to open for business without having to meet any regulatory standards'.[50] Despite individual examples to the contrary, high levels of non-compliance are reflected in qualitative studies across the board.[51]

In conclusion, it should briefly be noted that some existing statutory regulation, for example in the areas of health and safety or anti-discrimination, can extend into the operation of work agencies. The actual status of workers or employers

---

[40] Countouris and Horton, 'The Temporary Agency Work Directive: Another Broken Promise?' (n 38) 338.

[41] Agency Workers Regulations 2010, SI 2010/93. See P Leighton and M Wynn, 'Classifying Employment Relationships—More Sliding Doors or a Better Regulatory Framework?' (2011) 40 ILJ 5.

[42] Agency Workers Regulations 2010 (n 41) regs 12 and 13.

[43] Agency Workers Regulations 2010 (n 41) reg 5.

[44] Eversheds LLP, 'Terms and Conditions for the Supply of Services from an Employment Business to an End-User Client' (PLC Employment and PLC Commercial, Practical Law Company, London 2012) 2.10.

[45] Agency Workers Regulations (n 41) reg 14.

[46] McGaughey, 'Should Agency Workers be Treated Differently?' (n 13) 12.

[47] eg Employment Act 2008, s 16 (increased EASI inspection powers).

[48] Wynn, 'Regulating Rogues?' (n 35) 72.

[49] Equality and Human Rights Commission ('EHRC'), 'Inquiry into Recruitment and Employment in the Meat and Poultry Processing Sector' (EHRC 2010) 31.

[50] E Markova and S McKay, 'Understanding the Operation and Management of Employment Agencies in the UK Labour Market' (TUC Commission on Vulnerable Employment, London 2008) 8.

[51] Aziz et al, 'Hard Work, Hidden Lives: The Full Report' (n 1) 127.

for employment law purposes is not defined, however; an omission that is in clear violation of ILO norms.[52] The specific industry regulation seen here will therefore be mostly excluded from future chapters,[53] as it merely tinkers 'at the edges of the problem rather than dealing with the matter at the heart of this area of law [viz] . . . the issue of the employment status and protective employment rights of agency workers'.[54]

B. The Emergence of Multiple *Loci* of Employer Functions

Discussion thus turns to the first step in the practical illustration: the following paragraphs look at agencies and end-users as key actors in the triangular setup, briefly explore the potential motivations for the use of agency labour, and analyse how the multi-partite relationship is structured through contracts for the supply of labour. The variety of motivations, legal organization, and work arrangements under scrutiny is puzzling, and presents perhaps the clearest challenge to the received unitary concept of the employer, as Section 3 of Chapter 3 will demonstrate.

Employment Agencies

Employment agencies recruit workers on an ongoing basis in order to provide labour to clients on individual 'assignments'. In a highly fragmented market, over half of the temporary work agencies in the United Kingdom are very small operations, directly employing fewer than five people; less than one per cent have staff exceeding 200.[55] The majority of agencies operate from a single establishment.[56] Forde and Slater have identified at least three different typologies,[57] beginning with agencies' geographical span: whilst some operate only in a limited area, others have branches across the country. Second, whilst some large firms operate as general workforce providers, most agencies have a specific occupational and sectoral focus. Finally, agencies vary as regards the nature of their contractual relationships with end-users, from one-off short-term hires to 'in-house' labour agencies at large corporations.[58] Qualitative fieldwork reports confirm this high degree of factual variation.[59] It is also mirrored in the broad range of different jobs done by agency workers,[60] from providing cleaning services to piloting commercial passenger aircraft.[61]

---

[52] ILO Private Employment Agencies Convention 1997 (No 181).
[53] Notably the Employment Agencies Act 1973 and the Conduct Regulations 2003 (n 27).
[54] P Leighton and M Wynn, 'Temporary Agency Working: Is the Law on the Turn?' [2008] Company Lawyer 7, 8.
[55] EMAR, 'Agency Working in the UK' (n 5) [1.3].
[56] EMAR, 'Agency Working in the UK' (n 5) [1.3].
[57] Forde and Slater, 'The Role of Employment Agencies in Pay Setting' (n 12) 10ff.
[58] Aziz, 'Hard Work, Hidden Lives: The Full Report' (n 1) 188.
[59] See eg the list of different agencies reviewed by McKay and Markova, 'Understanding the Operation and Management of Employment Agencies in the UK Labour Market', 16–21.
[60] EMAR, 'Agency Working in the UK' (n 5) 11–12.
[61] See eg the agency recruiting for Ryanair: <http://www.mcginleyhr.co.uk/h/about-us/aviation/47/> accessed 28 August 2014.

End-Users or Clients

Nearly one-fifth of workplaces in the United Kingdom rely on the services of temporary agency workers,[62] with a fairly clear concentration in larger enterprises: over 50 per cent of temporary agency workers are seconded to work in enterprises with more than 50 employees.[63] BERR figures suggest that production industries (including, for example, agriculture, construction, and manufacturing) make up 25 per cent of agency clients, and private sector service companies 33–45 per cent.[64] Other sources suggest a different makeup, leaving the overall picture rather unclear.[65] The role of the public sector in procuring the services of labour agencies should also not be underestimated: several of the leading cases to be discussed in subsequent chapters involve public authorities, and fieldwork reports give numerous examples, such as a London local authority which sources nearly 20 per cent of its staff from agencies.[66]

When enquiring into the use of agency work,[67] different studies have uncovered a wide range of potential motivations, with considerable divergence between the answers offered by end-users and agencies. Users' arguments range from numerical flexibility to meet peaks and troughs in demand to obtaining specific skills or ensuring temporary leave and maternity cover.[68] Markova and McKay summarize these reasons under a series of categories.[69] Flexibility is considered to be of prime importance, though it is not always clear to what extent this is limited to complementarity, ie the use of agency workers in situations where required staff numbers rise temporarily, or whether there is an increasing move towards substitution of permanent employees and the long-term hiring of a workforce through agencies. Cost savings are a second factor frequently identified, though a considerable number of end-users suggest that there are little, if any, overall savings. Legal factors, finally, also loom large. Some studies suggest that employers' primary motivation is not the avoidance of employment law regulation as such, but rather the possibility of shifting liability for immigration law violations, with the agency in charge of organizing work permits, checking workers' documents, and ensuring ongoing compliance.[70] Other studies, however, have found that up to a quarter of end-user

---

[62] B Kersley et al, *Inside the Workplace: First Findings from the 2004 Workplace Employment Relations Survey* (Routledge 2005), as cited in Forde and Slater, 'The Role of Employment Agencies in Pay Setting' (n 12) [2.1].

[63] EMAR, 'Agency Working in the UK' (n 5) 4–5.

[64] EMAR, 'Agency Working in the UK' (n 5) 3–4.

[65] Markova and McKay, 'Agency and Migrant Workers: Literature Review' (n 15) 17.

[66] Markova and McKay, 'Understanding the Operation and Management of Employment Agencies in the UK Labour Market' (n 50) 18.

[67] See also S McKay, 'Employer Motivations for Using Agency Labour' (2008) 37 ILJ 296.

[68] See eg EMAR, 'Agency Working in the UK' (n 5) Table 4.1.

[69] Markova and McKay, 'Agency and Migrant Workers: Literature Review' (n 15) 19ff, drawing on L Gramm and J Schnell, 'The Use of Flexible Staffing Arrangements in Core Production Jobs' 2001 (54) Industrial and Labour Relations Review 245; K Hakansson and T Isidorsson, 'Flexibility, Stability and Agency Work: A Comparison of the Use of Agency Work in Sweden and the UK' in B Furaker, K Hakansson, and J Karlsson, *Flexibility and Stability in Working Life* (Palgrave 2007) 123; P Allan, 'The Contingent Workforce; Challenges and New Directions' (2002) American Business Review 103.

[70] Markova and McKay, 'Understanding the Operation and Management of Employment Agencies in the UK Labour Market' (n 50) 24–5.

firms rely on agency labour specifically in order to avoid incurring employment law obligations.[71]

Contractual Setup

The formal relationship between agencies and end-users can be structured in myriad ways,[72] from ad hoc contracting to increasingly common long-term relationships between a particular agency and end-user.[73] Some agencies have preferred-, or even sole-supplier, status with individual clients; others rely on framework agreements to standardize individual one-off hires.[74] A more recent development is temporary work agencies that act as third party vendors to coordinate other agencies, organizing external workforces for clients, without providing any workers directly. Greenwich London Borough Council, the defendant in the now infamous case of *James*,[75] for example, employed more than 10 per cent of agency workers at the time of the litigation, and had to retain the services of a large national employment agency to manage its various supplier agencies.[76]

The analysis of an anonymized sample contract used as the basis for negotiations between agencies and end-users[77] suggests that key terms between agency and end-user will usually go beyond the legally required minima, such as fee calculation and termination procedures.[78] The agencies' duties may be set out in great detail, including as to where and how workers should be recruited, which background and immigrations checks are to be completed, any additional licences, authorizations, and references that may be required, and the details of information about each temporary worker to be supplied to the end-user.[79] These information provisions are generally mutual, ie the end-user's obligations will cover provision of information about what workers are required and when.[80] There are, however, also reports of situations where end-users have little knowledge of the terms and conditions offered by agencies to workers.[81] Both parties will usually enjoy strong termination rights,[82] and be

---

[71]   EHRC, 'Inquiry into Recruitment and Employment' (n 49) 22.

[72]   Forde and Slater, 'The Role of Employment Agencies in Pay Setting' (n 12) 11–14.

[73]   See K Purcell, J Purcell, and S Tailby 'Temporary Work Agencies: Here Today, Gone Tomorrow?' (2004) 42 BJIR 705; Markova and McKay, 'Understanding the Operation and Management of Employment Agencies in the UK Labour Market' (n 50) 30–1 offer practical illustrations.

[74]   I Kirkpatrick et al, 'Professional Agency Working in Health and Social Services: Implications for Management' (CERIC Policy Report Number 3, CERIC 2009).

[75]   *James v Greenwich LBC* [2008] EWCA Civ 35, [2008] ICR 545.

[76]   McGaughey, 'Should Agency Workers be Treated Differently?' (n 13) 26.

[77]   Eversheds, 'Terms and Conditions for the Supply of Services from an Employment Business to an End-User Client' (n 44).

[78]   Conduct of Employment Agencies and Employment Businesses Regulations (n 28) reg 17.

[79]   Eversheds, 'Terms and Conditions for the Supply of Services from an Employment Business to an End-User Client' (n 44) cl 2.

[80]   Eversheds, 'Terms and Conditions for the Supply of Services from an Employment Business to an End-User Client' (n 44) cl 3.

[81]   Markova and McKay, 'Understanding the Operation and Management of Employment Agencies in the UK Labour Market' (n 50) 8.

[82]   Eversheds, 'Terms and Conditions for the Supply of Services from an Employment Business to an End-User Client' (n 44) cl 5.4.

subject to confidentiality, audit, record-keeping, and indemnity requirements. The contractual agreements, finally, will include detailed arrangements for fee and transition payment and tax structures, as well as the already referenced clause limiting the length of any individual assignment in order to avoid the application of the 2010 Agency Workers Regulations.[83]

C. The Shared Exercise of Employer Functions

In moving from a summary of the organizational and regulatory setup of the employment agency industry to a detailed account of how the five employer functions under scrutiny are jointly exercised, discussion in the present subsection draws on a broad range of sources that document the day-to-day operation across different sectors. There is, first, a considerable body of litigation concerning the status classification of temporary workers, which frequently summarizes the relevant involvement of different entities.[84] As Barmes has noted, however, even where such summaries can be found in reported decisions, they are usually limited to a small cross-section of the actual factual scenario, and can present a very abstract image of work arrangements.[85] It is therefore necessary to rely on additional field studies in scrutinizing the five functions. A range of such sources has recently become available, most notably in the form of a report on the 'Operation and Management of Employment Agencies in the UK Labour Market',[86] a sector-specific study on working conditions in the meat processing industry,[87] and several profile-based case studies found throughout the full report of the Commission on Vulnerable Employment.[88] One interesting effect of relying on these sources can be noted at the outset: while the case law frequently suggests a clear parcelling out of functions between different entities, the qualitative field work reports show a much more diffuse picture, with agencies and end-users both involved (albeit to different degrees) in the exercise of the full range of employer functions.

[1] Inception and Termination of the Contract of Employment
As regards the first function, this will usually be the primary task of the employment agency: a worker is taken on its books, and sent out to end-users at the agency's discretion.[89] Agencies can also shortlist and select candidates on the end-user's

---

[83] Eversheds, 'Terms and Conditions for the Supply of Services from an Employment Business to an End-User Client' (n 44) cl 2.10: 'The Employment Business shall not provide any Temporary Worker for a period in excess of 11 weeks without the prior written consent of the Client.'

[84] Barmes, 'Learning from Case Law Accounts of Marginalised Working' (n 7).

[85] Barmes, 'Learning from Case Law Accounts of Marginalised Working' (n 7) 314.

[86] Markova and McKay, 'Understanding the Operation and Management of Employment Agencies in the UK Labour Market' (n 50).

[87] EHRC, 'Inquiry into Recruitment and Employment' (n 49).

[88] Aziz, 'Hard Work, Hidden Lives: The Full Report' (n 1).

[89] Markova and McKay, 'Understanding the Operation and Management of Employment Agencies in the UK Labour Market' (n 50) 39ff.

behalf,[90] and be in charge of organizing work permits and checking other qualifications and documents.[91] End-users are, however, also sometimes involved in the selection of individual workers, and there are reports of instances where they do so for illegal purposes, for example by specifying a particular race or nationality of the agency worker to be supplied.[92]

As regards influence over the setting of terms, there is again a wide variety of different models, though end-users generally seem to have only 'limited knowledge of agency workers' terms and conditions'.[93] At least one report suggests that end-users 'found that they had no influence on changing terms and conditions, and indeed agency workers had been forbidden [by their agencies] from even talking to the [clients] about their pay rates'.[94] Public sector users are an exception in this context, with most local authorities insisting on direct control over agency workers' terms and conditions.[95]

General human resource (HR) functions including appraisals will usually be exercised by the agency.[96] Termination and replacement is likewise via the agency itself,[97] usually upon the end-user's request,[98] and without significant notice periods.[99] Some clients, however, may retain a direct right to dismiss the employee,[100] again with several reports of this function being exercised for inappropriate reasons, such as dismissing a female line worker on grounds of her gender.[101]

[2] Receiving Labour and its Fruits

While it could be suggested that agencies' profit margins are a result of workers' labour,[102] the second function rests firmly with the end-user; indeed this is usually the very reason for the triangular relationship. The extent to which this is an actual legal duty owed directly to the client varies, however,[103] as the agency will not normally rely on the worker to provide services for its internal purposes. Indeed, some

---

[90] Markova and McKay, 'Agency and Migrant Workers: Literature Review' (n 15) 20; citing C Stanworth and J Druker, 'Human Resource Solutions? Dimensions of Employers' Use of Temporary Agency Labour in the UK' (2006) 35 Personnel Review 175.

[91] Markova and McKay, 'Understanding the Operation and Management of Employment Agencies in the UK Labour Market' (n 50) 24–5.

[92] EHRC, 'Inquiry into Recruitment and Employment' (n 49) 8.

[93] Markova and McKay, 'Understanding the Operation and Management of Employment Agencies in the UK Labour Market' (n 50) 40.

[94] Markova and McKay, 'Understanding the Operation and Management of Employment Agencies in the UK Labour Market' (n 50) 42.

[95] Markova and McKay, 'Understanding the Operation and Management of Employment Agencies in the UK Labour Market' (n 50).

[96] Forde and Slater, 'The Role of Employment Agencies in Pay Setting' (n 12) 12.

[97] Aziz, 'Hard Work, Hidden Lives: The Full Report' (n 1) 189.

[98] Leighton and Wynn, 'Temporary Agency Working: Is the Law on the Turn?' (n 54) 9.

[99] McGaughey, 'Should Agency Workers be Treated Differently?' (n 13) 2.

[100] *Muschett v HM Prison Service* [2010] EWCA Civ 25, [2010] IRLR 451, 14.

[101] EHRC, 'Inquiry into Recruitment and Employment' (n 49) 11–12.

[102] Forde and Slater, 'The Role of Employment Agencies in Pay Setting' (n 12).

[103] Suggested to exist in *Tilson v Alstom Transport* [2010] EWCA Civ 1308, [2011] IRLR 169; cf *James* (n 75), where no duties were owed to the employer.

end-users increasingly report concerns about the quality of work received, with some linking it to a lack of temporary workers' loyalty to the client.[104]

[3] Provision of Work and Pay

The division of this third employer function is amongst the more difficult to analyse, as it varies drastically between different scenarios. Looking first at the obligation to provide work, the agency will normally not be under any obligation to do so. Leighton and Wynn cite the following sample contractual clause:

We, the agency, will do our best to find you work that suits you and you, the temp, will in turn agree not to unreasonably refuse suitable work when offered.[105]

The situation of the end-user is less clear. While an obligation to provide work is rarely found on the facts,[106] there have been decisions to the contrary, especially where the employee was deeply integrated in the end-user's undertaking, up to and including managerial control over the end-user's permanent employees.[107] Whilst the provision of day-to-day work is therefore clearly a role of the end-user, for example in choosing the allocation of particular jobs,[108] such findings will be rare. In reality, workers will frequently turn up at an end-user's site in the morning only to find that on that particular day no work is available.[109]

The provision of pay, on the other hand, is usually a function exercised by the agency, together with general payroll and tax services. Suggestions that an employment agency merely acts as the end-user's agent in this regard no longer seem to feature in the most recent case law.[110] While wages are nearly always paid to workers by their agency or a payroll company associated with it,[111] the question as to who actually determines the levels of remuneration yields a much more mixed response, as a recent report for ACAS shows. The traditional assumption, backed up by early empirical studies, was that pay levels were driven primarily by how much the end-user paid the agency.[112] In *James*, on the other hand, it was pointed out that different agencies sometimes offer distinct pay levels for identical jobs: the claimant was found to have 'changed agencies rather than employers in order to obtain a higher wage'.[113]

It has also been suggested that during positive economic climates agencies will have more power to set pay levels[114] as well as additional benefits, such as holiday pay.[115] Any suggestions of a clear overall picture, however, betray immense factual

---

[104] Aziz, 'Hard Work, Hidden Lives: The Full Report' (n 1) 190.
[105] Leighton and Wynn, 'Temporary Agency Working: Is the Law on the Turn?' (n 54) 12.
[106] See eg *James* (n 75).   [107] *Alstom* (n 103).
[108] EHRC, 'Inquiry into Recruitment and Employment' (n 49) 10.
[109] Aziz, 'Hard Work, Hidden Lives: The Full Report' (n 1) 14 (John's story).
[110] Though cf Munby J's dissent in *Cable & Wireless Plc v Muscat* [2006] EWCA Civ 220, [2006] ICR 975.
[111] EHRC, 'Inquiry into Recruitment and Employment' (n 49) 16.
[112] Forde and Slater, 'The Role of Employment Agencies in Pay Setting' (n 12) 19.
[113] *James* (n 75) [41], [15].
[114] Forde and Slater, 'The Role of Employment Agencies in Pay Setting' (n 12) 30.
[115] Forde and Slater, 'The Role of Employment Agencies in Pay Setting' (n 12) 35.

variation and complexity. This is frequently illustrated in situations where problems arise once an end-user has paid its fees to an agency, without workers' ever receiving their wages,[116] or being paid late and only after incurring much hassle.[117]

[4] Managing the Enterprise-Internal Market

The facts of most reported cases suggest that function four rests firmly with the end-user. In *James*, for example, the council conceded at the outset that it had exercised full control over the claimant.[118] In *Alstom*, counsel for the end-user went even further in agreeing with the court that on the basis of a 'significant degree of control', there had been 'a direct contractual relationship between Alstom and the appellant, [identifiable] as a contract of service'.[119] But agency involvement frequently goes further than these reports suggest. The starkest illustrations of this are agency offices on the client site as seen in *Astbury v Gist*.[120] Other reports suggest that this was by no means an isolated incident,[121] and that some local authorities even have more than one agency physically represented on their premises.[122]

Agencies may also influence what work is done and how, for example when a cleaning agency instructs its workers how to prepare and apply certain chemicals.[123] Agency involvement may even go as far as the selection of employees for specific tasks or other clients, to the potential frustration of the original end-user where 'the agencies . . . "skim off" the best workers or move them on, even when the company was keen to keep them'.[124] As regards time worked, it will usually be the end-user who sets the hours where workers' presence is required, with control exercised right down to when toilet breaks may be taken.[125] Again, however, there is also evidence of agency involvement, for example where workers are forced to leave their accommodation and go to work in the morning, or the case of the 'agency managers standing at the factory exit and turning back agency workers to force them to work overtime when they tried to leave the factory after their shift had ended'.[126] Working-time opt-out signatures under the Working Time Regulations 1998[127] are usually required by both agency and end-users.[128]

---

[116] Aziz, 'Hard Work, Hidden Lives: The Full Report' (n 1) 133 (Michael's story).

[117] Aziz, 'Hard Work, Hidden Lives: The Full Report' (n 1) 116 (Pietr's story).

[118] *James* (n 75) [12].   [119] *Alstom* (n 103) [4].

[120] *Astbury v Gist Ltd* [2007] UKEAT/0619/06/DA.

[121] Including the public sector: K Hoque et al, 'New Contractual Relationships in the Agency Worker Market: the Case of the UK's National Health Service' (2008) 46 BJIR 389.

[122] Aziz, 'Hard Work, Hidden Lives: The Full Report' (n 1) 14.

[123] Aziz, 'Hard Work, Hidden Lives: The Full Report' (n 1) 18 (Angela's story).

[124] Markova and McKay, 'Understanding the Operation and Management of Employment Agencies in the UK Labour Market' (n 50) 29.

[125] EHRC, 'Inquiry into Recruitment and Employment' (n 49) 11.

[126] EHRC, 'Inquiry into Recruitment and Employment' (n 49) 14.

[127] SI 1998/1833, reg 5.

[128] EHRC, 'Inquiry into Recruitment and Employment' (n 49) 12.

Wynn and Leighton suggest that agencies will rarely be involved in managing their clients' internal affairs, on the basis of a distinction between the end-user's operational control over specific tasks performed (category [1] in the present classification), and transactional controls such as immigration status checks, which are left to the agency.[129] As the present discussion has demonstrated, on the other hand, agencies may frequently be involved in a client's enterprise-internal market, with examples reaching as far as the reported requirement by an agency that its end-user client install on-site washing machines and shower facilities.[130]

[5] Managing the Enterprise-External Market

The allocation of the final function is likewise distributed in myriad ways: when measured against the common law criterion of undertaking an economic activity in return for potential profit whilst also under the risk of direct exposure to loss, it can be seen as, in some sense, shared between end-user, agency, *and the worker herself*. In *Alstom*, for example, the claimant had repeatedly refused to be engaged under a contract of employment with the end-user directly, as 'he was on a significantly higher rate of pay under the agency arrangements' and 'also perceived there to be tax advantages'.[131] The oft-cited provision of tools, including health and safety equipment and relevant training, is sometimes seen as the task of the agency,[132] and at other times as that of the end-user, who may even force workers to share particular items.[133] There are also frequent reports of workers having to provide their own uniforms and protective equipment.[134] Specific training will usually be provided by the end-user,[135] though generally at a lower level than for permanent staff,[136] whereas some agencies also provide broader skills training.[137]

The chance of making profits or incurring losses, for example due to a contractual obligation to keep paying workers even when there is no work available, will usually be born by *neither* agency nor end-users, thus shifting the risk directly onto individual workers who will not get paid when no work has been offered.[138]

In conclusion, then, it has been seen how extremely 'varied and variable'[139] the arrangements between different *loci* of employer functions in the triangular agency

---

[129] Leighton and Wynn, 'Temporary Agency Working: Is the Law on the Turn?' (n 54) 9.

[130] Markova and McKay, 'Understanding the Operation and Management of Employment Agencies in the UK Labour Market' (n 50) 34 (Food Company G).

[131] *Alstom* (n 103) [5].

[132] Markova and McKay, 'Understanding the Operation and Management of Employment Agencies in the UK Labour Market' (n 50) 33 (Food Company A vs Food Company G)

[133] Aziz, 'Hard Work, Hidden Lives: The Full Report' (n 1) 22 (Victor's story).

[134] Aziz, 'Hard Work, Hidden Lives: The Full Report' (n 1) 27 (Imran's story).

[135] eg Markova and McKay, 'Understanding the Operation and Management of Employment Agencies in the UK Labour Market' (n 50) 34 (Local Authority B); 26 (Food Company A).

[136] Aziz, 'Hard Work, Hidden Lives: The Full Report' (n 1) 188.

[137] *Heatherwood and Wexham Park Hospitals NHS Trust v Kulubowila* [2006] UKEAT/0633/06/LA; Forde and Slater, 'The Role of Employment Agencies in Pay Setting' (n 12) 36.

[138] J Hacker, *The Great Risk Shift: the New Economic Insecurity and the Decline of the American Dream* (OUP 2008).

[139] Leighton and Wynn, 'Temporary Agency Working: Is the Law on the Turn?' (n 54) 8.

work context can be—far beyond the unitary paradigm model of single-entity employment. It should furthermore be remembered that the joint exercise of employer functions takes place on a spectrum ranging from complete parcelling out, where different entities have exclusive competence in certain areas, to a high degree of overlap. A single triangular setting will usually involve a combination of these. A good illustration of this arose on the facts of *Dacas v Brook Street Bureau (UK) Ltd*,[140] where the claimant was an agency worker employed to clean hostels for a local authority (the end-user). Under the arrangement, the agency paid the worker (function [1]), while day-to-day control over her work (function [4]) was exercised by the local authority. An example of shared exercise, on the other hand, can be found in situations were both agency and end-user have the right to terminate the worker's engagement,[141] or indeed the many diffuse situations encountered above.

Section 2: Private Equity

Discussion thus turns to a second example of multi-entity employer function exercise: the Private Equity industry. As the traditional model of dispersed shareholdings has increasingly come under pressure,[142] industry analysts have noticed a strong trend towards concentrated ownership, from block holdings to outright subsidiary ownership. Private Equity funds are a prime example of this shift towards relational, or 'insider',[143] systems of corporate governance. Concentrated share ownership is particularly challenging in the employment context, as it leads to multiple parties' potentially exercising traditional employer functions. Once the majority, or at least a significant proportion of, voting rights are vested in a single shareholder, it will be able to exert considerable power over management. Gospel and Pendleton, drawing on research by Holland,[144] describe this power as the result of a two-way relationship:[145] through individual, usually private, meetings with senior management, detailed information about the company flows to its owners. This information covers both matters of long-term strategic planning and daily operational details (thus covering all elements of the employment relationship), and forms the basis of investors' effective control, in 'a clear break with

---

[140] [2004] EWCA Civ 217, [2004] ICR 1437.

[141] *Muschett* (n 100); see also *Construction Industry Training Board v Labour Force Ltd* [1970] 3 All ER 220 (HC).

[142] H Gospel and A Pendleton, 'Markets and Relationships: Finance, Governance, and Labour in the United Kingdom' in H Gospel and A Pendleton (eds), *Corporate Governance and Labour Management: An International Comparison* (OUP 2005) 71.

[143] Gospel and Pendleton, 'Markets and Relationships: Finance, Governance, and Labour in the United Kingdom' (n 142) 62.

[144] J Holland, 'The Corporate Governance Role of Financial Institutions in Their Investee Companies' (Research Report No 46, Chartered Association of Certified Accountants 1995) 19.

[145] Gospel and Pendleton 'Markets and Relationships: Finance, Governance, and Labour in the United Kingdom' (n 142) 75.

the traditional view of investor passivity in corporate governance'.[146] The firm's management will pay close attention to investors' opinions, even if not voiced expressly, as this 'network of relationships . . . provides an effective means . . . for investors to force changes on management'.[147] This is an important addition to the more traditional company law tools of control, such as replacing directors on the company's board—another example of controlling action that is available to majority shareholders.

In a strict technical sense, Private Equity refers to an asset class that comprises the entirety of equity investments not quoted on public exchanges.[148] In commercial reality, on the other hand, there is consensus that the meaning of the term is much more limited—even if its exact boundaries remain unclear. PE financiers are said to 'provide capital to invest in unquoted companies including public companies that are de-listed as part of the transaction. These investments may take the form of a purchase of shares from an existing shareholder (a buy-out if control is acquired) or an investment in new shares providing fresh capital to the investee company (development capital)'.[149] The value of these equity stakes in high risk/potentially high reward projects is protected by undertaking careful due diligence before making the investments and retaining powerful oversight rights afterwards.[150] The industry is further divided between funds providing capital to companies in their early life, with a focus on growth and expansion (venture capital), and investments in mature companies, usually in form of a buy-out: the meaning of Private Equity that is most relevant for present purposes. Mature companies are acquired by PE funds directly from public markets in so-called Public to Private (P2P) transactions, from private ownership, or increasingly from other investment funds through secondary buyouts. The same interest groups usually represent both branches of the industry;[151] in economic terms, however, buy-out activity is significantly more important than venture capital. A range of other alternative investment funds are sometimes mistakenly characterized as, or equated to, Private Equity partnerships. Confusion arises most frequently as to the relationship between hedge funds and PE. The main difference here is that the former focus on an infinite variety of relatively liquid trading strategies, moving quickly in (usually) public markets.[152] While some activist hedge funds do seek to influence company managers, they usually do so with only a small stake in

---

[146] Gospel and Pendleton, 'Markets and Relationships: Finance, Governance, and Labour in the United Kingdom' (n 142) 75.

[147] Gospel and Pendleton, 'Markets and Relationships: Finance, Governance, and Labour in the United Kingdom' (n 142) 79.

[148] T Jenkinson, 'Private Equity' in European Economic Advisory Group (ed), *Report on the European Economy* (CESifo 2009) 124.

[149] J Gilligan and M Wright, *Private Equity Demystified: An Explanatory Guide* (2nd edn ICAEW Corporate Finance Faculty 2010) 16.

[150] P Gompers and J Lerner, *The Venture Capital Cycle* (MIT Press 2004) 1.

[151] The British Venture Capital and Private Equity Association (BVCA) on a national level; a member of the EVCA (European Private Equity and Venture Capital Association).

[152] For a taxonomic overview, see P Myners, *Institutional Investment in the United Kingdom: A Review* (HM Treasury 2001) 157–8.

the company, and their influence is never *contractual*: the primary way of putting formal pressure on management is by divesting shares. As Private Equity management companies seek to build larger investment portfolios and hedge funds move into less liquid investment strategies there is considerable room for convergence between different types of alternative investment funds;[153] for present purposes, however, the focus remains on 'traditional' PE management companies involved in the acquisition and restructuring of mature businesses.

The underlying economic rationale of this industry can be summarized in three main strands. The first of these rejects traditional models of firms built on managerial discretion and shareholder deference to professional managers,[154] focusing on the agency costs that arise from a misalignment of owners' and managers' interests.[155] Private Equity, it is suggested, can overcome this problem by giving senior management a significant equity stake in the enterprise, thus closely aligning the interests of all parties.[156] The sharp incentive structure thus set up is usually reinforced by considerable levels of debt, requiring optimization rather than maximization of the underlying business.[157] Second, a clearly defined and closely monitored obligation to service creditors[158] settles what could otherwise be a constant struggle between owners and managers over the allocation of free cash-flow;[159] thus removing further inefficiencies that are said to result from the public corporation's split between ownership and control. Finally, the much more detailed and regular provision of information about the company to investors considerably reduces the price of financing operations by overcoming the 'lemons market' problem, where uncertainty about the true quality of a product impedes otherwise beneficial market transactions.[160] As traditional retail banks lack the institutional capacity for this sort of monitoring and oversight, the Private Equity industry has come to fill the niche role.[161] There are three ways for Private Equity investments to create returns in practice.[162] First, business performance can be improved, specifically by increasing the free cash flow of the enterprise.[163] This in turn is necessary to fund the second driver of increased returns, financial leverage: as long as the

[153] J Bevilacqua, 'Convergence and Divergence: Blurring the Lines between Hedge Funds and Private Equity Funds' (2006) 54 Buffalo Law Review 251, 253.

[154] A Berle and G Means, *The Modern Corporation and Private Property* (Macmillan 1939).

[155] A Alchian and H Demsetz, 'Production, Information Costs, and Economic Organization' (1972) 62 The American Economic Review 777; W Meckling and M Jensen, 'A Theory of the Firm: Managerial Behavior, Agency Costs and Ownership Structure' (1976) 3 Journal FE 4.

[156] I Clark, 'The Private Equity Business Model and Associated Strategies for HRM: Evidence and Implications?' (2009) 20 International Journal of Human Resource Management 2030, 2033.

[157] Jenkinson, 'Private Equity' (n 148) 132.

[158] M Jensen, 'The Eclipse of the Public Corporation' (1989) 67 HBR 61, 64; 1997 revision 18.

[159] Gilligan and Wright, *Private Equity Demystified: An Explanatory Guide* (n 149) 84.

[160] G Akerlof, 'The Market for "Lemons": Qualitative Uncertainty and the Market Mechanism' (1970) 84 Quarterly Journal of Economics 488.

[161] Gompers and Lerner, *The Venture Capital Cycle* (n 150) 4–5.

[162] T Franklin, 'What Private Equity Investors Look For: Investments, Managers, Advisers and Professionals' in M Soundy, T Spangler, and A Hampton (eds), *A Practitioner's Guide to Private Equity* (City & Financial 2009) 13–14.

[163] The financial measure for this is usually EBITDA (Earnings Before Interest, Taxes, Depreciation, and Amortization).

overall price of an asset remains stable, the value of its equity is set to increase as debts secured against it are being paid off. Finally, operational changes and new business environments can increase the overall value of a company, by increasing the multiple at which it can be sold on.[164] The following sections focus on the first of these value drivers, as it is here that *management* skills are at the core of what PE management companies do. Business performance has traditionally been improved by focusing on revenue growth, consolidation, and cost reduction;[165] with the latter not necessarily as the primary driver of efficiency gains.[166]

Before turning to a detailed examination of the industry and the resulting joint exercise of employer functions, it should be noted that Private Equity is a good example, *pars pro toto*, in the present context of inter-corporate control of corporate groups more generally. Despite a range of differences between Private Equity funds and the corporate group as economic entities—for example, as regards the longevity of the involvement, or the extent to which some functions are centralized in the parent entity—there are two key similarities that warrant comparative treatment for present purposes: the external decision-making powers of a sole, or at least majority, shareholder, and a close economic incentive alignment. As regards the former, a central group (or holding) company will normally own all the shares in its subsidiaries, either directly or through a chain of other companies, thus being able to exercise close control over its boards. This is mirrored in the PE partnership's control, albeit usually via a sophisticated chain of Special Purpose Vehicles (SPVs) headed by a Private Equity management company, of the portfolio company's board and senior executives. Subject to the temporal limitations of PE ownership over a three- to ten-year cycle, the economic incentive alignment is equally powerful in corporate groups and portfolio companies. Traditional shareholders suffer considerable agency cost losses due to their inability to act collectively.[167] As a block- or single shareholder, the fund or central group company has direct control over an entity that shares its economic aims, and may therefore be able to generate substantial additional value from the underlying entity. Corporate groups share key features with Private Equity, such as the exercise of employer functions at multiple levels and close economic incentive alignment. As a result, examples can be drawn from both areas, with relevant links explained at the appropriate juncture in subsequent chapters.

The key challenge for present purposes, viz the involvement of external shareholders in detailed management as an example of multiple *loci* of control, comes out most starkly in the Private Equity context. The relationships to be discussed sit on a particularly salient point along different axes of inter-corporate

---

[164] One way of valuing businesses is by multiple of EBITDA.

[165] Franklin, 'What Private Equity Investors Look For: Investments, Managers, Advisers and Professionals' (n 162) 20.

[166] Ernst & Young, 'How Do Private Equity Investors Create Value? A Study of 2006 Exits in the US and Western Europe' (2006).

[167] For analysis in the company law context see Kraakman et al, *The Anatomy of Corporate Law* (2nd edn OUP 2009) 36.

relationships,[168] combining each relevant facet in its strongest possible instantiation. The key points of subsequent findings will therefore also hold true for corporate groups. As regards the allocation of control between insider and outsider models of corporate governance, for example, Private Equity is identical to corporate groups in a strong focus on insider control, with a single shareholder drawing on a range of sources from company law and contractual agreements to commercial pressure. As regards the incentive alignment between management and shareholders, there are similar parallels. The intensity, purpose, and actual exercise of a shareholder's control over an underlying entity, finally, can be at an abstract, general (strategic) or detailed, day-to-day (operational) level. In corporate groups this will depend on different areas of the business, individual management structures and sometimes even historical accident. The hands-on approach of control-oriented Private Equity management companies, on the other hand, provides the clearest possible example of external control.

Operations in the PE industry thus provide a particularly salient subset in which to illustrate the conceptual tension in the concept of the employer. Given the financial and reputational constraints prevalent throughout the industry, however, there has been comparatively little litigation on which an exploration of practical implications in the following chapter could draw. By carefully moving along the various axes just identified, any differences identified will be ones of degree, rather than of kind. On the basis of the foregoing observations, the relevant subset will therefore be extended in Chapter 3 to include corporate groups more generally.

A. The Operation of Private Equity Investments

Private Equity has a long history in the United Kingdom. It has been suggested that PE funds have existed since the 1930s,[169] with the earliest leading institution—the Industrial and Commercial Finance Corporation (ICFC)—founded in 1945.[170] Today, the majority of UK-based funds specialize in the buy-out market for mid-cap enterprises, comprising a substantial part of mergers and acquisitions activity.[171] The BVCA estimates that three million workers, the equivalent of 21 per cent of private sector employees, are employed in British companies that have PE backing.[172]

---

[168] E Berglöf, 'Reforming Corporate Governance: Redirecting the European Agenda' (1997) 12 Economic Policy 91; B Cheffin, 'Corporate Law and Ownership Structure: A Darwinian Link?' (2002) 25 University of New South Wales Law Journal 346.

[169] A full historical overview is given in Myners, *Institutional Investment in the United Kingdom* (n 152) [12.22]–[12.34].

[170] Today the fund is known as 3i.

[171] Gilligan and Wright, *Private Equity Demystified: An Explanatory Guide* (n 149) 19–20.

[172] IE Consulting, 'The Economic Impact of Private Equity in the UK' (n 6). This report was compiled on the basis of just over 1,000 companies surveyed by IEC and the BVCA. By comparison, House of Commons Treasury Committee, *Interim Report on Private Equity* (10-I, 2006–07) puts the figure at 8 per cent of the UK workforce being employed in PE-owned companies.

In the mid-2000s, the UK Private Equity industry, along with the rest of Europe (and indeed the world), enjoyed extremely benign economic and regulatory conditions, leading to record investments in 2006.[173] The demise of this rapidly maturing industry has been predicted by economic and academic commentators,[174] and current statistics do show a contraction of the Private Equity sector in line with the retreat of global financial markets during the recession:[175] overall, BVCA members' investment in the United Kingdom fell from £12 billion in 2007 to £8.2 billion in 2008.[176] Figures for total global investment of UK-based firms show an even more drastic decline, from £20 billion in 2008[177] to £12.6 billion in 2009.[178] By 2012, these numbers had begun to stabilize, with BVCA members investing £5.7 billion and £12.2 billion respectively.[179] The industry's significance is therefore unlikely to diminish in future: a key forward-looking measure—the amount of new funds raised—showed a significant upturn during 2012, with £5.9 billion in fresh capital committed to Private Equity (and venture capital) funds.[180]

The Socio-Economic Impact of Private Equity

The oft-reported picture of Private Equity value creation has not gone unchallenged. In their extensive study of the role of Private Equity investors in the United States, Appelbaum and Batt conclude that the 'financial structure and light legal regulation of private equity firms allow them to much more aggressively pursue shareholder value at the expense of others with a stake in the company—its suppliers, employees, customers, and creditors'.[181] Froud and Williams similarly argue that the returns achieved by PE firms are based on the capture and extraction of existing value, with a small group of investors reaping a disproportionate benefit of a company's economic activity.[182] Funds are said to rely on financial engineering to rearrange 'ownership claims for value extraction, particularly for the benefit of the few who are positioned as private equity principals or senior managers in the operating businesses'.[183] The legacy effect of this is a 'cultural shift which

---

[173] K Raade and C Dantas Machado, 'Recent Developments in the European Private Equity Markets' (2008) 319 European Commission Economic Papers 27.

[174] B Cheffins and J Armour, 'The Eclipse of Private Equity' (2008) 33 The Delaware Journal of Corporate Law 1.

[175] E Appelbaum and R Batt, *Private Equity at Work—When Wall Street Manages Main Street* (Russell Sage Foundation 2014) Ch 4 (The Effects of the Financial Crisis).

[176] PriceWaterhouseCoopers, 'PE and VC Performance Measurement Survey' (BVCA 2008) 12.

[177] PriceWaterhouseCoopers, 'Private Equity and Venture Capital Report on Investment Activity 2008' (BVCA 2008).

[178] BVCA, 'February Briefing' (BVCA 2010) 26.

[179] PriceWaterhouseCoopers, 'Private Equity and Venture Capital Report on Investment Activity 2012' (BVCA 2013) 4.

[180] PriceWaterhouseCoopers, 'Private Equity and Venture Capital Report on Investment Activity 2012' (n 179) 3.

[181] Appelbaum and Batt, *Private Equity at Work—When Wall Street Manages Main Street* (n 175) 2.

[182] J Froud and K Williams, 'Private Equity and the Culture of Value Extraction' (2007) 12 New Political Economy 405.

[183] Froud and Williams, 'Private Equity and the Culture of Value Extraction' (n 182) 407.

normalises value capture insofar as it helps to institutionalise and normalise value extraction for the few as a practice and motivation for investors and managers within and beyond the Anglo-Saxon economies'.[184]

Reliable quantitative evidence of the impact of Private Equity funds on employment can be hard to compile, given 'considerable variation in the amount and quality of evidence and research'.[185] Whilst a detailed engagement of competing arguments is therefore beyond the scope of the present chapter,[186] labour outcomes generally appear to be slightly negative. Gospel and Pendleton report that '[s]maller scale studies in . . . the UK . . . find employment reductions',[187] and that 'pay grows more slowly in PE-owned firms than in the wider economy'.[188]

Turning first to employment levels, early studies found that 44 per cent of buyouts led to more or less instant redundancies,[189] with later job reductions in the case of Management Buy-Outs (MBOs) and Management Buy-Ins (MBIs) reported at 25 per cent[190] and 38 per cent respectively.[191] More recent research shows a somewhat conflicting picture: across a wide range of PE transactions, Amess and Wright report minimal employment growth (0.51 per cent) in management-led buy-outs, whereas new incoming senior executives seem to decrease the workforce by 0.81 per cent.[192] A second study on the same dataset confirms these results,

---

[184] Froud and Williams, 'Private Equity and the Culture of Value Extraction' (n 182) 407. The authors suggest that this is not necessarily on the back of workers alone, but rather through financial engineering such as re-financings, where debt can be used to pay dividends to PE investors. This is reminiscent of the idea that in hostile takeovers value comes from shareholders' reneging on implicit contracts with stakeholders, with the resulting gains cast as redistributions from stakeholders to shareholders: A Shleifer and L Summers, 'Breach of Trust in Hostile Takeovers' (1987) NBER Working Paper No 2342.

[185] H Gospel and A Pendleton, 'Financialization, New Investment Funds, and Labour' in H Gospel, A Pendleton, and S Vitols (eds), *Financialization, New Investment Funds, and Labour—An International Comparison* (OUP 2014) 28. The following paragraphs ignore primarily financial matters, from risk-adjusted financial returns in comparison to other markets to the impact of leverage on distressed companies: additional extensive summaries of PE-related academic research can be found in Gilligan and Wright, *Private Equity Demystified: An Explanatory Guide* (n 149) 61 and Appendix Table 3 Panel A [employment] and B [wages]; the following paragraphs draw on material set out there. Another summary of various PE studies can be found in M Wright et al, *The Implications of Alternative Investment Vehicles for Corporate Governance: a Survey of Empirical Research* (OECD 2007) 53 (Table 19).

[186] A country-specific overview of relevant studies can be found in A Pendleton and H Gospel, 'Financialization, New Investment Funds, and Weakened Labour: The Case of the UK' in H Gospel, A Pendleton, and S Vitols (eds), *Financialization, New Investment Funds, and Labour—An International Comparison* (OUP 2014).

[187] Gospel and Pendleton, 'Financialization, New Investment Funds, and Weakened Labour: The Case of the UK' (n 186) 29–30 (citations omitted).

[188] Gospel and Pendleton, 'Financialization, New Investment Funds, and Weakened Labour: The Case of the UK' (n 186) 30 (citations omitted).

[189] M Wright and J Coyne, *Management Buy-Outs* (Croom Helm 1985).

[190] M Wright et al, 'Management Buy-Outs, Trade Unions and Employee Ownership' (1990) 21 Industrial Relations Journal 137.

[191] K Robbie, M Wright, and S Thompson, 'Management Buyins in the UK' (1992) 20 Omega 445; K Robbie and M Wright, 'Managerial and Owernship Succession and Corporate Restructuring: the Case of Management Buy-Ins' (1995) 32 Journal of Management Studies 527.

[192] K Amess and M Wright, 'The Wage and Employment Effects of Leverage Buyouts in the UK' (2007) 14 International Journal of the Economics of Business 179.

whilst pointing out that even if employment levels remained constant, job security was lowered drastically.[193] At plant level, increases in economic efficiency and productivity are often tied to substantial job reductions.[194] On the other hand, there are studies to suggest that after an initial decline in employment, which may last for up to four years, higher job numbers ensue eventually.[195] Finally, it has also been suggested that PE involvement results in overall employment growth;[196] the EVCA's own suggestion that the industry has created more than 630,000 new jobs in venture capital and 420,000 through LBOs across Europe,[197] however, is highly questionable given flaws in the underlying methodology.[198]

When it comes to the impact of PE involvement on wages, the evidence is similarly conflicting. There are some findings of wage growth post-buy-out;[199] a majority of the studies surveyed, however, find generally lower average wages,[200] and significantly lower wage growth.[201] In terms of employment relations more generally, 'harder Human Resource Management' has been identified as a main cause of deteriorating substantive and procedural terms and conditions of employment.[202] This is opposed to findings that MBOs have a positively empowering effect on employees, both through increased training,[203] and more discretion over work practices.[204] As regards the collective dimension, trade union recognition post-buy-out fell in early studies;[205] with more recent evidence again split. Some commentators argue that collective representation levels have stabilized, with statistically irrelevant changes to both trade union recognition and membership density;[206] others suggest that levels continue to fall, with 40 per cent of managers actively hostile to organized labour and only 10 per cent openly supportive.[207]

---

[193] P Thornton, *Inside the Dark Box: Shedding Light on Private Equity* (The Work Foundation 2007).

[194] R Harris, D Siegel, and M Wright, 'Assessing the Impact of Management Buy-Outs on Economic Efficiency: Plant-Level Evidence from the United Kingdom' (2005) 87 The Review of Economics and Statistics 148.

[195] R Cressy, F Munari, and A Malipiero, 'Creative Destruction? Evidence that Buyouts Shed Jobs to Raise Returns' (2011) 13 Venture Capital: An International Journal of Entrepreneurial Finance 1.

[196] N Bacon, M Wright, and N Demina, 'Management Buy-Outs and Human Resource Management' (2004) 42 BJIR 325.

[197] A-K Achleitner and O Kloeckner, 'Employment Contribution of Private Equity and Venture Capital in Europe' (EVCA Research Paper 2005).

[198] Jenkinson, 'Private Equity' (n 148) 133.

[199] M Wright et al, *The Implications of Alternative Investment Vehicles* (n 185).

[200] Thornton, *Inside the Dark Box* (n 193).

[201] Amess and Wright, 'The Wage and Employment Effects of Leverage Buyouts in the UK' (n 192).

[202] Clark, 'The Private Equity Business Model and Associated Strategies for HRM: Evidence and Implications?' (n 156) 2034.

[203] Bacon, Wright, and Demina, 'Management Buy-Outs and Human Resource Management' (n 196).

[204] K Amess, S Brown, and S Thompson, 'Management Buy-Outs, Supervision and Employee Discretion' (2007) 54 Scottish Journal of Political Economy 447.

[205] M Wright et al, 'Management Buy-Outs and Trade Unions: Dispelling the Myths' (1984) 15 Industrial Relations Journal 45: from 65 per cent to 60 per cent post-buy-out; Wright et al, 'Management Buy-Outs, Trade Unions and Employee Ownership' (n 190): from 58 per cent to 51 per cent.

[206] N Bacon et al, 'Assessing the Impact of Private Equity on Industrial Relations in Europe' (2010) 63 Human Relations 1343.

[207] Thornton, *Inside the Dark Box* (n 193).

In considering this very diffuse picture, it is important to bear in mind Jenkinson's comments on the methodological challenges facing PE research: samples can easily be biased, for example by only focusing on exited (successful) investments.[208] Furthermore, it can often be near impossible to come up with relevant comparators or counterfactuals, especially following a restructuring where a single enterprise is carved up into several new entities,[209] or where the creation of new employment disrupts existing industries.

The Regulatory Context

By dealing exclusively with large, sophisticated investors, Private Equity funds are only subjected to a limited array of general financial markets regulation on both national and EU levels.[210] This is justified by the policy idea that major institutional investors are capable of bargaining for their own protection, and supported by very few reports of investor problems in the PE industry.[211] The only recent exception to this hands-off regulatory stance are pension funds belonging to investee company employees.[212] Following a pensions regulator investigation in 2008, the PE house Duke Street Capital contributed £8 million to the Focus DIY pension scheme, despite having sold the company on to another fund, Cerberus Capital, in the previous year.[213]

Domestic regulation is therefore primarily self-imposed. *The Walker Guidelines* for increased industry transparency were published in November 2007. Their scope is reasonably limited,[214] covering less than 15 per cent of the industry in the United Kingdom, given that reporting obligations only apply to investee companies if more than 50 per cent of revenues stem from the UK, there are in excess of 1,000 employees, and the enterprise value at acquisition exceeded £500 million, or £300m in the case of P2P transactions. As regards substantive obligations, a first set lies directly with the portfolio company:[215] in a public annual report, it has to identify its PE shareholders, as well as their senior executives or advisers in the UK who have oversight of the company on behalf of the fund or funds. There must furthermore be disclosure on board composition, a business review along the lines of public companies,[216] and financial reviews that cover risk-management objectives. Investing funds are equally obliged to produce public reports,[217] describing their basic structure and investment approach, listing UK portfolio companies,

---

[208] Jenkinson, 'Private Equity' (n 148) 131.

[209] Jenkinson, 'Private Equity' (n 148) 132–3.

[210] S Firth and O Watkins, 'The Regulatory Environment for Funds and Private Equity Houses' in M Soundy, T Spangler, and A Hampton (eds), *A Practitioner's Guide to Private Equity* (City & Financial 2009).

[211] Jenkinson, 'Private Equity' (n 148) 136.

[212] G Brafman and J Wheeler, 'Due Diligence—Management/Employees' in M Soundy, T Spangler, and A Hampton (eds), *A Practitioner's Guide to Private Equity* (City & Financial 2009) 158.

[213] Linklaters, 'Hot Topic: Duke Street Capital's £8m Pension "Hit"' (2008).

[214] Linklaters, 'Hot Topic' (n 213) V3.   [215] Linklaters, 'Hot Topic' (n 213) V4.

[216] Companies Act 2006, s 417.

[217] D Walker, 'Guidelines for Disclosure and Transparency in Private Equity' (2007) V 7.

management, and investors categorized by type and geography. Finally, all parties are to provide the BVCA with detailed data covering their financial and business activities,[218] and are subject to external supervision.[219]

Responses to the Guidelines were critical, with Jack Dromey of Unite (T&G) voicing the fear that self-regulation was 'worse than useless'.[220] Other commentators questioned whether the benefits of limited additional disclosure would outweigh the costs of producing materials 'on average . . . about as interesting as the glossy annual reports from public companies that are often assigned rapidly to the re-cycling bin'.[221]

On a European level, attacks on the industry were considerably more vehement, ranging from a critical report of the European Parliament[222] to more explicit attacks equating Private Equity firms with 'locusts'.[223] In 2009, the European Commission presented draft proposals for a Directive on Alternative Investment Fund Managers, aimed primarily at the regulation of 'significant systemic risk in financial markets'.[224] The Directive was finally adopted in late 2010 and published in the Official Journal on 1 July 2011.[225]

As regards PE funds' operational aspects, the major focus is on increased transparency and the prevention of asset stripping.[226] Chapter V, Section 2 of the Directive sets out new obligations for Alternative Investment Funds (AIFs) acquiring controlling influence in non-listed companies,[227] which is defined as holding more than 50 per cent of voting rights,[228] even if as part of several funds' coming together in a so-called club deal.[229] Funds must notify the acquisition of such control to the investee company and its shareholders,[230] and disclose the acquisition to a wider stakeholder group including to employees or their representatives via the investee's board.[231] Information on operational and financial developments must be included in firms' annual reports. [232] Article 30 of the Directive sets out a list of distribution requirements designed to avoid asset stripping within the first 24 months following the acquisition of control.

---

[218] Walker, 'Guidelines' (n 217) V6 (portfolio company) and V9 (Private Equity firms).

[219] By the so-called Walker Guidelines Monitoring Group.

[220] HC Treasury Committee, *Interim Report on Private Equity* (n 172) [76].

[221] Jenkinson, 'Private Equity' (n 148) 137.

[222] P Rasmussen, 'Report of the European Parliament with Recommendations to the Commission on Hedge Funds and Private Equity' (A6-0338 2008).

[223] Anon, 'Locust, Pocus—German Capitalism' (*The Economist*, 7 May 2005).

[224] Commission (EC), 'Proposal for a Directive of the European Parliament and of the Council on Alternative Investment Fund Managers and amending Directives 2004/39/EC and 2009/ . . ./ EC' COM(2009) 207 final ('AIFM Draft Directive').

[225] Directive (EU) 61/2011 of the European Parliament and of the Council on Alternative Investment Fund Managers and amending Directives 2003/41/EC and 2009/65/EC and Regulations (EC) No 1060/2009 and (EU) No 1095/2010 [2011] OJ L 174/1 ('AIFM Directive').

[226] AIFM Directive (n 225) preambles (58), (89).

[227] AIFM Directive (n 225) art 26–30.

[228] AIFM Directive (n 225) art 26(5). This changed from 30 per cent in the AIFM Draft Directive (n 224) art 26(1)(a).

[229] AIFM Directive (n 225) art 26(5)(b).   [230] AIFM Directive (n 225) art 27(1).

[231] AIFM Directive (n 225) art 28(4).   [232] AIFM Directive (n 225) art 29(2).

The Directive's regulatory design is interesting, as certain obligations do not rest with individual investee companies but are to be borne centrally by the PE management company.[233] The extent to which this approach addresses actual issues within the industry is, however, questionable. As Jenkinson notes, any 'push to increase transparency . . . is likely to have a limited impact'.[234] The asset stripping provisions are equally unlikely to have a significant impact, as Private Equity income is increasingly structured via the repayment of debt, which, professional advisers suggest, is likely to fall outside the Directive's scope.[235]

B. The Emergence of Multiple *Loci* of Employer Functions

In order to demonstrate the distribution of employer functions amongst different entities inherent in the Private Equity business model, the present chapter turns to a detailed technical analysis of buy-out transactions.[236] It introduces the key parties involved before focusing on the legal structures behind a buy-out transaction. This is the backdrop against which multiple employer function *loci* emerge, specifically through PE management companies' legal control rights and operational oversight.

Variations in the Private Equity Business Model

Two important caveats remain to be made: first, as to the range of issues under consideration, and second, as to the practical relevance and consistency of the specific model used. Private Equity investments have come to be analysed in various stages of a cycle spanning the life period of an investment from acquisition to divestment, yet the following discussion will be centred on the management of portfolio companies in between these points, including only those acquisition issues, such as company structuring and debt covenants, that continue to overshadow the operational phase. This focus means that a lot of other contentious issues related to the PE industry will not be scrutinized,[237] ranging from tax-transparent fund structures, leverage, and systemic risk to the incentives and remuneration of fund managers and their interaction with institutional investors, such as major pension funds. This limitation is analytically justified: it is during the active management stage that the relationship with a Private Equity management company has its strongest impact on investee companies. As one of the leading business school casebooks puts it, 'interactions between PE investors and the entrepreneurs they finance . . . are at the core of what PE investors do'.[238]

---

[233] AIFM Directive (n 225) art 29(1). It is however unclear to what extent this cross-portfolio view is a deliberate regulatory strategy: Interviews with Officials at DG Market (Brussels 23 March 2010).

[234] Jenkinson, 'Private Equity' (n 148) Executive Summary, 139.

[235] Clifford Chance, 'AIFM Directive and Private Equity' (Client Briefing, January 2011) 1.

[236] See also Appelbaum and Batt, *Private Equity at Work—When Wall Street Manages Main Street* (n 175) Ch 3 ('The Business Model: How Private Equity Makes Money').

[237] Jenkinson, 'Private Equity' (n 148) 128 ff.

[238] Gompers and Lerner, *The Venture Capital Cycle* (n 150) 7.

Finally, it is important never to forget the limitless variety within the Private Equity industry—both as regards the orientation of funds in general, and their specific structuring of individual transactions. As regards the former, PE transactions where only a minority stake in an enterprise is acquired, or where several funds share a single acquisition (so-called club deals), are examples of different approaches to essentially the same business model. The organizational chart in Figure 2.1 is drawn up on the basis of an existing fund; there are however no two funds exactly like one another. As structural differences are primarily driven by tax and securitization considerations, such distinctions are of little relevance in the practical control aspects.

The use of financial jargon in the Private Equity industry can be bewildering,[239] and while most terms will be addressed as discussion evolves, three terms surrounding the concept of buy-outs warrant immediate explanation. The first of these is the LBO, or leveraged buy-out. In a leveraged (geared) transaction, a majority of the purchase price does not come from the fund itself, but is provided by banks in various forms of debt. Whilst not all PE transactions have to be leveraged, and levels of debt have indeed been falling recently, this is very much the norm in buy-out transactions today. Where a business, or part thereof, is acquired by the existing management team with the backing of external investors, reference is made to an MBO (management buy-out); if a new team of managers is brought in, the same transaction will be classified as an MBI (management buy-in).

Key Actors

The most significant parties[240] to a buy-out deal are equity capital providers, viz the limited partnership between fund managers (General Partners, or GPs) and investors (Limited Partners, or LPs);[241] debt capital providers, viz banks and the debt syndication markets; the acquisition fund and its associated special purpose vehicle (SPV) structure; and professional advisers including accountants and lawyers.[242]

The lifetime of the *Limited Partnership* is limited to a fixed duration of usually ten years.[243] Its key terms are set out in a partnership agreement concluded between the GP and LPs. The parties' obligations include the personal service of key GP employees,[244] basic economic terms, such as fees and management

[239] Extensive explanatory lists can be found at <http://www.evca.eu/toolbox/glossary.aspx> accessed 1 September 2012; Gilligan and Wright, *Private Equity Demystified* (n 149) Glossary Section; Myners, *Institutional Investment in the United Kingdom* (n 152) 152.

[240] Gilligan and Wright, *Private Equity Demystified: An Explanatory Guide* (n 149) 30 and T Spangler, 'Private Equity Fund Structures' in M Soundy, T Spangler, and A Hampton (eds), *A Practitioner's Guide to Private Equity* (City & Financial 2009) 31ff.

[241] Technically speaking there are normally *several* limited partnerships in place, eg the GPs themselves are often organized as a partnership, which in turn forms part of the partnership with LPs.

[242] Financial Services Authority, *Private Equity: a Discussion of Risk and Regulatory Engagement* (Discussion Paper 06/6, 2006) [2.16] and [2.28] respectively.

[243] A reasonably long period in financial industry terms.

[244] So-called 'key-man' provisions: Spangler, 'Private Equity Fund Structures' (n 240) 44.

remuneration (the 'carry'), indemnities and other limits on the GP in relation to investment activity in other funds. Other investment vehicles, such as direct investment [semi-]'captive funds' and investment trusts exist, but their market penetration is comparatively low.[245] A final investment variant are listed Private Equity trusts, with considerably lower minimum commitments—the price of a single share, and ready liquidity over the course of the investment cycle.[246]

A fund's *General Partner* is the legal entity representing the interests of the Private Equity house, with detailed management roles often devolved into a separate management company, which in turn also serves as the regulated entity.[247] GP remuneration is based on a 2/20 structure: two per cent of assets under management are charged annually to cover fees and other expenses of the fund; this number has increasingly come under pressure as larger and larger funds are raised. Once an exited investment has exceeded a minimum rate of return (the so-called 'hurdle rate'), GPs receive 20 per cent of any remaining profit as carry, taxed as capital gains.[248]

The *Limited Partners*, on the other hand, are usually large institutional investors[249] looking for long-term, illiquid assets for their investment portfolios.[250] A potential for somewhat ironic incentive structures has been noted in this connection where workers' pension funds are at stake.[251] At fund closure, limited partners will commit considerable amounts of capital—minimum investments in excess of £10 million are not unheard of—without however transferring any money other than advance fees. The bulk of invested sums are received only once the GPs issue draw-down notices in order to fund a specific investment.[252] In legal terms, LP liability for the partnership's actions is capped at the initially contributed amount.[253] However, it is interesting to note that this protection can be lost if an LP becomes too closely involved in the management of the partnership's investment,[254] for example through close monitoring or control.[255] A final source of equity is the direct investment expected of both PE principals and investee company senior management. The latter's 'hurt equity' is usually the equivalent of a year's salary, or 50 per cent of the personal gains from a previous sale of the company. Considerably higher management stakes are equally possible.[256]

---

[245] Myners, *Institutional Investment in the United Kingdom: A Review* (n 152) [12.12]–[12.21].

[246] HgCapital Trust plc, *Annual Report and Accounts* (London 2009) 9.

[247] L Gullifer and J Payne, *Corporate Finance Law: Principles and Policy* (Hart 2011) 658.

[248] Memorandum of Understanding between the BVCA and Inland Revenue on the Income Tax Treatment of Venture Capital and Private Equity Limited Partnerships and Carried Interest (2003).

[249] Gilligan and Wright, *Private Equity Demystified: An Explanatory Guide* (n 149) 45. This is to limit investment to eligible counterparties. Sources of investment are discussed in detail by Myners, *Institutional Investment in the United Kingdom* (n 152) [12.64]–[12.75].

[250] Gompers and Lerner, *The Venture Capital Cycle* (n 150) 1.

[251] Jenkinson, 'Private Equity' (n 148) 126, quoting Phillip Jennings (UNI Global Union): 'Unions need to be aware that the money they are paying into pension funds is feeding the beast that may devour them.'

[252] Spangler, 'Private Equity Fund Structures' (n 240) 37.

[253] Limited Partnership Act 1907, s 4(2).   [254] Limited Partnership Act 1907, s 6(1).

[255] Spangler, 'Private Equity Fund Structures' (n 240) 33.

[256] E Rigby and A Felsted, 'Pessina to Boost Alliance Boots Skincare Brands' (*Financial Times*, 28 April 2010): CEO investment of £1.27 billion in a £12.4 billion deal.

Banks provide the debt element in a purchase; before the 2008 crisis in bond markets, this often constituted 70 per cent or more of the overall price.[257] A lead bank would syndicate the loan, packaged into a variety of collateral debt obligations (CDOs), amongst several financial institutions and hedge funds,[258] thus increasing overall amounts of liquidity. Debt financing is coupled with a host of obligations, going well beyond prioritized repayment: through detailed covenants, banks can closely monitor a portfolio company's ability to repay its debts.[259] Indeed, monitoring compliance with bank covenants may quickly become a CEO's primary task following a leveraged buyout.[260] If covenants are breached, the bank has several options, from renegotiating loan terms with the shareholder fund to stepping in and selling the remaining assets of the investee.

The interaction between these various groups is organized and supported by a large number of *External Professional Advisors*.[261] Industry studies suggest that close to 15,400 service industry professionals are engaged in Private Equity-related activities in the United Kingdom.[262]

Fund Structure

The model Private Equity fund structure in Figure 2.1 shows the operation of a variety of relationships between the parties identified above. Whilst developed on the basis of an existing fund, it has been modified both in order to maintain investor and investee anonymity, and to remove more complex arrangements relevant only for tax and debt securitization purposes.

The life cycle of a PE investment commences when the Limited and General Partners come together in a partnership that owns and controls the *Master Fund*, PE Fund I Ltd.[263] This fund then enters into further partnerships, specific to each investment project, with a management company and other investment-specific co-investors, most notably the target company's senior management team. PE Fund I Ltd and the co-investors are LPs in this partnership; with the management company taking on the GP's operational duties. Together they set up the *Deal Fund*, nominally controlled by an investment specific nominee. It is this entity which then sits on top of a long chain or web of Special Purpose Vehicles (SPVs).

These companies, sometimes also referred to as Alternative Investment Vehicles (AIVs) are created by the GP in order to give security to the holders of more junior debt (so-called mezzanine facilities), and structure the transaction

---

[257] Froud and Williams, 'Private Equity and the Culture of Value Extraction' (n 182) 407. The equity/debt ratio in an average UK FTSE company was the opposite.

[258] Gilligan and Wright, *Private Equity Demystified: An Explanatory Guide* (n 149) 54. Several PE firms have benefitted from the financial crisis by repurchasing these loan packages at significant discounts from distressed debt funds.

[259] Gilligan and Wright, *Private Equity Demystified: An Explanatory Guide* (n 149) 88.

[260] Interview with former Investee Company CEO (Oxford 23 February 2010).

[261] Franklin, 'What Private Equity Investors Look For: Investments, Managers, Advisers and Professionals' (n 162) 26.

[262] AS Associates, 'The Impact of Private Equity as a UK Financial Service' (BVCA 2008) 7.

[263] The numbering of funds traditionally refers to previous successful ventures by the GP.

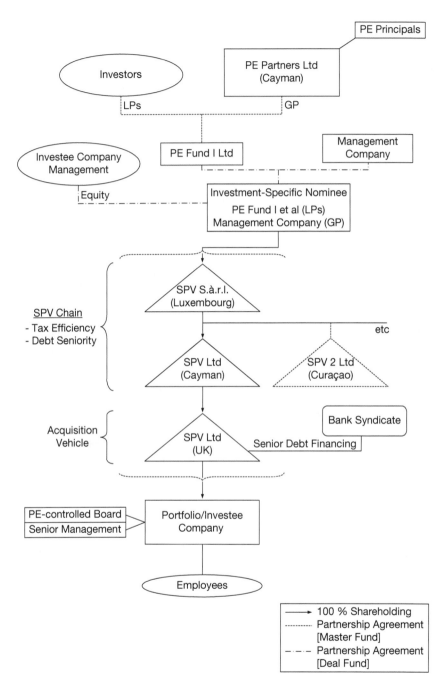

Figure 2.1 *Private Equity Fund Structure*

as tax efficiently as possible.[264] Shareholdings across multiple jurisdictions, and cross-holdings amongst different SPVs are common. Control over each entity is exercised through majority shareholding, usually as a single member. Offshore trust companies in the relevant jurisdictions will provide the necessary administrative facilities; in most cases (again dictated primarily by tax considerations), an employee of the PE management company is also represented on the SPV board.

At the end of this arrangement sits the Acquisition Special Purpose Vehicle (ASPV). Usually incorporated in the target company's jurisdiction, its purpose is the acquisition of a controlling (or exclusive) stake in the enterprise.[265] The consideration for this is raised from two sources—the deal fund (via the various SPVs), and public debt markets (via the syndicate leader bank). In the ASPV, all streams of funds are united for the first time: neither the fund nor the partnerships take on any debt directly.

Management Control

Two aspects of management control will be discussed in the remainder of this subsection: its legal organization through the company's constituent documents, and the various tools for its practical exercise. It is in this context that the specific examples to be explored are set, thus illustrating the serious challenges posed by the Private Equity model to the common law's traditional concept of the employer: a second entity exercises employer functions, up to and including control over the supposedly singular counterparty to the contract of employment itself.

Management control is the unique selling point of the Private Equity industry: in order to ensure the success of their investments, GPs must carefully work with and oversee entrepreneurs and portfolio companies.[266] There is some disagreement about this hypothesis—some argue that profits were driven for a long time by leverage and multiple growth, with operational improvements becoming more and more important only in the twenty-first century,[267] while other commentators place the shift from a 'hands-off, eyes-on' approach to an involved management style and sector specialization as early as the 1980s.[268] Today, there is a clear consensus that even funds that traditionally specialized in the financial aspects of buy-out deals are taking a strong interest in management control. In fact, nearly all funds surveyed employ a dedicated team of professional managers and consultants, or are in the process of setting up specific portfolio interaction teams.

From a legal perspective, the relationship between investors and senior company management is regulated by the investee company's constituent documents;

---

[264] This is a power explicitly laid down in the Master Fund Partnership Agreement.
[265] Gilligan and Wright, *Private Equity Demystified: An Explanatory Guide* (n 149) 76.
[266] Gompers and Lerner, *The Venture Capital Cycle* (n 150) 70.
[267] Interview with Partner in City Law PE practice (London 10 March 2010).
[268] Gilligan and Wright, *Private Equity Demystified: An Explanatory Guide* (n 149) 17.

specifically the investment or shareholders' agreement, and the company's articles. In the Private Equity context, there will usually be extensive management undertakings given to both the investee company and the PE management company; these are analytically distinct from the company's key documents and will accordingly be discussed as illustrative examples in the next subsection. The investment or shareholders' agreement sets out key terms of the subscription arrangement, followed most importantly by governance details. These include the structure of the company board and its various sub-committees (eg for remuneration, risk, and compliance), and the procedures for replacing directors and the appointment of additional ones. A detailed schedule attached to the agreement will specify key decisions which cannot be taken without the formal approval of the Private Equity management company, give ample information rights to investors, and list a series of warranties and restrictive covenants given by the management team. The company's articles, on the other hand, focus on the target's capital structure and various classes of equity and debt. It is nevertheless an important control tool due to the share transfer rules laid down in it: management can be forced to exit an investment at any moment chosen by the investors (drag-along provisions), may lose its investment (bad leaver clauses) or gain additional equity stakes at the fund's discretion (ratchet).

Legally speaking, the portfolio company board is therefore a major location for the exercise of investor control. In addition to a public company board's normal function as a decision-making and strategy-setting authority, boards in Private Equity backed enterprises become one of the major interfaces between investors and management.[269] Executive directors are supplemented by PE-appointed non-executives in order to represent investor interests: whilst this might be legally different from reporting lines in group subsidiaries, for example, it is not far off in practice: the alternative governance arrangement 'does not mean that the [management] team does not have a "boss" . . . ultimately, the investor will have the authority to make major changes in the interests of shareholders or the company as a whole'.[270] In practice, Private Equity funds and their board representatives deploy a series of specific governance tools at board level and beyond, four of which will now be examined more closely.[271]

Board Setup

As a first step, a PE management company will normally 'consider carefully the composition of the [investee company] board, and the ability to control it'. This specifically refers to using the appointment and removal of directors 'in the event of a disagreement with the executives and other non-executive directors'.[272]

---

[269] G Sharp, *Buyouts: A Guide for the Management Team* (Montagu Private Equity 2009) 102.
[270] Sharp, *Buyouts* (n 269) 104.
[271] A Hampton, 'Corporate Governance/Risk Management' in M Soundy, T Spangler, and A Hampton (eds), *A Practitioner's Guide to Private Equity* (City & Financial 2009), on which the following paragraphs draw for basic structure.
[272] Hampton, 'Corporate Governance/Risk Management' (n 271) 331.

Information Access

This is regulated both through formal arrangements and management practice. As regards the former, both the shareholders' agreement and loan covenants will set out a series of reporting requirements (cash-flow statements, balance sheets, executive reports) due at regular intervals anywhere between daily and monthly set points and when certain key events arise. Informal arrangements, however, are considerably more important: 'directors appointed by a PE house will spend a significant amount of time with the company and its managers, discussing strategy and performance issues'.[273] This is further supported by 'a steady flow of e-mail and telephone exchanges',[274] allowing analyst teams within the investing fund constantly to monitor each investment.

Veto Rights

It has already been noted that the shareholders' agreement will normally include a schedule setting out an extensive list of issues on which the investee company's board of directors, or sometimes even the Private Equity management company itself, must be consulted by the management team and consent before a proposed course of action can be taken. Examples of such events range from material business plan changes and major financial decisions, including new loans, the payment of dividends, or a change of accounting policies to the hiring of individuals paid more than a certain amount.[275] A liability risk can arise from these veto rights, however, as a PE management company could conceivably be found to have become a shadow director of the investee company—an especially challenging issue in the insolvency context, where conflicting interests between shareholders and other stakeholders crystallize.[276] Under section 251(1) of the Companies Act 2006, an individual or entity can acquire this status if they become a 'person in accordance with whose directions or instructions the directors of the [portfolio] company are accustomed to act.' Sophisticated PE management companies therefore make sure that the veto schedule is kept to exceptional items only, and that any other guidance is phrased as advice, which 'the directors are free to consider . . . and adopt . . . or alter . . . as they think best for the company'.[277]

Direct Interventions

A combination of the above factors enables Private Equity investors to spot potential issues arising in investee companies early on, and provides them with a full range of powerful remedies, from giving general advice and challenging particular decisions to a complete renewal of the management team. It is important to

---

[273] Hampton, 'Corporate Governance/Risk Management' (n 271) 332.
[274] Sharp, *Buyouts* (n 269) 104.
[275] £50,000 seems to be the most frequent threshold.
[276] D McCahill and S Willcock, 'Restructuring Issues for Private Equity Houses' in M Soundy, T Spangler, and A Hampton (eds), *A Practitioner's Guide to Private Equity* (City & Financial 2009) 397.
[277] Hampton, 'Corporate Governance/Risk Management' (n 271) 334.

remember that interaction goes well beyond formal board sessions or sporadic meetings: there is a strong culture of 'regular [investor representative] attendance at ad hoc meetings to address specific issues'.[278]

In summary, management is rarely, if ever, left alone in its core tasks following the buy-out, be it an increase in post-tax profits by upping gross margins and sales volumes or a reduction in overheads.[279] Academic studies have found a very high level of investor interaction with executives through active boards and beyond. Whilst specific details might vary between different funds or even investment teams,[280] the overall difference from traditional models is striking: an intense leadership of management strategy leads to a focus on value creation rather than more general compliance and risk management issues.[281] Whereas executives in public companies act more or less autonomously, Private Equity shareholders wield 'significant influence over aspects of the running of the business such as budget approvals, capital investment decisions and management appointments; . . . such control [being] one of the defining elements of PE ownership'.[282] Indeed, economic analyses[283] show that performance change in investee companies results not only from additional financial constraints imposed by high debt levels,[284] but from economically more effective management,[285] and increased reliance on control systems that help the buy-out team to meet business plan targets and stay within financial covenants.[286] Global studies show overall efficiency improvement in management,[287] especially where PE funds specialize in the relevant industry.[288] Clark has presented two sets of findings at the firm level that could explain this increased economic efficiency: considerably less managerial discretion once executives' decisions are driven by quantifiable measures such as improved cash-flows or reduced head counts, and the 'more overtly aggressive management of Human Resources'.[289]

---

[278] Sharp, *Buyouts* (n 269) 104.

[279] Gilligan and Wright, *Private Equity Demystified: An Explanatory Guide* (n 149) 83.

[280] F Cornelli and O Karakas, 'Private Equity and Corporate Governance: Do LBOs Have More Effective Boards?' in J Lerner and A Gurung (eds), *The Global Impact of Private Equity Report 2008* (World Economic Forum 2008) for example find that as a PE fund becomes more experienced, its post-LBO board size decreases significantly.

[281] V Archarya, C Kehoe, and M Reyner, 'Private Equity vs PLC Boards: A Comparison of Practices and Effectiveness' (2009) 21 Journal of Applied Corporate Finance 45.

[282] Franklin, 'What Private Equity Investors Look For: Investments, Managers, Advisers and Professionals' (n 162) 25.

[283] See Gilligan and Wright, *Private Equity Demystified: An Explanatory Guide* (n 149) Appendix Table 11 and 12 for a full overview of studies.

[284] J Franks and C Mayer, 'Governance as a Source of Managerial Discipline' (2002) National Bank of Belgium Working Paper 31, 2.

[285] S Green, 'The Impact of Ownership and Capital Structure on Managerial Motivation and Strategy in Management Buy-Outs: A Cultural Analysis' (1992) 29 Journal of Management Studies 513.

[286] C Jones, 'Accounting and Organizational Change: An Empirical Study of Management Buy-Outs' (1992) 17 Accounting, Organizations and Society 151.

[287] N Bloom, J van Reenen, and R Sadun, 'Do Private Equity-Owned Firms Have Better Management Practices?' in J Lerner and A Gurung (eds), *The Global Impact of Private Equity Report 2008* (World Economic Forum 2008).

[288] Cressy, Munari, and Malipiero, 'Creative Destruction?' (n 195).

[289] Clark, 'The Private Equity Business Model and Associated Strategies for HRM: Evidence and Implications?' (n 156) 2044.

C. The Shared Exercise of Employer Functions

Having thus seen the emergence of a second *locus* of managerial control, especially as regards traditional employer functions, in the specific context of Private Equity-led leveraged buy-outs, discussion returns to the inherent tension identified in the conclusion to the first chapter: what will happen if various employer functions are no longer exercised by a single entity? To illustrate this tension in the present context, the final subsection draws on a range of case studies from London-based PE houses. The emerging picture—of employer functions shared between different entities, parcelled out to various parties, or exercised jointly in a host of different ways—confirms the observation that different facets of the concept of the employer, whilst not problematic in the unitary paradigm of single employer cases, may stand directly opposed to each other in scenarios where control is exercised by more than one entity.

The Case Studies

In order to demonstrate the division of traditional employer functions in practice, it is necessary to identify various *loci* of control, and then look in detail at their interaction. The first of these tasks is relatively straightforward in the Private Equity setting: following a buy-out, a fund management team representing investor interests joins the investee company management in directing the portfolio enterprise. The second step, on the other hand, is rather more challenging: there is little detailed qualitative research on the actual modes of interaction between funds and their investee companies. Aggregate data is of limited use, as each fund deploys different strategies, sometimes even varying them as between different investments. Finally, even practical analyses in practitioners' handbooks focus more or less exclusively on the technicalities of *legal* mechanisms of control in company law. This perspective ignores the majority of less formal interactions between the two *loci* of control, which are crucial in illustrating the day-to-day division of employer functions.

In order to obtain the relevant information several case studies were conducted amongst London-based Private Equity funds.[290] In a series of semi-structured interviews, participants were asked first to explain the basic financial and legal structure of their fund, before focusing on the list of employer functions identified in the first part. In this context, interviewees identified how various functions were exercised in practice. Relying on illustrations from current or recently divested investments, this function-by-function analysis explored the roles and incentives of the various participants in the two *loci* of control.

In order to obtain as accurate a picture as possible, at least one interviewee was chosen from each group of key parties in a typical Private Equity transaction: investors, PE funds, portfolio company management, legal advisers, and

---

[290] This fieldwork was approved by the University of Oxford's Social Sciences and Humanities Inter-Divisional Research Ethics Committee (IDREC) on 20 January 2010: SSD/CUREC1/10-285.

investment banks. Different funds were chosen to reflect the breadth of the industry, both in terms of investment vehicle choice (limited partnerships and public investment trust funds) and management strategy (strong focus on operational improvements versus a more traditional hands-off approach based on financial engineering skills). The 'private' aspect of the Private Equity industry was noticeable insofar as it was initially challenging to identify individuals willing to provide information. All interviewees insisted on strict anonymity, and none of the funds or investee companies will be identified in the discussion below.[291] Whilst the overall sample size had to remain reasonably small, especially when considering the variety of structures and strategies within the industry, the examples below are nonetheless highly useful in illustrating the key argument put forward in this work: tensions inherent in different aspects of the traditional concept of the employing entity come to the fore as soon as various employer functions are exercised from more than one *locus* of control.

[1] Inception and Termination of the Contract of Employment

The first employer function was summarized earlier in functional terms as all aspects of power over the very existence of an employment relationship under a contract of service. There are four areas where this function is exercised in practice: actions before an actual contract is concluded, such as the advertisement of a post, selection of potential candidates and negotiations over their terms of employment; the actual hiring; powers of suspension and over disciplinary procedures more generally; and the termination of employment relationships. In the PE context, all of these functions are shared between the investee company management and its financial backers. The various case studies on this first function show the full variety of different modes of interaction between the two *loci* of control—from direct contractual arrangements and formal voting on the company board to investor veto rights and more informal discussions.

As regards actions even before an actual contract is concluded, several PE management companies maintain rosters of executives specializing in specific management tasks, from divisional restructuring to supply chain reorganization. If a portfolio company decides to hire employees in any of these fields, the fund will 'assist' its efforts by selecting an executive from its database, or sometimes even propose one of its own senior partners as an appropriate (temporary) manager.[292] These candidates will normally be interviewed and selected directly by the PE management company team, who are also often tasked with negotiating further particulars of employment. Other funds maintain a much smaller stock of experienced executives, but nevertheless retain the power to direct the portfolio company's hiring choices.[293] The actual conclusion of employment contracts with lower-tier employees is usually

---

[291] Full interview notes, including names and fund information for all interviews, and samples of contractual documents have been deposited in accordance with IDREC-notified procedures. No market-sensitive data were collected.

[292] Telephone Interview with Senior PE Operations Executive (15 February 2010).

[293] Interview with PE Business Development Partner (London 19 February 2010).

left to management itself. It is not unusual however to see explicit veto provisions reserved for the Private Equity management company: one common provision demands explicit fund approval for new employment contracts where the total value of annual remuneration and additional benefits exceeds £50,000.[294]

Whereas general human resource management in solvent companies is left to portfolio company executives on a day-to-day basis,[295] the PE investors usually retain powers of suspension and related disciplinary procedures for more senior employees through two distinct routes: executive directors can, first, always be ousted by shareholder representatives' votes on the company board. Second, there are contracts concluded directly between individual senior employees and the PE management company. In consideration for participatory drawing rights in the carry vehicle,[296] these agreements subject employees to both general underperformance clauses and more specific disciplinary procedures run by the Private Equity management company. The latter can extend as far as an individual's personal behaviour, such as an obligation to report even minor traffic offences.[297]

The right to terminate employment relationships is equally shared between both *loci* of control. Portfolio company management and investing funds can usually initiate redundancies, albeit through different processes. The former will retain the formal power to terminate most employment contracts, subject to key personnel clauses. Nonetheless, even minor terminations are usually discussed in informal phone calls between the PE operations team and the company's Chief Executive Officer (CEO) or Head of Human Resources.[298] If analysts within the Private Equity management company have identified potential redundancies, the next steps will depend on the fund's investment strategy: while some firms only initiate 'general conceptual discussions' with management,[299] others will provide detailed instructions on where and how changes to the workforce are to take place.[300] Investee company executives are fully aware that in the case of disagreement with PE investors, their contracts can be terminated more or less immediately.[301] Some funds regularly invoke the underperformance clause set out above to this end, containing potential employment law litigation through compromise undertakings given in return for the retention of small equity stakes in the investment.[302]

[2] Receiving Labour and its Fruits

The essential element underlying both aspects of this second function of the employer was identified earlier as the employer's ability to demand, and if so

---

[294] Interview with PE Partner (London 10 March 2010).
[295] Interview with former Investee Company CEO (Oxford 23 February 2010).
[296] And ratchet provisions (management equity increase triggers when performance targets are met).
[297] Interview with former Investee Company CEO (Oxford 23 February 2010).
[298] Interview with former Investee Company CEO (Oxford 23 February 2010).
[299] Telephone Interview with Senior PE Operations Executive (15 February 2010).
[300] Interview with PE Partner (London 10 March 2010).
[301] Interview with former Investee Company CEO (Oxford 23 February 2010).
[302] Interview with PE Partner (London 10 March 2010).

receive, the workforce's personal labour. In the vast majority of cases, this function will be exercised exclusively by the portfolio company itself: there is little scope for Private Equity investors' involvement in the actual day-to-day execution of work processes, as even traditional factory visits are an increasingly rare sight.[303] The right to receive any goods and materials resulting from the work processes was noted to include incidental benefits, such as intellectual property rights. In practice, however, it appears again that fund managers are in most cases content to leave such issues to the investee company.[304]

Two exceptions to this general observation should be noted: first, the direct contracts between senior management and Private Equity management companies, as already discussed in the first function. Through these arrangements, the investors are arguably entitled to demand and directly receive a considerable share of management employees' labour: regular reporting, both through formal documents and informal meetings and phone conversations, on cash-flows, covenant stress-testing, and divisional performance are a key part of executives' work, and have to be delivered directly to the relevant analyst teams within the management company.[305] A second area where Private Equity investors can sometimes get involved in the receipt of labour and its fruits is in troubleshooting operations for specific sections of the business. An example of this is the collection of receivables, particularly in overseas operations, where funds might rely on direct involvement to ensure that materials or services provided to customers are turned into stable incoming cashflows within a reasonable timeframe.[306]

[3] Providing Work and Pay

This third category is underpinned in functional terms by the work-taking party's reciprocal obligations to those of wage-takers in category [2]. The provision of regular work is usually parcelled out to the investee company—with the exception of senior management contracts as just discussed. In general, the Private Equity managers do not consider it their duty to provide work to employees. This becomes particularly evident when portfolio companies are on the brink of bankruptcy: whilst holding discussions on business strategy and employment level changes, or at least a sale as a going concern to a trade buyer or another Private Equity fund, to ensure the future viability of the enterprise, some funds will simultaneously retain professional advisers to prepare the winding down of the company.[307]

When it comes to the payment of wages, expenses, and other allowances, on the other hand, both company and PE *loci* of control will normally be involved, be it directly or indirectly. On one end of the spectrum there is the direct payment of regular wages by the Private Equity management company, usually for key employees of the portfolio company (on top of any eventual proceeds from the sale

---

[303] Interview with PE Business Development Partner (London 19 February 2010).
[304] Interview with former Investee Company CEO (Oxford 23 February 2010).
[305] Interview with PE Business Development Partner (London 19 February 2010).
[306] Interview with former Investee Company CEO (Oxford 23 February 2010).
[307] Interview with Investment Banking Associate (London 10 March 2010).

of equity stakes).[308] Most funds, however, avoid such direct links: operational partners have to relinquish their partnership in the investment vehicle before taking up executive management roles within the investee enterprise, with the latter also agreeing to pay the partner's wages and expenses during that period.[309] When it comes to the payment of external non-executive directors that represent the interests of the PE fund and its management company on the company board, there is a fairly even split between remuneration coming from the portfolio company and the funds. One regularly used technique to avoid direct cashflows between the Private Equity management company and its appointees is the payment of monitoring fees in the range of £15,000 to £50,000 from company funds.[310]

A final control tool over payment of wages is the board subcommittee on compensation. Several Private Equity management companies staff this entity exclusively with their representatives, preferably the 'toughest guys around'.[311] By setting the criteria along the lines of which management and sometimes even employees at large are evaluated, and deciding on the corresponding levels of pay and other benefits, the fund here exercises a crucial employer function, regardless of the actual accounts linked to payroll. Any discretionary bonuses management want to award as incentives to more junior employees will equally have to be considered and approved by the Private Equity management company, acting through the compensation committee.

[4] Managing the Enterprise-Internal Market

It will be recalled from the discussion in Chapter 1 that this function is central to the role of the entrepreneur-coordinator: only through the constant use of the directional powers founded on the employees' contractual obligations can management achieve the necessary control over all factors of production. The functional concept underpinning this category is an open-ended right to direct employees, regardless of the actual level of detail of that instruction. As set out earlier, the idea at the very core of the Private Equity business model is that as single majority shareholder, funds can seize control over their investment companies *in addition* to the existing management. Control over the enterprise-internal market is not shared in the sense expounded, for example, in the first function. Rather, the same sets of functions are in fact exercised at different levels in the PE context: the investing fund will traditionally focus on business plans and development, leaving more detailed execution to the company's executives. The precise levels of this stratification vary dramatically from fund to fund, and can in some instances even be inverted.

In nearly all investment agreements there is a clear list that sets out which strategic matters can only be initiated and in some cases even executed by the PE firm. This will cover decisions on senior management, group structures and financing,

---

[308] Interview with PE Business Development Partner (London 19 February 2010).
[309] Telephone Interview with Senior PE Operations Executive (15 February 2010).
[310] Interview with Partner in City Law PE practice (London 10 March 2010).
[311] Telephone Interview with Senior PE Operations Executive (15 February 2010).

from repayment priorities to additional loans.[312] Changes to the overall business plan, or any significant acquisitions or disposals of individual business units will equally be within the exclusive domain of the management company.[313] Depending on the latter's internal operations team, the target company's management may be tasked with drawing up detailed action plans: in one case, the fund simply provided executives with target employment figures 30 per cent below the existing level, and then approved management's suggestions as to how this should be achieved. Whilst strategic change is often addressed at formal board meetings there are other, more opaque, methods of communication between the two *loci* of control: the investors can, for example, request mere attendance rights at board meetings, with the minutes clearly reflecting that all decisions were taken by the executive directors alone. In other scenarios, particularly when it comes to reductions in employment levels, information is conveyed as informally as possible, from telephone calls to lunch conversations.[314]

Other funds take an even more active approach to managing the enterprise-internal market. The employment of operating partners as senior management has already been discussed; another frequently used technique is a direct secondment of junior analysts at all levels of the target company,[315] for example as chief of staff to key executives, in order to get 'very close to the operations' and deliver the strategic changes decided by the fund.[316] For a large fund, this can involve up to 30 of its employees acting as 'consultants' within a recently acquired business.[317] More regularly occurring management functions, such as ensuring that health and safety controls are in place and dealing with vicarious liability claims following accidents or deaths at work in hazardous environments, will often be delegated to the investee company despite board information and approval requirements.[318]

[5] Managing the Enterprise-External Market
The final function of the employer that emerged in the first part of this work was engagement with markets at large. Put differently, it is a key function of being an employer to enjoy the chance of financial profit and carry the risk of loss from investing in ventures undertaken by the enterprise. At a first glance, it might be assumed that it is on the investee company's account, and on this account alone, that all business activities take place. This is true insofar as—subject to what has just been said about the division of management functions in the enterprise-internal market—it is the company that has to sell its products and services on the open market. The key element, however, was investment in projects and facilities, as seen historically in the provision of tools and equipment. In the Private Equity context it is the investing fund that provides, or arranges for the external provision via debt markets, of all such investments through downstream cashflows, and enjoys the financial gains

---

[312] Interview with PE Partner (London 10 March 2010).
[313] Interview with Partner in City Law PE practice (London 10 March 2010).
[314] Interview with PE Partner (London 10 March 2010).
[315] Interview with PE fund General Counsel (London 11 March 2010).
[316] Telephone Interview with Senior PE Operations Executive (15 February 2010).
[317] Interview with Partner in City Law PE practice (London 10 March 2010).
[318] Interview with former Investee Company CEO (Oxford 23 February 2010).

from upstream payments. The following paragraphs take a closer look at these cash-flows, building on the fictional fund structure set out in Figure 2.1.

Financial movements take place in two directions within that investment structure: investments initially move downstream when cash flows from the master fund via the deal fund and its SPVs into the acquisition vehicle, and from there onwards to the target company vendors and the portfolio enterprise itself. During and at the end of the investment cycle, money moves back upstream, when the investee company's cash flow is distributed along similar pathways. Downstream financing is initiated by the General Partner's capital calls under the terms of the original Master Fund partnership agreement. The GP will then set up the Deal Fund (including the nominee company and subordinated entities) and start diffusing capital into the structure. In return, each SPV issues a mix of equity (shares), debt (especially in the form of loan notes) and hybrid securities. Only a relatively small part of the fund's investment is in the form of equity, however, as its amount is limited by the proportion of management investment. The majority of funds will therefore be structured as loans,[319] with tiered repayment priorities during the course of the investment. Once subordinated debt providers have injected their share of investment, the fund will arrange for the syndicate leader bank to transfer the most senior loan tranches directly to the acquisition vehicle, securing its interest on the target company's assets.[320] Using these funds, the Private-Equity controlled ASPV then acquires shares in the target company.

Upstream cash flows commence as soon the investee company's balance sheet meets or exceeds local dividend payment requirements. The board declares a dividend on the company's shares, which are duly paid to its sole shareholder, the ASPV, in order for it to meet its financing obligations to debt holders (banks) and loan note bearers (the PE fund). Capital is then moved up through the structure as various SPVs declare dividends, repay their debts, and redeem various hybrid securities. Once profit targets in the partnership agreement are met, 20 per cent of profits are paid out to the GP's carry vehicle, with the remainder distributed proportionally amongst LPs. A similar process, albeit on a much larger scale, takes place at investment exit: the ASPV sells its shares in the investee company, repays any outstanding debts, and returns the remaining investment and profits to the master fund.

The final employer function, risk of loss and chance of gain associated with the equity investment, is therefore shared between portfolio company and investing fund in a rather curious way: even as regards engagement with the market, any expansion or additional investment will usually be funded through drawdowns from new or existing lines of credit. The portfolio company will not normally reinvest any of its positive cashflows in the business, declaring dividends and repaying existing debts instead. If the portfolio company's financial performance deteriorates to the extent that it becomes unprofitable, it is the fund managers rather than portfolio company executives who negotiate loans and restructure the company's debts

---

[319] Gullifer and Payne, *Corporate Finance Law: Principles and Policy* (n 247) 665.
[320] The precise timing of this depends on the target jurisdiction's financial assistance laws.

when covenants have been breached.[321] The PE fund's financial commitment, however, is limited to its invested capital, which will usually be only a minor proportion of the overall purchase price. It is therefore the portfolio company (and its creditors) who will bear the majority of financial losses in a potential bankruptcy.

The summary survey of the complex operations of Private Equity investments in section 2 has therefore shown how the emergence of PE funds as an additional *locus* of control leads to employer functions' shared exercise between different entities, parcelled out to various parties, or even exercised jointly in a host of different ways. The case studies thus confirm the observation that different strands of the concept of the employer, whilst not problematic in the unitary paradigm of single employer cases, may stand directly opposed to each other in scenarios where control is exercised by more than one entity: the inherent tension has come to the fore.

Conclusion

Chapter 1 suggested that the concept of the employer in English employment law suffers from an inherent tension. The traditional unitary vision of the employer as a singular entity is firmly built on historical language and fact patterns, reinforced by contractual doctrines of bilateral relationships and, in the context of corporate employers, in line with economic theory as embodied in company law. Upon closer inspection, however, this orthodoxy was challenged by the fact that all tests traditionally used to determine the status of dependent workers, other than the enterprise integration test, do not command a unitary vision of the employer as a matter of logical necessity. Moreover, this orthodoxy is further challenged by the multi-functional approach prevalent in the case law. In concluding, it was suggested that the resulting tension might not be an issue in single-employer scenarios where all functions are exercised by one party, but that the concept could face serious challenges in situations outside this narrow paradigm.

The present chapter then turned to two such scenarios that are particularly challenging to the unitary element in the traditional concept of the employer: triangular agency work arrangements, and Private Equity portfolio companies. Following a brief introduction to each industry, discussion focused on two major aspects—how additional entities emerge as a second *locus* of control; and how this in turn leads to a joint exercise of nearly all of the employer functions identified in Chapter 1.

These arrangements bring the contradictions inherent in the concept of the employing entity to the fore: the assumption that only a single entity, the counterparty to the contract of employment, can exercise employer functions is incongruent with their continuous joint exercise by two *loci* of control in the contexts surveyed. It is to the practical implications of this tension for employment law coverage to which the second part of this work now turns.

---

[321] Interviews with Partner in City Law PE practice and Investment Banking Associate (London 10 March 2010).

PART II

THE IMPLICATIONS OF A CONCEPT UNDER PRESSURE

Introduction

The first part of this work identified a deep tension inherent in the concept of the employer in English law as multi-functional, yet unitary. It then demonstrated that the resulting conflict between the two strands is brought to the fore in situations beyond a narrow single-entity employer paradigm, with triangular work relationships and Private Equity controlled firms providing notable examples of situations where multiple entities exercise employer functions. The goal of the third and final part will be to respond to this problem, addressing the issue through a reconceptualization of the employer.

Before this task can be attempted, however, several intermediary steps have to be taken in order to explore the implications of the concept under the pressure. This exploration in the second part serves a dual purpose: first, to illustrate practical instances of the tension, and second, to collect evidence for the eventual construction of a reworked concept of the employer. In doing so, the chapters to follow form a logical link between Parts I and III.

Evidence that the identified tension is not merely an abstract theoretical problem, but one of the key causes of an ongoing crisis in labour law's fundamental concepts,[1] will support the claim that the problems identified are grave enough to warrant a reconsideration of the employer concept. The various examples explored in order to advance this argument will furthermore form the initial elements of a framework in which this reconceptualization is to take place. The previous part surveyed case law and academic material in search of different aspects of the functioning of the employer, operating on the assumption that it was in difficult borderline scenarios that the concept could best be teased out. This exercise is now, in a certain sense, to be repeated at a different level in order to prepare for the eventual reconceptualization in Part III.

---

[1] A term coined in K Wedderburn, R Lewis, and J Clark (eds), *Labour Law and Industrial Relations: Building on Kahn-Freund* (Clarendon Press 1983) vi.

Defining the Relevant Case Law

Having thus set out the main aim of Part II, two preliminary points remain to be made: explaining the subsequent discussion's move on to a broader plane in order to be able to look at the issue from multiple angles in different contexts, and elaborating on how this seemingly fragmented effort is nonetheless driving at a single concept of the employer. As regards the former point, there is a crucial dimension in which the material analysed moves beyond the work's general focus on multi-entity employment in English law, in which discussion has taken place thus far, by turning to a comparative excursion into German law.

This comparative analysis will be particularly fruitful due to that legal system's long-standing tradition of regulating block shareholdings and complex cross-holdings in corporate structures. Home to one of the largest European Private Equity industries outside the United Kingdom,[2] research in Germany has also allowed for the collection of illustrative fieldwork material where necessary.[3] German company and employment law have developed a series of legal mechanisms to address the challenges arising from multiple *loci* of control over subsidiary undertakings, for example, as regards the protection of different stakeholders in the subordinated entity; up to and including specific mechanisms for the protection of employees other than as wage creditors.

Two particular sets of employees will be excluded from further consideration: employees of Private Equity partnerships such as financial analysts or management advisers, and senior management at investee companies. As regards the former group, litigation has been brought directly against management companies for a wide range of issues, for example, to settle questions as to a redundant analyst's entitlement to a profit share in the carry vehicle.[4] From an analytical perspective such cases fall outside the current framework, however, as there is no tension in the traditional concept where the Private Equity fund exercises all employer functions in regard to the claimant. The litigation options of senior management at investee companies, on the other hand, are usually limited by contractual agreements and economic incentives. In the case of dismissal, for example, executives' primary motivation is to bargain with the management company to retain at least a small portion of their equity entitlements in consideration of comprehensive compromise and non-disclosure agreements.[5]

---

[2] J Haves, S Vitols, and P Wilke, 'Financialization and Ownership Change: Challenges for the German Model of Labour Relations' in H Gospel, A Pendleton and S Vitols, *Financialization, New Investment Funds, and Labour* (OUP 2014) 158ff.

[3] Approved by the University of Oxford's Social Sciences and Humanities Inter-Divisional Research Ethics Committee (IDREC) on 21 December 2010: SSD/CUREC1/10-451.

[4] *Aymard v SISU Capital Ltd* [2009] EWHC 3214 (QB).

[5] Furthermore, it might even be open to question whether senior management could be considered as being partners in the original fund: *Tiffin v Lester Aldridge LLP* [2012] EWCA Civ 35, [2012] IRLR 391.

A Single Concept of the Employer

The second preliminary point to be discussed concerns the development of a single concept of the employer through an analysis of different contexts. Given the wide range of sources to be analysed, it might be thought that at least two analytical juxtapositions arise: the concept of the employer at common law, as opposed to that in statute, and a domestic concept differing from one developed in the case law of the Court of Justice of the European Union (CJEU) and other Union-level legal developments. This is not the case, however. None of the above categories is a watertight compartment with a distinct concept of the employer. While such developments have been called for in other areas such as tort[6] or intellectual property law,[7] the concept of the employer is implicitly assumed to be identical across all areas covered in the following chapters.

This may be so in part because the apparently separate domains of statute and common law at domestic and European levels are in reality in constant interaction with each other, mutually shaping a unified concept of the employing entity. They are closely linked infra- and superstructures, each adding particular aspects to the overall concept. At points, this linkage becomes explicit, with amalgamations both in substance and in a jurisdictional sense.[8] Legislation will normally rely directly on common law concepts such as the contract of employment in defining key terms such as employee and employer,[9] and the existence of legislation will in turn influence the development of the common law.[10] As regards the relationship between common law and statute, it is therefore 'increasingly difficult to view [the two domains] as separate streams whose waters "do not mingle"'.[11]

The relationship between domestic and European law operates along similar lines,[12] in particular as regards the specific concept of the employer. Concepts of European Union law are to be applied uniformly by all Member State courts under principles of EU constitutional law.[13] Their precise nature, however, is frequently shaped by practices at domestic level. The Acquired Rights Directive[14] to be discussed in Chapter 3 serves as an illustration of this approach: key concepts are defined in direct reference to domestic law. The meaning of the term 'employee'

---

[6] E McKendrick, 'Vicarious Liability and Independent Contractors: A Re-Examination' (1990) 53 MLR 770.

[7] J Pila, '"Sewing the Fly Buttons on the Statute": Employee Inventions and the Employment Context' (2012) 32 OJLS 265.

[8] M Freedland, *The Personal Employment Contract* (OUP 2003) 3.

[9] Employment Rights Act 1996 ('ERA 1996'), s 230.

[10] See, most notably, Lord Hoffman in *Johnson v Unisys Ltd* [2001] UKHL 13, [2001] 1 AC 518.

[11] S Deakin and G Morris, *Labour Law* (6th edn Hart 2012) 138. For a broader perspective, see A Burrows, 'The Relationship between Common Law and Statute in the Law of Obligations' (2012) 128 LQR 232.

[12] J Prassl, 'Three Dimensions of Heterogeneity' in M Freedland and J Prassl (eds), *EU Law in the Member States: Viking, Laval and Beyond* (Hart 2014).

[13] P Craig and G de Búrca, *EU Law* (6th edn OUP 2015) ch 7.

[14] Council Directive (EC) 23/2001 on the approximation of the laws of the Member States relating to the safeguarding of employees' rights in the event of transfers of undertakings, businesses or parts of undertakings or businesses [2001] OJ L82/16 ('ARD').

(and thus in turn the concept of the employer) covers 'any person who, in the Member State concerned, is protected as an employee under national employment law'.[15] The Directive furthermore explicitly operates 'without prejudice to national law as regards the definition of contract of employment or employment relationship'.[16]

Considered in the light of the second part's dual purpose, these different contexts are all equally relevant. As regards the first task of illustrating practical instances of the tension identified in Part I, it will be helpful to be able to show problems from across the employment law spectrum. As regards the second goal of collecting evidence for the eventual reconceptualization of the employer, the *functional concept* of the employer to be developed is not necessarily bound to a single area of regulation. Indeed, to some extent this is even true for the comparative enquiry, contributing to different aspects of the present discussion from distinct legal systems in order to provide additional external insights to the development of a unifying approach. As different facets of the concept of the employer come under strain in various contexts it is only by looking at a selection of issues in each area that an understanding of the implications of the concept under pressure can emerge. Indeed, the problems with the received concept could in this way be analysed as resulting precisely from a one-dimensional, contractual, analysis of a multi-dimensional issue.

Structure

In order to develop the steps thus outlined, the material in this part is structured as follows: Chapter 3 addresses specific problems in the United Kingdom and European Union context; with Chapter 4 being dedicated to an exploration of German labour law in corporate groups (*Arbeitsrecht im Konzern*). With minor variations as expedient (such as a brief excursion into comparative methodology), each chapter is generally structured first to set the scene and point out the problems that can arise from a split of employer functions, before analysing potential responses within existing frameworks and drawing tentative conclusions that will become guidelines for rethinking the concept of the employer in Part III.

---

[15] ARD (n 14) art 2(1)(d).   [16] ARD (n 14) art 2(2).

3

The Fragile Scope of Employment
Law Coverage

Introduction

Turning first to illustrations in domestic law (as significantly influenced by EU measures in certain areas), discussion will focus on two particular implications of the inherent tension: the complete breakdown of employment law coverage in triangular (agency work) scenarios, and the incomplete and incoherent extension of employee voice mechanisms, as illustrated in the Private Equity context with regards to consultation with employee representatives in collective redundancies and transfers of undertakings. This selection should not be taken as a suggestion that these are isolated instances: the tension arises, and is significant, in employment scenarios across the board. The examples are chosen *pars pro toto* to highlight a series of different types of problems, and enable discussion of a core group of issues from a variety of angles. Ideally, the contexts should cover several parts in the lifecycle of the employment relationship and draw on a wide variety of labour market regulation tools, including common law and statutory provisions of domestic and European Union origin. The two areas chosen meet this requirement, and have the additional advantage of considerable amounts of recent litigation which can be drawn on to illustrate key arguments.

The tension characterizing the concept of the employer makes employment law coverage fragile in multi-entity employment scenarios: it becomes unclear, incoherent, and open to easy manipulation. This is because the identification of the employer is driven by two conflicting strands with the potential to point in different directions. In multilateral employment relationships, the multi-functional aspect instinctively points towards the identification of several relevant entities, whereas various elements identified as parts of the unitary concept in Chapter 1 seem to fit only with a single entity conceptualization. The contractual aspect of this effect will be demonstrated in the context of parcelled-out employer functions in the triangular agency employment in section 1; section 2 focuses on the joint or shared exercise of employer functions across different entities.[1] As a direct consequence of the

---

[1] As noted previously, there are no clear-cut distinctions between these different mode of exercising employer functions; rather, they serve as a convenient sub-division for the purposes of the present analytical exposition.

concept's underlying tension, no employer can be identified in the former scenario; in the latter, identification is limited to a small subset, which may frequently be an inappropriate counterparty, or only one of several relevant entities.

The challenges arising from multiple employing entities to the very existence of a contract of employment have already been the subject of extensive scrutiny in litigation and scholarship. Discussion of the second set of implications will therefore be significantly more extensive in this chapter, particularly in order to demonstrate the importance of a coherent concept of the employer even in areas where significant problems may not have been readily perceivable to date.

Section 1: The Breakdown of Employment Law Coverage in Triangular Work Arrangements

Section 1 of Chapter 2 illustrated the different ways in which the five employer functions are in fact shared or parcelled out between agency and end-user in the temporary agency work context. This joint exercise of employer functions is a clear illustration of the 'profound difficulties' posed by complex triangular or multilateral employment relationships:[2] it challenges the very existence of a contract of employment, thus leaving individual workers without recourse to the majority of domestic employment protective legislation. The complete breakdown of employment law coverage is a consequence of 'contractual arrangements that split, on the one hand, day-to-day control of work processes and, on the other hand, day-to-day securing and paying of people to work, [thus] prima facie prevent[ing] those working from being legally classified as anyone's "employees" '.[3] The present section sets out to explore the mechanisms behind this outcome, tracing it back to the inability of the traditional common law tests for the existence of the contract of service to cope with the joint exercise of multiple functions: as the inherent tension between the multi-functional and the unitary strands of the concept of the employer is brought to the fore, no responsible employer can be identified.

The existence of a contract of employment is a necessary precondition for the claimant's success in a large number of employment tribunal cases, most notably in unfair dismissal claims;[4] the absence of any contract at all, however, can also have an impact in wider areas such as discrimination claims.[5]

---

[2] M Freedland, *The Personal Employment Contract* (OUP 2003) 36ff.

[3] L Barmes, 'Learning from Case Law Accounts of Marginalised Working' in J Fudge, S McCrystal, and K Sankaran (eds), *Challenging the Legal Boundaries of Work Regulation* (Oñati International Series in Law and Society, Hart 2012) 308.

[4] The issue at stake in the majority of cases to be discussed below, including *James v Greenwich LBC* [2008] EWCA Civ 35, [2008] ICR 545; *Tilson v Alstom Transport* [2010] EWCA Civ 1308, [2011] IRLR 169; and *M&P Steelcraft Ltd v Ellis* [2008] IRLR 355 (EAT).

[5] *Muschett v HM Prison Service* [2010] EWCA Civ 25, [2010] IRLR 451: in addition to unfair dismissal, a claim was brought under the wider definition of employment (including contracts for services) under anti-discrimination legislation; the absence of any contract at all with the end-user was fatal to the applicant's claim.

Given the large number of possible factual variations as seen in the previous chapter, it is important to note that there is nothing *prima facie* to exclude the existence of a contract of employment under all circumstances, be it with an employment agency (some major industry players explicitly make a point of providing their workers with such contracts)[6] or end-users.[7] As discussion in the following section will show, however, this is still not a guarantee for complete regulatory coverage. The same point applies to various kinds of specific statutory interventions to be discussed extensively in Chapter 5.

McCann has suggested[8] that workers' exclusion from key employment rights, triggered by the absence of a contract of employment, can be traced back to two dimensions of triangular agency work's divergence from standard employment. The first dimension revolves around the multilateral nature of the work setup. Indeed, in early cases such as *Construction Industry Training Board v Labour Force Ltd*, this seemed to lead the courts to the conclusion 'that there is much to be said for the view that, where A contracts with B to render services exclusively to C, the contract is not a contract for services, but a contract *sui generis*, a different type of contract from either of the familiar two'.[9] While this analysis is generally no longer considered appropriate today, a second dimension, viz the fact that the worker's relationship with the agency is a casual working arrangement, has become increasingly important. For present purposes, discussion is therefore broken down into analyses of the two potential relationships involved: that between the temporary worker and the agency, and that between the temporary worker and the agency's client or end-user.

A. No Contract with the Agency

In their analysis of the relationship between worker and employment agency, Wynn and Leighton suggest that '[i]t is clearly understood that the agreement between a temp who is on the books of an agency is essentially a pre-contractual or collateral one'.[10] This result is borne out in some early cases such as *O'Sullivan v Thompson-Coon*,[11] where the court held that there was no contract at all between agency and worker. With respect, however, this will no longer be the case in most scenarios today: a contract is frequently in place between the parties, and there is nothing in principle to stop it from being characterized as a contract of employment; indeed, the Court of Appeal so found in *McMeechan*.[12]

In reality, however, it is unlikely 'that many agency contracts will turn out to be contracts of employment [even if] the possibility should not be overlooked'.[13]

---

[6] *McMeechan v Secretary of State for Employment* [1997] ICR 549 (CA).
[7] *Motorola Ltd v Davidson* [2001] IRLR 4 (EAT).
[8] D McCann, *Regulating Flexible Work* (OUP 2008) 147.
[9] [1970] 3 All ER 220 (QBD) 225 (Cooke J).
[10] M Wynn and P Leighton, 'Will the Real Employer Please Stand Up? Agencies, Client Companies and the Employment Status of the Temporary Agency Worker' (2006) 35 ILJ 301, 319.
[11] *O'Sullivan v Thompson-Coon* (1972) 14 KIR 108 (DC).   [12] *McMeechan* (n 6).
[13] HMRC, *Employment Status Manual*, ESM2002, <http://www.hmrc.gov.uk/manuals/esm-manual/ESM2002.htm> accessed 28 August 2014.

Instead, while a contract with the agency will be found, it will usually be characterized as one for services. In *Wickens v Champion Employment*,[14] for example, it was held that the claimant could not bring an unfair dismissal claim, as temporary agency workers were not engaged under contracts of employment; the relevant business size threshold had therefore not been met.

The explanation behind these findings can be found in the traditional common law tests as set out in Chapter 1; in particular the tests of control and mutuality of obligation.[15] As the previous chapter has demonstrated, the employer functions most relevant under these criteria are usually exercised jointly, or by the end-user rather than the agency. The Court of Appeal's decision in *Bunce v Postworth*[16] neatly illustrates this point. The applicant was a welder on the books of an employment agency, Skyblue. While the vast majority of engagements were for one particular end-user, a railway company, the relationship there was not exclusive, and the Employment Tribunal's decision as to the absence of an employment contract with any particular end-user was never appealed. The employment agency exercised a range of employer functions, including payment, training, and the provision of certification materials and tools.[17] Once at the actual job sites, however, the welder worked directly under the control of each client. As Keene LJ put it '[t]hat is really fatal to [the claimant's] case'.[18] The mutuality of obligation test can play a similarly lethal role, as the decision in *Montgomery v Johnson Underwood* shows:[19] an agency-supplied receptionist was not an employee working under a contract of service because of the absence of reciprocal obligations.

Despite exceptions on the facts of specific cases[20] or in the practice of individual agencies that explicitly 'employ' their temporary workers,[21] it is therefore unlikely that temporary workers will come within the protective scope of a contract of employment with their agency.

B. No Contract with the End-User

The situation with respect to end-users is similar, if not even more difficult. There is generally no direct contractual arrangement in place between the parties, although factual exceptions are again possible.[22] The traditional tests for

---

[14] *Wickens v Champion Employment* [1984] ICR 365 (EAT).

[15] The latter being especially important since *Carmichael v National Power Plc* [1999] 1 WLR 2042 (HL).

[16] *Bunce v Postworth Limited t/a Skyblue* [2005] EWCA Civ 490, [2005] IRLR 557.

[17] *Bunce* (n 16) [9].

[18] *Bunce* (n 16) [29]–[30]. For lack of control over day-to-day work see also *Dacas v Brook Street Bureau (UK) Ltd* [2004] EWCA Civ 217, [2004] ICR 1437.

[19] [2001] EWCA Civ 318, [2001] ICR 819; confirmed in *Bunce* (n 16).

[20] *McMeechan* (n 6).

[21] C Forde and G Slater, 'The Role of Employment Agencies in Pay Setting' (ACAS Research Paper 05/2011) 14; K Ward, 'Making Manchester "Flexible": Competition and Change in the Temporary Staffing Industry' (2005) 36 Geoforum 223.

[22] In *Dacas* (n 18), a contract with the client was found to have been established. In *Motorola* (n 7), the end-user's high level of control over aspects of the employment relationship, including training and sanctions for misconduct, supported a finding that the individual was an employee.

employment status are the by now familiar starting point, as seen for example in Elias J's decision in *Stephenson v Delphi Diesel Systems Ltd*.[23] There, an employee's previous service under an agency arrangement was held not to have been under a contract with the end-user, thus negating the possibility of an unfair dismissal claim. In so doing, Elias J's focus was firmly on mutuality of obligation as the test for the existence of a contract: '[t]he significance of mutuality is that it determines whether there is a contract in existence at all'.[24] Given the absence of a duty to pay the assigned worker continuously or to provide any future work there could therefore be no contract of any kind; the issue of control, in this analysis, having been relegated to the classification of any contract that may be found to exist.

At the time of Elias J's judgment in the EAT, however, a crucial development had already begun, with courts initially surprisingly willing to explore other ways of establishing a contractual relationship with the end-user. The absence of a written contractual document between the parties has never been a problem in this context, as section 230 of the Employment Rights Act 1993 explicitly provides that a contract of service can be 'express or implied, and (if it is express) . . . oral or in writing'.[25]

In *Dacas v Brook Street Bureau*,[26] a Court of Appeal led by Mummery LJ had picked up earlier foundations in cases such as *Franks v Reuters*[27] and developed the use of implied contracts in triangular work scenarios. On the facts of the case, this aspect of the decision was strictly *obiter dictum*, as the claimant had never appealed the employment tribunal's finding that there was no contract of employment with the end-user, Wansborough Council. Nonetheless, in overruling the EAT's finding that the cleaner had been employed by the agency, the court found that, as a matter of law, an implied contract between the parties was a possibility that tribunals ought to consider.[28]

The majority opinion in *Dacas* was approved in 2006 by the Court of Appeal in *Cable & Wireless Plc v Muscat*.[29] The most important thing to note about the latter decision, however, is the court's explicit linking of previous *dicta* that a contract could only be implied where necessary[30] to the business reality test of necessity as espoused by Bingham LJ in *The Aramis*.[31] This was an early sign of a shift in focus—soon to be taken up by Elias J in the EAT,[32] and culminating in the Court of Appeal's ruling in *James v Greenwich London Borough Council*.[33]

In that case, the applicant had been seconded by her agency to the respondent council as a housing support worker for nearly three years. When Ms James attempted to return to work after an extended period off for health reasons, she

---

[23] [2003] ICR 475 (EAT).
[24] *Stephenson* (n 23) [11]. Picked up by Munby J dissenting in *Dacas* (n 18).
[25] Employment Rights Act 1996 ('ERA 1996') s 230(2).   [26] *Dacas* (n 18).
[27] *Franks v Reuters* [2003] EWCA Civ 417, [2003] ICR 1166.
[28] The case law on implied contracts will be discussed extensively in Chapter 5.
[29] *Cable & Wireless Plc v Muscat* [2006] EWCA Civ 220, [2006] ICR 975 [45].
[30] *Dacas* (n 18) [16].   [31] *The Aramis* [1989] 1 Lloyd's Rep 213 (CA).
[32] *National Grid Electricity v Wood* [2007] UKEAT/0432/07.
[33] *James* (n 4). See also *Cairns v Visteon UK Ltd* [2007] ICR 616 (EAT).

found that her function had been filled by another temporary worker. There was no contention for a contract of employment directly with the agency.[34] Mummery LJ took the opportunity to review the existing case law on employment relations in triangular setups,[35] and made it clear that the threshold for implication was a high one: as the council's exercise of employer functions over Ms James could be explained by the parties' 'respective contracts with the employment agency, . . . it was not necessary to imply the existence of another contract in order to give business reality to the relationship between the parties'.[36]

The resulting difficulty in establishing a contract of employment with end-users is evident in a series of subsequent EAT decisions,[37] and was confirmed by the Court of Appeal two years later in *Alstom*.[38] Whilst the Employment Tribunal in *Alstom* had analysed the agency arrangements as merely a payment mechanism and therefore implied a direct contract with the end-user, Elias LJ in the Court of Appeal held that the other contractual relationships in the multi-agency arrangement were a sufficient explanation of Mr Tilson's service; consequently, no contract of employment could be implied.[39] The implications and possible interpretations of this line of cases will be discussed extensively in Chapter 5; suffice it to say for the moment that it is increasingly unlikely that a contract of employment would readily be implied between an agency worker and the end-user of the agency's services.

The starkest implication of shared exercise across multiple *loci* has thus become visible: a worker can find herself without recourse to the most significant employment protective rights in triangular settings, as neither the arrangement with the agency nor the relationship with the end-user is classified as a contract of employment. This situation is not infrequently exacerbated by the fact that many individuals in non-standard employment relationships have little understanding of their legal status.[40]

Section 2: Incomplete and Incoherent Coverage in Multilateral Organizational Settings

The second set of implications will be discussed in a different regulatory context, with examples chosen from statutory provisions that facilitate and

---

[34] *James* (n 4) [18]. There usually is a contractual nexus between worker and agency, but it will rarely be one of service: *Wickens v Champion Employment* (n 14).

[35] *James* (n 4) [46]–[52]. Agency worker cases at the tribunal stage had been stayed in anticipation of the decision.

[36] *James* (n 4) [42].

[37] For example in *East Living Ltd v Sridhar* [2007] UKEAT/0476/07/RN (carer not employed as other explanations for work negate necessity test) or *Vidal-Hall v Hawley* [2007] UKEAT/0462/07/DA (social worker in relationship with charity, no need also to imply relationship with HM Prison Service).

[38] *Alstom* (n 4).　　　[39] *Alstom* (n 4) [49].

[40] B Burchell, S Deakin, and S Honey, *The Employment Status of Individuals in Non-Standard Employment* (DTI 1999) 84.

protect employee voice in the workplace. The section will draw in particular on employers' duties to consult employees before specific events in a company's life cycle, with a view to influencing the exercise of related employer functions: collective redundancies, and the transfer of undertakings. Whilst consultation duties have today been extended to a more general plane,[41] these areas are closely linked examples of two such duties that continue to provoke litigation at the highest levels.[42] A multi-functional concept of the employer would point to all entities that are actual decision-makers under such circumstances. In corporate groups, however, the distinct legal personality of each entity confines the identification of the employer to the immediate contractual counterpart alone.

In line with the overall design of Part II, this section is organized as follows. A first subsection outlines the basic regulatory motivation and frameworks, before looking at the difficulty of identifying the relevant employer in the two contexts: the person or persons taking the decision leading to collective redundancies, and the transferor entity in the transfer of undertakings. The discussion's initial focus will be on the difficulty of identifying the employer for purposes of collective redundancy consultation. As the two areas are reasonably similar for present purposes this is then followed by an analysis of recent important developments concerning the concept of the employer in the context of the Acquired Rights Directive. Subsection B continues an exploration of that context, with a view to demonstrating why the corporate veil may continue to operate so strongly in shaping a unitary concept and denying a successful multi-functional identification of the employer, as well as showing up the deep flaws of such analyses. This material then provides the basis for Section 3, which sets out the key conclusions to be drawn from this chapter.

A. Employee Consultation in Collective Redundancies and Transfers of Undertakings

Discussion thus turns to the substantive areas under review: the information and consultation of employees in cases of collective redundancies and transfers of undertakings. The principal goal of statutory regulation in the former area is to avoid or reduce the need for redundancies or, failing that, to limit the impact of layoffs. The economic idea underpinning an obligation on employers to consult with employees is that the party taking a restructuring decision will be able to identify its most efficient choice

---

[41] Directive (EC) 14/2002 of the Council and the European Parliament of 11 March 2002 establishing a general framework for informing and consulting employees in the European Community [2002] OJ L80/29 ('Information and Consultation Directive').

[42] Information and Consultation Directive (n 41) pr 5: 'Information, consultation and participation for workers must be developed along appropriate lines, taking account of the practice in force in the various Member States. Such information, consultation and participation must be implemented in due time, particularly in connection with restructuring operations in undertakings or in cases of mergers having an impact on the employment of workers.'

only in dialogue with individuals directly affected. In order to ensure this, all stakeholders must be able to signal correctly their range of preferences, which in turn is only possible if their representatives have access to all the relevant information.

As regards the motivation underpinning the second area, changes in the structure and composition of enterprises were one of the key economic consequences envisaged by the creators of the European Single Market.[43] With the changes in economic activity there was to come an increase in productivity and wealth—but also an increase in the uncertainty faced by individual workers: as new shareholders and management took over, implicit bonds between the existing owners and employees were bound to break down.[44] The (then) Community therefore saw a need to provide for the protection of employees' rights in the resulting organizational changes,[45] primarily through 'the principle of the retention of employment contracts despite a change in the legal personality of the employer'[46] and by imposing a range of related obligations such as information and consultation with employees affected by a reorganization.[47] The relative weight accorded by the Community to the policy goal of safeguarding employees' rights in enterprise restructuring from early on was significant, thus justifying the imposition of 'a major limitation on . . . the power of employers to arrange their commercial and corporate affairs in such a way as to minimise or fragment their employment law liabilities'.[48]

These goals will be defeated by problems in identifying the employer: in the transfer of undertakings, the crucial question is as to whether the transferor of the undertaking was also the worker's employer, as the protective regime is otherwise inapplicable. In the context of redundancy consultations, wrong identification places obligations on parties other than those who are contemplating dismissals and will eventually take the relevant decisions. As the Court of Justice of the European Union has pointed out, one cannot comply with the Directive and avoid or reduce the number of terminations if consultation of workers' representatives comes subsequent to the redundancy decision.[49]

---

[43] Council Directive (EC) 23/2001 on the approximation of the laws of the Member States relating to the safeguarding of employees' rights in the event of transfers of undertakings, businesses or parts of undertakings or businesses [2001] OJ L82/16 ('ARD') pr (2).

[44] A Shleifer and L Summers, 'Breach of Trust in Hostile Takeovers' (1987) NBER Working Paper No 2342. The same is said to be true in Private Equity transactions today: D Hall, 'Methodological Issues in Estimating the Impact of Private Equity Buyouts on Employment' (Public Services International Research Unit, UNITE 2007).

[45] ARD (n 43) pr (3).

[46] Commission Report on Council Directive 2001/23/EC of 12 March 2001 on the approximation of the laws of the Member States relating to the safeguarding of employees' rights in the event of transfers of undertakings, businesses or parts of undertakings or businesses (Brussels, 18 June 2007) COM(2007) 334 final [6].

[47] ARD (n 43) ch III.

[48] S Deakin and G Morris, *Labour Law* (6th edn Hart 2012) 234. A summary of substantive provisions can be found at [3.67]ff.

[49] Case C-188/03 *Junk v Kühnel* [2005] ECR I-885 [38].

The Regulatory Frameworks

While the policy considerations and general context are therefore reasonably similar, the regulatory frameworks must be set out separately. The duty to consult with employee representatives in the case of collective redundancies, first, is found in section 188 of TULRCA 1992,[50] which implemented the Collective Redundancies Directive (98/59/EC).[51] Where more than 20 employees are to be made redundant at an establishment within a period of 90 days, the employer has to commence negotiations, 'with a view to reaching agreement', on ways of avoiding the dismissals, reducing the numbers of employees to be dismissed, and mitigating the consequences of the dismissals.[52] In so doing, relevant information needs to be provided to the employees' representatives, including details about the reasons for redundancies and the proposed method of selecting those to be dismissed;[53] these requirements have increasingly been interpreted as encompassing broader economic reasons for the employer's decision.[54] If an undertaking is found to have breached these obligations, the employees can apply for a protective award.[55]

The regulation of transfers of undertakings, on the other hand, stems from the Acquired Rights Directive 1977,[56] as implemented in the United Kingdom four years thereafter.[57] A series of politically controversial amendments and re-enactments followed;[58] the provisions in force today are set out in the Acquired Rights Directive of 2001,[59] to which the 2006 TUPE Regulations give domestic effect.[60] The Regulations apply if there is a relevant transfer of an undertaking, business, or part thereof, 'where there is a transfer of an economic entity which retains its identity'.[61] The precise scope of this requirement has been the subject of extensive litigation and academic writing. As the issues under discussion there are not specific to the PE or corporate group setting, the application of TUPE to a subsection of the scenarios under discussion (management buy-out of a unit in a large, solvent business) will be assumed for present purposes. Once TUPE applies, there are two crucial consequences, the latter of which is particularly relevant: contracts of employment will not terminate in a transfer of

---

[50] Trade Union and Labour Relations (Consolidation) Act 1992 ('TULRCA 1992'), pt IV ch II: Procedure for Handling Redundancies (ss 188–198).

[51] Council Directive (EC) 59/1998 on the approximation of the laws of the Member States relating to collective redundancies [1998] OJ L225/16 ('Collective Redundancies Directive').

[52] TULRCA 1992 (n 50), s 188(2).

[53] TULRCA 1992 (n 50), s 188(4)(a) and (d) respectively.

[54] *UK Coal Ltd v NUM* [2008] IRLR 4 (EAT) [84, 87] (Elias J).

[55] Which is of penal rather than compensatory nature: *Susie Radin Ltd v GMB* [2004] IRLR 400 (CA).

[56] Directive (EC) 187/1977. Today consolidated in the ARD (n 43).

[57] Transfer of Undertakings (Protection of Employment) Regulations 1981, SI 1981/1794.

[58] S Hardy and R Painter, 'Revising the Acquired Rights Directive' (1996) 25 ILJ 160, 165.

[59] ARD (n 43).

[60] P Davies and M Freedland, *Towards a Flexible Labour Market: Labour Legislation and Regulation since the 1990s* (Oxford Monographs on Labour Law, OUP 2007) 92.

[61] Transfer of Undertakings (Protection of Employment) Regulations 2006 ('TUPE 2006'), SI 2006/246, reg 3(1)(a).

the business (or part thereof), but take effect 'as if originally made between [the employee] and the transferee'.[62] The same general principle applies to collective agreements[63] and trade union recognition.[64] The parties are furthermore subject to a reasonably wide range of duties, including the provision of information on 'the fact that the transfer is to take place, the date or proposed date of the transfer and the reasons for it; the legal, economic and social implications of the transfer for any affected employees; [and] the measures [to be taken] in connection with the transfer';[65] and a duty to 'consult the appropriate representatives of [the employees to be made redundant] with a view to seeking their agreement to the intended measures'.[66]

B. Identifying the Relevant Employer

The existence of a second *locus* of control gives rise to two potential issues in the context of collective redundancy consultation: the most appropriate entity, first, may not be under an obligation to consult with employee representatives. If this obligation is placed on an investee company alone, for example, the scope of consultation would become vastly under-inclusive in the Private Equity context: it is at, or more precisely in the run-up to, the decision-making stage that consultation will be at its most effective, by making a broad range of information available to the decision-maker, and challenging them to come up with a plan that takes all stakeholders' interests into account. Depending on a PE fund's internal organizational structure, the primary information available to the PE analyst team preparing a redundancy decision will often be limited to the portfolio company's financial and strategic data. Its decision, which will frequently be final, may therefore be inefficient, both in terms of its impact on employees and the financial performance of the fund, as there was no obligation to consult with worker representatives. The second potential issue arises in relation to the contractual employer (viz, the portfolio company), who may attempt to use superior but formally external decisions as a defence to excuse its non-compliance with the consultation regime: the CEO of a portfolio company may not have contemplated redundancies until informed thereof by the PE management company but nonetheless has to give effect to these orders as a clear expression of shareholder interest. As subsequent discussion will show it is only the latter of these issues (the 'defence question') that is successfully addressed by the current redundancy consultation regime.

The issue of external influence is clearly addressed in the Directive's preamble, where the Community institutions note that:

> it is necessary to ensure that employers' obligations as regards information, consultation and notification apply independently of whether the decision on collective redundancies emanates from the employer or from an undertaking which controls that employer.[67]

---

[62] TUPE 2006 (n 61) reg 4(1).   [63] TUPE 2006 (n 61) reg 5.
[64] TUPE 2006 (n 61) reg 6.   [65] TUPE 2006 (n 61) reg 13(2)(a)–(d).
[66] TUPE 2006 (n 61) reg 13(6).
[67] Collective Redundancies Directive (n 51) [11].

This desire is reflected in Article 2(4), which decrees that the Directive's obligations 'shall apply irrespective of whether the decision . . . is being taken by the employer or by an undertaking controlling the employer', ie even in circumstances where the latter has not provided the relevant information to its subsidiary. At first sight these provisions appear to give effect to the goals of the Directive—the obligations 'apply' even where decisions are not taken by the employing entity's executives or board of directors. The wording of the preamble covers two distinct problems: first, that a company could rely on external decisions imposed on it as a defence to avoid consultative obligations; and, second, that no meaningful consultation with the appropriate decision-making body takes place at all as the relevant employer cannot be identified.

Upon closer inspection it becomes apparent that, while the provisions may be successful in addressing the first problem, they fail to attain the Directive's goals, as the second issue is not considered. *Ex-ante* consultation with the relevant decision-maker is considerably more important than the *ex-post* imposition of a punitive award.[68] There are several sources of this limitation: a particularly narrow transposition of Article 2(4) in section 188(7) of TULRCA 1992 in the United Kingdom and, on both domestic and Union levels, an unduly restrictive interpretation of the Directive and its implementing provisions.

The consultative obligations in Article 2(4) of the Directive are transposed in the United Kingdom as section 188(7) of TULRCA 1992. This provision sets out a defence available to the employing entity if special circumstances make it not reasonably practicable for it to have informed and consulted the workforce before the collective redundancies took place: it will only have to take such steps as are reasonably necessary. It is not difficult to envisage how binding orders from a superior company (acting if necessary as a sole shareholder) could be invoked as such a special circumstance, in effect negating the section 188 duties; the defence is therefore subject to an exception. Subsection (7) stipulates that:

[w]here the decision leading to the proposed dismissals is that of a person controlling the employer (directly or indirectly), a failure on the part of that person to provide information to the employer shall not constitute special circumstances rendering it not reasonably practicable for the employer to comply with such requirement.

It is not immediately obvious where this 'special circumstances' defence and the exceptions to it are grounded in the Directive; it appears to be a uniquely British approach to transposition.[69] The key problem for present purposes is the fact that the section 188(7) arrangement will only ever address the defence point, which was identified as one of two problematic issues in the Directive's preamble: there is nothing to guide consultative efforts towards the party best placed to discharge this duty. As regards the defence question, repeated decisions have emphasized that 'special circumstances' is a high threshold indeed: the events in question need to be something out of the ordinary; even a very significant event such as

---

[68] *Susie Radin Ltd v GMB* (n 55).   [69] Deakin and Morris, *Labour Law* (n 48) 936.

insolvency, which may regularly occur in the business world, is not enough.[70] The futility of consultation (an argument at hand in most PE situations) will likewise not constitute a special circumstance by itself.[71]

Even where a court heeds the legislation's worker-protective purpose and attempts to look beyond this reductive interpretation towards effective consultation, however, there is very little space to manoeuvre within that framework. In *GMB v Beloit Walmsley*,[72] the UK subsidiary of a US paper conglomerate had ceased trading following the parent entities' surprise collapse; two separate rounds of redundancies consequently took place. A breach of the section 188 consultation requirements was conceded before the court, the focus of the argument thus shifting onto the special circumstances defence. The Employment Tribunal held that the unexpected announcement had indeed constituted such special circumstances, and that the second part of section 188(7) was not applicable as the decision leading to the dismissals had not been that of the American parent company, nor had the latter failed to provide relevant information.

The Employment Appeal Tribunal, having noted that this was the first time it had been asked to interpret these particular provisions, first turned to the Directive's preamble to discover the purposes of consultation. With this in mind, it proceeded to construe widely the requirement of 'information' to be provided, and held that the parent companies' actions may well have been decisions with 'the causal effect of requiring dismissals by reason of redundancy by the employers, and that the person or persons who made them must have contemplated that they would have that consequence'.[73] The trade union's appeal was therefore successful, with the matter remitted for a further hearing to determine the relevant facts.

Seen through the narrow perspective of the defence question, this decision is to be welcomed: it ensures that the general high threshold (which excludes economic events such as insolvency) is equally applied in group settings. Towards the end of the appeal tribunal's judgment, however, Mitting J suggested that it was 'delay in communicating [the redundancy] decision which is the mischief at which the exception to the special circumstances defence in section 188(7) is aimed'.[74] It is submitted, with respect, that this constitutes far too narrow an interpretation of the provision, particularly in light of the material extensively cited in the earlier parts of the appeal tribunal's judgment.

At the European Union level, the first opportunity to clarify the application of Directive 98/59 to situations where decisions are taken by entities other than the undertaking's management arose in *Fujitsu Siemens*.[75] Here, control was exercised by Fujitsu Siemens Computers (Holding) BV, a company incorporated and

---

[70] *Clarks of Hove Ltd v The Bakers' Union* [1978] IRLR 366 (CA).
[71] *Iron & Steel Trades Confederation (ISTC) v ASW Holdings plc* [2004] IRLR 926 (EAT); *Middlesborough BC v TGWU* [2002] IRLR 332 (EAT); but cf *Amicus v GBS Tooling Ltd (in administration)* [2005] IRLR 683 (EAT).
[72] *GMB (AEEU & MSF) v Beloit Walmsley Ltd* [2003] ICR 1396 (EAT).
[73] *GMB v Beloit* (n 72) [23].   [74] *GMB v Beloit* (n 72) [22].
[75] Case C-44/2008 *Akavan Erityisalojen Keskusliitto AEK ry and Others v Fujitsu Siemens Computers Oy* [2009] ECR I-8163, Opinion of AG Mengozzi [50].

resident in the Netherlands, over manufacturing plants in Kilo, Finland and various locations in Germany. On 7 December 1999 the executive team of the parent company held a telephone meeting to discuss the potential disengagement from the Kilo plant, and resolved to propose the measure to the parent company's board. The latter supported the proposal on 14 December without, however, deciding on a specific plan of action. Local management in Kilo consulted with employee representatives from 20 December 1999 to 31 January 2010, before ceasing activity on 1 February, and terminating the employment of 350 workers from 8 February onwards. The trade unions representing the claimants alleged that these steps meant that Fujitsu Siemens had failed to comply with the Directive's obligations as transposed into Finnish law.

At first instance it was held that consultation amongst Kilo employees had been genuine. Upon appeal, several questions were referred to the CJEU, including (questions 3 and 4) whether the obligation to inform and consult originated at the point in time when the controlling parent undertaking discussed a general need for action, or only once collective redundancies were contemplated specifically in the subsidiary company; and (questions 5 and 6) whether consultation needed to be finalized before the parent took general commercial or strategic specific decisions that might lead to redundancies, or only before the need for dismissals was certain.

AG Mengozzi's opinion started with a detailed examination of the scope *ratione personae* of the Directive, asserting that this was firmly restricted to the employing entity itself.[76] Whilst the Advocate General then conceded that compliance with the information requirement might be impossible without assistance from the controlling entity, he nonetheless went on to suggest that this could not be read as a duty on the latter to hold direct consultations. Indeed, the *travaux préparatoires*[77] to the Directive had made it clear that its provisions were not to be used as a 'bypass' mechanism.[78] In following this line of reasoning, the Court affirmed that the Directive's obligations were squarely based on the 'employer, in other words a natural or legal person who stands in an employment relationship with the workers who may be made redundant'.[79] An undertaking, even if capable of controlling the employer through binding decisions, did not have that status. The Directive's goal was not to restrict the commercial freedom of corporate groups to choose their organizations' management structures, and none of its provisions could be interpreted as imposing any obligations on the controller.[80]

The Court then turned to its comparatively brief answers to the specific questions referred. A duty to start consultation, first, only arose once the specific subsidiary had been identified. If that company had not been immediately and properly informed by the controlling entity this would constitute a breach of

---

[76] *Fujitsu Siemens* (n 75) Opinion of AG Mengozzi [35].

[77] European Commission, *Explanatory Memorandum to the Proposal for a Council Directive amending Directive 75/129* COM(91) 292 final OJ 1991 C310, 5 [16].

[78] *Fujitsu Siemens* (n 75) Opinion of AG Mengozzi [40], [42].

[79] *Fujitsu Siemens* (n 75) [57]–[58].   [80] *Fujitsu Siemens* (n 75) [59], [68].

the Directive's provisions, with the consequences to be borne by the subsidiary alone.[81] As regards the timing of the final decision to dismiss workers, on the other hand, 'in the context of a group of undertakings . . . [the] decision by the parent company which has the direct effect of compelling one of its subsidiaries to terminate the contracts of employees . . . [could] be taken only on the conclusion of the consultation procedure within that subsidiary'.[82] These answers express an unease in dealing with the issue at stake: while the Court was mindful of not rendering the duties fictional, it nonetheless refused to give the information and consultation obligations full effect by including in their scope the party best placed to discharge them—an impasse created by a unitary understanding of the concept of the employer.

It should be noted that the wording of the decision throughout, and especially in answer to the questions referred, is relatively unclear, as the Court of Appeal's initial decision in the *USA v Nolan* saga shows:[83] there, the respondent had made some 200 civilians redundant as a consequence of the decision to close RSA Hythe, a military base in Hampshire, in September 2006. Ms Nolan alleged that the USA had failed to consult with representatives of the civilian workforce, in particular by not consulting before, and about, the operational decision to close the base.[84] In November 2010, the Court of Appeal referred a series of questions to the Court of Justice, in particular as to the distinction between the adoption of business and operational strategies and consequent redundancy decisions. In March 2012, AG Mengozzi suggested that consultation was to begin as soon as a strategic decision compelled the contemplation of collective redundancies;[85] the Court of Justice, on the other hand, refused to address the point as it declared itself not to have jurisdiction, as Article 1(2)(b) of the Directive 'provides an exclusion from the scope of Directive 98/59 [which therefore] does not apply to workers employed by public administrative bodies or by establishments governed by public law . . . [including] the civilian staff of a military base.[86] The Court of Appeal's subsequent decision focused on the scope of the domestic implementing legislation alone, thus leaving the '*Fujitsu* question' to be determined at a future hearing.[87]

In the Private Equity context (and indeed many forms of corporate groups), several of the distinctions drawn by the CJEU in *Fujitsu Siemens* may be entirely fictional: as opposed to the board of holding companies, PE fund teams will always take decisions directly for each investment—identifying the relevant subsidiary will rarely be a distinct step.[88] Applying the wording of the answer to questions

---

[81] *Fujitsu Siemens* (n 75) [63], [69].   [82] *Fujitsu Siemens* (n 75) [71].

[83] *The United States of America v Christine Nolan* [2010] EWCA Civ 1223, [2011] IRLR 40.

[84] *USA v Nolan* (n 83) [3].

[85] Case C-583/10 *United States of America v Christine Nolan* [2013] 1 CMLR 32, Opinion of AG Mengozzi of 22 March 2012. The 'compelling force' of individual decisions is to be determined by the Member State courts: AG Mengozzi [49].

[86] Case C-583/10 *United States of America v Christine Nolan* [2013] 1 CMLR 32, Decision of 18 October 2012 [33]–[34].

[87] *The United States of America v Nolan (No 2)* [2014] EWCA Civ 71, [2014] ICR 685 [33].

[88] Essentially only where the investee itself is a group of companies.

5 and 6 in the judgment,[89] therefore, it would appear that the immediate implementation of a fund's decision to dismiss a group of employees would be in direct contravention of section 188 of TULRCA 1992. This conclusion holds true even if the decision was transmitted informally to portfolio company management, as the tests focus on the 'factual level' of control exercised.[90] While the fact that the resulting protective award can only be made against the investee company might matter in certain groups of companies with distinct accounts and liabilities, it is of little relevance to the Private Equity operator whose returns are directly linked to cashflows from the portfolio company.

The law's inability to identify the appropriate employing entity or combination of entities where there has been a split of employer functions across multiple corporate entities is a result of an interpretation conflicted between the two competing strands of the concept of the employer. Its problematic consequences extend to both employees and management, as the most appropriate entity may be under no duty to become involved in dialogue with employee representatives. As regards PE management companies, there is the potential of liability where fund-internal procedures mean that 'workers would be presented with a fait accompli, and the provision would be deprived of any practical effect'.[91] For employees, on the other hand, there is little chance that their representatives will be able to engage in meaningful consultations as to the workforce's future.

Potential Solutions

The issue thus identified exists at both Union and domestic levels: the problems that can arise from complex corporate setups in informing and consulting employees are twofold, yet only the reliance on external (shareholder) instructions as a potential defence is successfully addressed. The differences at various regulatory levels are, however, not ones of degree, but of kind. In the CJEU, a broader interpretation of the Directive's provision would be feasible, whereas given the UK implementation in section 188(7) the possibilities for an effective solution within the existing framework are few. For the information and consultation duties to operate effectively in subsidiary-parent or portfolio company-PE fund circumstances, the very duties created by the collective redundancy regime would need to be able to identify the relevant counterparty as the employer: the obligations have to rest on the body from which the decision to effect collective redundancies emanates, regardless of whether parent and subsidiary entities are acting independently or jointly.

Within the existing domestic framework, there is but one potential route to achieving this result: a challenge to the proper transposition of the Directive under EU law principles. It has long been established that the UK government

---

[89] *Fujitsu Siemens* (n 75) [71].

[90] J Heinsius, 'Commentary on the EU Court's Decision in *Fujitsu*' (2010) 7 European Company Law 165, 168.

[91] [91] *Junk* (n 49) Opinion of AG Tizzano [60].

showed particular reticence in the transposition of various employee consultation Directives;[92] the European Commission first instituted infringement proceedings in 1992.[93] These were primarily focused on the consultative mechanism and the remedial regime, however, and did not address the peculiarity of section 188(7). The same is true for another series of judicial discussions, this time on the temporal element of the consultative requirement, a decade later.[94] It is therefore unlikely that such an avenue for reform will be pursued.

Before the Court of Justice, on the other hand, there is at least some possibility that *Fujitsu Siemens* may not be followed in its narrow confinement of the consultative obligation to the subsidiary entity and formal counterparty to the contract of employment. The CJEU's general approach in the area of employee consultation has frequently been a purposive one, both generally to achieve the proclaimed harmonization goals of various Directives,[95] and specifically in order to support their worker-protective stance.[96] In the present context, this general stance would suggest a functional approach to the interpretation of the Directive's requirements; that is a finding of consultative obligations' resting on whichever entity will in fact take the eventual redundancy decision. It is against this backdrop that the judgment in *Fujitsu Siemens* must be evaluated.

The relevant sections of Advocate General Mengozzi's opinion, endorsed by the Court, begin with an examination of the 'scope *ratione personae* of Directive 98/59, and in particular the question . . . whether that Directive lays down obligations incumbent not only on the employer but also on the undertaking controlling that employer'.[97] This question is answered primarily by reference to the actual wording of the provisions, with a major emphasis on the practicality of needing a *single* entity on whom the various duties (information, notification, and consultation) in the run-up to the proposed redundancies rest, which is to discharge them, and accept liability for the failure so to do. This last part of the AG's argument is not necessarily contentious—indeed, it harks back to the defence point already discussed at length: in a multi-entity scenario it is crucial to avoid the exploitation of the corporate group in order to escape regulatory obligations. In cases where the redundancy decision is taken jointly by two entities, it will always be possible for an employment tribunal to decide on the facts which company was the primary *locus* of decision-making—or impose AG Mengozzi's solution as a default outcome unless displaced by factual evidence.

The case for the single entity on which the obligations are imposed always to be the subsidiary, on the other hand, is a much weaker one, even if construed purely on the wording of the Directive: whilst this might be the appropriate solution in

[92] P Davies and M Freedland, *Labour Legislation and Public Policy* (OUP 1993) 576 ff.

[93] Case C-383/92 *EC Commission v United Kingdom (collective redundancy infringement)* [1994] ECR I-2479.

[94] See eg *MSF v Refuge Assurance plc* [2002] 2 CMLR 27 (EAT).

[95] Case C-242/09 *Albron Catering BV v FNV Bondgenoten* [2011] All ER (EC) 625.

[96] See eg Case C-55/02 *EC Commission v Portuguese Republic* [2004] ECR I-9387 [50]; Case C-449/93 *Rockfon A/S v Specialarbejderforbundet i Danmark* [1996] ECR I-4291.

[97] *Fujitsu Siemens* (n 75) Opinion of AG Mengozzi [35].

the majority of cases, there is nothing to suggest an inherent need for a focus on any particular entity. Indeed, the Advocate General concedes that 'the fact remains that, if the parent company takes the decision leading to collective redundancies, it is required to provide the necessary information to the relevant employer under its control',[98] thus directly contradicting the later assertion that 'the fulfillment of [the consultative obligation] falls exclusively on the employer even if the parent company controlling that employer takes the decision leading to collective redundancies'.[99]

A second set of reasons offered for the narrow confinement of the consultative obligation to the contractual work-taking employer is traced back to a quote from the *travaux préparatoires*, giving the impression that the Commission's original focus was to protect corporate groups' freedom to organize their management structure internally. Upon a detailed reading of the cited document, however, this is not the case.[100] Instead, it states explicitly that the Directive is designed to 'ensure that the information, consultation *and* notification requirements are met *whatever the identity of the undertaking* which takes the relevant decisions leading to the collective redundancies'.[101]

The defence question is merely seen as an addendum to this:

The main changes [in the consolidated version] are to fulfil the aim of ensuring the enforcement of the existing directive . . . Thus, it is provided that the information and consultation requirements laid down by the directive apply irrespective of whether the decisions entailing collective redundancies are taken by the employer himself, by a controlling undertaking or by the central administration of a multi-establishment undertaking. *In order to reinforce* this central obligation it is *also* established that an employer's failure to comply with the directive's requirements can not be condoned on the ground that the undertaking taking the decision leading to collective redundancies failed to inform the employer in due time.[102]

While the AG is therefore correct to suggest that the Directive 'does not directly impose any obligation on controlling undertakings *as such*',[103] the conclusion that no obligation must be imposed under any circumstance is, with respect, fallacious. Indeed, the Commission's explanatory notes seem to support the development of a functional approach by emphasizing that all obligations are to apply substantively regardless of the corporate structure in question—the opposite of the reductive view emerging from *Fujitsu Siemens*, where an emphasis on compliance with the Directive's obligations sits uneasily with the unwillingness to identify the most appropriate entity.[104]

[98] *Fujitsu Siemens* (n 75) Opinion of AG Mengozzi [40].

[99] *Fujitsu Siemens* (n 75) Opinion of AG Mengozzi [42].

[100] Even though it had become, somewhat ironically, the Commission's position by the time of *Fujitsu Siemens* (n 75) [59].

[101] European Commission, *Explanatory Memorandum* (n 77) 6 [15]. Emphasis supplied.

[102] European Commission, *Explanatory Memorandum* (n 77) 6 [14]. Emphasis supplied.

[103] European Commission, *Explanatory Memorandum* (n 77) 5 [16] as cited by the AG; 6 [16] in the version available to the author. Emphasis supplied.

[104] Indeed, the Commission's main concern with imposing liability seems to have been the difficulties arising from extraterritorial regulation; this is no longer considered as a serious obstacle to legislative harmonization.

A final strand of reasoning, prevalent particularly in the Court's decision, focuses on the Directive's repeated use of the word 'employer' in the singular. The CJEU goes on to suggest that this ought to be construed as 'a natural or legal person who stands in an employment relationship with the workers who may be made redundant. An undertaking which controls the employer, even if it can take decisions which are binding on the latter, does not have the status of employer'.[105] This narrow definition of the employer has not been a consistent element in the Court's jurisprudence, as its recent decision in *Albron* shows.[106] There, the court interpreted the concept of the employer in complex group scenarios very widely indeed, by seeing it as independent of direct contractual arrangements.[107] When looking for potential solutions within the existing framework, therefore, it may be possible to read *Fujitsu Siemens* as a case confined in its larger impact to a reasonably narrow set of facts—which may of course in turn inform the Member State courts' duty of compliant interpretation in a possible challenge to the UK's highly limited transposition of the Directive.

The much more flexible approach to identifying the employer arose in the context of a question as to which party in a large multi-entity group was the relevant transferor for ARD purposes. In *Albron*,[108] the court applied a strongly purposive interpretation to the definition of the transferor under Dutch ARD implementation measures and found that a service company without direct contractual links to the employees could nonetheless be an employer and thus a relevant transferor.

As illustrated in Figure 3.1, the claimant Mr Roest (R) had been an employee of Heineken Nederlands Beheer BV (B), a staff service company within the Dutch beer-brewing group, for over 20 years. He was permanently assigned to Heineken's catering entity (H). In early 2005, H's activities were taken over by Albron Catering BV (A), and Mr Roest commenced employment with A. With the support of his trade union, he subsequently claimed that this change had fallen within the remit of the Dutch ARD provisions, and that he was therefore entitled to the same contractual terms as before the outsourcing.

The national court referred the question to the CJEU whether H could be regarded as a transferor under the Directive despite the absence of a direct contractual relationship of employment with Mr Roest, given the context of a group of companies.

The Court of Justice, following the AG's opinion,[109] answered the question in the affirmative. It arrived at this result having considered the purpose and wording of Directive 23/2001, finding that whilst the transferor was the party losing the capacity of employer, 'in the mind of the Union legislature, a contractual link with the transferor [was] not required in all circumstances for employees to be able to benefit from the protection conferred by [the Directive's provisions]'.[110] In

---

[105] *Fujitsu Siemens* (n 75) [57]–[58].   [106] *Albron* (n 95).

[107] A decision in the context of the ARD (n 43), which is similar enough for present purposes: Deakin and Morris, *Labour Law* (n 48) 913.

[108] *Albron* (n 95).

[109] *Albron* (n 95) Opinion of AG Bot of 3 June 2010.   [110] *Albron* (n 95) [24].

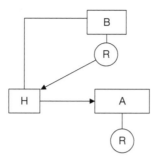

Figure 3.1 *Albron*

complex group situations with a 'plurality of employers', there was nothing to suggest that 'the contractual employer must systematically be given greater weight'.[111] Indeed, as the transfer regime was designed to 'protect employees in the event of a change of "employer"', 'a change in the legal or natural person . . . responsible for the economic activity' could be a relevant transfer despite the absence of direct contractual relationships, 'even [where] there exists within [the corporate] group an undertaking with which the employees concerned were linked by . . . a contract of employment'.[112]

This finding that the meaning of 'transferor' was not necessarily limited to the claimant's contractual employer, but also extended to a third party exercising economic control over the worker, led to a considerable flurry of practitioner comment.[113] Its precise impact remains unclear, especially given the apparent focus on the permanent nature of Mr Roest's assignment to H,[114] and the Court's emphasis on the corporate veil's protection of internal group structures in other contexts.[115] The position in the United Kingdom after *Albron* is equally unclear: as has been seen, the courts have traditionally refused to pierce the veil in TUPE transfers.[116] Depending on the context of future cases, it is possible to envisage a split between the private (where the employment tribunal is under a strong interpretative obligation, but no more) and public sectors (where an employee could attempt to rely on the direct effect of the Acquired Rights Directive).

The crucible of a potential solution lies in the Court of Justice's recognition that parties other than a contractual counterparty to the contract of service can

---

[111] *Albron* (n 95) [25].   [112] *Albron* (n 95) [30], [28], and [32] respectively.
[113] See, eg DLA Piper, 'TUPE: *Albron Catering BV v FNV Bondgenoten*' (2010); Freshfields Bruckhaus Deringer, 'Simplifying the Application of the Acquired Rights Directive to Complex Corporate Structures?' (2010); Allen & Overy, 'ECJ Confirms its Broad Interpretation of the Scope of Transfer of Undertakings Protection' (2010) and Thompsons Solicitors, 'An Acquired Taste: *Albron Catering BV v FNV Bondgenoten*' (2010).
[114] Though this aspect is much more pronounced in the AG's reasoning, eg *Albron* (n 95) Opinion of AG Bot [61], than in the Court's final judgment.
[115] *Fujitsu Siemens* (n 75) [59].
[116] *Brookes v Borough Care Services Ltd and CLS Care Services* [1998] ICR 1198 (EAT); *Clifton Middle School Governing Body v Askew* [2000] ICR 286 (CA).

be responsible for employees' sphere of economic activity, and therefore the regulatory consequences attached to it, and that the status of 'contractual employer' does not automatically take precedence over such external control. There is little in the judgment to suggest that this purposive interpretation of the ARD is limited to the transferor concept. Even in that case, however, it may have an impact in the present context: where a PE fund divests a portfolio company, for example in a secondary sale to another investor, it could be seen as a transferor, in addition to or instead of the investee enterprise. The primary benefit to employees of such an extension would be unlikely to relate to the existence of the contract of employment (as, unlike in *Albron*, this issue would not arise), but rather would consist of the additional information and consultation duties contained in TUPE. Going beyond this narrow impact, the principles espoused by the Court may in addition mean that the strict separation of shareholders and contractual employers as seen in *Fujitsu Siemens* is now open to serious questioning.

C. Shareholders as Employers?

The tension underpinning the concept of the employer is thus increasingly coming to the fore: while its multi-functional strand implicitly recognizes that relevant employer functions are exercised by multiple parties, the strong unitary assumption limits the imposition of duties to a singular entity. One particularly strong instantiation of this assumption is the idea that shareholders must generally be kept clearly distinct from employers. The transfer of an undertaking provides a salient illustration of how the identified tension creates problems in identifying the employer. As the precondition for triggering the operation of the protective regime is a *change in employer*, the unitary strand of the concept leads to very arbitrary distinctions as to when a relevant event takes place.

This significant limitation to the scope of TUPE protection has already been briefly touched upon: the definition of relevant transfer in Regulation 3 does not encompass situations where the legal personality of the target company is unaffected, such as for example a change of its members. This has the effect of '[p]aradoxically . . . exclud[ing] . . . the most important kind of change of ownership in our system of company law, namely takeover by share purchase'.[117] The following paragraphs explore this exclusion in terms of its statutory origin and application in the common law, and contrast it with situations where TUPE does apply. Against this background, a discussion of PE transactions highlights a further problem in defining the employer: the current concept leads to an entirely arbitrary application of particular norms. In the present context, the justifications given for the share transfer exclusion are incongruent with its effect where the shareholder is a Private Equity fund.

---

[117] P Davies and M Freedland, 'The Effects of Receivership upon Employees of Companies' (1980) 9 ILJ 95, 109.

In its initial proposals of 1973, the European Commission explicitly included share transfers within the ambit of the (then draft) Acquired Rights Directive.[118] The protective regime was designed to apply 'also to concentrations by which control was acquired in an undertaking, so affecting the most common form of share mergers, without a change in the identity of the employer, in Great Britain'.[119] This was to be achieved by including in its scope transactions where control was acquired, which in turn was defined very widely, including the 'power to influence the composition, voting or decisions of the organs of an undertaking'.[120] Pressure exerted by the United Kingdom and other Member State governments,[121] however, succeeded in excluding share transfers from the ARD's scope; and the UK did not make use of its power to enact a higher level of protection (which would have been far more intrusive than the existing common law position) in the 1981 transposition.[122]

The exclusion's operation is strict.[123] In *Brookes*,[124] a large group of care home workers who had previously been employed directly by a local council were transferred to a limited company operated by the latter in 1992 (BCS Ltd). Several years later, the council decided to sell its care homes to a provident society. The purchaser was aware of the (then) recent decision in *Wilson*,[125] and decided that the only way it could modify the employee's terms and conditions was if the transaction were structured as the equivalent of a share sale, rather than a transfer of the undertaking. Despite this explicit intention to avoid the application of TUPE, the EAT held that the Regulations had not been triggered. Relying on *Adams v Cape Industries plc*,[126] the tribunal found that as the company's arrangement had not been a mere façade, the corporate veil could not be pierced. Similarly, in *British Nursing v Peterson*[127] the applicant had worked for Goldsborough (G), a subsidiary company of health care provider BUPA. In 2001, the entire share capital in G was sold to BNA (B), itself a subsidiary of another major company in the industry, Nestor. Mr Peterson was made redundant following a reduction in the number of field manager positions. In somewhat unclear proceedings, the tribunal at first instance found that the transaction had not merely been a share sale, but that following it there had been a separate transfer of G's undertaking to B.[128] The Employment Appeals Tribunal relied on *Brookes* in holding that the first

---

[118] [1973] OJ C104, as cited by S Hardey, *Understanding TUPE—A Legal Guide* (Chandos 2001) 12.

[119] B Hepple, 'Recent Legislation: European Economic Community' (1977) 6 ILJ 106.

[120] B Hepple, 'Workers' Rights in Mergers and Takeovers: The EEC Proposals' (1976) 5 ILJ 197, 205.

[121] Davies and Freedland, *Labour Legislation and Public Policy* (n 92) 579.

[122] B Hepple, 'The Transfer of Undertakings (Protection of Employment) Regulations' (1982) 11 ILJ 29, 31.

[123] Though note the potential departure in *Millam v Print Factory (London) 1991 Ltd* [2007] EWCA Civ 322, [2007] IRLR 526.

[124] *Brookes* (n 116). Similarly *SI (Systems and Instrumentation) Ltd v Grist* [1983] ICR 788 (EAT).

[125] *Wilson v St Helen's Borough Council* [1995] ICR 711 (EAT).

[126] *Adams v Cape Industries Plc* [1990] Ch 433 (CA).

[127] *British Nursing Co-Operations Ltd v Peterson* (unreported, 16 January 2004) (EAT).

[128] *British Nursing v Peterson* (n 127) [33].

instance tribunal had erred in law. The idea that a change in factual control over the enterprise could be sufficient was rejected in explicit terms:

[B] acquired the means to influence and control [G]'s policies and decisions as to the employment and retention of staff. [G] had, by reason of the share purchase, become a part of the [B] stable. However, of course, the fact that by reason of the share transfer [B] had become the owner of the shares in [G] and had thus acquired the ability to decide, in effect, whether [G] carried on in business did not have the effect that [G]'s undertaking was transferred to [B] and, if it did, how it would carry on its business . . . None of that control indicates that [G]'s business or part of it (as opposed to the ability to control that business) had been transferred to [B].[129]

The basis of the share transfer exception, therefore, is the argument that a change of shareholder does not change the employer's identity. This idea, however, conflates a change of identity with a change of legal personality, as the juxtaposition of two examples from the Private Equity context shows. A change in the employer's identity is frequently what PE management companies hope to achieve in a buyout transaction. Where the target company is part of a larger corporate group, and is acquired via a share sale from the target parent to the domestic acquisition special purpose vehicle (ASPV), TUPE will not apply.

Another common way for Private Equity funds to source new deals is to work with the management of a particular department within a large company, such as R&D or particular services,[130] towards a spin-off into a new company. Contrary to the share sales discussed above, TUPE does apply in such situations. The sale of a part of an undertaking falls within the definition of an economic entity as 'an organised grouping of resources which has the objective of pursuing an economic activity, whether or not that activity is central or ancillary'.[131] The CJEU held in *Botzen* that 'the decisive criterion regarding the transfer of employees' rights and obligations [was] whether or not a transfer takes place of the department to which [the employees] were assigned and which formed the organizational framework within which their employment relationship took effect'.[132] Put differently, while the group of individuals transferring is reasonably limited, there is no doubt that TUPE will apply to the core group of the departmental employees.

This 'arbitrary impact of the Directive'[133] and the resulting incongruence between regulatory aims and the effects of the relevant provisions is by no means confined a Private Equity subset of cases: in *Brookes*,[134] for example, the applicants were in fact subject to two changes in the structure of their employing entity. The first was a transfer of the care homes from the Council to BCS Ltd. While the factual identity of the employer remained unaffected, BCS Ltd was a

---

[129] *British Nursing v Peterson* (n 127) [21].

[130] Interview with former Investee Company CEO (Oxford 23 February 2010).

[131] TUPE 2006 (n 61) reg 3(2).

[132] Case C-186/83 *Arie Botzen and Others v Rotterdamsche Droogdok Maatschappij BV* [1985] ECR 519 [15].

[133] P Davies, 'Transfers—The UK Will Have to Make Up Its Own Mind' (2001) 30 ILJ 231, 234; there criticizing the impact of the CJEU's decision in Case C-172/99 *Oy Liikenne* [2001] ECR I-475.

[134] *Brookes* (n 116).

new legal entity (a company limited by guarantee), and TUPE therefore applied. The subsequent share transfer to CLS Care Services Ltd, an entity harbouring intentions of changing the nature of the employer, on the other hand, was not capable of triggering the employee-protective regime.[135] In the PE context the distinction is even starker, especially where various kinds of transactions are economically identical from the fund's perspective. The split of employer functions between the buyout firm and its portfolio company management is equally applicable, regardless of how a fund acquired a particular investment. The structure of the investment (P2P or a spin-off transaction), on the other hand, will expose the fund to very different levels of potential employment law liability.

From the employees' perspective, the joint exercise of employment functions which comes into existence following a Private Equity investment is therefore a prime example of the situation envisaged by Elias and Bowers where workers 'may be significantly affected by a change in the control of the company in which they work'. The incongruence in identifying the relevant employer, however, 'has the effect that employees have no right to be informed or consulted about most takeovers even though the nature of the new controllers may be of great importance to their working lives'.[136]

Despite these problems, as long as the concept of the employer is characterized by the strong influence of the elements constituting the unitary strand, effective change is unlikely: separate legal personality is at the heart of anthropomorphic perceptions of the company. As noted by the UK government's consultation paper on TUPE in 2001, 'the scope of the legislation is the most extensively debated and litigated aspect of the current regulations'.[137] Indeed, public stances on the share exclusion continue to be divided across the spectrum: a House of Lords Select Committee in 1995, for example, found in favour of extending TUPE's scope to cover share transfers; a 2001 DTI consultation paper, on the other hand, suggested that the government's opposition to an extension remained unchanged.[138] The most recent discussion of the issue at the European level is found in the Commission's impact report pursuant to Article 10 of the ARD. After a survey of Member States and consultation with relevant interest groups, it clearly affirmed the status quo, suggesting that:

[t]he transfer of ownership of the majority of the shares in an undertaking or a change in the majority of shareholders does not constitute a transfer because the legal personality of the employer is unchanged. The Commission considers that a revision of the Directive,

---

[135] *Brookes* (n 116) 1201.

[136] P Elias and J Bowers, *Intelligence Report. Transfer of Undertakings: The Legal Pitfalls* (6th edn FT Law & Tax 1997) 33 [2.4.1].

[137] Employment Relations Directorate, 'Transfer of Undertakings (Protection of Employment) Regulations 1981: Government Proposals for Reform. Detailed Background Paper' (DTI 2001) [5].

[138] House of Lords Select Committee on the European Communities, Fifth Report, Session 1995–96: *Transfer of Undertakings: Acquired Rights* (HL Paper (1995–96) No 38, 11 July 1995); Employment Relations Directorate (n 137). For full discussion of these sources, see J McMullen, 'An Analysis of the Transfer of Undertakings (Protection of Employment) Regulations 2006' (2006) 35 ILJ 113, 119.

extending the definition of 'transfer' to include a change of control, as proposed by the European Confederation of Trade Unions . . . is not justified at this stage. Although a change of control can lead to changes in the undertaking, the employees' legal position vis-à-vis the employer is unchanged.[139]

Significant change to the regulatory provisions on a domestic level is equally unlikely. In early 2008, John Heppell MP introduced a Private Equity (Transfer of Undertakings and Protection of Employment) Bill.[140] Having noted the potential impact of PE takeovers on employees and the fact that transactions structured as share sales would fall outside the scope of the existing TUPE provisions, the Bill sought to extend the TUPE regime to the acquisition, transfer or disposal of substantial shareholdings by PE funds. The latter terms were not explicitly defined in the Bill, with 'Private Equity Company' to be accorded such meaning as prescribed by the Secretary of State in a statutory instrument,[141] and 'Substantial Shareholding' linked to the definition of controlling undertakings in regulation 3 of the Transnational Information and Consultation of Employees Regulations 1999.[142]

The Bill then targeted the incongruence just set out: by widening the relevant definition of the employer, PE-controlled transactions are brought within the scope of TUPE, and employees and their representatives are accorded most information, consultation, and protection rights directly against the controlling Private Equity shareholder in addition to the employing enterprise. Some natural limitations apply, for example as there is no need to transfer or novate contracts of service in the case of a share sale.[143] The rights accorded to employees go further than the scope of TUPE, a fact apparently not intended by the Bill's sponsor, who indeed offered to withdraw these at the (hypothetical) committee stage when challenged in the House of Commons.[144] Examples include additional information and consultation rights, including employee representatives' entitlement to commission external expert studies and a *quasi*-works council setup for the first five years after the transaction,[145] the requirement to seek employee agreement before the transaction can take place, and an additional remedy in the form of injunctive relief in the High Court.[146]

The Bill's initiative was welcomed by the Trade Union movement; indeed it closely mirrored the substantive suggestions set out by Jack Dromey, the (then) Deputy General Secretary of the Transport and General Workers Union in a *Financial Times* article calling for increased regulation of Private Equity

---

[139] Commission Report (n 46) [2.2.1].

[140] Private Equity (Transfer of Undertakings and Protection of Employment) Bill, Bill 28/07–08: 'A Bill to extend the application of the Transfer of Undertakings (Protection of Employment) Regulations 2006 to the acquisition and disposal of substantial shareholdings by private equity companies; and for connected purposes' ('The PE Bill').

[141] The PE Bill (n 140) cl 1(4).   [142] SI 1999/3323.

[143] V Keter, 'Private Equity (Transfer of Undertakings and Protection of Employment) Bill 2007–08: Research Paper 08/23' (House of Commons Library 2008) 9.

[144] HC Deb 7 March 2008, col 2031.

[145] The PE Bill (n 140) cl 4(5) and 4(3), respectively.   [146] The PE Bill (n 140) cl 5(2).

'employers' the previous year.[147] The BVCA, a Private Equity industry body, unsurprisingly came out strongly against the proposed measure, suggesting that no substantive changes, including as regards employee protections, were brought about by share sales: '[i]n relation to any concerns regarding potential job losses there is existing employment legislation [to protect employees—TUPE] . . . There is no basis in logic or law for such an extension. It is unnecessary and would be grossly unfair'.[148] This stance was supported by leading PE practitioners, notwith-standing their contradictory (and probably more truthful) advice that the enact-ment of the draft Bill 'would have made the restructuring and renegotiation of employment terms on or post completion much more difficult'.[149]

This strong opposition, in combination with its sponsor's own admission that there were significant 'technical difficulties in the Bill'[150] and a lack of support from the government, meant that the Bill failed to reach its committee stage on 7 March 2008.[151] Until its promised return in a refined version,[152] the identified 'anomaly' in the law therefore remains.[153]

Section 2 has thus identified some of the implications of the conflict inherent in the received concept of the employer in the context of multiple entities' joint exer-cise of employer functions, be they shared or parcelled out. The multi-functional aspect of the current conceptualization would easily permit the identification of relevant entities, but different elements in the unitary strand limit the enquiry to a single entity. The distinct legal personality of group entities was seen as a par-ticular obstacle: obligations are placed on a limited subset, which may frequently contain only one of the relevant decision-making entities, or even an inappropri-ate one that was merely executing decisions taken elsewhere. The unitary strand furthermore drives a strong perception that the corporate entity employer must under all circumstances be completely distinct from its shareholders, despite the illogic consequences to which this can lead, for example in determining whether a change of employer has taken place in a corporate restructuring.

Conclusion

Having set out a broad range of practical examples, discussion thus returns to the second goal of Part II: to collect first guidelines for the reconceptualization of the employer to follow in the final part. Three such lessons can be identified at this stage.

---

[147] J Dromey, 'Protect Workers from Private Equiteers' (*Financial Times* 3 July 2007).
[148] BVCA, 'TUPE Briefing Note' (London 2008).
[149] C Wynn-Evans, 'TUPE or not TUPE?' (2008) 94 Dechert Comment: Private Equity Europe 8.
[150] HC Deb 7 March 2008, col 2031.
[151] HC Deb 7 March 2008, col 2092 (Motion and bill, by leave, withdrawn).
[152] L Peacock, 'MP vows to carry on fighting for TUPE private equity deals' (*Personnel Today* 10 March 2008).
[153] HC Deb 7 March 2008, col 2029.

First, the extent to which the concept of the employer is shaped by an unconscious assumption of *excessive homogeneity*. Second, that in resolving the tension between the *formalist or unitary* and the *functional strands*, the latter may be the more promising avenue to pursue: a strict attachment to contractual formalism can quickly lead to the breakdown of coverage, leaving the concept of the employer vulnerable to changing socio-economic circumstances. A cautious functional approach, on the other hand, is less susceptible to such developments, as first judicial pronouncements in that direction show. The third lesson, finally, is that if the legal framework within which a particular problem is set up is itself problematic it can only be addressed by a *careful departure that remains within existing frameworks*. The TUPE (PE) Bill discussed earlier is an example of how on-the-spot solutions frequently fail for that very reason; a similar point applies in the context of purposive judicial intervention, which is not immune from this problem, either, as an analysis of the CJEU's decisions in *Rockfon* and subsequent cases shows.[154]

Avoiding Excessive Homogeneity

There are two clear illustrations of the first observation, viz that the concept of the employer is currently shaped by an unconscious assumption of a high degree of homogeneity. As Section 1 has demonstrated, once a work arrangement such as triangular agency work falls outside the narrow unitary paradigm, individuals will be left without recourse to the majority of employment protective norms. Furthermore, it is not accurate to assume that regulatory coverage will be complete even in situations where there is a contract of service in any particular employment relationship. The examples given in Section 2 are stark reminders of how substantive compliance can quickly be defeated where the exercise of employer functions is shared between multiple entities. A second, related, insight derives from a specific aspect of regulatory technique: as the analysis of the ARD and TUPE provisions has shown, it is crucially important to address fundamental distinctions within the field to be regulated instead of assuming an artificial homogeneity throughout the group. In the present context this could be achieved, for example, by focusing on the different economic incentives of distinct groups of shareholders: at its most basic, the difference between individual dispersed and disinterested shareholders, and sophisticated block owners with a direct interest in the management of their portfolio company.

The current approach sees shareholders as a homogenous group at the former end of the spectrum. As a result, the shareholder exception conflates 'change in shareholder' with 'no change in the employer's identity'. It is true to say that the first step in this reasoning, that a change in shareholder does not affect the company's legal personality, is correct. However, not every change of a company's identity requires a change of legal personality. The reasoning therefore only works in a particular subset, dispersed shareholders, where the underlying premise of

---

[154] *Rockfon* (n 96).

the shareholder exception is true: legal personality and the realities of control (and hence the identity of the employing entity) remain unchanged when shares are bought or sold on a public exchange. In the case of block or majority share ownership, on the other hand, there is no such link: with the shareholder change comes a change in control, and thus in identity—indeed that will frequently be the purpose of acquiring a controlling block in the first place.[155]

To put the same point differently, it is accurate to say that a sale of shares does not affect the legal personality of the company, but merely its beneficial ownership.[156] It is then fallacious, however, to jump from this to the assertion that '[s]hare transfers do not change the identity of the employer' under any circumstance,[157] as even the (then) Minister for Employment Relations, Pat McFadden, suggested in setting out the government response to the Private Equity (TUPE) Bill.[158] When a principle that is correct for a particular sub-group is artificially stretched to encompass a larger, heterogeneous group, the door is opened for it to produce paradoxical results in situations that do not fit with the assumptions of the original paradigm. In the context of different groups of shareholders, other areas of the law have long realized this principle and given effect to it: company law, for example, treats block or majority shareholders differently in a number of instances, from acquisition reporting requirements to additional duties towards other (minority) shareholders.[159]

Towards a Functional Approach

The second lesson that emerges from the material surveyed is that in resolving the tension between the unitary and the multi-functional strands, the former may have to give way more than the latter. The utility of the current unitary approach has come under particular scrutiny, as the consequences of a strict attachment to its inherent formalism can quickly lead to the breakdown of employment law coverage, as demonstrated in the context of agency work. A functional approach to the concept of the employer, on the other hand, would avoid precisely those pitfalls which currently exclude triangular work arrangements from the scope of employment law: more than one entity could be recognized as exercising relevant employer functions.

In corporate groups, on the other hand, the present state of the law may from a formalist perspective appear to be entirely satisfactory: corporate groups should be able to partition their assets and liabilities as they see fit; any downsides, such as potential regulatory costs arising from such actions, will be priced into the value of the firm.[160] Employees will always be able to claim a monetary award if their

---

[155] Equity markets price this distinction into block acquisitions as the control premium.
[156] Keter, 'Private Equity Bill' (n 143) 13.
[157] Keter, 'Private Equity Bill' (n 143) 14.   [158] HC Deb 7 March 2008, col 2088.
[159] P Davies and S Worthington, *Gower and Davies' Principles of Modern Company Law* (9th edn Sweet & Maxwell 2012) ch 19.
[160] H Hansmann and R Kraakman, 'The Essential Role of Organizational Law' (2000) 110 Yale Law Journal 387.

representatives can prove that key decisions had been made by the PE management company and that portfolio company management simply went through the motions of consultation once it had been instructed to effect the layoffs: the superior entity's anterior decision cannot be invoked as a defence. The punitive element of the damages awarded, finally, ensures that firms will not engage in such behaviour on a repeated basis.

This approach—reflected to a large extent, for example, in the United Kingdom's reductive interpretation of what employee consultation is about—is unsatisfactory on a number of levels. Both the economic goals of majority shareholders and the personal interests of individual workers would be better fulfilled by a *functional* approach, ie one that looks at consultation as the underlying goal, independent of formal technicality. On this view, the *ex post facto* imposition of punitive awards for failure to consult with employee representatives about the avoidance or reduction of redundancies is the least desirable outcome: for the majority shareholder, because value is lost not only by the absence of employee voice, but additionally the regulatory fines;[161] for the employee, because it will be very difficult, if not impossible, to weigh up the value of his or her employment in simple monetary terms. A functional approach to this problem would be designed to achieve compliance with the consultation provisions by adjusting the *locus* of the consultative obligation in line with the relevant decision-making power, thus engaging both positive and negative aspects of employee protection.

There is therefore a clear need for a cautious functional approach in moving beyond restrictive concepts of the employer. At the European Union level, the CJEU's decision in *Albron* achieved precisely this result: what mattered there was being responsible for the economic activity.[162] This approach, independent of group companies' formal arrangements, allowed the Court to sidestep the potential *lacuna* in worker protection that could arise from a strictly technical or formalistic interpretation. A focus on 'the substance and not the form of the transaction'[163] is similarly possible at the domestic level, as a recent decision in the present context demonstrates.

In *Millam v Print Factory*,[164] the Court of Appeal had to decide by way of a preliminary question whether the claimant's employment had transferred from F, his original employer, to M, when the former's parent entity had sold its shares in F to M.[165] Buxton LJ set out the basic rules in such situations, viz that a share transfer does not normally involve a transfer of the underlying business that could trigger TUPE,[166] and that even in group or parent–subsidiary relations there was

---

[161] For recent research on which see J Armour, C Mayer, and A Polo, 'Regulatory Sanctions and Reputational Damage in Financial Markets' CELF conference paper, Oxford 13 April 2011.

[162] *Albron* (n 95) [31].

[163] Elias and Bowers *Intelligence Report* (n 136) 43; citing Case C-24/85 *Spijkers v Gebroeders Benedik Abbatori CV* [1986] ECR I-2479.

[164] *Millam* (n 123). For an early note, see Anon, 'TUPE: When is a Share Sale Not a Share Sale?' (Linklaters 2007).

[165] In which case its successor entity, the defendant, could potentially be liable.

[166] *Brookes* (n 116).

no assumption of control being exercised over a company's business by its share-holder.[167] However, his Lordship went on to note that these were 'merely reminders that the question is whether as a matter of fact the business . . . has been transferred'.[168] On the facts, the tribunal at first instance had found that there had been a transfer despite the share sale, as:

[t]he buyer of the shares did far more than a simple shareholder would have done following a simple sale, or in our experience, a parent company of a subsidiary would have done in similar circumstances. In particular, [M]'s handling of a significant element of the management of [F] set its actions apart from those of a mere shareholder. It made key decisions . . .[169]

The Employment Appeals Tribunal subsequently overturned this decision, on the basis that the ET had effectively pierced F's corporate veil. The high 'sham' requirement for this to be possible had not been met, as the two companies continued to have separate boards, accounts, and VAT registration.[170] On the analysis of Moses LJ, however, this was not to be understood as a case of piercing the veil: M was not to be liable for F's activities as a shareholder per se. Instead, the ET's finding was to be correctly understood as the shareholder, due to its close control and involvement in F, actually having carried out various business activities *through* F. In the course of his judgment, Buxton LJ also noted the key advantage of a successful functional approach: 'The legal structure is of course important, but it cannot be conclusive in deciding the issue of whether, within that legal structure, control of the business has been transferred as a matter of fact.'[171]

Developing Existing Frameworks

The final lesson to be taken away from the present chapter is the realization that framework problems such as the current tension underpinning the concept of the employer cannot easily be solved by on-the-spot interventions. Neither purposive judicial interpretation nor individual legislative interventions in response to a particular facet of the problem will provide effective solutions. As the frame is bent to fit into one corner, it snaps apart at another: the ad-hoc fix has actually caused further problems. The UK's implementation of the Agency Work Directive[172] is a clear illustration on point: its protective effect is easily avoided by structuring individual assignments to fall below the 12-week threshold,[173] whilst the measure completely fails to address the real underlying problem of employment status, as discussed in Section 1. A second legislative context in which this can be seen is

---

[167] Case C-234/98 *GC Allen v Amalgamated Construction Co Ltd* [1999] ECR I-8643.
[168] *Millam* (n 123) [3].   [169] *Millam* (n 123) [4], quoting the ET's decision at [5.9].
[170] *Millam* (n 123) [20]–[24].   [171] *Millam* (n 123) [9].
[172] Directive (EC) 104/2008 of the European Parliament and of the Council of 19 November 2008 on temporary agency work [2008] OJ L 327/9.
[173] Agency Workers Regulations 2010, SI 2010/93, reg 5. See Chapter 2.1A for further discussion.

the failure of the Private Equity (TUPE) Bill.[174] To build on the frame metaphor, whilst a new part to be inserted into an existing frame might in itself be different from the element it is to replace, it must nonetheless fit into the pre-existing structure in order to achieve its purpose. Seen through this angle, the Bill's key problems quickly emerge: it foundered on its (initial) departure from the existing information and consultation regime, as well as on its attempt to regulate but one particular phenomenon, without taking account of the larger context—as its sponsor admitted before the House of Commons.[175] First, whilst attempting to introduce considerable change by expanding the overall application of TUPE, core concepts are reaffirmed in their narrow-most conception: '[r]eferences to employees of the transferor or transferee are to be read as references to employees of the employer'.[176] The emphasis on such orthodoxy should not be underestimated: the CJEU's decision in *Albron*, for example, would have been impossible under this provision, as the claimant employee there did not stand in any direct contractual relationship of employment with the transferor.

The failure to engage with large parts of the underlying problem is visible, second, from a failed attempt to define key terms. As the research report accompanying the Bill notes, '[i]n non-legal language the term "private equity" covers a very wide range of businesses. It may be difficult to define with legal certainty which companies should be caught by the Bill's provisions'.[177] This is the case because the Private Equity business model allows the exploitation of an arbitrage opportunity that exists between different forms of economic organization.[178] Any attempt at reform that does not engage directly with this question[179] will soon run into the third problematic issue: a host of unintended consequences that arise as a result of the conceptual distortion. As Christopher Chope MP noted during the second reading of the Bill, its proposed definition could mean that 'a private equity organisation would be any organisation that is incorporated, other than a public listed company'.[180] Another unintended consequence, discussed at length, related to the possibility of injunctive relief creating considerable delays in the takeover process, which could increase uncertainty for workers, for example in the case of an enterprise nearing bankruptcy.[181]

Purposive judicial interpretation in a limited area is just as vulnerable to framework problems, as can again be illustrated in both contexts scrutinized. Early

---

[174]   The political background to the Bill, which has already been alluded to above, may of course be invoked as part of the answer to the charges which follow, but is not immediately relevant for the present doctrinal-analytical purpose.

[175]   HC Deb 7 March 2008, col 2032 (John Heppell MP). The Bill furthermore included significantly increased consultation and consultation duties,

[176]   The PE Bill (n 140) cl 4(2).   [177]   Keter, 'Private Equity Bill' (n 143) 7.

[178]   The basic idea is that the gains resulting from the elimination of one agency problem (shareholders-management) are higher than the resulting cost in other agency relationships, because only one of the affected stakeholders (creditors) can impose their cost on the controlling shareholder. The resulting price differential represents a potential arbitrage opportunity to PE investors.

[179]   For example, by leaving the relevant definitions to the Secretary of State: Bill, cl 1(4).

[180]   HC Deb 7 March 2008, col 2053.

[181]   HC Deb 7 March 2008, col 2064 ff (Jonathan Djanogly MP).

attempts at developing the implied contract as a solution to agency workers' plight, for example, were soon faced with provisions from the general law of contract, and thus left unable to grapple with multi-contractual arrangements such as those found in *Alstom*.[182] As Hugh Collins so memorably put it:

In trying with the best of motives to rescue temporary agency workers from their plight of being excluded from employment law almost entirely, the courts have resorted to fictions such as the implied contract of employment, and subsequently received their just reward: incoherence in the law followed by ignominious retreat to orthodoxy.[183]

A second illustration can be drawn from the context of Directive 59/1998. One of its trigger requirements is a minimum number of employees affected by the planned mass redundancy. There are two alternative formulations of this threshold, either as a percentage or as an absolute number; it is up to each Member State to choose which option to implement.[184]

In *Rockfon*,[185] the CJEU had to address the definition of 'establishment' on the facts of a case arising from dismissals within the Rockwell Group, the employers of more than 300 workers in several sub-units that shared a single personnel department. Given the Danish transposition option and the size of the enterprise, the claimants had to show that a certain percentage within the establishment had been affected in order to claim under the collective redundancy provisions. It was undisputed that if Rockfon, one of the three units, were found to be an establishment, the relevant member state provisions would apply. The Danish Labour Council defined establishment as the Rockwell Group as a whole, and held that no obligations had therefore been triggered.

The Court of Justice set out by affirming that the Directive was not aimed at restricting the freedom of undertakings to organize their activities, nor intended to lay down rules relating to the internal organization of undertakings or the management of their personnel.[186] Based on the AG's opinion, it went on to suggest that as the wording of different language versions was unclear, regard had to be had to the 'purpose and general scheme of the rules'—in this particular instance, the 'greater protection of workers in the event of collective redundancies'.[187] An interpretation that would allow companies to make the Directive's application more difficult would allow companies 'to escape the obligation to follow certain procedures for the protection of workers and large groups of workers could [thus] be denied the right to be informed and consulted'.[188] It was therefore not surprising that the Court defined the meaning of the term 'establishment' as narrowly as possible. On the facts of the case, this purposive interpretation produced a worker-productive result. Given its position in the larger statutory framework, however, problems soon emerged. As opposed to Denmark, the United Kingdom had chosen the trigger requirement in Article 1(a)(ii) of Directive 59/1998: the

---

[182] *Alstom* (n 4).
[183] H Collins, 'Book Review: D McCann *Regulating Flexible Work* (Oxford, OUP 2008)' (2009) 72 MLR 141, 143.
[184] Collective Redundancies Directive (n 51) art 1.   [185] *Rockfon* (n 96).
[186] *Rockfon* (n 96) [21].   [187] *Rockfon* (n 96) [28]–[29].   [188] *Rockfon* (n 96) [30].

dismissal of at least 20 workers over a period of 90 days, whatever the normal size of the establishment. In this context, the *Rockfon* jurisprudence (as confirmed in subsequent cases[189]) was to have the very opposite effect: the narrower the definition of enterprise, the easier for an employer to compartmentalize its workforce to avoid triggering the provisions of section 188.

In *MSF v Refuge Assurance*,[190] two companies consolidated their headquarter and field staff following a merger. The employment tribunal found that the meaning of term 'establishment' covered the entire field staff at each company, thus triggering a duty to consult. On the employer's cross-appeal, the EAT (having questioned the validity of the transposition) cited the CJEU's decision in *Rockfon* that an 'establishment' did not necessarily need to have separate management which could independently effect the collective redundancies.[191] Despite the ET's warning that if each branch were held to be an establishment productive industrial relations would be rendered fictional as the employers could avoid consultation by not identifying specific branches in time, the EAT considered itself bound by the CJEU's case law, and allowed the employer's appeal.

The final lesson to be drawn from the present chapter, therefore, is that even openly purposive interpretation by the courts will not necessarily be enough to address the problems that can arise once the exercise of employer functions is shared by several entities: the framework itself must be able to take account of complex scenarios beyond a narrow paradigm. Before the insights thus gathered can be applied to a reconceptualization of the employer, however, a further step is required: the exploration of the concept from a comparative perspective. It is to that task that the next chapter now turns.

---

[189] See also Case C-270/05 *Athinaiki Chartopoiia AE v Panagiotidis* [2007] ECR I-1499.
[190] *MSF* (n 94).   [191] *MSF* (n 94) [52]–[53].

4

Complex Employment Structures in Germany

A Comparative Perspective

Introduction

The second part of Chapter 3 explored the practical implications of the tension inherent in the concept of the employer in the context of collective redundancies and the transfer of undertakings. This analysis served a dual purpose: to give examples of potential problems, and to start gathering guidelines for the eventual task in the final part of this work: the development and evaluation of an updated concept of the employer, able to take into account the economic realities of complex employment relationships. The present goals are similar: the concept of the employer in German law will be explored to determine how key rules and institutions have developed to take account of the challenges posed by complex *Konzern* (corporate group) structures. Seen from an employment law perspective, the *Konzern* turns one of the discipline's most vexing questions—that as to the nature of the employee—on its head, asking instead: who is the employer? The existence of multiple entities on the employing side leads to a search for the 'lost employer, . . . *le patron introuvable*'.[1]

The basic structure of this chapter loosely mirrors that of the previous one, despite its setting in a different context: after an introductory discussion of comparative methodology, the concept of the employer in German law is set out, followed by a discussion of the *Konzern* concept as the context of multiple *loci* of corporate control. Analysis then focuses on the modification of general employment law standards in the *Konzern*. The results of this comparative study will demonstrate that some of the deeper problems underpinning modern economic phenomena, such as their potential to frustrate the full application of employee rights, are not limited to the United Kingdom and provide further insight and background material for the work's ultimate task.

---

[1] C Windbichler, *Arbeitsrecht im Konzern* (Beck 1989) 25, quoting G Lyon-Caen, 'Arbeitsrecht und Unternehmenskonzentration' (1984) 36 RdA 285, 298. The following sections draw on this *Habilitation* work (especially with regard to their general framework and analysis of the individual employment relationship). The author gratefully acknowledges Professor Windbichler's support in his comparative endeavour, as well as subsequent discussions with Leopold Bauer and Professor Horst Call.

Before embarking on that task, however, an apparent omission remains to be explained: whereas discussion in previous chapters was concerned with both triangular agency work and Private Equity-driven corporate group structures as illustrations of multilateral employment contexts, the present chapter focuses on the German regulation of employment structures within the *Konzern*. This shift in emphasis is due to the fact that the main academic and judicial debates about the identification of the employer have taken place in that area. Since the legalization of agency work in 1972, and subsequent liberalization in the *Arbeitnehmerüberlassungsgesetz 2003* ('AÜG 2003'),[2] the multilateral problems associated with such arrangements have found a comparatively straightforward solution in statutory regulation: a contract of employment is deemed to exist between the agency and the worker, and the client end-user's control rights are heavily circumscribed.[3] This separate statutory regulation means that the treatment of triangular agency work situations is of little comparative relevance for present purposes.

Section 1: The Concept of the Employer in German Law

A. A Methodology of Comparative Law

Zweigert and Kötz have suggested that comparative scholarship may to a large extent always remain an area where 'only sound judgment, common sense, or even intuition can be of any help'.[4] Even if one were to agree with this assessment, however, both choice of subject *and* method must be conscious ones,[5] as questions of structure and methodology are closely linked and of heightened importance in the comparative context.

As regards general methodology, debate has raged about the ongoing validity and utility of a *functional* method of comparative law. This covers a range of techniques and outcomes with varying degrees of normative force;[6] an unsurprising discussion given the wide variety of approaches that underpin the functional method.[7] Whilst it may therefore be characterized as a *chimera* of sorts,[8] there are several core aspects on which most functionalists agree, and which will therefore

---

[2] M Lembke, 'Neue Rechte von Leiharbeitnehmern gegenüber Entleihern' (2011) 28 NZA 319, 320: amendments in line with Directive (EC) 104/2008 of the European Parliament and of the Council of 19 November 2008 on temporary agency work OJ L327/9 will not lead to a substantive redesign.

[3] J Kirchner, P Kremp, and M Magotsch (eds), *Key Aspects of German Employment and Labour Law* (Springer Verlag 2010) 47–9.

[4] K Zweigert and H Kötz, *Introduction to Comparative Law* (Tony Weir tr, 3rd edn Clarendon Press 1998) 33; recalling the earlier warning that 'sciences which have to busy themselves with their own methodology are sick sciences': G Radbruch, *Einführung in die Rechtswissenschaft* (12th edn Köhler 1969) 253.

[5] O Kahn-Freund, 'Comparative Law as an Academic Subject' (1966) 82 LQR 40, 41.

[6] M Freedland and N Kountouris, *The Legal Construction of Personal Work Relations* (OUP 2011) 49.

[7] R Michaels, 'The Functional Method of Comparative Law' in M Reiman and R Zimmermann (eds), *The Oxford Handbook of Comparative Law* (OUP 2007) 340, 345ff, 360.

[8] Michaels, 'The Functional Method of Comparative Law' (n 7) 340.

inform the present effort:[9] first, the comparative focus is not only on individual rules of a particular system, but also their aggregate effects. It follows, second, that law cannot be seen in a vacuum, isolated from society. Third, function itself serves as the *tertium comparationis*: institutions, both legal and non-legal, even doctrinally different ones, are comparable if they are functionally equivalent. Functionality, finally, may also serve as an evaluative criterion in and of itself, subject to objections to be discussed, below.

The field of comparative labour law more specifically covers a range of genres,[10] from mostly descriptive 'academic tourism'[11] and purely theoretical treatises to efforts predictive of future social or economic problems and purposive comparative work. A combination of the latter two may 'cause the reader to think and see outside his or her accustomed frame of reference; to learn that there are other ways for the law to deal with an economic or social question, ways that may actually be more protective of values the reader's system professes, that are more effective, that have lower transaction costs or fewer negative externalities';[12] it is in this area that the present chapter is situated.

The necessity and value of comparative labour law has been recognized in leading generalist works for a considerable period,[13] and despite some warnings against comparative efforts in at least one leading German textbook,[14] it is evidently clear today that 'labour law in Europe is no longer local'.[15] Historically, the majority of comparative research was found in the collective domain.[16] More recently, and not least as a result of the rapid growth of EU employment law[17] and its deep interaction with the legal systems of the Member States,[18] there has been a resurgence in comparative analyses of the individual employment relationship in different European legal systems, both in books[19] and leading journals.[20]

---

[9] Michaels, 'The Functional Method of Comparative Law' (n 7) 342 for a full overview.

[10] M Finkin, 'Comparative Labour Law' in M Reiman and R Zimmermann (eds), *The Oxford Handbook of Comparative Law* (OUP 2007) Taxonomy 1129 ff.

[11] Finkin, 'Comparative Labour Law' (n 10) noting that the term had originally been coined by Clyde Summers.

[12] Finkin, 'Comparative Labour Law' (n 10).

[13] H Gutteridge, *Comparative Law: An Introduction to the Comparative Method of Legal Study & Research* (CUP 1946) 31.

[14] Finkin, 'Comparative Labour Law' (n 10) 1149.

[15] Finkin, 'Comparative Labour Law' (n 10) 1150. This trend is clearly evidenced by the wide-spread treatment of comparative topics in domestic and European labour law journals. See eg J Prassl, 'Die Suche nach dem Arbeitgeber im Englischen Recht' (2013) Europäische Zeitschrift für Arbeitsrecht 472; J Prassl, 'L'emploi multilatéral en droit anglais: à la recherche du patron perdu' (2014) Revue de Droit du Travail 236.

[16] P de Cruz, *Comparative Law in a Changing World* (3rd edn Routledge-Cavendish 2007) Ch 13. For a notable early exception, see B Waas, *Konzernarbeitsrecht in Großbritannien* (Nomos 1993).

[17] B Bercusson, *European Labour Law* (2nd edn CUP 2009) 99ff.

[18] M Freedland and J Prassl (eds), *EU Law in the Member States: Viking, Laval and Beyond* (Hart 2014); E Kohlbacher, *Streikrecht und Europarecht* (Linde 2014) 253ff.

[19] Freedland and Kountouris, *The Legal Construction of Personal Work Relations* (n 6); N Countouris, *The Changing Law of the Employment Relationship: Comparative Analyses in the European Context* (Ashgate 2007).

[20] See eg L Mitlacher and J Burgess, 'Temporary Agency Work in Germany and Australia: Contrasting Regulatory Regimes and Policy Challenges' (2007) 23 International Journal of Comparative Labour Law and Industrial Relations 401.

The range of methodological issues to be confronted in a comparative enquiry is tightly linked to its purpose; in the present context, primarily to gather thoughts from German law to inform and evaluate the proposals to be set out in Part III. This recourse to comparative law as an '*école de vérité*', to extend and enrich the domestic 'supply of solutions'[21] is not without its own controversies, particularly as regards the normative force of its outcomes. While '[c]omparative legal enquiries are frequently made as part of an effort to improve a legal rule or institution which has been suspected or recognized as a source of problems',[22] it has also been suggested that within a functional framework, 'recognizing different solutions abroad does not show us deficiencies at home. Functionalist comparison can open our eyes to alternative solutions, but it cannot tell us whether those solutions are better or not'.[23] This stance conflates two distinct points—the reliance on comparative law as a source of fresh ideas from a common fund, which is a long way removed from its 'hard' use in explicit value judgments.[24] The subsequent focus on comparative law as a tool to improve one's own (understanding of) domestic law[25] thus brings with it few of the traditional legitimacy problems.[26] Indeed, it has been suggested that in the specific context of labour law, comparative ventures can 'significantly enrich the reformers' imagination of what could be done'.[27]

Having thus situated the chapter in the broad field of comparative law, its specific methodology falls to be developed—keeping in mind the object decided upon at the outset.[28] The approach will be a multi-axial one, building on Schmidt,[29] whose suggested axes include both functional as well as doctrinal aspects; thus covering both specific outcomes, and the rules and debates behind them. The *microcomparisons*, or 'focus on specific legal . . . problems'[30] will centre on the extent to which employment law coverage is affected by complex corporate structures as the 'factual situations . . . which arise in connection with the topic under comparison'.[31] Given the deep connection of labour law with broader social and political norms, it has been suggested that there would be little space for comparison;[32] Scheiwe on the other hand has demonstrated that this can be counteracted with an expansion

---

[21] Zweigert and Kötz, *Introduction to Comparative Law* (n 4) 15.

[22] G Dannemann, 'Comparative Law: Study of Similarities or Differences?' in M Reiman and R Zimmermann (eds), *The Oxford Handbook of Comparative Law* (OUP 2007) 403.

[23] Michaels, 'The Functional Method of Comparative Law' (n 7) 379.

[24] T Annus, 'Comparative Constitutional Reasoning: The Law And Strategy Of Selecting The Right Arguments' (2004) 14 Duke Journal of Comparative and International Law 301.

[25] Kahn-Freund, 'Comparative Law as an Academic Subject' (n 5) 60.

[26] J Smits, 'Comparative Law and its Influence on National Legal Systems' in M Reiman and R Zimmermann (eds), *The Oxford Handbook of Comparative Law* (OUP 2007) 525, 528.

[27] M Weiss, 'The Future of Comparative Labor Law as an Academic Discipline and as a Practical Tool' (2003–2004) 25 CLLPJ 169, 178.

[28] The test advocated by AE Örücü, 'Methodology of Comparative Law' in J Smits (ed), *Elgar Encyclopedia of Comparative Law* (Edward Elgar 2006) 451.

[29] F Schmidt, 'The Need for a Multi-Axial Method in Comparative Law' in H Bernstein, H Kötz and U Drobnig (eds), *Festschrift für Konrad Zweigert* (Mohr 1981) 534.

[30] Zweigert and Kötz, *Introduction to Comparative Law* (n 4) 5.

[31] Dannemann, 'Comparative Law: Study of Similarities or Differences?' (n 22) 407.

[32] Zweigert and Kötz, *Introduction to Comparative Law* (n 4) 38.

of the functional equivalence term:[33] as every rule or system will always have more than one function, there can be no functional equivalents in every aspect.[34] By focusing on aspects such as a measure's aim (eg allowing the free development ressof company law structures, but then ensuring employee representation within what has economically grown[35]) it will nonetheless be possible to assemble valuable information for subsequent chapters.

Comparative Steps

The fundamental elements of comparison should include considerations as to the objectives, subject matter, and method of comparison *stricto sensu*.[36] Hugh Collins, writing in the context of comparative contract law, develops the following five steps:

1. Identification of some aspect of domestic law which seems confused or lacks a clear rationale.

2. Identification of the social problem which this aspect of domestic law addresses.

3. Examination of the legal doctrines and techniques by which one or more foreign legal systems tackle or avoid the same problem.

4. Evaluation of the foreign solution to decide whether its approach is superior, be it in technique or result.

5. Re-analysis of the domestic legal system in order to reveal the conceptual obstacles to the achievement of more satisfactory results, be it in technique or policy goals.[37]

Several of these steps are outside the scope of the present chapter, or even Part II more broadly: a legal problem (the split of employer functions in complex corporate structures) and its practical implications in domestic law have already been identified. The final step will run through Part III. Steps 3 and 4, the examination (and, to a lesser extent, evaluation) of foreign legal techniques and solutions are thus at the heart of the present chapter. At this stage, they remain to be broken down into two further methodological points—selection, and description.[38]

The one explicit choice that remains to be explained is that as to the comparator legal system. While it has been suggested that in solution-seeking, the closer two

---

[33] K Scheiwe, 'Was ist ein funktionales Äquivalent in der Rechtsvergleichung? Eine Diskussion an Hand von Beispielen aus dem Familien- und Sozialrecht' (2000) 83 Kritische Vierteljahresschrift für Gesetzgebung und Rechtswissenschaft 30, 33.

[34] Scheiwe, 'Was ist ein funktionales Äquivalent in der Rechtsvergleichung?' (n 33) 36–7.

[35] M Kort, 'Der Konzernbegriff i.S. von §5 MitbestG' (2009) 36 NZG 81.

[36] A de Roo and R Jagtenberg, *Settling Labour Disputes in Europe* (Kluwer 1994) 8; drawing on JH Merryman, 'Comparative Law and Scientific Explanation' (1974) Reports to the Academie Internationale du Droit Comparé 121.

[37] H Collins, 'Methods and Aims of Comparative Contract Law' (1989) 11 OJLS 396, 399.

[38] Following Dannemann, 'Comparative Law: Study of Similarities or Differences?' (n 22) 406ff.

legal systems are related the better a source of comparison,[39] the lack of radically different solutions can also be an obstacle, thus requiring a search for 'controlled difference'.[40] Indeed, the choice of comparators is highly topic-sensitive; the more specific the enquiry, the more freedom one is allowed, though a general preference for 'parent' system remains.[41] German law clearly fits this purpose: as a legal system, it has developed the necessary conceptual and technical apparatus across company and employment law to address both complex inter-related corporate ownership and employee involvement within these structures. The comparison of civil and common law is therefore 'the most fruitful field to till'.[42]

With the choice of Germany as the comparator system there comes a linguistic issue: in working with German texts, it will not only be important to watch out for *faux amis*,[43] but also to ensure consistency in the use of foreign terms while maintaining readability. It is hoped that this will be achieved by translating into the text all materials other than relevant key terms, which will be explained (and sometimes abbreviated) at their first occurrence. Turning to the second issue, the appropriateness of the descriptive effort, Dannemann's warning to beware of immediately seeing differences or falling for similarities by slotting material into known (domestic) legal categories will be kept firmly in mind. Whilst description will be focused on the aims and effects of different rules, the broader context cannot be ignored.[44] The functional specificity emphasized earlier does not limit one's understanding of wider issues, but focuses it where necessary.[45] Heeding Eichendorff's warning as recalled to the novice comparativist,[46] account will thus be taken not only of the 'law in the books' but also of general conditions of business, customs, and practices[47] in the ambition of treating as a source of law all those factors moulding or affecting the living law in the chosen system.[48] Such a move beyond the text of generalist Codes is particularly important in employment law. As Zweigert and Kötz note, the 'legal values of bourgeois liberalism' embodied in the *Bürgerliches Gesetzbuch* ('BGB')[49] mean that the vast majority of employee-protective norms have been developed through additional action by courts and the legislature.

[39] Dannemann, 'Comparative Law: Study of Similarities or Differences?' (n 22) 410, building on common law judges' preference for authorities from other common law jurisdictions.

[40] Dannemann, 'Comparative Law: Study of Similarities or Differences?' (n 22) 411.

[41] Zweigert and Kötz, *Introduction to Comparative Law* (n 4) 41–2.

[42] FH Lawson, '*The Field of Comparative Law*' (1949) 61 Juridical Review 16, 35 (as cited by J Cairns, 'Development of Comparative Law in Great Britain' in M Reiman and R Zimmermann (eds), *The Oxford Handbook of Comparative Law* (OUP 2007) 164).

[43] M Ancel, *Utilité et Méthodes du Droit Comparé: Eléments d'Introduction Générale à l'Étude Comparative des Droits* (Ides et Calendes 1971) 92.

[44] Dannemann, 'Comparative Law: Study of Similarities or Differences?' (n 22) 412–13.

[45] B Markesinis and J Fedtke, *Engaging With Foreign Law* (Hart 2009) 320.

[46] Zweigert and Kötz, *Introduction to Comparative Law* (n 4) 36: '*Hüte Dich, sei wach und munter!*' ('Be careful, alert, and cheerful!').

[47] Zweigert and Kötz, *Introduction to Comparative Law* (n 4) 11.

[48] Zweigert and Kötz, *Introduction to Comparative Law* (n 4) 35. See also R Fahlbeck, 'Comparative Law—Quo Vadis?' (2003–2004) 25 CLLPJ 7 for an emphasis on the importance of comparative labour law working with other disciplines.

[49] Zweigert and Kötz, *Introduction to Comparative Law* (n 4).

This broad context, finally, matters not just in what is analysed, but also in how the results are used. Part III will not suggest any direct legal 'transplants' from German employment (or indeed company) law.[50] Even if a particular approach works well in one jurisdiction one cannot assume that a more or less direct translation would fulfil a similar purpose successfully in another.[51] A series of ad hoc transplants could furthermore lead to an unnecessary fragmentation of domestic legal scholarship, and thus a 'bland convergence with the theoretical discourse of other national systems of labo[u]r law such as those of continental European countries'.[52]

The 'borrowing' of legal ideas, however, can also be a dynamic process over an extended period of time, with initial phases involving no more than the identification of appropriate models.[53] It is with this goal of influence, inspiration, and cross-fertilization[54] in mind that relative weight will be accorded to comparative and domestic thought about new 'ways of ensuring that workers are not excluded from employment protections by conceptual or structural rigidities in doctrinal reasoning'.[55]

Subsequent discussion is thus organized as previously indicated: section 2 outlines the basic concept of the employer in German law generally, including elements from both individual and collective domains. Discussion then turns to the *Konzern* as the legal paradigm grouping of multiple *loci* of corporate control, before focusing on examples of situations where employment law norms have been modified to take account of the *Konzern* context.

B. The Concept of the Employer

Despite the narrow focus of the comparative venture as just outlined, it will be important to situate the discussion in its broader legal context. The following paragraphs thus cover key features of German labour law as well as, to the extent that enterprise co-decision and the notion of the *Konzern* are situated there,

---

[50] As has happened in domestic labour law: O Kahn-Freund, 'On Uses and Misuses of Comparative Law' (1974) 37 MLR 120.

[51] Discussed in an analysis of Kahn-Freund's 1973 Chorley lecture at the LSE: M Freedland, 'Otto Kahn-Freund (1900–1979)' in J Beatson and R Zimmermann (eds), *Jurists Uprooted— German Speaking Émigré Lawyers in Twentieth-century Britain* (OUP 2004) 311. The issue is not a new one: Montesquieu, *De L'Esprit des Lois*, vol I, ch 3 'Des lois positives': '*les lois politiques et civiles de chaque nation. . . doivent être tellement propres au peuple pour lequel elles sont faites, que c'est un grand hazard si celles d'une nation peuvent convenir à une autre.*'

[52] M Freedland and P Davies, 'National Styles in Labor Law Scholarship: the United Kingdom' (2001–2002) 23 CLLPJ 765, 787.

[53] J Fedtke, 'Legal Transplants' in J Smits (ed), *Elgar Encyclopedia of Comparative Law* (Edward Elgar 2006) 435. cf the account in B Markesinis, *Comparative Law in the Courtroom and Classroom: The Story of the Last Thirty-Five Years* (Hart 2003), which is closely focused on utility to practitioners.

[54] M Graziadei, 'Comparative Law as the Study of Transplants and Receptions' in M Reiman and R Zimmermann (eds), *The Oxford Handbook of Comparative Law* (OUP 2007) 443.

[55] M Freedland, 'Developing the European Comparative Law of Personal Work Contracts' (2006–2007) 28 CLLPJ 487, 490.

company law, in order to ensure that the subsequent enquiry avoids an improper conflation of legal issues and approaches.[56] In so doing, however, it would be impossible to provide a complete précis of the legal system. Instead, the following gives a brief account of the standard approach to selected examples in order then to permit an exploration of variations in the *Konzern* scenario, viz situations where the second *locus* of control over the employment relationship is a majority shareholder in the employing entity. These limitations are primarily ones of scope; it will nonetheless be important to outline and explain several choices at the outset.

Three topics in particular will be excluded from further consideration: the role of collective bargaining (*Tarifverträge*), senior management, and the extra-territorial application of German law. As regards the first of these, its exclusion might at first appear surprising—after all, collective bargaining is one of the three central categories of employment law statutes.[57] There is however little scope for its involvement in the *Konzern* field: as Boehm and Pawlowski flatly note, 'there is no such thing as a *Konzern-Tarifvertrag*'.[58] Even where there is theoretical room in individual provisions of the *Betriebsverfassungsgesetz* 1972 ('BetrVG 1972') for collective bargaining agreements to determine co-decision structures,[59] its organizational patterns are too far removed from the area of discussion to be of significant relevance.[60]

The role of senior management, second, is excluded because of its anomalous and highly fact-specific treatment across different areas. Some senior managers (the so-called *Leitende Angestellte*) are in fact employees, but do not enjoy the full set of employment rights.[61] Others, notably the CEO (*Geschäftsführer*) of a GmbH are not employees despite being subject to direct control,[62] but nonetheless enjoy a legislative extension of individual employment protective measures, such as minimum dismissal periods.[63]

The impact of German law on corporate group setups crossing international borders, third, will also not be discussed to a significant extent. The general

---

[56] Windbichler, *Arbeitsrecht im Konzern* (n 1) 582.

[57] de Cruz, *Comparative Law in a Changing World* (n 16) 475.

[58] W Boehm and H Pawlowski, 'Konzernweite Beschäftigungsgarantien bei Umstrukturierung—aber was, wenn die "Heuschrecken" kommen?' (2005) 22 NZA 1377, 1380; cf BAG decision of 11.09.1991, (1992) 9 NZA 321 (*Goetheinstitut*), 323 where the BAG held that whilst a German mother entity should try to influence foreign subsidiaries, no direct enforcement was possible.

[59] M Kort, 'Bildung und Stellung des Konzernbetriebsrats bei nationalen und internationalen Unternehmensverbindungen' (2009) 26 NZA 464, 466; discussing §3 *Betriebsverfassungsgesetz* 1972 ('BetrVG 1972').

[60] Windbichler, *Arbeitsrecht im Konzern* (n 1) 582.

[61] Kirchner, Kremp, and Magotsch (eds), *Key Aspects of German Employment and Labour Law* (n 3) 3. They are also excluded (with very few exceptions) from the scope of the BetrVG 1972 (n 59): §5III 1.

[62] The *Gesellschafterversammlung*'s *Weisungen*. This power stems from the *Gesetz betreffend die Gesellschaften mit beschränkter Haftung* (GmbHG 1892) §37 I, rather than the contract of employment.

[63] W Zöllner, K Loritz, and C Hergenröder, *Arbeitsrecht* (Beck 2008) 40: *Bürgerliches Gesetzbuch* ('BGB') §622.

position, in both company and employment law, is one of strict territoriality:[64] co-decision in an international *Konzern*, for example, will only cover employees located in Germany.[65] If the controlling enterprise is overseas, on the other hand, there will be no scope for co-decision mechanisms there;[66] the possibility of a *Konzern*-works council under such circumstances has been the subject of intense academic debate,[67] but was eventually denied by the Federal Labour Court (*Bundesarbeitsgericht*, 'BAG').[68] As the issue also touches on questions of international private law, and was not pursued in the domestic legal enquiry in previous chapters, it will not be investigated further.

Turning from exclusion to selection, finally, there are two areas in which specific norms were chosen to illustrate, *pars pro toto*, underlying points. In the area of individual employment law rights flowing from the contract of employment, this is unfair dismissal protection (in the form of the *Kündigungsschutzgesetz* 1969, 'KSchG 1969'): the *Konzern*-situation may have a direct impact on its provisions, and has been the subject of fairly recent academic and judicial discussions.[69] In the field of enterprise co-decision, the example to be discussed will be the *Mitbestimmungsgesetz* 1976 ('MitbestG 1976'), which is applicable to companies with more than 2,000 employees, covering all industries and including (inter alia) both AGs and GmbHs.

The Employer as Counterparty to the Arbeitsverhältnis

As Mehrhoff suggests, the concept of the employer (*Arbeitgeber*) in German law has historically been constructed around a duty to protect the weaker party to the *Arbeitsverhältnis* (employment relationship), despite many developments in line with social and economic structures of society.[70] There is no explicit definition of the employer; the starting point of any enquiry is the contract of employment (*Arbeitsvertrag*) as the central legal organizing device (*Rechtsfigur*) of employment law,[71] to which the employer is the work-taking counterparty. This is mirrored by

---

[64] BAG decision of 14.02.2007, (2007) 24 NZA 999.

[65] A seat may sometimes be offered to a foreign representative: M Gentz, 'Das Arbeitsrecht im Internationalen Konzern' (2000) 17 NZA 3, 5 (noting the presence of a US trade union representative on the board of DaimlerChrysler).

[66] cf the (limited) anti-avoidance provision in §5III *Mitbestimmungsgesetz* ('MitbestG 1976'), discussed below.

[67] Kort, 'Bildung und Stellung des Konzernbetriebsrats bei nationalen und internationalen Unternehmensverbindungen' (n 59) 467.

[68] BAG decision of 14.02.2007 (n 64). For critical discussion, see H Buchner, 'Konzernbetriebsratsbildung trotz Auslandssitz der Obergesellschaft' in H Konzen et al (eds), *Festschrift für Rolf Birk* (Mohr Siebeck 2008) 11 ff.

[69] BAG decision of 26.9.2002, (2003) 20 NZA 549 (*Rheumaklinik*).

[70] F Mehrhoff, *Die Veränderung des Arbeitgeberbegriffs* (Schriften zum Sozial- und Arbeitsrecht Band 75, Duncker & Humblot 1984). Reviewed by R Becker (1986) 3 NZA 190.

[71] Zöllner, Loritz, and Hergenröder, *Arbeitsrecht* (n 63) 1. The CJEU's decision in Case C-242/09 *Albron Catering BV v FNV Bondgenoten* [2011] All ER (EC) 625 is unlikely to upset this: H Willemsen, 'Erosion des Arbeitgeberbegriffs nach der Albron-Entscheidung des EuGH? Betriebsübergang bei gespaltener Arbeitgeberfunktion' (2011) NJW 1546.

a lack of a clear definition of the employee, with uncertainty continuing despite a long historical track record,[72] including even a constitutional challenge.[73]

The contract of employment needs to be a contract of service, with a focus on the employee's effort rather than outcome.[74] It is defined via the status of the wage-taking party,[75] the key criterion being personal subordination or a lack of independence.[76] Despite ample criticism of this approach,[77] no alternative criteria, such as a version of the business integration test,[78] have been accepted.[79] For these and a host of additional reasons,[80] then, the contract of employment itself cannot suffice as a regulatory tool. Indeed, as Simitis notes, it was the path away from an undisputed priority of the contract of employment that gave the discipline its distinct form.[81] Where labour law was thus seen as failing in its protective function, both courts and statute intervened to extend it beyond contract alone to ensure a *Schutzzweckerfüllung* (fulfilment of protective purpose).[82] These additional areas included the field of collective bargaining and a close involvement in the employer's decision-making, both at the level of individual measures (through works councils) and entrepreneurial choices more generally (co-decision).[83]

The totality of legal relationships springing from the contract of employment is thus subsumed into the notion of the *Arbeitsverhältnis*. As employment law is seen as concerning employers as much as employees, the concept of the employer in the *Arbeitsverhältnis* is simply the party other than the employee to it.[84]

C. Key Areas and Sources

There is no one code regulating the entirety of German employment law. Instead, it can be found in a wide range of relevant sources, from the *Bürgerliches Gesetzbuch* and the *Grundgesetz* (Basic Law) to individual statutes (such as the BetrVG

---

[72] Zöllner, Loritz, and Hergenröder, *Arbeitsrecht* (n 63) 27, 29: first mentioned in 1794, *Allgemeines Landrecht für die preußischen Staaten*, II.8 §423.

[73] BVG decision of 20.05.1996, AP Nr 82 zu §611 BGB Abhängigkeit. Discussed in W Däubler, 'Working People in Germany' (1999–2000) 21 CLLPJ 77.

[74] Zöllner, Loritz, and Hergenröder, *Arbeitsrecht* (n 63) 35–7.

[75] Equally across all areas, other than social security and tax: Däubler (n 73).

[76] *Unselbstständigkeit* or *persönliche Abhängigkeit*: BAG decision of 20.08.2003, (2004) 21 NZA 39.

[77] Zöllner, Loritz, and Hergenröder, *Arbeitsrecht* (n 63) 42.

[78] eg E Molitor, *Das Wesen des Arbeitsvertrages: eine Untersuchung über die Begriffe des Dienst- und Werkvertrags, sowie des Vertrags über abhängige Arbeit* (Deichert 1925) 82.

[79] See now also the new term 'Beschäftigte' as a specifically gender-neutral attempt: R Richardi, 'Arbeitnehmer als Beschäftigte' (2010) 27 NZA 1101, 1103.

[80] Zöllner, Loritz, and Hergenröder, *Arbeitsrecht* (n 63) 2–3.

[81] S Simitis, 'Juridification of Labor Relations' in G Teubner (ed), *Juridification of Social Spheres* (de Gruyter 1987) 114.

[82] Mehrhoff, *Die Veränderung des Arbeitgeberbegriffs* (n 70).

[83] Zöllner, Loritz, and Hergenröder, *Arbeitsrecht* (n 63) 3–4.

[84] Zöllner, Loritz, and Hergenröder, *Arbeitsrecht* (n 63) 33–4, 44. There can be exceptional situations where an employment relationship is formed by means other than the contract of employment, for example in agency work relationships conducted without a permit.

1972) and labour court judgments (*Richterrecht*).[85] There is a fairly clear division, in both doctrine and practice, between the areas of individual and collective employment law, despite a clear acknowledgment that clean dividing lines are difficult to draw.[86] Subsequent paragraphs loosely adopt this division in setting out relevant provisions, turning first to the individual employment relationship. Organized around the contract of employment, key questions in this area (other than those as to the very existence and classification of a contractual relationship) include the mutual duties of the parties, the modification of general private law (*Zivilrecht*) standards, and the termination of the relationship.[87]

The Individual Dimension: das Arbeitsverhältnis

The employer is the party which can demand and control the employee's efforts.[88] This right of control, based on a contract of employment, is a central component of the *Arbeitsverhältnis*.[89] There are few, if any, requirements beyond the criteria set out above, either in terms of form or substance: the contract of employment does not need to be in writing,[90] and the parties can, in principle, agree to any terms.[91] One important set of norms that builds directly on the contract of employment relates to general dismissal protection, as set out in §§ 1–14 of the *Kündigungsschutzgesetz* 1969.[92] In order to be 'socially justified', an individual dismissal needs to take place on the basis of a specific range of reasons (the 'positive reasons')[93] and must not contravene a further set of 'negative reasons', including previously agreed selection criteria, the existence of other employment opportunities, and selection according to social criteria.[94]

The Collective Dimension: Mitbestimmung

The fundamental idea underpinning this area is that stakeholders affected by an entity's decision should have a voice in the process leading up to it. While an involvement of all groups potentially affected by a company's actions would be impossible, German law has recognized employees' special role through a system of involvement in company decision-making. Whilst the advantages (including

---

[85] Zöllner, Loritz, and Hergenröder, *Arbeitsrecht* (n 63) 31; Windbichler, *Arbeitsrecht im Konzern* (n 1) 58.

[86] Zöllner, Loritz, and Hergenröder, *Arbeitsrecht* (n 63) 65.

[87] Zöllner, Loritz, and Hergenröder, *Arbeitsrecht* (n 63) 124.

[88] J Bauer and D Herzberg, 'Arbeitsrechtliche Probleme in Konzernen mit Matrixstrukturen' (2011) 28 NZA 713.

[89] U Preis, *Erfurter Kommentar zum Arbeitsrecht* (11th edn Beck 2011) §611 BGB rn 233.

[90] Zöllner, Loritz, and Hergenröder, *Arbeitsrecht* (n 63) 137; citing M Kliemt, *Formerfordernisse im Arbeitsverhältnis* (Müller 1998).

[91] S Morgenroth, 'Employment Contracts and Further Legal Sources' in J Kirchner, P Kremp, and M Magotsch (eds), *Key Aspects of German Employment and Labour Law* (Springer Verlag 2010).

[92] Zöllner, Loritz, and Hergenröder, *Arbeitsrecht* (n 63) 279.

[93] §1II and III *Kündigungsschutzgesetz* 1969 ('KSchG 1969').

[94] Kirchner, Kremp, and Magotsch, *Key Aspects of German Employment and Labour Law* (n 3) 5–7.

additional perspectives, control and explanation mechanisms, and the legitimization of decisions through proper procedures) and disadvantages (notably the expense, administrative effort, and supposed inefficiency of a highly complex system) have been discussed at length, a general consensus seems to have emerged that positive factors outweigh negative ones.[95] In the context of corporations, two kinds of employee involvement mechanisms are of interest: works councils, created under the provisions of the BetrVG 1972 as a mechanism of co-decision 'from below', and the representation of employee representatives on the company's board under the *Mitbestimmungsgesetz* 1976 as an example of co-determination 'from above'.[96] The concept of the employer is broken down into a distinction between two units: the *Betrieb* and the *Unternehmen*. The line is an inherently difficult one to draw—indeed, it has in this regard been compared to the very notion of the *Arbeitnehmer* itself.[97] Whilst both are organizational units within the enterprise, the aims pursued are different: the *Betrieb* focuses on specific, task-related aims; the *Unternehmen*, on the other hand, on the enterprise's broader economic goals.[98] The former is a factual unit, with only the latter having legal personality (*Rechtssubjekt*). The distinction follows from a (legal) doctrinal framing of (economic) business realities, looking at the level at which decisions are taken. In deciding to which level to attribute particular decisions, the primary focus is on the relative proximity to either *Betrieb* or *Unternehmen*.[99]

The Works Constitution: Betriebsverfassung

Turning first to the *Betrieb*-level, co-decision here takes place via the *Betriebsrat* (works council) as an independent organ of the *Betriebsverfassung* (works constitution), as regulated by the BetrVG 1972. The purpose of its provisions is to ensure the organizational involvement of employees in key questions at the works level, as well as the protection and fostering of individual employees. These aims play an important role both in the interpretation of BetrVG 1972 norms, but also in guiding worker representatives when participating in individual decisions.[100]

The central institution of the works constitution is the *Betriebsrat*. An odd number of members are elected for four-year terms from amongst the *Betrieb*-employees, depending on the overall size of the unit.[101] Whilst technically independent from trade unions, there will in reality be a significant overlap between members of the works council and trade union representatives.[102] The BetrVG 1972 specifies that the works council's interlocutor be the employer, which, in the absence of contrary

---

[95] Zöllner, Loritz, and Hergenröder, *Arbeitsrecht* (n 63) 456.

[96] Kirchner, Kremp, and Magotsch, *Key Aspects of German Employment and Labour Law* (n 3) 305ff.

[97] U Preis, 'Legitimation und Grenzen des Betriebsbegriffs im Arbeitsrecht' (2000) 52 RdA 257.

[98] Zöllner, Loritz, and Hergenröder, *Arbeitsrecht* (n 63) 458–9.

[99] D Joost, *Betrieb und Unternehmen als Grundbegriffe im Arbeitsrecht* (Beck 1988).

[100] Zöllner, Loritz, and Hergenröder, *Arbeitsrecht* (n 63) 461; M Heinze and A Söllner, *Arbeitsrecht in der Bewährung: Festschrift für Otto Rudolf Kissel* (Beck 1994) 1269.

[101] §9 BetrVG 1972 (n 59).

[102] Kirchner, Kremp, and Magotsch, *Key Aspects of German Employment and Labour Law* (n 3) 59.

legislative provisions is the contractual counterparty of the works employees. The employer can however nominate representatives for such negotiations,[103] as long as they are fit for the purpose (eg by being in possession of specific knowledge as regards the topics under discussion).[104]

The wide range of information, consultation and participation rights accorded to the works council by the BetrVG 1972 can be divided into specific and general duties. As regards the former, there are three main areas: social (§87ff), personnel (§92ff), and economic matters (§106ff). The majority of the works council's day-to-day work is on social and personnel topics, such as on working conditions, or the inception and termination of individual employment relationships.[105] There is however also scope for involvement in important one-off events, such as significant changes to the *Betrieb* itself.[106] The employer must inform the works council of such plans, consult on the parties' different interests,[107] and conclude a social plan to compensate for, or at least mitigate, the resulting economic disadvantages.[108] A range of fundamental principles including faithful cooperation, a duty to ensure the welfare of both workers and the *Betrieb*,[109] and strict neutrality guide the works council's efforts.[110] Whilst the detailed procedural apparatus is beyond the scope of the present discussion, it is important to note at this point the possibility of several works councils coming together in the formation of a *Gesamtbetriebsrat*[111] and even a *Konzernbetriebsrat*.[112] The general rules for and duties of these bodies are to be interpreted in accordance with the system just set out.[113]

Co-Determination: Unternehmerische Mitbestimmung

In the second area under consideration, employees are directly involved in entrepreneurial decisions taken at the level of the undertaking. There are two key differences to be noted. First, as regards the institutional setup of co-decision, the entity in question is no longer specific to employee issues; worker representatives participate directly in a company organ. Indeed, this explains why co-determination is situated at the intersection of company and employment law.[114] The second shift

---

[103] M Franzen, *Gemeinschaftskommentar zum Betriebsverfassungsgesetz: GK-BetrVG* (9th edn Beck 2010) §1 rn 91.

[104] BAG decision of 11.12.1991, AP Nr 2 zu §90 BetrVG 1972.

[105] Zöllner, Loritz, and Hergenröder, *Arbeitsrecht* (n 63) 477.

[106] §111 BetrVG 1972 (n 59); Kirchner, Kremp, and Magotsch, *Key Aspects of German Employment and Labour Law* (n 3) 220ff.

[107] §112 BetrVG 1972 (n 59) ('Interessensausgleich').

[108] §112, 112a BetrVG 1972 (n 59). See further C Gillen and O Vahle, 'Personalabbau und Betriebsänderung' (2005) 22 NZA 1385, 1391.

[109] §§2I and 74I BetrVG 1972 (n 59).

[110] §75I BetrVG 1972 (n 59); Zöllner, Loritz, and Hergenröder, *Arbeitsrecht* (n 63) 469ff.

[111] §47 BetrVG 1972 (n 59). [112] §§54, 55 BetrVG 1972 (n 59).

[113] E Salamon, 'Die Konzernbetriebsvereinbarung beim Betriebsübergang' (2009) 26 NZA 471.

[114] As shown by treatment in key texts in both areas: Zöllner, Loritz, and Hergenröder, *Arbeitsrecht* (n 63) §53 ('Mitbestimmung in Unternehmensorganen'); V Emmerich and M Habersack, *Konzernrecht* (9th edn Beck 2008) §4.V ('Mitbestimmung im Konzern'). The following paragraphs draw on accounts given there. See also Kirchner, Kremp, and Magotsch, *Key Aspects of German Employment and Labour Law* (n 3) 308.

is one in purpose: to involve employees in a high-level determination of all commercial decisions, rather than issues related to a specific *Betrieb*.[115] Whilst both the legal and economic merits of this approach are hotly debated in domestic and international literature,[116] such questions are beyond the scope of the present discussion.

Which of the three models of co-determination available under German law applies in any given situation is determined by the industry, size, and legal form of an undertaking. The provisions to be discussed in this chapter are taken from the *Mitbestimmungsgesetz*, instead of either the *Drittelbeteiligungsgesetz* 2004 ('DrittelBG 2004') or *Montanmitbestimmungsgesetz* 1951 ('MontanMitbestG 1951'), as the former best illustrates the issues at stake. In terms of substantive co-decision powers, it ranges in the centre of the employee voice spectrum; likewise in terms of the applicability of its norms: while the MontanMitbestG 1951 enjoys technical priority,[117] it is limited in practical impact due to its exclusive focus on mining-related companies; the MitbestG 1976 is then to be applied in preference to the DrittelBG 2004.[118]

Co-determination is exercised by elected employee representatives,[119] who hold the same number (one-half of 12, 16, or 20, depending on company size) of seats on the supervisory board as shareholder representatives.[120] If the company's legal structure does not mandate the existence of a separate supervisory entity (eg in the case of a GmbH), a board is to be formed for co-determination purposes.[121] Employee representatives are thus involved in all decisions within the powers of the co-deciding board.[122] Whilst the distribution of board seats suggests exact parity between employee and shareholder representatives, a complex set of voting arrangements avoids deadlocks: by allocating an additional vote to the board's presiding member (who will usually have been chosen by the shareholders[123]) following an initial draw, the latter will prevail in case of conflict.[124]

Section 2: The Shared Exercise of Employer Functions

German law's conception of the employer thus set out is not immune to variation.[125] One set of such challenges that has become frequently discussed is a split

---

[115] Zöllner, Loritz, and Hergenröder, *Arbeitsrecht* (n 63) 567.
[116] Zöllner, Loritz, and Hergenröder, *Arbeitsrecht* (n 63) 573; More generally: J Rogers and W Streeck (eds), *Works Councils: Consultation, Representation, and Cooperation in Industrial Relations* (University of Chicago Press 1995).
[117] §1 II MitbestG 1976 (n 66).   [118] §1 III MitbestG 1976 (n 66).
[119] Chosen through a highly complex election system: §9ff MitbestG 1976 (n 66).
[120] §7 MitbestG 1976 (n 66).   [121] §§6I, 7I MitbestG 1976 (n 66).
[122] This is dependent on the nature of the company, there being slightly more powers in an AG as opposed to a GmbH.
[123] §27II MitbestG 1976 (n 66).
[124] §29II MitbestG 1976 (n 66). The procedures for electing executive officers differ slightly.
[125] H Konzen, 'Arbeitsrechtliche Drittbeziehungen: Gedanken über Grundlagen und Wirkungen der "Gespaltenen Arbeitgeberstellung"' (1982) 13 ZfA 259.

of employer functions.[126] Whilst the label suggests a unified series of problems, there are in fact several groups of issues: the joint involvement of different kinds of employees, of different kinds of employers, and the utilization of labour by parties other than the contractual employer. In rare circumstances, this split of employer functions can lead to certain employee rights' becoming enforceable against third parties, both via contract and other legal constructions—not least the already-mentioned statutory regulation of temporary agency work.[127] None of these piecemeal approaches can, however, be understood as embracing a fully-fledged functional concept of the employer.[128]

A. The *Konzern*

The *Konzern* is therefore the most appropriate context in which to explore the split of employer functions in multilateral organizational settings. The fundamental idea underpinning this notion is that a company under the controlling power of another enterprise will deviate from the independent control over its business, the concept on which much of German company law is premised.[129] As the external entity's influence is organized through company law measures (as opposed to supply contracts, for example) it will be consistently strong and reasonably permanent,[130] giving the parent company control that can range from a direct exercise of key management functions to a more general influence on the broader setting and direction of stakeholder relationships. The relationships between Private Equity management companies and portfolio companies in German law are a clear example of such setups.[131]

Given the high density of corporate groupings in Germany, it is unsurprising that a specific legal approach to these issues has developed in German law: it knows of *Konzernrecht*[132] as a distinct subset of company law. Despite the *Konzern* label, this area of the law focuses on a wide range of connections between companies, with the *Konzern* as the closest form of integration (short of a fusion) at its very core in §18 of the *Aktiengesetz* 1965 ('AktG 1965'). There is no single code or law regulating the area; judicial pronouncements have played a significant role in developing the law both in terms of substance and scope. As regards the former, for example, new doctrines addressing specific problems not explicitly considered by the legislature remedied judicially recognized issues.[133] As regards the latter, there is nothing in the *Gesetz betreffend die Gesellschaften mit beschränkter Haftung*

---

[126] Zöllner, Loritz, and Hergenröder, *Arbeitsrecht* (n 63) 306ff.

[127] Zöllner, Loritz, and Hergenröder, *Arbeitsrecht* (n 63) 307.

[128] Zöllner, Loritz, and Hergenröder, *Arbeitsrecht* (n 63) 45.

[129] §761 *Aktiengesetz* 1965 ('AktG 1965').

[130] This is sometimes questioned in the context of franchising or just-in-time contracts.

[131] R Schmidt and G Spindler, *Finanzinvestoren aus Ökonomischer und Juristischer Perspektive* (Nomos 2008) 139ff.

[132] Emmerich and Habersack, *Konzernrecht* (n 114) §1ff.

[133] eg the notion of *Existenzvernichtungshaftung* (liability for destroying the very existence of an entity), developed in the BGH decision of 17.09.2001, II ZR 378/99 (*Bremer Vulkan*); BGH decision of 16.07.2007, II ZR 3/04 (*Trihotel*).

1892 ('GmbHG 1892'; the law regulating one of two major company forms found in German law, as explained below) mirroring the *Konzern*-specific considerations of the AktG 1965; the BGH (Federal Supreme Court) nonetheless developed the application of relevant rules in parallel.[134]

In the context of this parallel development, it is appropriate briefly to address the distinction between the *Aktiengesellschaft* (AG) and the *Gesellschaft mit beschränkter Haftung* (GmbH) as relevant to subsequent discussion: there is a wide range of important distinctions between the two forms as organizational models of business enterprise. For the purposes of this chapter, however, these will frequently be negligible, as a similar purpose is pursued. As has already been seen, for example, the range of substantive co-determination powers differ depending on whether a company is organized as an AG or a GmbH. The underlying principle, on the other hand, is the same: employee representatives can become involved in the same range of topics as owner representatives.

Discussion now turns to a brief exposition of the technical construction of the legal notion of the *Konzern* in German company law, the universality of its application across different legal areas, and an outline of the specific (economic) problems arising from connected companies as a key to the purposes of (legal) regulatory measures in the *Konzern*-context.

It is crucial to clarify at the outset that the economic unity inherent in the *Konzern* as an enterprise organizational model does not have a general impact on the law's perception of the corporate grouping: as Windbichler notes, 'there is no such thing as the *Konzern* as a subject, for example as a legal person'.[135] Limited exceptions, for example in the area of group accounting,[136] should not be interpreted as moves in a contrary direction.

§18 AktG 1965 sets out the criteria for the *Konzern* as the closest possible connection between legally distinct corporate entities. Different kinds of the wide economic variety of company group arrangements are envisaged by §18, depending on the relative relationship between the companies: §18I applies to situations where the relationship is one of subordination; §18II where they are equal.

§18, however, is not a free-standing provision, building instead on a set of criteria and presumptions laid down in §§15–17 AktG 1965.[137] Two criteria are usually identified for a subordinated *Konzern*: there must, first, be connected undertakings (in the sense of §15 and §17 AktG 1965), which are, second,[138] brought together under the unified control of one of the shareholder companies. The application of each of these elements on the facts of a particular grouping can be contentious. As a result, German law has developed an intricate cascade of presumptions (building on notions such as control and dependency) to determine whether a particular corporate grouping constitutes a *Konzern*. These presumptions are irrebuttable

---

[134] Especially in its second *Senat Zivil* chamber.
[135] Windbichler, *Arbeitsrecht im Konzern* (n 1) 14: '*Den Konzern als Rechtssubjekt, etwa als juristische Person, gibt es nicht.*'
[136] *Konzern-Rechnungslegung*: §290ff, esp §297III 1 *Handelsgesetzbuch* 1897.
[137] Emmerich and Habersack, *Konzernrecht* (n 114) 57.
[138] This is on (rare) occasion suggested to be an independent criterion.

where contractual or other integration arrangements are in place;[139] they may on the other hand be rebutted (albeit only by clearing a rather high threshold[140]) in other kinds of dependency.[141] In essence, as Emmerich and Habersack note,[142] unified control in §18 AktG 1965 is actual control in the sense of §17 AktG 1965, which will always be applicable in the case of majority shareholdings.[143] How this control, based on general company law rights, is exercised (or indeed whether it is exercised at all) is of little relevance for the existence of the *Konzern*.[144]

Within the category of subordinated groups (*Unterordnungskonzern*), one further division should be noted: that between the *Vertrags-* or *Eingliederungskonzern* (corporate grouping by contract or integration) and the *Faktischer Konzern* (de facto corporate grouping). In the former, unified control is based on one of the contracts mentioned in §18I 2 AktG 1965, that is to say, either a *Beherrschungs- und Gewinnabführungsvertrag*[145] or an *Eingliederungsvertrag*.[146] If one of these contracts has been concluded, §18I 3 AktG 1965 decrees a rebuttable presumption of *Vertragskonzern*.[147] In the latter, unified control is the result of other arrangements, from majority shareholdings to vote control contracts. All that matters in this regard is the possibility to enforce the implementation of parent entity decisions.[148]

In summary, then, the application of the general presumption cascade in the specific setting of the *Unterordnungskonzern* requires the connected undertakings to be in a relationship of subordination and the real control of dependent companies through unified direction.[149] For the first criterion, the mere possibility of control, directly or indirectly, is enough; it will be presumed for example in the case of a majority shareholding (§17II AktG 1965). This control will usually be exercised, though it is again (§18I 3 AktG 1965) presumed unless rebutted. Unified direction, finally, can come from the majority shareholder, integration, contractual arrangements, or de facto subordination.[150]

In spite of these sophisticated arrangements, the notion of the *Konzern* does not serve as a gateway into a wide range of regulatory regimes.[151] Crucially for present purposes, however, the two key provisions to be discussed make direct reference to §18 AktG 1965: §5 MitbestG 1976 (on *Unternehmerische Mitbestimmung im Konzern*), and §54 BetrVG 1972 (on the *Konzernbetriebsrat*).

---

[139] §18I 2 AktG 1965 (n 129).

[140] Kort, 'Bildung und Stellung des Konzernbetriebsrats bei nationalen und internationalen Unternehmensverbindungen' (n 59) 466.

[141] §18I 3 AktG 1965 (n 129).

[142] Emmerich and Habersack, *Konzernrecht* (n 114) 59.

[143] §17II AktG 1965 (n 129).

[144] LG Oldenburg decision of 14.03.1991, ZIP (1992) 1632, 1636.

[145] §291 AktG 1965 (n 129): contract of control and profit redistribution.

[146] §319 AktG 1965 (n 129): integration contract.

[147] R Richardi et al, *Betriebsverfassungsgesetz: BetrVG* (10th edn Beck 2006) §54 rn 8.

[148] BAG decision of 22.11.1995, (1996) 13 NZA 706.

[149] BAG decision of 16.08.1995, (1996) 13 NZA 274.

[150] B Schwab, 'Der Konzernbetriebsrat—Seine Rechtsstellung und Zuständigkeit' (2007) 24 NZA 337, 338.

[151] Indeed, Emmerich and Habersack, *Konzernrecht* (n 114) 63 note its primary importance as a gateway to the MitbestG 1976.

B. A Single *Konzern* Notion?

Given the generally purposive approach to the interpretation of statutory norms in German law,[152] and the distinct regulatory aims in company and employment law, the question has arisen whether the notion of the *Konzern* applies equally across these contexts. In the context of §5 MitbestG 1976, this question has been the subject of recent litigation.[153] As Kort notes, however, given the existence of co-determination within company law, statutory references to §18I AktG 1965 are to be understood in the company law sense; the §15/16/17/18I AktG 1965 definition and their cascade of presumptions apply in full.[154] He goes on to dismiss suggestions that contractual control outside the company law tools just set out could suffice to fulfil the *Konzern* presumptions; such setups are admitted only in the context of, for example, minority shareholdings.[155] Once within the company law framework, however, there is no need for the actual exercise of unified control power: the arrangement itself suffices.[156] How control is exercised in reality is equally irrelevant; there is no need to give actual orders.[157]

The picture is slightly more difficult in the context of §54 BetrVG 1972:[158] it is an employment law norm, but makes direct reference to the (company law concept of the) subordination *Konzern* in §18I AktG 1965.[159] The Federal Labour Court has held that for the existence of a *Konzern* under §54 BetrVG 1972, the legal form of controlling and subordinate enterprise is irrelevant—even a natural person as head entity would come under its provisions, lest the co-decision duties be voided of significance.[160] In a recent decision,[161] the BAG affirmed that there was no independent notion of the *Konzern* in the BetrVG 1972, and that in applying its provisions the company law definition of subordination mattered.[162] The court left it open, however, whether in exceptional circumstances subordination may also be found beyond the realm of company law. While the Federal Court of Justice ('BGH') had in the past emphasized this limitation as a way of avoiding deep intrusions into the market economy, it had done so specifically in the context of company law.[163] The BAG, on the other hand, had focused on the possibility of subordination, regardless of means;[164] the academic literature was divided.[165] The desire for legal

---

[152] Windbichler, *Arbeitsrecht im Konzern* (n 1) 48, 50.

[153] Discussed in Kort, 'Bildung und Stellung des Konzernbetriebsrats bei nationalen und internationalen Unternehmensverbindungen' (n 59).

[154] Kort, 'Bildung und Stellung des Konzernbetriebsrats bei nationalen und internationalen Unternehmensverbindungen' (n 59) 82; Windbichler, *Arbeitsrecht im Konzern* (n 1) 518.

[155] cf Windbichler, *Arbeitsrecht im Konzern* (n 1) 519.

[156] K Hopt and H Wiedemann, *Großkommentar Aktiengesetz* (4th edn de Gruyter 1999) §18 rn 29, 32.

[157] U Hüffer, *Aktiengesetz* (8th edn Beck 2008) §18 rn 12.

[158] Schwab, 'Der Konzernbetriebsrat—Seine Rechtsstellung und Zuständigkeit' (n 150).

[159] BAG decision of 22.11.1995 (n 148).

[160] BAG decision of 22.11.1995 (n 148); BAG decision of 05.05.1988, (1989) 6 NZA 8.

[161] BAG decision of 09.02.2011, (2011) 28 NZA 866.

[162] BAG decision of 27.10.2010, (2011) 28 NZA 524.

[163] BGH decision of 26.03.1984, (90) BGHZ 381.

[164] BAG decision of 30.10.1986, AP BetrVG 1972 §55 Nr 1.

[165] BAG decision of 30.10.1986 (n 164) [27].

coherence and certainty could in certain individual cases be outweighed by a need to ensure effective co-decision when required, especially given the legislative aim that a *Konzern-Betriebsrat* should counteract impairments to worker participation resulting from factual and legal external control opportunities.[166] Bäck and Winzer make two important points about these guidelines.[167] They note, first, the high threshold to prove control outside of company law structures: it would not suffice, for example, if such powers were temporary, or partial. They note furthermore that whilst the judgment denies the existence of co-decision mechanisms within broad functional groups, it does clearly confirm the existence of a *Konzernrecht* doctrine, the so-called *Konzern im Konzern*,[168] in employment law, despite its very contentious position in company law.

C. The Purpose of *Konzernrecht*

German law thus gives special recognition to the *Konzern* as a particular model of economic organization. In concluding, the question should briefly be asked why this is the case, especially as the answer may provide clues as to the general aims and purpose of *Konzernrecht*. The specific recognition, it is frequently suggested, is due to both the advantages and dangers inherent in the *Konzern* model. Turning first to the advantages of economic integration,[169] there are significant efficiency gains from the coordinated approach of multiple entities, with an increase in overall size leading to additional economies of scale. In bringing these advantages about without complete integration, a wide range of stakeholders can benefit: shareholders and customers receive a share in the resulting surplus, creditors benefit from specific capital allocation,[170] and even employees may see advantages in working for a large *Konzern* instead of an individual company.[171] These advantages, however, face an equally important list of countervailing factors.[172]

The general provisions of German company law are designed around the assumption of a collective action problem amongst shareholders: given the high cost of individual shareholder control whilst benefits would be spread widely, an undertaking's management is independent. The same is not true for subordinated companies in the *Konzern*; the balanced system of the AktG 1965 is thus thrown out of kilter once a single entity manages to exert pressure in its own interest on the administrative organs of another—indeed, this influence can go as far as the

---

[166] BAG decision of 27.10.2010 (n 162); BAG decision of 13.10.2004, (2005) 22 NZA 647 [30].

[167] U Bäck and T Winzer, 'BAG: Konzernbetriebsrat—Möglichkeit eines Spartenkonzern-betriebsrats?' (2011) 38 NZG 944.

[168] A model where a subordinate company still has relevant control over subordinates in lower tiers: BAG decision of 14.02.2007 (n 64).

[169] For an extensive overview, see K Martens, 'Grundlagen des Konzernarbeitsrechts' (1984) 12 ZGR 417.

[170] H Hansmann and R Kraakman, 'The Essential Role of Organizational Law' (2000) 110 Yale Law Journal 387.

[171] Windbichler, *Arbeitsrecht im Konzern* (n 1) 41.

[172] Emmerich and Habersack, *Konzernrecht* (n 114) 10–11. For an extensive list, see Windbichler, *Arbeitsrecht im Konzern* (n 1) 40.

pursuit of aims directly contrary to those of other shareholders, creditors, and even the company itself.[173] *Konzernrecht* maps itself onto these issues by developing detailed rules[174] to protect various identified parties and to provide clear boundaries as to when and how concentration can be achieved. It is against this background that the purpose of separate *Konzernrecht* rules becomes clear:[175] they provide the necessary *organizational* framework for deep changes in enterprise structure, thus facilitating the concentration of control powers, while at the same time *protecting* minority shareholders, creditors, and even the subordinated entity and shareholders in the parent company itself.

Section 3: *Arbeitsrecht im Konzern*

Discussion thus turns to employment law in the corporate group, to set out and analyse examples of specific modifications to the general framework which have taken the *Konzern* context into account in shaping their regulatory design. A linguistic point should be noted at the outset: whilst the topic under scrutiny was historically discussed under the label of *Konzernarbeitsrecht* (corporate group employment law),[176] it has become clear today that the questions are more appropriately framed as concerning *Arbeitsrecht im Konzern* (employment law in corporate groups). This is notably reflected in the title of the first,[177] and to date only, comprehensive investigation of all related phenomena in this *terra incognita*.[178]

The question as to the *patron introuvable* in the corporate group context can only be answered within the existing frameworks of employment and company law, which explains a methodology that focuses on problems and solutions specific to the form instead of attempting a complete restatement of employment law for corporate groups. The first point that arises is as to the difference between employment in an independent company, and one subordinated to others in a *Konzern*: does the structural difference lead to changes in risk profile? Being embedded in a group structure influences a company in general—but does it also influence the company as an employer in particular? This point matters as regards the joint or shared exercise of employer functions, but is equally important even in the absence of such arrangements, given the general influence of another entity over the employing company.

---

[173] See Emmerich and Habersack, *Konzernrecht* (n 114) and Windbichler, *Arbeitsrecht im Konzern* (n 1) for examples.

[174] See eg §291AktG 1965 ff (n 129). A detailed analysis of their operation is beyond the scope of the present discussion.

[175] Hüffer, *Aktiengesetz* (n 157) §15 rn 3.

[176] The term used in Martens, 'Grundlagen des Konzernarbeitsrechts' (n 169). Early topics included the application of the contract of employment, the *Betriebsbedingte Kündigung*, and, after the *BetrVG* of 1972, the possibility of creating a *Konzern*-Works Council.

[177] Windbichler, *Arbeitsrecht im Konzern* (n 1).

[178] BAG decision of 18.10.1976, AP Nr 3 §1KSchG 1969.

It has already been seen that company law reacts to the *Konzern* with a range of general stakeholder-protective mechanisms. As Konzen has noted,[179] there can only be an employment law-specific extension of such protection if there is a '*lacuna* in the regulatory regime' (*Regelungslücke*), ie if employees are sufficiently different from other stakeholders, such as creditors. Discussion thus turns to a brief comparison of these groups,[180] focusing on the interests of employees other than as wage creditors.[181]

At a first glance, both groups will share a primary interest in the solvency of the company, thus benefitting equally from a range of measures designed to protect the daughter company.[182] Henssler suggests that a first difference may arise from the possibility that whilst the fruits of the employees' labour can easily be whisked away to solvent controlling companies, reciprocal employer obligations will remain in a lightly capitalized lower entity.[183] This danger, however, is equally applicable to general creditors' contributions to the company.[184]

Upon further consideration it emerges that employees have a much stronger interest in the protection of the employing company's 'economic individuality' and ongoing existence because of their *existentielle Wirtschaftsabhängigkeit* (existence-critical economic dependence).[185] Individual *Konzernrecht* measures do of course protect the subordinated company to a certain extent; it is however doubtful whether this will always see creditor and employee interests aligned. Indeed, it is not difficult to imagine a situation where the protection of the enterprise as such could lead to the dismissal of workers in order to lower wage expenditure.

Having reviewed these comparisons as well as the relevant economic and legal literature, Windbichler concludes that there are three *Konzern*-specific threats to employees:[186] decisions taken outside of co-decision mechanisms; detrimental influence,[187] and the closure of independently viable economic units. Unsurprisingly there is no one, clear solution to all these issues; the individual approaches will now be explored in turn. It will emerge that while there is little response in terms of individual employment law (other than in exceptional circumstances, which will frequently be highly fact-specific), a broad range of firm regulatory responses can be observed in the collective domain. At first sight, the focus of the present section might therefore appear to be rather out of line with

---

[179] H Konzen, 'Arbeitnehmerschutz im Konzern' (1984) 36 RdA 65, 66.

[180] Windbichler, *Arbeitsrecht im Konzern* (n 1) 29–42. This difficulty and importance of the right choice of comparator will matter throughout the evaluative exercise to follow: Martens, 'Grundlagen des Konzernarbeitsrechts' (n 169) 423ff.

[181] Employees can claim first priority as wage creditors: H Staab, 'Der Arbeitnehmer-Gesellschafter der GmbH im Spannungseld zwischen Arbeitnehmerschutz und gesellschaftsrechtlichem Gläubigerschutz' (1995) 12 NZA 608.

[182] Windbichler, *Arbeitsrecht im Konzern* (n 1) 32–3: indirect creditor protection ('*Schadenersatz, Nachteils- und Verlustausgleich*').

[183] Windbichler, *Arbeitsrecht im Konzern* (n 1) 59.

[184] H Konzen, 'Arbeitsverhältnisse im Konzern' (1987) 151 ZHR 566, 572.

[185] H Wiedemann, *Die Unternehmensgruppe im Privatrecht* (Mohr Siebeck 1988) 97, 108.

[186] Windbichler, *Arbeitsrecht im Konzern* (n 1) 42.   [187] '*Nachteilige Einflussnahme*'.

the results presented in Chapter 3. They are nonetheless crucial for the purpose of the present discussion—to add further considerations and methodological evidence to the guidelines for the eventual reconceptualization of the employer, a task specifically addressed in Section 4 immediately subsequent.

A. Individual Employment Law

As has already been noted, there is no general scope for seeing the *Konzern* as a contractual employer under German law.[188] The following paragraphs analyse this position, as well as criticisms of the approach, before turning to other potential solutions, such as piercing the corporate veil.[189] Finally, the scope of unfair dismissal protection mechanisms will be tested in the *Konzern* context. Despite some potential avenues and small modifications, the answer there will again be negative,[190] unless additional external factors prevail.[191] The range of solutions introduced in the collective dimension (or even as regards triangular agency employment relationships) has no significant impact on the individual dimension.

The Contract of Employment

As Windbichler points out, there is a real danger of incongruence between contractual and de facto risk allocation in situations where the close connection of the contractual employer to other undertakings directly influences the individual employment relationship.[192] This does not mean, however, that the *Konzern* can somehow become a singular legal entity, and thus a contractual counterparty.[193]

Various attempts to remedy the resulting incongruence draw on a range of 'exceptional' contractual approaches, for example by suggesting a unified employment relationship involving multiple employers, or multiple connected employment relationships.[194] The advantage of such analyses lies in the fact that all non-wage taking parties to the relationship(s) would become subject to the duties placed on employers. The key problem, however, is that for such a relationship to come about, all parties must have taken active steps towards it, which will be rare in reality.[195] Similar considerations speak against a range of related solutions

---

[188] T Liebscher, *Münchener Kommentar zum Gesetz betreffend die Gesellschaften mit beschränkter Haftung—GmbHG* (Beck 2010) rn 1100, drawing on Windbichler, *Arbeitsrecht im Konzern* (n 1) 69. There is a possibility of exceptional contracts for senior management and sending employees across units: ibid rn 1113, 1112.

[189] BAG decision of 14.12.2004, (2005) 22 NZA 697. The only possible routes are outside employment law, for example in the law of delict ('*Existenzvernichtungshaftung*').

[190] See eg most recently BAG decision of 23.03.2006, (2007) 24 NZA 30.

[191] For example '*Vertrauensgesichtspunkte*': see eg BAG decision of 27.11.1991, (1992) 9 NZA 644; and potentially where the group parent actually runs the *Betrieb* in question: R Richardi, *Münchener Handbuch zum Arbeitsrecht* (Beck 2009) §32 rn 33.

[192] Windbichler, *Arbeitsrecht im Konzern* (n 1) 166.

[193] Windbichler, *Arbeitsrecht im Konzern* (n 1) 70, 202ff.

[194] Windbichler, *Arbeitsrecht im Konzern* (n 1) 71: '*einheitliches Arbeitsverhältnis*'.

[195] Windbichler, *Arbeitsrecht im Konzern* (n 1) 79.

proposed, for example, by Heinze, Fabricius, and Müllner.[196] As the BAG has repeatedly and consistently found, external influence alone cannot suffice for the construction of an employment relationship with the third entity.[197]

Another potential model is that of a partial employer position, for example by identifying the party who reaps the economic benefit of the workers' efforts, and/ or can offer the best levels of social protection.[198] In the *Konzern* setting, the controlling entity could be such a partial employer;[199] again, however, the mere exercise of certain rights cannot suffice *se ipso* to create an employment relationship.[200]

Dismissal Protection: the Kündigungsschutzgesetz

Turning from the very existence of the contract of employment to regulatory frameworks in the individual employment law dimension that build directly upon it, unfair dismissal protection is an interesting further illustration of attempts to infuse individual employment law with the notion of the *Konzern*.

The power to terminate an employment relationship under the KSchG 1969 lies firmly with the contractual counterparty. The *Konzern*-dimension can nonetheless give rise to two sets of questions in the dismissal context: first, as to the role of entity-external pressure exerted by other group companies; and second, as to the significance of a subordinated company's relationships with other group members in the application of the various protective steps mandated by the KSchG 1969 (especially as regards the social selection process, and the possibility of continuing employment in different functions).[201]

The answer to the former question appears settled: even if an explicit shareholder order led to the termination, it will be effective as long as the dismissal is otherwise correct.[202] Put differently, the factual source of the dismissal decision in such a *Druckkündigung* is not an important consideration in the light of other procedural criteria. Turning to the latter point, there is no general *Konzern* dimension to dismissal protection.[203] This is because each *Konzern-Unternehmen* is a legally independent employer; the KSchG 1969 norms attach directly to the contract of employment.[204] In the case of social selection, the relevant unit is the

---

[196] M Heinze, 'Rechtsprobleme des sog. echten Leiharbeitsverhältnisses' (1976) 7 ZfA 183, 205; F Fabricius, *Rechtsprobleme gespaltener Arbeitsverhältnisse im Konzern: Dargestellt am Rechtsverhältnis der Ruhrkohle Aktiengesellschaft zu ihren Betriebsführungsgesellschaften* (Luchterhand 1982) 40; W Müllner, *Aufgespaltene Arbeitgeberstellung und Betriebsverfassungsrecht* (Duncker & Humblot 1978) 62.

[197] BAG decision of 08.08.1958, AP Nr. 3 §611 BGB; BAG decision of 26.11.1975, AP Nr 19 §611 BGB; cf BAG decision of 04.07.1979, AP Nr 10 §611 BGB (*Rotes Kreuz*); M Henssler, *Der Arbeitsvertrag im Konzern* (Duncker & Humblot 1983) 58, 66.

[198] T Ramm, 'Die Aufspaltung der Arbeitgeberfunktionen (Leiharbeitsverhältnis, mittelbares Arbeitsverhältnis, Arbeitnehmerüberlassung und Gesamthafenarbeitsverhältnis)' (1973) 4 ZfA 263.

[199] Windbichler, *Arbeitsrecht im Konzern* (n 1) 80.

[200] Windbichler, *Arbeitsrecht im Konzern* (n 1) 79.　　　[201] §1 KSchG 1969 (n 93).

[202] Windbichler, *Arbeitsrecht im Konzern* (n 1) 252: '*Druckkündigung*'. BAG decision of 10.02.1977, AP Nr 8 §103 BetrVG 1972 bl 4.

[203] BAG decision of 13.06.2002, (2002) 19 NZA 1175.

[204] BAG decision of 14.10.1982, (1984) NJW 381.

even smaller *Betrieb*, thus denying any broader interpretation.[205] As regards the possibility of continuing employment, the reference unit was traditionally understood to be each individual company,[206] rather than the larger corporate group.[207] The *Rheumaklinik* judgment of 2002 created considerably uncertainty on this last point:[208] while the overall position remains unclear, a spectacular extension seems unlikely.[209]

The only clear set of exceptions, on the other hand, fits into the pattern that has already begun to emerge: the *Konzern* dimension only becomes relevant if entities other than the contractual employer have taken additional steps in that direction,[210] from explicit contractual promises to conduct giving rise to legitimate expectations via the contractual employer.[211]

In summary, the identity of the employment relationship is determined by the contractual parties to it. As the *Konzern* lacks legal personality, it can therefore not be an employer. In exceptional circumstances a third party may become legally involved with the employment relationship.[212] Such circumstances would, however, be highly fact-specific, requiring at the very least specific third party interventions into the employment relationship, rather than being based on control over the contractual counterparty more generally. As Windbichler concludes, 'the individual dimension of employment law [therefore] remains firmly independent of the legal and economic organization of the employer, its entrepreneurial goals and choices'.[213]

B. *Betriebsverfassung*

Turning next to the collective dimension,[214] the *Betriebsverfassungsgesetz* is a prime example of a labour law regime which explicitly takes the *Konzern* dimension into account.[215] The logical need for the creation of a *Konzern* works council ('KWC') arises from the fact that different companies within the group will not necessarily form a large, joint *Betrieb*, which would have to consult with a

---

[205] Bauer and Herzberg, 'Arbeitsrechtliche Probleme in Konzernen mit Matrixstrukturen' (n 88) 716.

[206] BAG decision of 23.04.2008, (2008) 25 NZA 939.

[207] M Henssler, *Münchener Kommentar zum Bürgerlichen Gesetzbuch: BGB. Band 4: Schuldrecht* (6th edn Beck 2012); KSchG 1969 §1 rz 278.

[208] *Rheumaklinik* (n 69); noted G Annuß, 'Die rechtsmissbräuchliche Unternehmerentscheidung im Konzern' (2003) 20 NZA 783.

[209] Bauer and Herzberg, 'Arbeitsrechtliche Probleme in Konzernen mit Matrixstrukturen' (n 88) 785.

[210] BAG decision of 23.11.2004, (2005) 22 NZA 929.

[211] Bauer and Herzberg, 'Arbeitsrechtliche Probleme in Konzernen mit Matrixstrukturen' (n 88) 713: '*Vertrauenstatbestand*'.

[212] For example by signing additional contractual agreements.

[213] Windbichler, *Arbeitsrecht im Konzern* (n 1) 585: '*Individualarbeitsrecht ist grundsätzlich unabhängig von Rechts- und Finanzierungsform, Unternehmenszweck und –gegenstand des Arbeitgebers.*'

[214] The descriptive elements in the following build primarily on Zöllner, Loritz, and Hergenröder, *Arbeitsrecht* (n 63) 454ff.

[215] Windbichler, *Arbeitsrecht im Konzern* (n 1) 26.

Gesamtbetriebsrat.[216] §54 BetrVG 1972 thus envisages the (voluntary) creation of a separate body to consult on matters that are of relevance across the entire *Konzern.*[217] It is constituted following an affirmative vote of the *Betriebsräte* representing at least 50 per cent of employees of all *Konzern* companies;[218] this threshold was lowered from 75 per cent in 2001 in order to facilitate and encourage the creation of KWCs. A European works council,[219] if constituted within the same corporate group, exists on a complementary basis—neither regime is exclusive. KWC membership is regulated by §55 BetrVG 1972, in parallel to the provisions for the *Gesamtbetriebsrat:*[220] there is no maximum number of members; each works council sends two representatives, who will be subject to the same duties and rights as other works council representatives.[221]

The duties of the KCW are laid out in §58I BetrVG 1972 and can be broadly summarized as areas that cannot be covered meaningfully by individual works councils, and those where the *Konzern* situation leads to a mandatory requirement of unified rules across the *Konzern,* or at least the *Unternehmen.* The latter power depends on concrete evidence of the circumstances; a mere desire for efficient coordination will not suffice.[222] When it comes to the distribution of powers, §58I BetrVG 1972 is deliberately designed along the lines of §50 BetrVG 1972 on the relationship between *Betriebs-* and *Gesamtbetriebsrat:* pursuant to the principle of subsidiarity, each function should be exercised at the lowest level possible.

To illustrate this distribution in each of the three main co-decision areas, for social matters any arrangements will only fall within the ambit of the KWC if their effect reaches across the entire *Konzern.*[223] In the field of personnel matters, the divide will usually mean that the KWC cannot get involved in individual measures (§99ff), focusing instead on matters of general policy and planning across the *Konzern.* In the economic dimension, finally, KWC can only get involved when there is a need for an *Interessensausgleich* or *Sozialplan* on the *Konzern*-level. Despite academic commentary to the contrary,[224] the KWC can furthermore not create a *Wirtschaftsausschuss* pursuant to §106I BetrVG 1972.[225]

In addition to these *inherent* powers, the KWC can also exercise functions delegated to it by the *Gesamtbetriebsrat* (§58II BetrVG 1972), as well as individual works councils in turn (§50II BetrVG 1972). Its work in this context is conceptually

---

[216] Liebscher, *Münchener Kommentar* (n 188) rn 1098.
[217] §58I BetrVG 1972 (n 59). This is different from §47 (*Gesamtbetriebsrat*).
[218] As very widely defined: BAG decision of 11.08.1993, AR Blattei ES 530.12.1 rn 5.
[219] Directive (EC) 38/2009 of the European Parliament and of the Council of 6 May 2009 on the establishment of a European Works Council or a procedure in Community-scale undertakings and Community-scale groups of undertakings for the purposes of informing and consulting employees [2009] OJ L122/28. Implemented in German law by the *Gesetz über Europäische Betriebsräte* 1996.
[220] §47II–VIII BetrVG 1972 (n 59).
[221] BAG decision of 20.12.1995, (1996) 13 NZA 945.
[222] BAG decision of 20.12.1995 (n 221).
[223] BAG decision of 21.56.1979, AP Nr. 1 §87 BetrVG 1972.
[224] W Trittin and others, *BetrVG—Kommentar für die Praxis* (10th edn Bund 2006) §58 rn 37: 'planwidrige Gesetzeslücke'.
[225] BAG decision of 23.08.1989, (1990) 7 NZA 863.

entirely different, however, as one entity merely acts as an agent for another.[226] The difference can be illustrated briefly in the context of *Betriebsvereinbarungen* (works agreements). Whether such agreements could exist on the *Konzern*-level was for a long time unclear,[227] until the BAG settled the matter in favour of KWCs, who may now conclude agreements that will apply throughout the corporate group in spite of its legal separation.[228] If negotiations are conducted on the basis of delegated authority, on the other hand, the resulting agreement will only be binding on the individual employer in question.[229]

In concluding, it should be re-emphasized that the KWC is an independent entity, neither above nor below other works councils in the works constitution.[230] Similarly, *Betriebsräte* at different levels are not subordinated to each other.[231] Their relative powers, however, are regulated by §58I BetrVG 1972, and limited to those issues that cannot be meaningfully addressed elsewhere.[232] This cross-entity focus becomes possible because of a shift in regulatory design: the BetrVG 1972 is based on an organizational and functional model of employee representation. The extent to which works constitution structures can transcend enterprise borders is directly linked to the *Konzern*'s degree of integration.[233] The reverse aspect of this model is that the *Konzern* dimension has no fundamental impact on whether there should be co-decision on certain matters, or the extent to which it should take place: the set of rights and duties as set out earlier should be subject only to logically required modifications.

C. *Mitbestimmung*

In the already contentious legislative history of the *Mitbestimmungsgesetz*, co-determination's impact on *Konzern* structures stands out as a particularly controversial area.[234] As the subsequent exposition of three *Konzern*-specific questions will show, this is to a significant extent reflected in the very different goals pursued by the relevant provisions of §§5 and 32 MitbestG 1976.

The first *Konzern*-specific danger under the co-determination provisions is the deliberate use of economic structures by employers trying to avoid the application of the MitbestG 1976:[235] by carving up a company into individual units, employee numbers could artificially fall beneath the relevant thresholds, thus

---

[226] The Courts have suggested that there is consequently no impact on the concept of the employer: BAG decision of 12.11.1997, (1998) 15 NZA 497.

[227] K Biedenkopf, 'Konzernbetriebsrat und Konzernbegriff' in P Zonderland (ed), *Liber amicorum Sanders* (Kluwer 1973) 1, 11ff.

[228] BAG decision of 22.01.2002, (2002) 19 NZA 1224.

[229] BAG decision of 12.11.1997 (n 226); Schwab, 'Der Konzernbetriebsrat—Seine Rechtsstellung und Zuständigkeit' (n 150).

[230] §58I 2 BetrVG 1972 (n 59).   [231] BAG decision of 12.11.1997 (n 226).

[232] Salamon, 'Die Konzernbetriebsvereinbarung beim Betriebsübergang' (n 113) 472.

[233] Windbichler, *Arbeitsrecht im Konzern* (n 1) 587, 592.

[234] T Raiser, 'Einleitung' in K Forster and others (eds), *Festschrift für Bruno Kropff. Aktien- und Bilanzrecht* (IDW 1997).

[235] Zöllner, Loritz, and Hergenröder, *Arbeitsrecht* (n 63) 575–6.

denying any avenue for employee voice on the supervisory board. The provisions in §5 control this danger through a series of attributions:[236] based on the contract of employment, individual workers are counted towards their *Unternehmen*, and in turn tallied up in line with each entity's membership of the corporate group.

From the workers' perspective, the second and arguably more fundamental danger to co-determination in a *Konzern* is as to its very effectiveness. It will be recalled that the MitbestG 1976 is designed to provide a system of economic employee co-determination, ie direct involvement in important entrepreneurial decisions.[237] In a chain of externally controlled enterprises, co-determination at the level of the subordinate company will however be of comparatively little value, as decisions are (at least substantively) taken elsewhere. By providing that co-determination is to take place at the highest *Konzern*-level, viz the *locus* of relevant decision-making,[238] the provisions of §5 MitbestG 1976 counteract the potential distortions resulting from group subordination.

Turning to the third *Konzern*-specific issue, it should be noted that attribution of employees under §5I MitbestG 1976 does not stop subordinate units from also having co-determination if their employee numbers exceed the threshold.[239] As a result of this cumulative approach, co-determination can end up going further than its proclaimed goal of employee-owner parity:[240] on the board of a large subordinated entity, the shareholder representatives will have to exercise their voting rights as instructed by the parent company board, thus giving effect to the will of both employees and owners as represented there. The fear is that this could result in two problems—employee voice on topics that are purely a matter for the shareholders and an excessive proportion of employee participation overall, as the employee representatives' voting on the subordinated company's supervisory board is not co-determined from above.

As the Federal Constitutional Court has held, in order for co-determination to be in line with the *Grundgesetz*, it must not represent a direct threat to shareholders' interests as the company's owners.[241] Property rights are constitutionally superior, however slightly. Indeed even the choice of co-determination on the supervisory board can be interpreted as a deliberate one in this context, by limiting the scope of co-determined matters primarily to executive officer selection and supervision.[242] It is therefore important to ensure that co-determination does not take place at the expense of the owners generally, and to avoid so-called employee 'over-parity' (*Überparität*)

---

[236] Windbichler, *Arbeitsrecht im Konzern* (n 1) 590.

[237] BVG decision of 01.03.1979, (1979) NJW 699. As Emmerich and Habersack, *Konzernrecht* (n 114) 68 note, the main historic reason for placing this at board level was to ensure employee involvement in the selection of executive officers.

[238] This is an *additional locus* of co-determination: Liebscher, *Münchener Kommentar* (n 188) rn 1115.

[239] Emmerich and Habersack, *Konzernrecht* (n 114) 73 go as far as describing this setup as 'against the system' ('*systemwidrig*').

[240] Zöllner, Loritz, and Hergenröder, *Arbeitsrecht* (n 63) 575–6.

[241] BVG decision of 01.03.1979 (n 236); R Schmidt, 'Das Mitbestimmungsgesetz auf dem verfassungsrechtlichen Prüfstand' (1980) 19 Der Staat 235, 254.

[242] §31 and §25I MitbestG 1976 (n 66) respectively.

in particular. §32 MitbestG 1976 ensures this protection of shareholders rights, by providing that certain decisions can only be taken by a majority of shareholder representatives on the supervisory board, especially as regards the selection of shareholder representatives in lower entities, and enterprise contracting.[243]

Conclusion

The results of the comparative enquiry in the present chapter have been in line with much more extensive German research on the subject:[244] in the individual employment law dimension, *Konzernrecht* does not generally influence the legal fundamentals of the contract of employment.[245] This is a major difference from the *Betriebsverfassungs-* and *Unternehmensmitbestimmungs-*contexts, where provisions such as §54ff BetrVG 1972 and §5 MitbestG 1976 operate across legally separate entities. Under the former, a *Konzern*-works council can be created as a separate body to consult on matters that are of relevance across the entire *Konzern*, and would therefore not be captured by consultation obligations on subsidiary units.[246] In the latter context, employee numbers in each subsidiary are attributed to the parent entity through a process of counting individual workers first towards their *Unternehmen*, and then tallying up those numbers in line with each entity's membership of the corporate group. The provisions furthermore ensure that co-determination can take place at the real *locus* of relevant decision making, up to and including the highest *Konzern* level, thus counteracting the potential distortions resulting from group subordination. Throughout, the economic and legal implications of the *Konzern* grouping are the explanation for the adaptation of general norms, as the impact of structurally inherent and temporally (reasonably) permanent subordination fundamentally changes the relationships between different stakeholder groups.

Having thus seen a cross-section of German employment law and tested the extent to which some of its provisions have come to be modified for application in complex corporate structures, the final part of this chapter returns to draw some broader conclusions from the material surveyed in Part II, and to note important pointers for the development and evaluation of potential solutions in domestic law. In concluding the previous chapter, three key lessons emerged to guide the eventual reconceptualization of the employer in the final part. The results of the comparative analysis confirm and further develop each of these points.

Avoiding Excessive Homogeneity

One of the underlying flaws that was identified as inherent in the received concept of the employer in English law was the assumption of homogeneity built

---

[243] §§291, 292 AktG 1965 (n 129).
[244] Windbichler, *Arbeitsrecht im Konzern* (n 1) 581ff.
[245] Windbichler, *Arbeitsrecht im Konzern* (n 1) describes this as group-proof ('*konzernfest*').
[246] §581 BetrVG 1972 (n 59).

into it, both as regards the concept itself (ie that it is substantively identical across all different regulatory domains) and the underlying matter to be regulated. The scrutinized aspects of German *Konzernrecht* avoid this to a certain extent, by focusing regulation on particular aspects of complex multilateral relationships.[247] It therefore recognizes the *intra-group specificity* of the joint exercise of employer functions, and relies on this observation to distinguish the corporate group or controlling block shareholder scenario from other situations such as dispersed ownership. It is this distinction, furthermore, which is then used to justify and shape a differentiated legal response.

An employing company's membership of a corporate group is not in and of itself an issue that requires legal remedies.[248] The above discussion, on the other hand, has identified a series of particular opportunities and dangers that can arise from such connections, and explored the purpose of various rules in addressing them. The unifying theme throughout was influence or control: the external (corporate) block shareholder has a strong enough impact on all facets of the subordinated enterprise to warrant a departure from standard legal rules.[249] The shared exercise of employer functions is on one end of a *Konzern* spectrum of control and subordination; contracts for partial control (*Teilbeherrschungsverträge*) on the other. Yet, as Däubler has demonstrated,[250] what all points on this spectrum have in common is an underlying lack of truly independent control given concentrated external direction powers. This deviation from the standard model serves both to justify a specific regulatory response in the first place, and explains the reliance on a combination of company and labour law mechanisms to achieve the desired goals.

Towards a Functional Approach

Previous chapters suggested that it is primarily the formalistic, not the multi-functional part of the tension inherent in the concept of the employer that constitutes the problem to be addressed. The selected examples at the intersection of German company and labour law have equally come to indicate that the key problem with a formalistic, purely contractual, approach is its vulnerability to changing economic structures. Even the presence of a contract of employment does not guarantee full employment law coverage where the exercise of employer functions is shared between, or divided up across, different entities. The solution to this issue lies in a shift to a functional approach, which must however be limited carefully in its operation and underpinned by a coherent conceptualization. The comparative enquiry in this chapter has

---

[247] As opposed to, for example, the regulation of temporary agency work: see text surrounding (n 2).

[248] Windbichler, *Arbeitsrecht im Konzern* (n 1) 592.

[249] Salamon, 'Die Konzernbetriebsvereinbarung beim Betriebsübergang' (n 113); Richardi, *Betriebsverfassungsgesetz: BetrVG* (n 147) §54 rn 4; Vor 54 rn 1.

[250] W Däubler, 'Ausklammerung sozialer und personeller Angelegenheiten aus einem Beherrschungsvertrag' (2005) 32 NZG 617, 619.

added a further dimension to this need for limits on any proposed functional reconceptualization.

First, by recognizing that, when attempting to modify the concept of the employer in complex multilateral work settings such as corporate groups, the concept can only be modified within the existing frameworks of employment and company law. This requires a methodology focused on problems and solutions specific to each situation instead of attempting the creation of distinct bodies of employment law. The functional approach, second, must be limited by existing concepts and approaches in neighbouring disciplines. This is illustrated in the individual dimension, where it is very clear that a combination of entities or even the whole group cannot become understood as a single-entity employer. The extension of specific obligations and liabilities to cover additional group companies, on the other hand, ensures a congruent scope of employment law coverage without threatening the fundamental setup of German group company law.

Developing Existing Frameworks

These observations are echoed in the earlier realization that any change must be logically linked to, and take account of, its point of departure in order to be successful. One crucial insight from the comparative work in this regard is the idea that a functional approach to the design and interpretation of the concept of the employer can achieve this balance of reconceptualization and respect for existing structures by relying on a combination of different regulatory methods, driven by the specific regulatory goals in different sub-domains of employment law.

The specific areas where modification of regulatory frameworks could be identified in the comparative work share similar goals: the effective, yet controlled, participation of workers in the management of their employing undertakings. At the same time, however, they rely on very different mechanisms to achieve these goals: §54 BetrVG 1972 creates a new entity, the *Konzernbetriebsrat*; §5 MitbestG 1976, on the other hand, adds employee representatives to an existing entity, the worker board representatives at the parent or holding company level. Two distinct regulatory models underlie these differences: one of managerial, and one of organizational, attachment.[251] A series of further distinctions between the two systems is frequently rehearsed:[252] the BetrVG 1972, for example, is firmly based in labour law, whereas the MitbestG 1976 has traditionally been claimed as a domain of company law. The former is limited to the *Betrieb* as the smallest organizational unit possible, and limits consultation to those areas which will have a direct impact on employees' lives; the level of co-decision however is direct and intense.

---

[251] Windbichler, *Arbeitsrecht im Konzern* (n 1) 582.
[252] Kort, 'Bildung und Stellung des Konzernbetriebsrats bei nationalen und internationalen Unternehmensverbindungen' (n 59) 466.

Under the MitbestG 1976, on the other hand, employees may participate in the full range of decisions concerning the undertaking, subject only to the limits on the role of the supervisory board. In return, the level of required cooperation, for example in dealing with a hostile employer, is limited to an advisory function. Neither of these distinctions necessitates a particular regulatory design. A potential answer may however become apparent from a simultaneous consideration of mechanisms and purpose.

The purpose of §54ff BetrVG 1972 is to ensure ongoing employee participation at relevant levels throughout the company, even if it is within a corporate group structure.[253] The place where this happens is crucial: at the *locus* of concrete exercise of an undertaking's control, which can be different according to the measure under consideration. A series of entities (works councils) is therefore created, following this function. This 'functional adaptation'[254] ensures a clear connection to the *Konzern*, whilst remaining flexible depending on the level of group centralization. At the same time it ensures that the modification does not go further than necessary:[255] there is no impact of the underlying structures of the enterprise.[256]

§5 MitbestG 1976, on the other hand, is aimed at ensuring the institutional attachment of co-determination to the employing organization.[257] Its technical focus is on the organizational connection to structures rather than individual circumstances. By putting employee representatives on the supervisory board, there is a direct impact on the underlying corporate structure, regardless of the actual exercise of different functions. Windbichler has analysed these differences as a gradation of legal responses to grouped companies, from the executive level (with no *Individualarbeitsrecht* consequences) via an organizational/functional mix (BetrVG 1972) to the purely organizational (MitbestG 1976).[258]

This final insight has an important implication for the subsequent chapter: it will have to survey a wide range of potential techniques that may be used in operationalizing a reconceptualized definition of the employer in English law, and consider in which contexts and combinations they are to be deployed. It is this task to which discussion now turns.

---

[253] BAG decision of 21.10.1980, (1982) NJW 1303.

[254] Windbichler, *Arbeitsrecht im Konzern* (n 1) 582: '*funktionale Anpassung*'.

[255] Kort, 'Bildung und Stellung des Konzernbetriebsrats bei nationalen und internationalen Unternehmensverbindungen' (n 59).

[256] Konzen, 'Arbeitnehmerschutz im Konzern' (n 179) 68 strongly disagrees. cf Kort, 'Bildung und Stellung des Konzernbetriebsrats bei nationalen und internationalen Unternehmensverbindungen' (n 59) 465.

[257] W Koberski and others, *Kommentar: Mitbestimmungsrecht* (4th edn Beck 2011) §5 rn 2–3.

[258] Windbichler, *Arbeitsrecht im Konzern* (n 1); C Windbichler, 'Unternehmerisches Zusammenwirken von Arbeitgebern als arbeitsrechtliches Problem. Eine Skizze auch vor dem Hintergrund der EG-Richtlinie zum Europäischen Betriebsrat in Unternehmensgruppen' (1996) ZfA 1.

PART III

TOWARDS A FUNCTIONAL CONCEPT OF THE EMPLOYER

Introduction

The goal of the third and final part of this work is to reconceptualize the employer in response to the problems identified in previous parts. Subsequent chapters will develop and test a new approach in a series of detailed steps; for present purposes it is important to set out a clear overarching goal against which the overall effort may eventually be evaluated. It is suggested that the only way a reconceptualization can be successful is by addressing the fundamental tension head-on: it is not possible simply to ignore either the unitary or the multi-functional strand, by radically departing from the existing case law or by proposing partial statutory intervention. Indeed, it is in this regard that previous attempts at grappling with the question at hand have struggled. In its place, a careful reconsideration of both functional and unitary aspects will be at the core of subsequent chapters. Before turning to this substantive discussion, two preliminary points should be made: a brief return to the key lessons observed in previous parts, and a reminder of the subtle methodological shift towards a normative approach, as first discussed in the Introduction.

Key Lessons from Earlier Parts

During the case law survey in Part I, as well as the results of the comparative enquiry into the legal mechanisms developed to address the specific problems arising from complex corporate groups in German law, a series of important lessons became apparent. These must be adhered to in order to ensure a successful reconceptualization of the employer.

As the investigation in Part II has shown, there is a strong assumption of homogeneity running in parallel with the conception of the employer as a unitary entity: that it must in fact always be the *same*, substantively identical, single entity throughout all areas of employment law. With the growth of statutory regulation of personal work relationships, the domains within the discipline have multiplied, from setting minimum wage levels and ensuring equal pay to trade union recognition and consultation and information of employees. Within each of these domains, the concept of the employer plays a crucial role, frequently as the key entity on which obligations fasten. In a complex multilateral employment scenario it is, however, a highly fictional assumption that it will always be the same entity (or combination of entities) that is best placed to operationalize the relevant function: given the possibility for shared exercise of key employer functions, this is a fictional concept derived directly from the unitary straitjacket as discussed in Chapter 1. In a Private Equity controlled company, for example, the worker's contractual counterparty will be best placed to ensure the payment of minimum wage levels if it is the entity operating payroll functions, whereas key decisions on redundancy may be taken elsewhere entirely, so that a limitation of consultation rights to the immediate contractual counterparty would hollow out the regime's protective purpose.

A second lesson to be recalled is that in the move towards a functional approach, both strands of the tension need to be addressed for a successful reconceptualization, even if in very different ways. The solution proposed below lies in a shift to a stronger functional approach, underpinned by a coherent single conceptualization. The primary problem with the current formalistic (ie purely contractual) approach is its vulnerability to changing economic structures: as previous chapters have shown, even the presence of a contract of employment does not guarantee full employment law coverage where the exercise of employer functions is shared between or divided up across different entities. There are, however, also some positive aspects of the unitary fiction, insofar as it provides doctrinal unity, gives employees a clear counterparty to sue for various claims and provides clear contours in causation enquiries. It will be important to maintain such positive facets in the process of removing a long-established conceptual straitjacket. On the functional side, a key temptation to be avoided is the initially simple thought that an answer to some of the practical problems identified could lie in the piecemeal creation of on-the-spot solutions, either through legislative intervention (with distinct and conceptually independent concepts of the employer in various contexts) or purposive judicial interpretation. Such an approach would quickly become incoherent, and could even prove counterproductive where compliance with employment law obligations is reduced to financial compensation.

Finally, it is important to remember at all stages that any change must be logically linked to, and take account of, its point of departure, instead of providing an ad-hoc attempt at remedying the problems in a particular situation, or set of work relations: as Chapter 2 demonstrated, difficulties encountered with the scope of employment law in complex multilateral arrangements are but symptoms of the deeper tensions inherent in the received concept of the employer. A functional approach to the design and interpretation of the concept of the employer should build directly on existing case law as identified in Part II, and must also be able to sit reasonably comfortably with other areas, notably company law.

The Shift Towards a Normative Approach

This final reminder is reflected in the second preliminary point that needs to be considered before embarking on the substantive task of the following chapters: the methodological departure from earlier parts. The approach thus far has been fundamentally analytical–descriptive, discovering a problem in the current law and explaining its implications. The third part is a careful move beyond earlier work into a deliberately normative stance: the proposed reconceptualization suggests that the only way of resolving the fundamental issue at stake is a novel approach to our conception of the employer. The following paragraphs give an account of this move by explaining the need for such a step, addressing potential concerns associated with it by demonstrating how it builds on existing foundations, and briefly locating the chosen approach in the light of methodological theory.

A shift towards a normative approach becomes necessary at this stage because the analytical–descriptive methodology deployed thus far has reached its limits. As earlier chapters amply demonstrate, the multi-functional and unitary strands currently implicit in the concept of the employer lead to a conceptual deadlock in situations beyond a narrow paradigm. Furthermore, it has already become clear that attempts at devising a piecemeal approach to solutions cannot work. The utility of an analytical–descriptive method in overcoming the problem is exhausted with its extensive presentation of the latter. The case for a departure might be put even more explicitly: continuing in a purely descriptive manner could preclude the present effort from arriving at a solution. Indeed, it has been suggested that sticking religiously to such an approach while working with traditional norms in rapidly changing contexts can lead to 'mental imprisonment, the walls of which are self-constructed'.[1] In keeping in line with the careful shift from what the current concept of the employer *is* towards what it *could*, and *should*, be as developed in the Introduction,[2] subsequent chapters will however not seek to suggest any radical departure, but rather focus on a gradual adaptation of existing principles.[3]

That said, two related terminological issues which are less easy to resolve within existing frameworks need to be acknowledged openly: first, as regards the 'common sense' or general linguistic approach to what the words 'the employer' mean in everyday usage. It is not suggested that the proverbial reasonable 'man on the Clapham omnibus'[4] would readily perceive the word 'employer' to mean anything other than the anthropomorphic unitary counterparty to a contract of employment as described extensively in Chapter 1. The proposed solution may in certain

---

[1] L Nogler, 'Die Typologisch-Funktionale Methode am Beispiel des Arbeitnehmerbegriffs' (2009) 10 ZESAR §459, 467: '*Sie geraten in ein geistiges Gefängnis, dessen Mauern sie selbst errichtet haben.*'

[2] C Harlow, 'Changing the Mindset: The Place of Theory in English Administrative Law' (1994) 14 OJLS 419, 426, citing A Dicey, *Introduction to the Study of the Law of the Constitution* (Macmillan 1885) Preface to the First Edition, vii.

[3] D Marsden, '"The Network Economy" and Models of the Employment Contract' (2004) 42 BJIR 659, 671.

[4] *McQuire v Western Morning News* [1903] 2 KB 100 (CA) 109.

factual scenarios lead to context-specific variations as to the precise identity of the entity, or indeed entities, on whom legal obligations fasten: a potentially radical departure in linguistic terms, insofar as the legal concept of the employer is extended beyond contractual privity to an array of relevant parties, will not always fit with 'the employer' as used in common parlance. It is of course not in and of itself problematic if legal concepts depart at points from the ordinary meaning of a concept, be it to broaden or narrow it.[5] Indeed, it is frequently already the case that the 'legal meaning of the employer is not synonymous with the sociological or economic idea of the "enterprise" or "organisation" '.[6]

Second, as regards the difference in the use of the word employer between previous parts and the remaining two chapters: in Chapters 1 through 4, 'employer' when used in a technical sense referred to the received common law concept. The methodological shift towards a normative analysis in this part will not be accompanied by a shift in terminology: it is the *meaning* of the legal concept of the employer that needs to change, rather than the label attached to it. In proceeding thus, the terminology deployed can fully reflect the underlying normative argument, as set out at the beginning of Chapter 5. A detailed explanation for this choice will be offered in the course of the final chapter; suffice it to say for the moment that any other approach, such as the coining of a new term, would serve only to confirm and thus perpetuate the underlying problems instead of addressing them head-on.

Without straying too far into the territory of methodological scholarship, it is suggested that the cautious normativity advocated sits comfortably in the centre of a spectrum of potential approaches: the aim of the overall work, and Chapters 5 and 6 in particular, is to move beyond the careful balancing of competing intellectual arguments;[7] its effort can thus be characterized as normative. On the other hand, this stance does not necessarily mean that it will go as far as putting forward strong claims for systemic change, in line with the clear sense of vocation for labour law scholarship advocated by Collins,[8] where drawing on the historic roots of the subject the 'main object of labour law [is] to be a countervailing force to counteract the inequality of bargaining power which is inherent . . . in the employment relationship'.[9] This limitation does not necessarily imply a fundamental disagreement with such an approach, but is imposed rather because the task at hand is a much narrower one: to reconceptualize the employer in response to a specific contradiction. The effect of restoring conceptual coherence may of course be the extension of employment law coverage to situations currently outside its regulatory scope;[10] it is, however, suggested that this will only be done to

---

[5] J Bell and G Engle, *Cross on Statutory Interpretation* (3rd edn Butterworths 1995) 72–5.

[6] S Deakin, 'The Changing Concept of the "Employer" in Labour Law' (2001) 30 ILJ 72, 73.

[7] J Smits, 'Redefining Normative Legal Science: Towards an Argumentative Discipline' in F Coomans, F Grünfeld, and M Kamminga (eds), *Methods Of Human Rights Research* (Intersentia 2009).

[8] H Collins, 'Labour Law as a Vocation' (1989) 105 LQR 468.

[9] Collins, 'Labour Law as a Vocation' (n 8) 469, citing P Davies and M Freedland (eds), *Kahn-Freund's Labour and the Law* (3rd edn Stevens 1983) 18.

[10] P Davies and M Freedland, 'The Complexities of the Employing Enterprise' in G Davidov and B Langile (eds), *Boundaries and Frontiers of Labour Law* (Hart Publishing 2006) 277.

the extent of restoring coverage in line with its original regulatory design, rather than actively expanding employment protection.

In this sense, the present approach is perhaps closest to what Harlow had in mind when advocating a stronger role for 'theory' in shaping and analysing the law. It is hoped that any potentially 'opprobrious resonance'[11] of such endeavours will be limited by staying within the realm of theory marked by a 'principled attitude to the development of . . . legal concepts'.[12] The proposed reconceptualization is thus in line with the role of theory as advocated by Jane Stapleton,[13] as the functional concept developed in Chapter 5 aims not only to explain the core but also the boundaries of liability scenarios by identifying relevant counterparties and explaining causal requirements; all in line with deeper underlying principles to be developed in the final chapter.

Structure

With these preliminary remarks in mind, the third part is structured around the functional and unitary strands of the concept of the employer, with a chapter broadly dedicated to exploring the necessary changes to each. Chapter 5 develops the multi-functional limb to show how a careful extension to a fully functional concept can be achieved. Chapter 6 then turns to addressing the unitary strand to show that, while some clear breaks have to be made from the existing setup (particularly as regards privity, and the operation of the employer concept across different substantive domains), there is a clear overarching concept of the employer which unifies even complex substantive manifestations.

---

[11] Harlow, 'Changing the Mindset: The Place of Theory in English Administrative Law' (n 2) 420.
[12] Harlow, 'Changing the Mindset: The Place of Theory in English Administrative Law' (n 2) 421.
[13] J Stapleton, *Product Liability* (Butterworths 1994) 95–6.

5

A Functional Concept

Introduction

In developing a functional concept of the employer, discussion in this chapter will be divided into three broad steps, each with further subdivisions according to the analysis pursued. Section 1 develops the meaning of a 'functional' concept on an abstract or conceptual level. Section 2 then turns to an exploration of different legal avenues that may be used to put a functional concept into operation under existing law. A concluding section, finally, evaluates the proposed reconceptualization of the first strand against the criteria developed in earlier parts.

Section 1: Functional Definitions

As suggested in the introduction, this chapter will argue for a shift in how English law conceptualizes the employer, moving from the current rigidly formalistic approach to a flexible, *functional* concept. In more concrete terms, the following working definition is offered in order to draw together the range of specific elements to be discussed in greater detail, below. It is submitted that employer should come to mean:

the entity, or combination of entities, playing a decisive role in the exercise of relational employing functions, as regulated or controlled in each particular domain of employment law.

The first section of this chapter is dedicated to an exploration, on a more abstract level, of the idea of a 'functional definition'. Three crucial implications of such a reconceptualization, as traced through the following subsections, should be made clear at the outset. First, that employment law obligations may be spread across multiple legal entities. This is the core of the reconceptualization's challenge to the received concept of the employer as a single entity. Second, as the functions of the employer can be subdivided into distinct groups, the employer is no longer exclusively defined as an entity exercising a single and simple function comprising all elements identified: exercising a particular subset of employer functions may suffice to trigger responsibility in that regard. Which of the functions are relevant depends on the particular area of legal regulation: the third implication of the functional approach proposed is that the attribution of employer responsibility will differ across distinct domains within employment law. The legal techniques for achieving such effects will be explored in the subsequent section; it is nonetheless important to elaborate on these potential consequences at an early stage.

A functional approach will, first, often identify a multiplicity of employers on the facts of multilateral employment situations. Historically, when faced with an array of potential counterparties in multi-employer scenarios, privity of contract guided decisions as to where employment law obligations would be placed. An important part of the reconceptualized definition of the employer is the fact that different entities, or even a combination of distinct legal entities, could now be faced with employment law obligations, depending on the particular function and context in question. Second, this distribution of employment law obligations is driven by the multi-functional mode of defining the employer: responsibility attaches to each subset of functions, regardless of whether they are exercised in combination with all other functions by a single legal entity, parcelled out between different parties, or shared across multiple entities.

The third important consequence to note results directly from the earlier observations. Under a functional approach, the identity of the employer acquires a degree of context- or domain-specificity: depending on the regulatory context, different subsets of the five employing functions will be of particular significance in identifying the responsible counterparty or counterparties. Whilst differences (potential or actual) in the concept of the employer across areas such as tax, tort, vicarious liability, and 'employment law proper' have long been the subject of academic and judicial discussion,[1] the proposed definition goes further: adopting a functional method allows for even more detailed differentiation within what may all too easily have become perceived as a single regulatory domain.[2] The resulting responsiveness to different regulatory goals of distinct domains of employment law should not be mistaken as an element of the definition of the employer. As subsection A explains immediately below, it will be important not to confuse the different senses in which a concept can be 'functional'.

Calling for a functional definition of the employer is not a completely novel approach to the problems identified in previous parts. Fudge, for example, has long noted the 'need to go beyond contract and the corporate form, and adopt a relational and functional approach to ascribing employment-related responsibilities in situations involving multilateral work arrangements in employing enterprises'.[3] The present chapter hopes to contribute to that effort, by providing both theoretical foundations and practical illustrations for the workings of such a reconceptualization. Indeed, as subsequent paragraphs will show, the link between the 'relational' and the 'functional' aspects mentioned by Fudge are

---

[1] See eg E McKendrick, 'Vicarious Liability and Independent Contractors: A Re-Examination' (1990) 53 MLR 770.

[2] Though cf a notable countermove: M Freedland and N Kountouris, *The Legal Construction of Personal Work Relations* (OUP 2011) 17, 25ff.

[3] J Fudge, 'Fragmenting Work and Fragmenting Organizations: the Contract of Employment and the Scope of Labour Regulation' (2006) 44 Osgoode Hall Law Journal 609, 636.

crucial stepping-stones in the process. Writing in the domestic context of agency workers some ten years ago, Deakin similarly suggested the development of a functional concept of the employer, focusing on the functions of 'coordination', 'risk', and 'equity' as guiding principles.[4] The present effort may at first sight appear somewhat different from this work, both in terms of terminology and scope; it is nonetheless in line with Deakin's suggestion that 'obligations which would normally attach to the exercise of employer functions are to be imposed upon the relevant parties in each case'.[5]

With this background in mind, discussion turns to the development and close scrutiny of the idea of a functional concept of the employer: an initial subsection draws together the existing foundations for a functional approach, before explaining and developing it in the light of theoretical models. Attention will then be given to the crucial limitations of the proposed functional reconceptualization.

A. From Multiple Functions to a Functional Concept

The foundations for a functional concept of the employer can be traced back to the traditional tests for employment status. As the review of existing case law in Chapter 1 showed, the law already identifies and regulates a wide range of employer functions, which have been grouped together for analytical purposes into the following five categories:

[1] **Inception and Termination of the Contract of Employment**

> This category includes all powers of the employer over the very existence of its relationship with the employee.

[2] **Receiving Labour and its Fruits**

> Duties owed by the employee to the employer, specifically to provide his or her labour and the results thereof, as well as rights incidental to it.

[3] **Providing Work and Pay**

> The employer's obligations towards its employees.

[4] **Managing the Enterprise-Internal Market**

> Coordination through control over all factors of production.

[5] **Managing the Enterprise-External Market**

> Undertaking economic activity in return for potential profit, whilst also being exposed to any losses that may result from the enterprise

A 'function' of being an employer was earlier defined as one of the various actions employers are entitled or obliged to take as part of the bundle of rights and duties falling within the scope of the open-ended contract of service. The common law,

---

[4] S Deakin, 'The Changing Concept of the "Employer" in Labour Law' (2001) 30 ILJ 7279.
[5] Deakin, 'The Changing Concept of the "Employer"' (n 4) 81.

it was suggested, recognizes these different functions in order to identify and classify employment relationships, and thus indirectly the concept of the employer. In revisiting the functional groups, it can be noted further that each function is in some way regulated by at least one domain of employment law. Indeed, as the following examples show, there are frequently several distinct or overlapping areas, each with different sources and regulatory techniques, involved in regulating or controlling the exercise of such functions.

As regards function [1], *Control over the Inception and Termination of the Employment Relationship*, for example, the employer's power over the very existence of a contract of services is regulated in a host of different areas, from anti-discrimination provisions and individual dismissal (both in statute and at common law) to consultation obligations in the case of employer decisions affecting larger groups of workers. Function [3], *Providing Work and Pay*, is regulated at common law under doctrines springing from the law of the contract of employment, ranging from a duty to pay, sometimes even when no work is done,[6] to potentially even a duty to provide work,[7] and a range of statutory provisions, including for example minimum wage levels.[8] Even function [4], the *Management of the Enterprise-Internal Market*, which could be seen as driven by contractual direction rights,[9] is subject to limitations at common law,[10] as well as a host of legislative interventions, for example through provisions on workers' health and safety.[11]

Despite the increasing recognition of these groups of functions and the application to them of different regulatory techniques in employment law, the problems identified in earlier parts continue to exist. This, it has already been suggested, is because their use as a criterion is overshadowed by historical assumptions leading to a unitary straitjacket in anything beyond the narrow factual paradigm situation of an independent single entity exercising all five functions. Refocusing attention on a functional definition of the employer will allow the concept to break free from this single view through a detailed analysis of each individual function or groups of functions: from an array of legal entities linked to the employee, employment law obligations will be attached to whichever entity, or combination of entities, is exercising that very function, or plays a decisive role in its exercise. Whilst the outcome of applying a functional approach may therefore on occasion be radically different from the current, purely contractual, solutions, it is an approach fundamentally grounded

---

[6] *Clark v Oxfordshire HA* [1998] IRLR 125 (CA).

[7] *Nethermere (St Neots) Ltd v Gardiner* [1984] ICR 612 (CA) 632F (Dillon LJ). Although it has also been suggested that it might not be necessary for the courts to decide if an employer's duty is to provide a reasonable amount of work, or merely to pay an agreed and reasonable sum (Kerr LJ in dissent).

[8] National Minimum Wage Act 1998.

[9] R Coase, 'The Nature of the Firm' (1937) 4 Economica 386.

[10] *Simmons v Heath Laundry* [1910] 1 KB 543 (CA). The right need not be unrestricted: *Ready Mixed Concrete Ltd v Minister of Pensions* [1968] 2 QB 497 (HC).

[11] Construction (Working Places) Regulations 1966, SI 1966/94, reg 28(1): *Ferguson v John Dawson Ltd* [1976] 1 WLR 1213 (CA).

in existing legal avenues, yet carefully developing particular aspects of employment regulation.

B. Functional Typology

In order to embrace a functional approach, the law's underlying methods of reasoning need to evolve in part. The following discussion takes a step back to consider the meaning of 'functional' in the proposed functional concept on a more abstract level, in the hope that this will allow for a clearer account of that approach. It further aims to develop functional typology as a richer concept than simply a contrast to the perceived formalism of the current bilateral-contractual approach,[12] thus avoiding at least some of the dangers of the 'transcendental nonsense' which can result from the indiscriminate use of the 'functional approach' as a panacea to various analytical problems, 'often . . . with as little meaning as any of the magical legal concepts against which it is directed'.[13]

At the outset, it is crucial to note the relationship of the functional approach to be proposed with another prominent use of that label.[14] Academic work frequently describes itself as analysing law from a functional perspective, 'ie, in terms of the economic functions it seeks to perform, instead of simply describing the contents of the laws'.[15] It has already been suggested that an important consequence of reconceptualizing the employer will be its reflexivity to the aims, or socio-economic functions, of particular domains or layers of employment law. It could therefore be said that the concept of the employer also becomes a functional one, in the second sense of being aligned with those aims.

This, however, is an *analytical description* of the results of the functional approach in the present sense, where the exercise of a particular function is the basis for *defining* an entity as an employer. The two uses of the term are thus not mutually exclusive; they simply describe very different aspects of the reconceptualization. This can be illustrated by a brief attempt to use functionality in its analytical-descriptive sense for definitional purposes: the concept of the employer would simply become 'whatever it should be' for the purposes of, say, unfair dismissal or non-discrimination legislation. Such a definition would be hopelessly imprecise and unworkable. By recognizing the dual meanings of the term 'functional', however, it is possible to avoid this trap. Whilst the proposed definition can thus be said to be functional in both senses, they are relevant for different endeavours: the definition of the employer, and an *ex post facto*

---

[12] J Fudge, 'The Legal Boundaries of the Employer, Precarious Workers, and Labour Protection' in G Davidov and B Langile (eds), *Boundaries and Frontiers of Labour Law* (Hart 2006) 310–13.

[13] F Cohen, 'Transcendental Nonsense and the Functional Approach' (1935) 35 Columbia Law Review 809, 822.

[14] Frequently used, for example, in corporate law scholarship: W Douglas, 'A Functional Approach to the Law of Business Associations' (1928–29) 23 Illinois Law Review 673.

[15] J Payne, 'Book Review: the Anatomy of Corporate Law' (2010) 11 EBOR 477. In a sense, the same is true of 'functionalism' as used in sociology: L Nogler, 'Die Typologisch-Funktionale Methode am Beispiel des Arbeitnehmerbegriffs' (2009) 10 ZESAR 459, 463.

analytical description of the socio-economic consequences of adopting the new concept.

The account of functionalism proposed for purposes of identifying and defining the employer builds on the sociological concept of functional typologies, relying on the exercise of particular functions to determine the status of potential counterparties. A full exploration of the relevant sociological literature is beyond the scope of this work; the focus will instead be on Nogler's writing in a closely related area, applying different typological models to the determination of employee status.[16] In order to arrive at the functional typology proposed, two competing models will be evaluated and illustrated with examples from the domestic context. Approached thus, the inherent limitations of the current approach quickly become evident, and form the stepping-stones for a functional approach.

Nogler identifies two traditional approaches to the legal classification of complex factual patterns in employment law, both elements of which can be found in the contradictory strands of the current concept of the employer. Indeed, it could be argued that the current approach combines some of the worst features of the two models.

On one level, English employment law simply hopes to categorize employers according to a very simple scheme through the use of 'abstract-generalist terms',[17] ie a definition which rigorously lays down specific criteria to be met in each case. The limitations of this approach are not difficult to see: faced with endless variations of facts and changing circumstances, the application of specific criteria becomes increasingly capricious. The definition of the employer in section 230(4) of the Employment Rights Act 1996 as 'the person by whom the employee or worker is (or, where the employment has ceased, was) employed' is a clear example of the shortcomings of this abstract-generalist approach. Whether or not an entity is an employer becomes a question of the presence of specified element(s), which may not even be logically linked: in the domestic context these are the exercise of certain employer functions, combined with the existence of a particular link in the form of a contract of employment.

A shift to analytical typologies was initially perceived as a successful response to these shortcomings of abstract-generalist terms.[18] In its original conception,[19] this approach offers several relative advantages: the categories (or typologies) are open, in the sense of there being no fixed list of criteria, all of which are to be met; at the same time their openness allows for gradation within each category. Nogler, however, identifies a range of problems for the legal classification of complex factual patterns: first, there is still a deep underlying assumption that a category such as 'the employer' has a single, clear definition, universally applicable and

---

[16] Nogler, 'Die Typologisch-Funktionale Methode' (n 15). The following paragraphs draw extensively on this article and related work.

[17] Nogler, 'Die Typologisch-Funktionale Methode' (n 15) 460, citing Guardini, *Der Gegensatz. Versuch zu einer Philosophie des Lebendig-Konkreten* (4th edn Schoningh 1998) 17.

[18] Abstract discussions beyond the scope of the present work can be found eg in Hempel, 'Typological Methods in the Social Sciences' in M Nathanson (ed), *Philosophy of the Social Sciences* (Random House 1952) 46.

[19] Nogler, 'Die Typologisch-Funktionale Methode' (n 15) 461.

substantially identical, all components of which can be determined in advance in such a way that future real world scenarios will always fall within them. The English courts' struggle to develop various series of tests for employee status can be seen as a clear example of this difficulty. Second, it is questionable whether gradation (in the present context, for example, on a sliding scale of 'more of an employer' to 'less of an employer') is analytically useful in employment law regulation. As criticism of the judicial analysis of the worker concept (which attempted just such an approach) shows,[20] gradation will frequently lead to a lowest common denominator level of protection.[21] Indeed, it could even be argued that such gradation is a symptom of a deeper underlying problem, that of the currently insufficient recognition of subtle distinctions between different domains of employment law, by allowing for worker protective levels to be set on a general sliding scale instead of responding to the specific regulatory aims of a particular domain.

Having identified these flaws with existing classificatory attempts, Nogler expresses his conviction 'that in between the (too) strict approach of positivist analysis and the (too) unclear approach of classic typologies there exists a *tertium datur* which permits the development of solutions focussed on the structure of each individual scenario, whilst at the same time presenting a clear rule':[22] in other words, a functional typology.

The key idea of this *functional approach* is to focus on the specific role different elements play in the relevant context, instead of looking at the mere absence or presence of predetermined factors.[23] The presence of a contract of employment (or other contract),[24] for example, can thus be an important indicator in particular fields (for example the obligation to pay wages), but it is by no means the only one. To adapt Nogler's language to the present proposal, a functional concept of the employer is one where the employing entity or entities are defined not via the absence or presence of a particular factor, but via the exercise of specific functions.[25] This exercise of specific functions extends to include a decisive role in their exercise, in order to take account of the judicial recognition in existing cases that as regards employer functions the right to play a decisive role in a particular function is as relevant as the actual exercise thereof.

The working definition set out initially suggested that the concept of the employer should be understood as the entity, or combination of entities, playing a decisive role in the exercise of relational employing functions, as regulated or controlled in each particular domain of employment law. There are several steps in putting this abstract conceptualization into practice. First is the

---

[20] Most notably *Redrow Homes Ltd v Wright* [2004] EWCA Civ 469, [2004] 3 All ER 98. Though cf now the Supreme Court's decision in *Clyde & Co LLP v Bates van Winkelhof* [2014] UKSC 32, [2014] 1 WLR 2047 [26].

[21] G Davidov, 'Who is a Worker?' (2005) 34 ILJ 57.

[22] Nogler, 'Die Typologisch-Funktionale Methode' (n 15) 462.

[23] Nogler, 'Die Typologisch-Funktionale Methode' (n 15) pt 3.

[24] This would be particularly true if the analysis were applied beyond the core 'employee' category under scrutiny, as discussed in the Introduction.

[25] Nogler, 'Die Typologisch-Funktionale Methode' (n 15) 463.

recognition that, for each employee, a functional approach to different models of inter-entity relationships will lead to an *array* of potential employing entities, from which one or several may emerge as employers. Being within this array of potential counterparties does not automatically bring any specific set of employment law obligations with it, even less so responsibility for the full domain of labour regulation. It is only as a consequence of the exercise of a particular regulated function that employer responsibilities are triggered; limited, however, to the relevant domain or domains. Without going into details of practical operation—the subject of extensive discussion in the subsequent section of this chapter—several fictional examples on the basis of fairly common factual patterns may serve to illustrate this further.

The array of those with a decisive role in management, particularly as regards the exercise of employer functions, will vary depending on the context in which the employing enterprises are organized. In triangular employment relationships, for example, it may include both agency and end-user, despite their difference in organizational integration or economic interest alignment. In a Private Equity setting, both the 'immediate' employer (ie the portfolio company) and the PE management company will find themselves within the array. It may also extend further, including for example a franchisor with very tight control over the operations of a particular franchisee.[26] Under the traditional approach, privity (or at most a specific statutory extension) would select the employer from this array of entities potentially able to exercise employer functions. In the reconceptualized definition of the employer this role is replaced by the exercise of various functions. As a result, different employers may bear (or share) a range of obligations, depending always on their specific roles.

A first possible illustration is the decision taken by a Private Equity management company to reorganize a large manufacturing plant by shutting down a particular production line. The selection of individual employees to be dismissed is left to the portfolio company management, who see this as an opportunity to terminate the employment of protected individuals (such as trade unionists, or members of a minority group). Even in this relatively simple example, different employer functions are exercised in different domains; the functional concept can nonetheless respond adequately: for the purposes of mass redundancy consultation, both the PE management company and company management will be 'employers', as they have exercised the regulated function (decisions affecting the employment of a certain minimum number of workers); as regards possible discrimination or protected dismissal claims, on the other hand, liability will fall on the portfolio company alone.

Another scenario could arise in the context of hotels operated as franchise businesses, with the franchisor laying down, monitoring, and enforcing strict regulations for the conduct of evening performances, including a uniform dress code for all dancers and the equipment to be used. As the dresses and equipment turn out

---

[26] D Weil, *The Fissured Workplace* (Harvard University Press 2014) 122ff.

to be highly impractical for their shows, entertainers in hotels regularly end up injured during performances—it is the franchisor on whom the relevant health and safety provisions would fall. In the case of a disabled receptionist whose wheelchair cannot fit under the hotel's front desk, on the other hand, the employer's duty of reasonable adjustments would lie with the hotel alone.

Building on Davidov,[27] a final multilateral example could be the end-user who contracts with an agency for the supply of labour at an incredibly low price, evidently well below the legal minimum wage. In this scenario, the agency itself is in breach of the relevant regulations and will be seen as the employer for that purpose. As the end-user is also involved in the remuneration function, even if only indirectly, it too will be considered as an employer. If, on the other hand, a temporary worker comes up with a particular invention, the employer for purposes of a subsequent claim over patent rights will be the end-user, as it alone exercised the relevant role of the employer (for example training and provision of facilities) in that field.[28]

A detailed discussion of potential avenues to operationalize each of these options follows imminently. For the time being, the breadth and flexibility of outcomes resulting from a functional concept have been demonstrated. The methodology thus proposed allows for a very subtle approach to effective employment law enforcement, as it is able to 'take account of inter-firm relationships so as to determine each firm's respective share of responsibility for such events as may occur over the course of the employment relationship'.[29] By looking at the full range of functions exercised across various relationships to determine actual responsibility, obligations are placed on the most relevant party or parties, but not beyond them. Whilst the advantages of a functional approach will be discussed more extensively below, suffice it to say at present that this conceptualization allows for flexibility across different regulatory domains, and can thus deal with the complexities arising from the fact that there are multiple entities, and multiple modes in which these entities can share the exercise of employer functions. It furthermore avoids several of the traps that other potential approaches to bringing more entities into employer status suffer from, from reliance on narrow external doctrines such as fraud to the artificial assimilation of formally independent entities into a single legal personality.

C. The Outer Limits of a Functional Concept

Having thus explored how the exercise of a relevant function can include a wider range of entities in the realm of employment law regulation, the question as to

---

[27] G Davidov, 'Joint Employer Status in Triangular Employment Relationships' (2004) 42 BJIR 727.

[28] M Freedland and J Prassl, 'Resolving Ownership Invention Disputes: Limitations of the Contract of Employment' in M Pittard (ed), *Business Innovation—A Legal Balancing Act* (Edward Elgar 2012).

[29] M Morin, 'Labour Law and New Forms of Corporate Organization' (2005) 144 International Labour Review 5, 15 (as quoted in Fudge 'The Legal Boundaries of the Employer, Precarious Workers, and Labour Protection' (n 12) 645).

how the array of potential counterparties may be limited arises. In order for the functional concept of the employer to be workable, there also need to be clear outer limits, in order to avoid a search for any factors that may have influenced the 'real decision-maker', or even any causative event leading up to the exercise of a relevant employer function. Indeed, if all such factors were to be included in the reconceptualized definition, it would render most existing norms unworkable.

Employment law generally does not regulate dealings between arm's length parties, such as, for example, the breach of a commercial supply of goods contract between two companies. At the same time, however, such decisions may have a knock-on effect on employment: without orders, the counterparty might no longer be able to sustain production levels, or in the worst-case scenario cease to exist, thus leading to collective redundancies. In order to avoid an extension of employment law into such situations, narrower limits need to be drawn. Indeed, amongst the few positive aspects of a strictly bilateral analysis of the employer-employee relationship was its ability to act as a clear safeguard, causation-wise: whilst frequently placed too narrowly, it nonetheless has the virtue of easily identifying limits of responsibility. It is suggested that the functional definition put forward fulfils this function equally well, without however distorting the scope of legal protection: by focusing on the exercise of, or decisive legal role in the exercise of, employer functions, it ensures congruent employment law coverage that is neither under- nor over-determinative.

The functional approach proposed is *not* purely causation-based. If such a model were adopted and taken to its logical extreme, a major customer not renewing a substantial order would be under a duty to consider its decision's impact on employees; indeed anyone in a causal relationship may be caught. The crucial limitation in the proposed definition is a relational one, looking at the relationship between the relevant parties, and focused on the exercise of regulated functions *quoad* these relationships: these are the crucial factors in determining which actions constitute 'the exercise of employer functions'. Termination of a commercial supply contract, for example, would therefore not be the exercise of an employer function, as neither the relationship between supplier and producer nor the action of not placing further orders falls within the scope of employment law.

In his work on the ascription of legal responsibility in multi-entity scenarios,[30] Collins identified three forms of 'bonding between productive organisations': ownership, contract, and authority. Ownership bonds, usually via an outright holding of the majority or even all shares in subsidiaries, describe what has already been seen in corporate groups and Private Equity fund structures. As regards contractual bonds, Collins suggests examples from construction and manufacturing industries, describing the creation of cores and peripheries. The most relevant instantiation of this linkage for present purposes are triangular work agency setups, which characterize situations of parcelled out employer functions even though the entities involved will not usually be economically

---

[30] H Collins, 'Ascription of Legal Responsibility to Groups in Complex Patterns of Economic Integration' (1990) 53 MLR 731, 733–4.

aligned. Finally, there are more diffuse 'authority relations', including sharehold-ers with a significant minority equity stake, but also creditors, anyone else on the powerful end of a relationship of economic dependence, and even professional advisers.

Collins rightly suggests that in general, none of these forms of bonding should be enough in and of itself to contradict basic group liability principles of each legal entity's individual responsibility. At the same time, reliance on the contract of employment alone will leave many relevant situations beyond the reach of protec-tive norms. A functional approach to the concept of the employer as developed in this chapter can strike a successful balance between these extremes, by drawing the line at entities' exercise of employer functions, including a legal right to have a decisive role in so doing.

The goal is to ensure congruent legal coverage in situations where multiple enti-ties exercise some form of direct control over the employment relationship—but drawing on the functional approach suggested, the precise kind or mechanisms of bonding matter less than what its function is: if it is to give a legal right to exercise an employer function, or a legal right to have a decisive role in the exercise of such a function, then the party will be within the realm of potential employers. As has been seen, a commercial supply contract, even if written in favour of a financially dominant company, will not usually come within this scope. The functional limi-tation is more than just a pragmatic choice: it remains flexible to adjust to the spe-cific role a combination of factors may play in a particular context. The fictional customer who decides to breach its supply agreement would not be performing a function of the employer (and is therefore beyond the potential array of coun-terparties), even though its actions will have causative impact on the employer's actual decision-making.

As the Court of Appeal's recent decision in *Shanahan Engineering* shows,[31] the courts are well equipped and comfortable to draw these sorts of distinctions on the facts of individual cases. There, the energy company Alstom had contracted with Shanahan, a labour supplier who was paid at cost plus arrangement fees, to construct a set of reactors. Upon a change in external circumstances, Alstom decided to switch from simultaneous to sequential construction, thus reducing its manpower requirements. It instructed Shanahan in writing to 'review the resources on site and optimise those resources in line with the new schedule. It is Alstom's expectation that this will result in an immediate reduction of both indirect and craft labour whilst maintaining compliance with the [relevant regu-latory] agreement'. Shanahan's local manager consequently selected a number of employees for redundancy, and presented the trade union representatives with a final decision, having failed to consult them previously. On the facts, the special circumstances defence in section 188 of TULRCA 1992 was not made out, as even though 'instructions given by Alstom made it inevitable that the workforce on the contract would have to be reduced', there had been a wide range of options

---

[31] *Shanahan Engineering Ltd v Unite the Union* [2010] UKEAT/0411/09/DM.

left to the company, thus placing them under a duty to consult with workforce representatives.[32]

The Court furthermore made it clear that no reliance could have been placed on the external control provisions, 'no doubt because, although Alstom controlled the contract and the work, Alstom did not control Shanahan'.[33] Even if a functional test were normally to place obligations on the party who actually took the decision leading to collective redundancies, rather than the immediate party to the contract of employment, there is no need to fear the liability floodgates.[34] Courts are able to draw appropriate distinctions between different situations, whether by using the language of 'control over contract and work versus control over the company' as developed in *Shanahan*, or the decisive legal role in exercising employer functions suggested in the preceding paragraphs: applying that test, Alstom's commercial decision to alter the construction schedule would not have fallen within the scope of exercising one of the regulated employer functions.

Section 2: The Functional Concept in Operation

The accurate mapping of regulatory obligations onto the entity or entities exercising the relevant functions is thus the key aim to be pursued. As the survey of multi-entity contexts in Part II demonstrated, English law is far from achieving this goal. This section returns to specific examples of the application of different legal norms to complex factual scenarios, this time, however, in order to demonstrate how the functional concept of the employer can successfully overcome the problems identified.

At first glance, it might be thought that a fundamental reconceptualization of the employer would require significant innovation in both statutory design and the courts' adjudication. In developing practical illustrations it quickly becomes apparent, however, that this is not necessarily the case. Indeed, it is hoped that, in addition to exploring different possible avenues for operationalizing a reconceptualized definition of the employer, the following discussion will demonstrate how relatively little, if any, need there is for radical innovation or departure from existing frameworks to achieve the functional outcome proposed. Many if not all of the required techniques can already be found in various pockets of case law, growing from seeds of the functional approach described in the last section. Depending on fact patterns and the purpose of the relevant area of employment legislation, a combination of techniques already found in the law of the contract of employment and the many statutory extensions to it can be developed to give employment law scope functional flexibility in complex multilateral scenarios.

The idea of looking to existing material for inspiration as to how a functional reconceptualization might operate in practice is not new. In 1990, Collins

---

[32] *Shanahan* (n 31) [31]; cf the decision in *Howlett Marine Services v AEEU* [1998] UKEAT/253/98.
[33] *Shanahan* (n 31) [11].   [34] *R v Associated Octel Co Ltd* [1996] 1 WLR 1543 (HL).

examined a range of piecemeal statutory interventions in search of a functional approach;[35] Fudge similarly found existing techniques in a number of statutory devices, notably those lifting corporate veils and ignoring privity for specific purposes in particular contexts.[36] Davies and Freedland went further, setting out examples as diverse as the Gangmasters (Licensing) Act 2004, section 13 of which makes it a criminal offence to be supplied with workers through gangmasters' unlicensed activities, and the case of *Dawnay*,[37] where the court dispensed with the artificial bilateral analysis of restrictive covenants in financial institution teams; noting at the same time that, while these different techniques may contain promising avenues, they were in and of themselves not enough to remedy the underlying problem.[38]

Having delved into the problem itself by looking at the tension between the unitary and functional strands of the current concept, the development of a functional concept in this chapter is the first of two steps in an attempt to address the underlying problem. It surveys the broad range of possible options specifically in order to show how a functional approach can be put into practice, frequently by building on familiar structures. Examples will be drawn from a wide variety of regulatory areas, including techniques sometimes analysed as extensions of the employee concept. This, however, is primarily due to the way accounts of the scope of employment law are classically framed: upon closer inspection, clear traces of the functional approach become apparent in attempts to include multiple entities within the scope of employment law obligations. In presenting practical illustrations of the theoretical model developed thus far, the necessary steps are hardly radical: even under a functional concept of the employer, a worker's primary contractual counterparty, such as a corporate entity, may frequently be the bearer of many key employment obligations. That, however, will merely constitute the *starting point* of enquiry, not its automatic end.

It is important to note that this emphasis on the use of existing techniques to operationalize the proposed functional concept should not be mistaken for the suggestion that a coherent approach already underpins the different piecemeal solutions—notably as regards the contractual avenues to be discussed in the first subsection. Whilst it may be true to say on a very abstract level that most illustrations are driven by a specific purpose, the current piecemeal approach is highly problematic for a range of reasons, to be fully explored in Chapter 6. Suffice it to say for the moment that these revolve around a strict adherence to the bilateral and unitary focus of the traditional approach. Indeed, it may be for this reason

---

[35] Collins, 'Ascription of Legal Responsibility to Groups in Complex Patterns of Economic Integration' (n 30) 738ff.

[36] Fudge, 'The Legal Boundaries of the Employer, Precarious Workers, and Labour Protection' (n 12) 305.

[37] *Dawnay Day & Co Ltd v De Braconnier D'Alphen* [1997] IRLR 285 (CA).

[38] P Davies and M Freedland, 'The Complexities of the Employing Enterprise' in G Davidov and B Langile (eds), *Boundaries and Frontiers of Labour Law* (Hart Publishing 2006) 277.

that many of the cases on which the following section builds were, at least initially, seen as exceptions to established norms.[39]

A related challenge to the proposed approach, particularly as regards the discussion of specific statutory measures, are frequent judicial pronouncements to the effect that regulatory intervention in one particular area should be taken as a clear sign that the legislator intended to go thus far and no further, and that specific provisions can therefore not be applied in analogous contexts,[40] or that there is little space left for common law measures once Parliament has occupied a particular turf.[41] The response, again, is to recall the purpose of this chapter: it is not its suggestion that a functional concept of the employer can already be found in English employment law, or even that the proposed approach has been a driver of specific statutory reforms. The functional approach does not argue for the extension of specific concepts as such—such piecemeal reforms are inevitably constrained by the underlying unitary conception, as one or two examples will demonstrate. As the introduction to Part III made clear, a normative step is proposed. It is not, however, one that would require a radical rethink of the techniques to be discussed.

With these considerations in mind, discussion is structured into three subsections to analyse representative illustrations of a functional approach to defining employers, drawn from across English employment law. In keeping, at least as regards the general scheme, with the historical approach, initial discussion will focus on various *contractual solutions*, with the exploration of implied bilateral or even multilateral contracts in the agency labour context as its starting point. It will be seen how, even at common law, there are potential avenues to embrace a functional approach: implied contracts are a leading example of how a functional approach can overcome existing stalemates in this area, whilst remaining solidly embedded in common law reasoning. A second subsection then turns to illustrations of the functional approach operating in many areas of *statutory regulation*, notably anti-discrimination and equality duties, as well as health and safety. In working through several specific examples, the discussion's focus will be on demonstrating the different ways in which a functional approach can overcome most of the issues that needlessly puzzle courts at the moment—from an individual working for multiple employers on the same job at the same time, to reconciling parties' freedom of contract with regulation in line with economic and social realities.

Finally, and in parallel with the discussion of different modes of sharing functions in Chapter 2, a third subsection will explore different *modes of ascribing liability* to more than one entity, from joint and several liability to domain-specific responsibilities of various entities. Throughout these

---

[39] Deakin, 'The Changing Concept of the "Employer"' (n 4) 77, commenting on *MHC Consulting Services Ltd v Tansell* [2000] ICR 789 (CA).

[40] *Dimbleby & Sons Ltd v National Union of Journalists* [1984] ICR 386 (HL).

[41] Most famously in the context of the statutory regulation of unfair dismissal: Lord Hoffmann in *Johnson v Unisys Ltd* [2001] UKHL 13, [2001] 1 AC 518.

subsections, two crucial advantages, or flexibilities, of the functional concept that have already been hinted at will begin to emerge more clearly, in preparation for evaluation in a concluding section: the functional approach is context-specific, ie it can lead to different answers to the 'who is the employer' question, depending on the goals of the regulatory sub-domain or layer in question. The answer to that question may furthermore frequently involve more than one entity, and in combination with the earlier point, potentially different constellations will appear in different areas: the actual operation of a functional concept is highly responsive to the reality of relationships within a broad employment nexus—which is not to say, however, that it cannot also offer clear outer boundaries.

A. Contractual Avenues

The key avenue to be considered in this subsection builds on implied contracts. Their potential to operate in multi-entity scenarios such as agency work or personal service companies has been the subject of much controversy in both judicial opinions and academic writing. It is important to recall, therefore, that the return to an analysis of the role of contractual avenues at this juncture should not be taken as a suggestion that the proposed functional concept continues to be wedded to received notions of the contract of service alone. Indeed, as Chapter 6 will demonstrate, contract is today often merely the starting point in determining obligations between parties. In line with the overall purpose of this chapter, subsequent discussion of these materials is selective, with a focus on techniques that could be used, for example, to apply a functional approach in extending the scope of implied contractual terms, or certain statutory rights that need contractual minimum periods.

The primary testing ground for implied contracts in recent years has been agency worker cases. The setup of triangular relationships in this context will be recalled from Part I of the work: a worker (in the non-technical sense of that word) is supplied by an agency to perform tasks for one of its clients. In case of employment law grievances there are, broadly speaking, two kinds of parties against whom the worker might attempt to bring his or her claim:[42] the employment agency,[43] and its client, commonly known as the end-user.[44] From a functional perspective, this situation does not present major difficulty: whoever exercises a particular regulated function should be held responsible for any regulatory consequences. As discussed earlier, however, the fact that this setup is beyond the narrow unitary paradigm means that the courts have struggled with finding an adequate legal response to the resulting division of employer functions: while the

---

[42] A duality highlighted by E Brown, 'Protecting Agency Workers: Implied Contract or Legislation?' (2008) 37 ILJ 178.
[43] For example, *McMeechan v Secretary of State for Employment* [1997] ICR 549 (CA).
[44] For example, *Dacas v Brook Street Bureau (UK) Ltd* [2004] EWCA Civ 217, [2004] ICR 1437.

problem may no longer be one of *sui generis* classification,[45] a very wide range of rights go unprotected in the standard analysis where no contract is found with the end-user[46] and, with increasing frequency, not even with the labour agency.[47]

In direct response to this lack of protection for an increasingly large sector of the workforce,[48] a string of cases began to draw on the foundations laid in *Franks v Reuters*[49] in developing the idea that a contract of employment may be implied between end-user and worker. Statutory provisions explicitly provide for this possibility; the oft-cited definitional provision in section 230(2) of the ERA 1996, for example, decrees that a contract of employment is 'a contract of service or apprenticeship, whether express or implied, and (if it is express) whether oral or in writing'.[50]

As outlined previously, Mummery LJ laid out the basic foundations for using implied contracts in multi-entity employment law scenarios in *Dacas*.[51] On the facts of that case, this aspect of the decision was strictly *obiter dictum*, as the claimant had never appealed against the employment tribunal's finding that there was no contract of employment with the end-user. Nonetheless, in overruling the EAT's holding that the cleaner had been employed by the agency, the court found that *as a matter of law*, an implied contract between parties was a possibility that tribunals ought to consider. Mummery LJ's judgment, underpinned by an understanding of the structural problems facing agency workers, is at pains to reconcile the seeds of a functional approach with traditional common law techniques. Its reasoning is firmly based in the classic law of the employment contract, as later cases have confirmed.[52] Starting with the observation that the above-cited statutory reference to employment contracts explicitly includes *implied* contracts,[53] his Lordship set out an approach to implication featuring both traditional tests of mutuality of obligation and control. While the former was included as a necessary element,[54] the objective fact and degree of control was suggested to be the crucial element in finding an implied contract of employment.[55] Sedley LJ agreed with Mummery LJ in a short judgment infused with ideas from another early area of functional reasoning, vicarious liability.[56]

Munby J, in dissent, voiced rather strong opposition to such functional ideas of a contract with the end-user. Having set out the 'industry['s] assumption' that a contract of employment could be avoided once remuneration and control

---

[45] Initially, *sui generis*: see *Construction Industry Training Board v Labour Force Ltd* [1970] 3 All ER 220 (HC).

[46] eg recently in *East Living Ltd v Sridhar* [2007] UKEAT/0538/07/RN.

[47] *Montgomery v Johnson Underwood Ltd* [2001] EWCA Civ 318, [2001] ICR 819; confirmed in *Bunce v Postworth Limited t/a Skyblue* [2005] EWCA Civ 490, [2005] IRLR 557.

[48] *Montgomery* (n 47) [9].   [49] [2003] EWCA Civ 417, [2003] ICR 1166.

[50] *James v Greenwich LBC* [2008] EWCA Civ 35, [2008] ICR 545 [5] allows for the possibility of a single work arrangement leading to multiple contracts.

[51] *Dacas* (n 44).

[52] *Cable & Wireless Plc v Muscat* [2006] EWCA Civ 220, [2006] ICR 975 [36].

[53] Employment Rights Act 1996 ('ERA 1996') s 230(3).   [54] *Dacas* (n 44) [49].

[55] *Dacas* (n 44) [53].

[56] For example *Dacas* (n 44) [72]. While Mummery LJ mentions (tortious) vicarious liability briefly at the outset of his judgment at [2], he does not conflate the two situations to the same extent.

were split,[57] his opinion referred back to Elias J's EAT decision in *Stephenson v Delphi Diesel Systems Ltd*.[58] There, an employee's previous service under an agency arrangement was held not to have been under a contract with the end-user, thus negating the possibility of an unfair dismissal claim. In so doing, Elias J's focus was firmly on mutuality of obligation as the sole test for the existence of a contract—with control relegated to classifying the contract as one of employment once established.[59] The precise opposite of Mummery LJ's functional reasoning, this approach betrays a firm commitment to analytical typology, illustrating the resulting problems as identified in Nogler's work, above. Munby J built on the President's opinion, finding that the employment agency could not be seen as an agent for the employer when it came to remunerating the worker. This concept of mutuality of obligation is closely linked—on the employer's side—to a duty to pay the worker's wages. As this was said to be independent from the end-user on the facts of the case,[60] no mutuality and consequently no contract of employment could be found.

This shift towards mutuality of obligation, in combination with an attempt to decrease the importance of various modern manifestations of the control test,[61] traps the court's reasoning in a narrow formalistic approach. Once attention is focused on the absence of individual factors, analysis can only deal with a single relationship at any given time, without appreciating the role each factor plays in a particular context. A factor such as day-to-day direction may, for example, be the most important employing function exercised by the end-user.[62] Yet with it excluded from initial consideration, and mutuality being defined in a way that protects end-users, workers could have easily found themselves without access to any statutory rights.

Despite this powerful dissent, and an increasing unease expressed by the President of the EAT, the functional approach continued to develop. In 2006, the Court of Appeal explicitly approved the majority opinion in *Dacas. Muscat* was not a triangular case as such—an important reminder of the practically unlimited number of potential factual constellations beyond the narrow paradigm setup.[63] The claimant had originally been employed directly by the end-user, before the relationship was restructured as a chain of different entities, including work agencies and personal service company owned and directed by the claimant himself, set up on instructions of the previous employer. For present purposes, the decision in *Dacas* is interesting for two reasons:[64] first, as effective control had been conceded by the end-user, discussion before the court centred on remuneration

---

[57] *Dacas* (n 44) [82]–[83].   [58] [2003] ICR 475 (EAT).

[59] *Stephenson* (n 58) [11]. This is an illustration of the confusion mentioned earlier.

[60] *Quaere*, however, whether this can really hold true: normally the agency will only pay the worker if and when work has been done for an end-user, with funds provided by the latter.

[61] *Franks v Reuters* (n 49) [102], cited with approval by Munby J in *Dacas* (n 44). The explanation of *Motorola v Davidson* [2001] IRLR 4 (EAT) (where an end-user was held to be the employer) as a case fought on control alone can be seen in the same light.

[62] M Freedland, *The Personal Employment Contract* (OUP 2003) 40.

[63] *Muscat* (n 52).

[64] See also *Royal National Lifeboat Institution v Bushaway* [2005] IRLR 675 (EAT).

arrangements—an employer function that had not yet been the subject of extensive judicial discussion. The company's claim that absent a duty to pay the worker directly there could be no mutuality of obligation failed.[65] Smith LJ took an openly functional approach in holding that pay arrangements could be both direct and indirect. The structures in place were only an element in the factual matrix, and could not in and of themselves be determinative of the outcome.

The second important step[66] was the court's explicit linking of previous *dicta* that a contract could only be implied where 'necessary'[67] to the business reality test of necessity as espoused by Bingham LJ in *The Aramis*.[68] This was a first sign of what some interpreted as a shift in focus away from an overtly functional approach; a development continued in the subsequent case of *James v London Borough of Greenwich*.[69] The claimant there was again an agency worker, who had for several years been assigned to an asylum hostel operated by Greenwich Council. From a functional perspective, most employer functions were carried out by the Council, though crucially not all: the claimant once changed supplying agencies to improve her hourly wage. On the basis of these facts, the Appeal Tribunal held that no contract of service could be implied between the claimant and the Council. In the course of his decision, Elias J set out a series of guidelines to suggest that contracts could be implied only in sham contexts, or '[w]here the express contract does not properly reflect the actual arrangements, and it is necessary to imply a contract in order to provide a proper explanation'.[70] The Court of Appeal's ruling in *James* explicitly approved these guidelines.[71] Led once more by Mummery LJ, it upheld the EAT's decision, including the emphasis placed on a strict application of the necessity test.

In response to these decisions, leading commentators were quick to pronounce 'the end of the road for the implied contract'.[72] At a first glance, concerns voiced in various quarters that the shift towards necessity in *James* closed down a previously promising avenue for worker rights seem warranted.[73] Yet, together with most arguments critical of the implied contract approach, for example as regards questions of documentation,[74] this is not directly relevant for the current discussion. Seen through this lens, it is suggested upon closer inspection that the only thing the Court explicitly recoiled from was a possible interpretation of cases such as *Franks* and subsequent *dicta* that the passing of time alone may be key to the finding of a contractual relationship—an approach that would run counter to the established approach to implication in the general law of contract, where even very long-term relationships, for example with suppliers, cannot give rise to

---

[65] *Muscat* (n 52) [35]. This has since been applied in several EAT decisions, for example in *Harlow v O'Mahony* [2007] UKEAT/0144/07/LA.

[66] *Muscat* (n 52) [45].   [67] *Dacas* (n 44) [16].

[68] *The Aramis* [1989] 1 Lloyd's Rep 213 (CA).   [69] [2007] IRLR 168 (EAT).

[70] *James* (EAT) (n 69) 'Guidelines' 3(b).   [71] *James* (CA) (n 50).

[72] Brown, 'Protecting Agency Workers: Implied Contract or Legislation?' (n 42).

[73] M Wynn and P Leighton, 'Agency Workers, Employment Rights and the Ebb and Flow of Freedom of Contract' (2009) 72 MLR 91.

[74] M Wynn and P Leighton, 'Will the Real Employer Please Stand Up? Agencies, Client Companies and the Employment Status of the Temporary Agency Worker' (2006) 35 ILJ 301, 311.

a contract simply on the basis of the duration of the engagement.[75] From a functional perspective, this limitation is not problematic—indeed, the existence of fixed factors such as the passage of time would bring their own problems.

The decision may in fact be characterized as rather helpful in several aspects: not least, by limiting the role of mutuality of obligation to the classification of contractual types, a paragon of the old formalistic approach. More importantly, and perhaps counter-intuitively, its emphasis on the necessity test opens up the possibility of a functional approach with clear guidance and limits. In *James*, Mummery LJ set out the *Aramis* test as suggesting that implication must be:

> necessary . . . in order to give business reality to a transaction and to create enforceable obligations between parties who are dealing with one another in circumstances in which one would expect that business reality and those enforceable obligations to exist.[76]

In the narrow context of triangular employment relationships alone, the implications of this formulation may often be negative. On one level, existing contractual relationships between the agency and the end-user can be said to explain the provision of work, thus negating the necessity of an implied contract between worker and end-user. This analysis has led to the failure of most subsequent claims in the lower tribunals.[77]

From the less analytical-descriptive angle of this chapter, however, the necessity test may warrant some further thought: it is suggested that its enquiry could also be understood as a very functional one, insofar as it looks at the reality of the parties' actions, rather than the formal structure of their relationships. A possible objection to this contention can be found in subsequent paragraphs of Bingham LJ's judgment, where his Lordship suggested that:

> it would be contrary to principle to countenance the implication of a contract from conduct if the conduct relied upon is no more consistent with an intention to contract than with an intention not to contract . . . Put another way, I think it must be fatal to the implication of a contract if the parties would or might have acted exactly as they did in the absence of a contract.[78]

The context in which this formulation was developed must be remembered, however: the *Aramis* was a commercial case in the shipping world. The actors involved were professional parties (such as stevedores and freight agents); the purpose of their contract a one-off transaction. In employment law, that transactional element—the wage/work bargain—is only a small part of the contract's purpose,

---

[75] *Baird Textile Holdings Ltd v Marks & Spencer Plc* [2001] EWCA Civ 274, [2002] 1 All ER (Comm) 737.

[76] *James* (n 50) [30], [45]; noting that 'in this case, the question of the presence of the irreducible minimum of mutual obligations [is] . . . not the essential point'.

[77] Including *East Living Ltd v Sridhar* (n 46): carer not employed as other explanations for work negate necessity test; and *Vidal-Hall v Hawley* [2007] UKEAT/0462/07/DA: social worker in relationship with charity, no need also to imply relationship with HM Prison Service.

[78] Drawing in particular on F Reynold, 'The Status of Agency Workers: A Question of Legal Principle' (2006) 35 ILJ 320 (a piece the conclusions of which the present author respectfully disagrees with).

which extends into a wide range of regulatory domains, not least the law of unfair dismissal. From a functional perspective, 'conduct' in the above quote cannot therefore be limited to the immediate presence of the employee on the end-user's premises, or even the receipt of wage payments.

This thinking is brought out in another formulation of the necessity test. In a case subsequent to the *Aramis*, Staughton LJ suggested that:

> it [was] not enough to show that the parties have done something more than, or different from, what they were already bound to do under obligations owed to others. What they do must be consistent only with there being a new contract implied, and inconsistent with there being no such contract.[79]

Applying this analysis in the specific context of a functional interpretation of the scope of employment law, it is suggested that the necessity requirement would be met in many situations. Illustration may even be found in existing law, such as *NGE v Wood*, a case decided by the EAT in the run-up to *James*, already applying the guidelines set out by Elias J.[80] The claimant payments manager had been supplied to the respondent company by an agency; on the basis of his subsequent tight integration into the respondent's business, the Employment Tribunal implied a direct contract of employment on the basis of the sham doctrine. The EAT reversed the finding on this point, reminding the Tribunal of the high thresholds involved, but went on to substitute its own reasoning in favour of an implied contract under the necessity test, relying on factors including the parties' direct negotiations over various terms, and an obligation on the claimant to provide personal service. The resulting reasoning was openly functional, looking at necessity through the parties' long-term actions rather than a formalistic account of why Mr Wood was in NGE's service: '[the company] has chosen to put itself in a direct relationship with the individual, affecting the future conduct between them. The company was not treating the Claimant as a semi-detached member of staff. They were in practice acting as though he were a wholly integrated member of staff.'[81]

This section set out to show how a functional approach might be put in place in English law, and furthermore to suggest that seeds of it can already be found in its various domains. The preceding analysis has given clear examples of functional approaches in those domains regulated directly through the contract of employment: the courts are able to follow employer functions with relevant regulation through the implication of contracts of service. Before turning to the next subsection, a residual point of criticism of

---

[79] *Mitsui & Co Ltd v Novorossiysk Shipping Co (The Gudermes)* [1993] 1 Lloyd's Rep 311 (CA) 320.
[80] *National Grid Electricity v Wood* [2007] UKEAT/0432/07/DM.
[81] *National Grid* (n 81) [40]. The developments set out in the preceding paragraphs are clearly in line with the Supreme Court's recent decision in *Autoclenz Ltd v Belcher* [2011] UKSC 41, [2011] 4 All ER 745 where Lord Clarke noted a 'critical difference' between ordinary commercial disputes and employment law litigation: [34]. A Bogg, 'Sham Self-Employment in the Supreme Court' (2012) 41 ILJ 328, 332 sees this as clear evidence 'that the common law has now started to dispense with . . . fictions and mystifications in respect of contracts for personal employment'.

this approach should briefly be addressed: the already-cited observation by Collins, that:

in truth the courts are often caught between a rock and a hard place. In trying with the best of motives to rescue temporary agency workers from their plight of being excluded from employment law almost entirely, the courts have resorted to fictions such as the implied contract of employment, and subsequently received their just reward: incoherence in the law followed by ignominious retreat to orthodoxy.[82]

This view serves as an important reminder that nothing in the foregoing discussion should be taken as a suggestion that a fully operational functional concept has already been developed by the courts, or that the material set out would fit squarely with the proposed reconceptualization. Indeed, the very reason why the courts are stuck in the way described by Collins is that any attempt at developing functional solutions can only work in combination with a carefully reasoned underlying concept, a task to which Chapter 6 will return.

B. Statutory Regulation

As noted at the outset, contractual solutions are the departure rather than the end point of this enquiry: indeed, they may frequently need to be used in combination with other regulatory provisions to ensure that each employer will bear the relevant responsibilities. Discussion thus turns to an exploration of potential avenues for operationalizing a functional definition of the employer, as developed in numerous statutes. Its goal is to add to the understanding of a variety of ways in which it would be possible to place obligations on entities other than the employer's immediate contractual counterparty.

Examples will be drawn from a range of different statutory extensions of employment rights, in particular from the areas of discrimination and equality law, and the field of health and safety regulations. Illustrations will by no means be limited to these, however—examples for different ways of operationalizing a functional approach can be found in topics as diverse as whistle-blower protection and the political troubles in Northern Ireland. In discussing these various areas, a full analysis of substantive provisions will usually be beyond the scope of this work; the focus will be on the application of various rights and duties to employers in multi-entity contexts. Where the law has moved on, particularly in the field of the Equality Act 2010, this focus on regulatory technique alone will also allow for reliance on partially obsolete older case law, as it is the underlying approach that is of primary interest. The dual purpose already seen in subsection A remains identical over the following pages: the examples serve to show how the courts may put a functional concept of the employer into practice, drawing on pre-existing pockets of functionality—without, however, suggesting that a

---

[82] H Collins, 'Book Review: D McCann, *Regulating Flexible Work* (Oxford, OUP 2008)' (2009) 72 MLR 141, 143.

coherent functional concept is already in place, as a brief mention of several negative examples will highlight.

As regards structure, this subsection deliberately eschews the mere listing and description of different techniques—both because a complete list of examples would be nearly impossible to condense into the available space, and because the creation of any such list would significantly distract from the open-ended nature of the functional approach. Instead, the focus is on several instantiations of a further crucial lesson that emerges from this chapter: once the courts embrace a functional approach, freed from the conceptual unitary straitjacket, many if not most analytical issues that have been puzzling courts and commentators fall away: whether it is the embrace of different regulatory aims in purposive interpretation, a focus on the reality of an activity rather than its structural organization, or the fact that courts are no longer torn between parties' freedom of contract and their evasion of regulatory obligations; even the idea that work is frequently done for a multiplicity of parties whose control over and benefit from the activity are not mutually exclusive—all these questions can be addressed in a much more accurate fashion.

Purposive Interpretation in Line with Different Regulatory Aims

A functional concept of the employer can much more readily accommodate specific regulatory aims. It furthermore allows the judiciary to be open about these considerations, keeping in line with constitutional propriety and allowing for greater scrutiny and academic discussion of individual decisions.[83] It is perhaps not surprising that anti-discrimination and health and safety provisions are amongst the earliest examples of the functional approach advocated. There, clear purposes are easy to state at an abstract level: to ensure that individuals are treated equally and that workers are not physically harmed or injured, respectively. Despite this, it is easily possible to envisage potential under-inclusion even in paradigm situations.

Both areas can be seen as intimately connecting employer's economic activity and important regulatory goals. Put differently, the fact that legal anti-discrimination efforts started in employment law is not 'random' but rather a clear function of the 'social powers of employers', which 'may well explain why the law regards it as right to place them under a duty not to discriminate, by contrast with other private actors'.[84] Gardner puts this point very clearly in an attempt to justify discrimination law against liberal criticism, noting the 'special institutional role' of the employment relationship both as regards the distribution of relative advantages and loss of individual control. On this basis, 'when the employer's social significance is recognized, requiring him not to discriminate indirectly is merely a proper response to current patterns of advantage and disadvantage, coupled with

---

[83] Nogler, 'Die Typologisch-Funktionale Methode' (n 15).

[84] N Bamforth, M Malik, and C O'Cinneide, *Discrimination Law: Theory and Context* (Thomson Sweet & Maxwell 2008) 5.

an understanding of the distribution of effective social power'.[85] The same is true, *mutatis mutandis*, in the health and safety context: the Robens Report,[86] leading up to Health and Safety at Work Act 1974, was keenly aware of the importance of the link between an employer's business activity and workers' health and safety: '[t]he broad objective is to improve the conditions in which people work—to protect workpeople from hazards and to ensure so far as practicable that their working environment is a healthy one. If legislation designed for this purpose is to be meaningful in practice it must allocate responsibilities realistically.'[87]

The purposive approach openly acknowledged by the courts in applying the relevant statutory provisions is a clear example of how the functional approach could work in practice, and of the advantages it would offer—most notably the explicit application of norms in line with their protective function. One of the strongest statements in this regard can be found in an oft-cited passage in *Harrods v Remick*, where Vice-Chancellor Sir Richard Scott noted that:

in approaching the construction of [the relevant provision] we should, in my judgment, give a construction to the statutory language that is not only consistent with the actual words used but also would achieve the statutory purpose of providing a remedy to victims of discrimination, who would otherwise be without one.[88]

Two related ideas come to the fore in this passage: that the ordinary understanding of work or employment covers a much broader range of situations than the narrow current legal construction of employment, and that the scope of protective legislation has to be interpreted widely in order to give effect to its underlying aims accordingly. These factors are both noted by Mummery LJ in returning to a similar point in *Tansell*; holding that such exercises did 'not involve any unconstitutional border crossing'.[89] Finally, it should be noted that, while the specific purpose may be different in distinct contexts, the basic model can be applied across employment law, even in such specific contexts as equal access to employment for workers drawn from across different religious groups in the Northern Irish context.[90]

Focus on Activity, not Structures

The fact that courts can successfully grapple with the core idea underpinning the functional approach, viz that regulation should focus on the activity in question rather than its formal structural setup, is best illustrated in the

---

[85] J Gardner, 'Liberals and Unlawful Discrimination' (1989) 9 OJLS 1, 11. See also J Gardner, 'On the Ground of Her Sex(uality)' (1998) 18 OJLS 167, 167.

[86] A Robens, *Report of the Committee on Health and Safety at Work*, Cmnd 5043 (1972), as cited in S Deakin and G Morris, *Labour Law* (6th edn Hart 2012) 355.

[87] Robens, *Report of the Committee on Health and Safety at Work* (n 86) 51 [163].

[88] *Harrods Ltd v Remick* [1998] ICR 156 (CA) 163.

[89] *MHC Consulting Services Ltd v Tansell* (n 39) 798.

[90] Fair Employment (Northern Ireland) Act 1976; *Kelly v Northern Ireland Housing Executive* [1999] 1 AC 429 (HL).

context of the provisions of the Health and Safety at Work Act 1974 ('HSWA 1974'). This Act imposes a wide range of general duties on 'every employer to ensure, so far as is reasonably practicable, the health, safety and welfare at work of all his employees'.[91] Furthermore (and crucially for present purposes), employers are to 'conduct [their] undertaking[s] in such a way as to ensure, so far as is reasonably practicable, that persons not in [their] employment who may be affected thereby are not thereby exposed to risks to their health or safety'.[92] On the one hand, this approach evidently still differentiates between employees defined in a narrow sense as working under a contract of employment,[93] thus reinforcing formalistic distinctions. On the other, it also includes within its scope all those 'doing work', a category defined to include the self-employed.[94] For present purposes, the provisions can however be treated as identical: as Howes suggests, the sections impose the same kind of 'basic duty . . . upon the defendant company to make sure that their business (undertaking) is operated (conducted) in such a way that employees and other people are not exposed to risk'.[95]

By focusing on the business activity itself, the provisions leave employers few chances to evade liability with technical arguments based on complex corporate or contractual structures. The point is well illustrated in *R v Mara*,[96] where a retail employee was injured by defective equipment (provided by a third party contractor) outside the store's opening hours. The Court of Appeal was quick to dismiss the contention that activity should be defined narrowly, which would have left the protective duty applicable during store opening hours only.

This functional focus on the activity is even more explicit in one of the leading cases under section 3(1) of the Act, *Octel*.[97] There, the employee of a specialist contractor was severely injured as a result of an explosion in a tank which he had been sent to repair. Under a narrow approach to business activities, it could be argued that the actions that led to the injury were merely ancillary: the defendant company operated a chlorine works, not a fibreglass repair business. This narrow interpretation was however rejected by the House of Lords.[98] Lord Hoffmann, with whom the other four Law Lords agreed, unambiguously held that the duty in question was 'defined by reference to a certain kind of activity, namely, the conduct by the employer of his undertaking. It is indifferent to the nature of the contractual relationships by which the employer chooses to conduct it'.[99] The cited provisions of the 1974 Act are thus an excellent example of the functional approach to defining

---

[91] Health and Safety at Work Act 1974 ('HSWA 1974') s 2(1).

[92] HSWA 1974 (n 91) s 3(1).   [93] HSWA 1974 (n 91) s 53.

[94] HSWA 1974 (n 91) s 52.

[95] V Howes, 'Commentary: Duties and Liabilities under the Health and Safety at Work Act 1974: A Step Forward?' (2009) 38 ILJ 306, 307; citing *R v Gateway Foodmarkets Ltd* [1997] IRLR 189 (CA) and *R v British Steel* [1995] IRLR 310 (CA).

[96] *R v Mara* [1987] IRLR 154 (CA).

[97] *Octel* (n 34). See B Barrett, 'Commentary: Employers' Criminal Liability Under HSWA 1974' (1997) 26 ILJ 149.

[98] *Octel* (n 34) 1548.   [99] *Octel* (n 34) 1547.

the employer in English law: they allow for purposive interpretation, and allow the court to assess the actual fact pattern to determine which entity, or combination of entities, has played a decisive role in the exercise of a regulated function.

Before turning to the next points, it will be helpful briefly to pause and set out an overview of the scope of the statutory scheme of discrimination law. Historically regulated under a wide variety of measures such as the Race Relations, Sex Discrimination, and Disability Discrimination Acts, the relevant provisions are now found in the Equality Act 2010; nearly all are, however, materially identical for present purposes. The Act crucially extends the concept of the employer in two distinct ways. First, by broadening the definition of employment to include 'employment under a contract of employment, a contract of apprenticeship *or a contract personally to do work*'.[100] Under this wording, temporary agency workers may find themselves classified as employees of their agency: in *EDS*,[101] the claimant was in a fairly standard agency setup with Brook Street Bureau when she was allegedly dismissed on grounds of her recently discovered pregnancy. On a preliminary hearing as to her eligibility to bring a sex discrimination claim under the relevant provisions,[102] it was held that, while she did not qualify as an employee of the end-user, such a relationship existed with the agency for the purposes of the Act. That said, the definitional extension nonetheless quickly runs into contractual shackles, especially as it has been interpreted as continuing to require mutuality of obligation. In rejecting a taxi driver's claim under the Race Relations Act 1976 because the relationship with the taxi company formally consisted of no more than an obligation to pay the weekly rent for the taxi meter and ancillary equipment,[103] Buxton LJ explicitly noted the narrowness of the contractual requirement as a key difficulty for discrimination law coverage.[104]

With a hint of ironic draftsmanship, the second extension, on the other hand, breaks free from this narrow limitation. Section 41 of the Equality Act 2010 decrees that:[105]

(1) A principal must not discriminate against a contract worker

. . .

(5) A 'principal' is a person who makes work available for an individual who is—
   (a) employed by another person, and

---

[100] eg Race Relations Act 1976 ('RRA 1976') s 78; equivalent provisions in the Sex Discrimination Act 1975 ('SDA 1975') s 82 and the Disability Discrimination Act 1995 ('DDA 1995') s 68. Emphasis supplied. Today all these are replaced by the Equality Act 2010, s 83(2) of which is materially identical.

[101] *EDS v Hanbury* [2001] UKEAT 128 00 2903, [2001] All ER (D) 369 (Mar).

[102] SDA 1975 (n 100) s 82(1).

[103] *Mingeley v Pennock and another (t/a Amber Cars)* [2004] EWCA Civ 328, [2004] ICR 727.

[104] *Mingeley* (n 103) [19]. See now also *Jivraj v Hashwani* [2011] UKSC 40, [2011] 1 WLR 1872; M Freedland and N Kountouris, 'Employment Equality and Personal Work Relations—A Critique of *Jivraj v Hashwani*' (2012) 41 ILJ 30.

[105] RRA 1976 (n 100) s 7; SDA 1975 (n 100) s 9; DDA 1995 (n 100) s 12; Equality Act 2010 (n 100) s 41. A full explanation of equivalence can be found, eg, in T Royston, 'Agency Workers and Discrimination Law: *Muschett v HM Prison Service*' (2011) 40 ILJ 92, fn 1.

  (b) supplied by that other person in furtherance of a contract to which the principal is a party (whether or not that other person is a party to it).

 . . .

 (7) A 'contract worker' is an individual supplied to a principal in furtherance of a
   contract such as is mentioned in subsection (5)(b).

The effect of these provisions is that 'contract workers' can bring claims against
'principals' for whom they work, despite the lack of a direct contractual relationship. This openly functional approach brings with it a range of additional
advantages.

Moving Beyond Contractual Formalism

It has already been seen how a functional approach allows the courts to focus on
regulating actual activity. The contract worker provisions show the other side of
that coin: once the function of a relationship, rather than its formal setup, is relevant, traditional puzzles such as who a particular contract is with, what precisely
each contract is for, or indeed how many contracts there are in the setup overall,
can safely be disregarded.

 The leading example for this proposition is the case of *Tansell*, a multi-entity scenario where the contract worker provisions were tested beyond the narrow agency
work paradigm. As opposed to the normal triangular setup (which is undoubtedly
caught by section 41), an additional company was present in the setup, linking Mr
Tansell with his own company to the defendant insurance company via MHC,
an employment agency. In reality, the computer technician worked directly on
Abbey Life's systems. In defending Mr Tansell's disability discrimination claim,
alleging that he had been dismissed following a diagnosis of diabetes, the insurance company argued that the relevant provisions did not apply in their setup, as
there was no direct supply contract. The Court of Appeal dismissed this assertion, focusing on the reality of the situation and thus avoiding an unduly narrow
interpretation of the provisions. The simple insertion of an additional contractual
layer could not defeat the entire anti-discrimination regime: 'the language of the
section is . . . reasonably capable of applying to the less common case in which an
extra contract is inserted.'[106]

 The rejection of contractual formalism went a step further in other cases, holding that the provisions applied well beyond the agency or 'supply of worker' setting. In *Harrods*, a franchise contract between the department store and individual
goods manufacturers provided the relevant contractual background;[107] in *Bassi*,
the contractual agreement was for the delivery of concrete.[108] The flexibility even
developed so far as to challenge mutuality of obligation, the very core of the traditional formalistic approach. In the recent decision in *Pegg*, the restrictive approach
taken in *Mingeley* (the taxi driver's case, above) was explicitly distinguished for the

---

[106] *Tansell* (n 39) 797. This point now made explicit by the Equality Act 2010.
[107] *Harrods* (n 88).   [108] *CJ O'Shea Construction Ltd v Bassi* [1998] ICR 1130 (EAT).

purpose of the 'contract worker' definition: the court found that there had been a duty to work personally once a particular assignment had been accepted by the claimant.[109]

This is a clear strength of the functional approach, as embodied in the notion of the principal in employment discrimination: what matters for regulatory purposes is the employer's activity, ie making work available. It is to that employer function that the relevant obligations attach, regardless of how their provision is contractually structured. The parties remain free to arrange their commercial relationships as they see fit; indeed they may even gain flexibility by no longer needing to consider the employment law implications of particular setups. Courts will of course continue to take contractual structures into account, but they are merely one factor in looking at the exercise of employer functions. The EAT's acceptance of counsel's submission that 'the tribunal erred in law in limiting its consideration to the formal contractual position'[110] in *Croke*[111] echoes the earlier words of Lord Hoffmann in *Octel* that a functional approach can legitimately be 'indifferent to the nature of the contractual relationships by which the employer chooses to conduct [its business]'.[112]

The Exercise of Employer Functions across Multiple Entities

The current concept of the employer is driven to a certain extent by functional thinking, for example insofar as it seeks to attach employer obligations to the party having control over an employee and benefitting from his or her work. The unitary strand, on the other hand, leads to a struggle once multiple entities become involved, with the intuitive response that in the absence of a single identifiable counterparty, no entity should be made to bear the protective obligations. A functional solution approaches this problem by turning it on its head: it recognizes that multiple entities can exercise employer functions such as having control over or receiving the benefits of an individual's work, and responds to this by holding each entity responsible accordingly.

A practical example of this point can be found in *Laing*,[113] where the claimant worked for a charity providing advocacy services to patients in a psychiatric hospital. As a preliminary point in a discrimination claim, the clinic argued that it could not be a principal, because the work done was not 'work for the principal' in the sense of the relevant Act, a predecessor provision to section 41 of the Equality Act 2010.[114] It submitted that Mr Laing had worked as an independent advocate, and that it was therefore not difficult to envisage situations where that work

---

[109] *LB Camden v Pegg* [2011] UKEAT/0590/11/LA, 2012 WL 1357842.
[110] *Croke v Hydro Aluminium Worcester Ltd* [2007] ICR 1303 (EAT). Note the different context of whistleblower protection under ERA 1996 (n 53) s 43K(1) which for present purposes can be considered equal to the other discrimination cases cited. See also *Woodward v Abbey National plc (No 1)* [2006] ICR 1436 (CA).
[111] *Croke* (n 110) [25], [41].   [112] *Octel* (n 34) 1547 B–C.
[113] *Partnership in Care (t/a The Spinney) v Laing* [2006] UKEAT/0622/06/DA, 2007 WL 1425705.
[114] RRA 1976 (n 100) s 7.

would be directed *against* the hospital; indeed given the nature of its patients, that was frequently to be expected. In addition to not benefitting from the claimant's efforts, the clinic furthermore had no right of control or direction over his work. The EAT disagreed with this narrow interpretation of employer functions, finding that inherent powers of control such as permitting the claimant access to its security facilities easily sufficed.[115] As regards the benefit of Mr Laing's work to the hospital, the fact that the work could also be seen as being for the benefit of others did in no way detract from the fact that the latter had also benefitted, even if only indirectly.[116]

In *Bassi*, a similar point was made in an entirely different context: the claimant lorry driver worked (in the broad sense of that term) for a company selling ready-mixed concrete. In the course of a delivery, he was allegedly racially abused by a banksman in the employment of the purchaser of the goods. The fact that he worked for the concrete vendor did in no way preclude the court's finding that his work was also for the company which received and used the concrete.[117] As regards work done for a multiplicity of employers, the Court of Appeal went even further in *Woodhouse*.[118] There, the claimant worked for a company providing management services to a local council under a complex housing outsourcing arrangement when the alleged racial abuse by a council staff member took place. It was held that control or even influence were not necessary ingredients of 'doing work for' a particular party, but rather that the situation had to be analysed in the round;[119] on that basis the Council clearly qualified as a principal for purposes of the Race Relations Act.

The Outer Limits of the Functional Approach

The final point which remains to be made in illustrating the operation of a functional approach concerns its inherent limitations. Previous discussion asserted that the functional approach had inbuilt limitations, and drew on the *Shanahan* case to show how tribunals are comfortable with the drawing of such boundaries. The contexts discussed in this section provide further illustration. One way in which the boundary issue can arise in the health and safety context, for example, is as to whether an employer's precautionary obligations are limited to activity taking place on its business premises; a clear limit akin in that sense to the received role of the contract of employment. As the answer is in the negative, critics of a functional approach may be worried about its potential to cast the net too wide, including in business activity items such as 'any repairs, cleaning or maintenance, wherever and by whomsoever they may be done, form part of the conduct by the employer of his undertaking . . . the cleaning of the office curtains at the dry cleaners; the repair of the sales manager's car in the garage, [and] maintenance work on machinery returned to the manufacturer's factory'.[120] As Lord Hoffmann

---

[115] *Laing* (n 113) [35].   [116] *Laing* (n 113) [34].   [117] *Bassi* (n 108) 1138.
[118] *Leeds City Council v Woodhouse* [2010] EWCA Civ 410, [2010] IRLR 625.
[119] *Woodhouse* (n 118) [22], [27].   [120] *Octel* (n 34) 1548.

made clear in *Octel*, however, this danger is significantly overstated. Applying the first elements of the relational-functional limits as outlined above, his Lordship held that activities such as those outlined could not be 'fairly described as the conduct by the employer of his undertaking',[121] and expressed confidence in the ability of courts at first instance to draw appropriate distinctions.

A broader point was made by Nicholson LJ in *Jones*, in confronting the suggestion that a purposive interpretation of the scope of the contract worker provisions would lead to too many spurious claims. The functional approach in and of itself provides a key limitation: only those with the power to take relevant decisions in the first place will be potential respondents to a discrimination claim.

I am not impressed by the 'floodgates' argument . . . If the principal is not in a position to discriminate against an 'employee' of the person who supplies that individual under a contract with the principal, any claim brought against the principal must, inevitably, fail. And it seems to me that an industrial tribunal should be able to deal with claims . . . [to] ensure that a genuine case of discrimination can be redressed.[122]

In combination with the previous subsection, discussion of these different statutory areas has thus served to illustrate from various angles what a functional approach would look like in practice. It may be worth re-emphasizing at this point that nothing in this chapter should be taken as a suggestion that a fully-fledged functional approach is already inherent in the current setup. Instead, the aim was simply to show how the courts would be able to implement a functional model, not least on the basis of existing techniques, and furthermore to demonstrate how such change would address many traditionally problematic questions. The purely domestic choice of examples here, finally, is complemented by similarly functional approaches on the European level. The CJEU's willingness to interpret employment law norms purposively was made clear in *Allonby*,[123] and the specific extension of this approach to the concept of the employer was discussed extensively in Part II: in *Albron*, the CJEU explicitly held that the Acquired Rights Directive should apply equally to 'non-contractual employers'.[124]

C. Allocating Responsibility

In exploring the implications of multi-entity employment, the final sections of Chapter 1 of this work set out different modes of sharing employer functions. The following paragraphs will explore whether the functional approach proposed can provide the conceptual apparatus for different modes of ascribing liability to more than one entity, in line with the multiplicity of possible scenarios. Three broad groups of fact patterns have previously been identified: functions might be bundled into one entity, shared between two or more entities, or parcelled out

---

[121] *Octel* (n 34) 1548.
[122] *Jones v Friends Provident Life Office* [2003] NICA 36, [2004] IRLR 783 [28].
[123] Case C-256/01 *Allonby v Accrington and Rossendale College* [2005] ECR I-873 (even though the Court's solution there did not necessarily carry that approach through consistently).
[124] Case C-242/09 *Albron Catering BV v FNV Bondgenoten* [2011] All ER (EC) 625.

between different entities. The first of these modes is the paradigm situation: a single individual or entity exercises all functions.[125] In *shared exercise*, some functions of the employer are simultaneously vested in more than one party. Such sharing of a decisive role in the management of labour functions can be found in contexts as diverse as the classic example in *Hill v Becket*,[126] where a coalyard employed a foreman to be in charge of a gang of workers, to Private Equity fund setups and corporate groups. When functions are *parcelled out*, on the other hand, distinct entities fulfil mutually exclusive roles. The best illustrations for this can be seen in the context of triangular work relationships. Finally, there is the possibility of multi-modality, ie that in the context of a single worker some functions are exercised jointly whilst others are parcelled out—such as in triangular situations where both agency and end-user have the right of dismissal.[127] If the functional approach proposed is to be neither under- nor over-determinative, it must be able to work successfully with multiple modes of attribution, in line with the complex realities of how multiple entities can share employer functions.

Before turning to a more detailed exploration of such avenues, however, it is important to clarify a point that has been obliquely running through the previous sections, without being explicitly brought to the fore. Whilst the general coverage of employment law norms would of course extend beyond its current narrow scope, the proposed functional reconceptualization does *not* lead to a major expansion of liability, in the sense that every entity which exercised, or had a decisive role in the exercise of, a particular function towards a worker will become liable as a counterparty to all employment-law related claims brought by the individual. Such a full liability approach is to a certain extent reflected in French 'legal doctrine and case law on economic and social unity',[128] and may have some superficial advantages: there would be no need for difficult causation enquiries, and the employee could go after whichever entity is the easiest one to sue,[129] be that on jurisdictional grounds or because of a particular entity's deep pockets. On closer consideration, however, it would not be a feasible, or indeed desirable, model to suggest under a functional approach.

First, as Collins explains in his seminal article, it would be very hard indeed to square such a wide extension of liability with the existing common law approach of ascribing responsibility, which is driven by capital boundaries even in complex economic organizations.[130] There is a crucial analytical distinction between holding multiple individual entities within a group or other multilateral setting liable, and ascribing responsibility for a particular action to the group as such. Muchlinski, writing in the context of enterprise entity theory, ie the idea

[125] Such as the franchisee in *Narich Pty v Commissioner of Payroll Tax* [1984] ICR 286 (EAT).

[126] *Hill v Beckett* [1915] 1 KB 578 (HC).

[127] *Construction Industry Training Board v Labour Force Ltd* [1970] 3 All ER 220 (HC).

[128] Morin, 'Labour Law and New Forms of Corporate Organization' (n 29), citing there G Teubner, 'Nouvelles formes d'organisation et droit' (1993) 96 Revue Française de Gestion 50.

[129] D Brodie, 'The Enterprise and the Borrowed Worker' (2006) 35 ILJ 87, 91 is critical on this point.

[130] Collins, 'Ascription of Legal Responsibility to Groups in Complex Patterns of Economic Integration' (n 30) 732.

recognizing 'corporate group[s] as a distinct form of specialized legal regime'[131] suggests a series of further concerns with such a 'full liability' approach, which can be extrapolated into all multi-entity settings. The determination of outer boundaries can become fiendishly difficult when 'contemporary ideas [of business organization are] used when constructing legal duties of care'.[132] Trying to place obligations directly on the 'group' or another cluster of multiple entities would furthermore fall back into the trap of assuming excessive homogeneity in the practical manifestations of the concept of the employer. Finally, as Teubner has noted,[133] the 'full liability' approach will quickly tend to become hierarchical, ie it will develop mechanisms that try to ascribe liability or impose obligations to some form of head or parent entity—and thus fail to take account of the many factual variations where different entities exercising employer functions are not in a hierarchical relationship.

Given the range of possible multi-modal combinations, a more flexible approach is required: just as employer functions can be divided up in different ways, so can different obligations be placed on entities exercising them. Subsequent paragraphs explore different avenues which could ensure that this happens—again emphasizing that, while traces may already be found in different parts of English law, it is not to be taken as a suggestion that a coherent underlying approach is already in place.

That the singular entity scenario is not a problem for the functional approach has already been amply discussed: as all functions are exercised together, appropriate obligations will point in the direction of the employer. The question does not change significantly where functions are cleanly parcelled out between different employers, for example where one entity controls the work and another entity pays the worker. A functional approach can easily grapple with this kind of scenario by allocating particular responsibilities to individual entities; indeed that approach is already evident in Agency Workers Regulation 2010,[134] and likely to become the default position in the model developed above. It is also in line with the functional model developed by Deakin, which, as already discussed, identifies functions of 'managerial coordination' and 'risk' and proceeds to attach the relevant obligations to the exercising entity.[135]

It is in the context of truly shared exercise of employer functions and the overlap of different modes that matters become somewhat more complicated. Davidov has developed his own high-level version of a functional account of the concept of the employer.[136] Whilst focused on other functional factors, such as democratic

---

[131] P Muchlinski, *Multinational Enterprise and the Law* (2nd edn OUP 2007) 317ff.

[132] Muchlinski, *Multinational Enterprise and the Law* (n 131) 320.

[133] Muchlinski, *Multinational Enterprise and the Law* (n 131) 321, citing G Teubner, 'Unitas Multiplex: Corporate Governance in Group Enterprises' in D Sugarman and G Teubner (eds), *Regulating Corporate Groups in Europe* (Nomos 1990) 67, 87–92.

[134] Agency Workers Regulations 2010, SI 2010/93, reg 14(1)–(2). See C Chacartegui, 'Resocialising Temporary Agency Work Through a Theory of "Reinforced" Employers' Liability' in N Countouris and M Freedland, *Resocialising Europe in a Time of Crisis* (CUP 2013).

[135] Deakin, 'The Changing Concept of the "Employer" in Labour Law' (n 4).

[136] Davidov, 'Joint Employer Status in Triangular Employment Relationships' (n 27).

deficits and dependency,[137] his account is similar enough to allow for a comparative discussion of different remedial approaches. In the context of what are termed 'truly triangular relationships', where different entities exercise various functions to overlapping degrees, Davidov does not appear to be convinced by the approach just outlined: the division of 'responsibilities is bound to be more complicated and might fail to ensure that workers are protected'. The only way to avoid this is the placing of 'all responsibilities on both [entities] jointly and severally'.[138]

Davidov goes on to concede that sometimes one specific entity may be required as a counterparty to avoid confusion, for example in the area of tax enforcement, but reaffirms that with 'employment standards and collective bargaining laws, the best solution seems to be the placing of joint responsibility'.[139] The present subsection advocates a refinement of this model: just as the functional approach is context-specific and domain-flexible in its identification of employing entities, so it should also be in its remedial stage: in some shared-exercise scenarios this may mean the imposition of joint and several liability (though at least at present, this will only work in a relatively small subset of cases as the next paragraphs show); in others, reliance on a regime of primary and secondary liability or even joint liability with contributory claims.

The possibility of dual or joint and several liability in a multi-employer context was discussed in *Viasystems v Thermal Transfer*.[140] There, the claimant had contracted for the installation of air conditioning in his factory; the work was done by a range of subcontractors. When a negligent fitter's mate of one such subcontractor caused a flooding of the premises while under the supervision of another subcontractor's employee, the question as to the identity of his employer or employers arose for the purposes of vicarious liability. The Court of Appeal was clearly aware that it was operating in novel territory; after a detailed survey of the authorities it found that traditional arguments in favour of single-entity liability were primarily based on unchallenged assumptions.[141] It therefore went on explicitly to embrace a functional approach, giving 'precedence to function over form'[142] in order to avoid 'an artificial choice required by an inflexible rule of law'.[143] On the facts, it was found that the relationships yielded dual control, ie that both the second and third subcontractors had exercised regulated employer functions.[144] Responsibility (in the sense of vicarious liability) fell in line with that: both employers were found to be liable for half the damage caused.

---

[137] Davidov, 'Who is a Worker?' (n 21).

[138] Davidov, 'Joint Employer Status in Triangular Employment Relationships' (n 27) 740.

[139] Davidov, 'Joint Employer Status in Triangular Employment Relationships' (n 27) 740.

[140] *Viasystems (Tyneside) Ltd v Thermal Transfer (Northern) Ltd* [2005] EWCA Civ 1151, [2006] QB 510.

[141] *Viasystems* (n 140) [76] (Rix LJ); [12], [46] (May LJ).

[142] *Viasystems* (n 140) [55]; cf also the references to function and purpose of the doctrine more broadly, eg [77]; R Stevens, 'A Servant of Two Masters' (2006) 122 LQR 201.

[143] *Viasystems* (n 140) [19].

[144] *Viasystems* (n 140) [79]–[80]. Rix LJ is somewhat more sceptical whether control is the only criterion, considering also the possibility of 'practical and structural considerations'.

Whilst *Viasystems* is an important case in showing potential avenues for the operationalization of the functional concept, it should—at least on present terms—not be read too far. The finding of a clear and equal sharing of employer functions will only be applicable to a reasonably small set of multi-modal employer function exercise,[145] particularly in some of the group structures under scrutiny. Furthermore, obligations placed on the employer cannot (and should not) be reduced to liability for the payment of financial compensation. Depending on the regulatory context and the factual setup, additional ways of sharing responsibility are required.

Indeed, upon reflection some of Davidov's own examples do not always go as far as suggesting the imposition of full joint and several liability, in the technical sense of that term, in all setups and contexts.[146] His model is underpinned by a more sophisticated approach, which may be termed a model of primary and secondary liability—an approach that is surprisingly close to some examples that can be found in English law. When it comes to the regulation of minimum wage levels in the agency labour context, for example, Davidov suggests coordination between entities, with the end-user under a duty to monitor the agency's compliance, and in the case of payment failure, a duty to step in and assure wages are paid, at least for the period of work with the end-user. There is a range of different ways to implement such an approach in practice.

The functional concept advocated can assure such a tiered approach to employee protection: with several of the employer functions identified, there will usually be one lead or primary party responsible for its exercise—even in a multi-entity setting. In the first instance, it is that entity which should bear the relevant employment law obligations; without undue deference to formalism, however, in case backup becomes required. The operation of such a tiered model can be illustrated through the National Minimum Wage Act 1998, section 34 of which is designed to ensure the protection of 'agency workers who are not otherwise "workers"'. Section 34(2) provides that:

... where this section applies, the other provisions of this Act shall have effect as if there were a worker's contract for the doing of the work by the agency worker made between the agency worker and—

(a) whichever of the agent and the principal is responsible for paying the agency worker in respect of the work; or

(b) if neither the agent nor the principal is so responsible, whichever of them pays the agency worker in respect of the work.

The tiered, functional approach is clearly visible in this provision: whoever is responsible for the exercise of the employer function, is under the primary obligation pursuant to subsection (2)(a). In the absence of clear responsibility, subsection 2(b) places responsibility on whichever entity actually effected the payments.

---

[145] A Dugdale and M Jones, *Clerk & Lindsell on Torts* (20th edn Sweet & Maxwell 2010) 4–29; see also Brodie, 'The Enterprise and the Borrowed Worker' (n 129).

[146] Davidov, 'Joint Employer Status in Triangular Employment Relationships' (n 27) 740.

It is furthermore not the only example of such regulation: a substantially identical approach applies in the working time provisions.[147]

Other contexts provide further illustrations of possible variations on the primary and secondary liability model that seems to be the unspoken thrust of Davidov's argument. One such variation can be found in the reasonable adjustments provisions, a duty placed on employers by the now historic section 4A of the Disability Discrimination Act 1995.[148] This duty extended to principals of contract workers under the model already discussed, above.[149] In terms of apportioning responsibility, however, principals only came under the obligation to make reasonable adjustments to the extent that the employer wasn't already required to do so.[150] A final possible variation under a functional approach would be to find different degrees of obligation placed on separate entities. This can be seen, for example, in the already discussed health and safety context: in *Swan Hunter Shipbuilders*,[151] a company was held to owe a higher duty to employees of subcontractors than to its own employees. The former had not been instructed in the proper use of oxygen tools, as a consequence of which several workers died: as the subcontractors could not be expected to have instructed their workers in the use of specific equipment, the higher duty fell on the principal.

This survey of how a functional concept of the employer may be put into practice has thus shown up a wide range of potential avenues, whether in contract, tort, or specific statutory provisions. It has been demonstrated how a functional approach would work both in terms of identifying employers and ascribing responsibility to them, and that several of the most vexing problems in the current setup could easily be solved. At the same time, it was not suggested that any of the examples identified come together to form a coherent doctrine. Indeed, it may be apt to recall at this point the warning noted by Davies and Freedland (in discussing the decision in *Tansell*) that piecemeal extensions, leading to a 'willingness to move directly along a chain of intermediaries [do not in and of themselves] satisfy the demand for imaginative legal recognition of complex multipolar work situations'.[152] Similarly, while activity liability in the health and safety context was seen as a good example of functional approach, many of its aspects continue to be hemmed in by the contractual framework, leading to 'serious doubts about the ability of the current regulatory framework for health and safety in Britain to adequately control the risks' to employees from the rise of 'networked forms of organisation encompassing the externalisation of work activities'.[153]

---

[147] Working Time Regulations 1998, SI 1998/1833, reg 36.

[148] In the Equality Act 2010 (n 100), this duty is squarely based on both entities by s 41(4): 'a duty to make reasonable adjustments applies to a principal (as well as to the employer of a contract worker).'

[149] DDA 1995 (n 100) s 4B(6).

[150] DDA 1995 (n 100) s 4B(7); H Johnson, 'Contract Workers—Disability Discrimination and Reasonable Adjustments' (2009) 90 Employment Law Bulletin 6.

[151] *R v Swan Hunter Shipbuilders Ltd* [1981] ICR 831 (CA).

[152] Davies and Freedland, 'The Complexities of the Employing Enterprise' (n 38) 290.

[153] P James et al, 'Regulating Supply Chains to Improve Health and Safety' (2007) 36 ILJ 163, 186.

As the introduction to Part III noted, the eventual solution to the underlying problem lies in a reconceptualization of *both* strands of the concept of the employer, its functional and its unitary one. The latter will be the task of Chapter 6; before discussion can move to that stage, however, one last task remains for the present reconceptualization of the functional strand. The examples developed in the preceding sections will be evaluated against the criteria developed in the conclusion to Part II, with particular attention to two crucial features of the functional concept as illustrated: it makes employment law coverage resilient against rapidly changing complex fact patterns, by allowing for the recognition both of different contexts or regulatory domains, and for the ascription of liability to multiple entities where necessary.

Conclusion

The overarching goal of this work is to explore the concept of the employer in English law and respond to any problems that may emerge with a coherent reconceptualization. In consequence, the eventual test to which Part III must stand up is whether it addresses the underlying tension head-on, by reforming both strands of the received concept of the employer so as to remove its inherent contradictions. At the present juncture, however it is too early to apply that criterion: the preceding enquiry only constituted the first of two steps in the reconceptualization. This observation is however not a suggestion that the functional concept developed thus far cannot be evaluated on its own terms. Three criteria emerged from the work in Part II as crucial preconditions for a successful rethink: the proposed reconceptualization has to avoid excessive homogeneity, by accommodating a differentiated view of different domains of employment law; the proposed change needs to be one of careful overall evolution to remain within existing frameworks, and the new functional concept needs to be able to be resilient to quick market-driven changes in the legal structures and commercial operations of enterprise. In concluding, these criteria are applied in turn; with a return to the larger underlying question postponed until the conclusion of Part III.

Domain Specificity

The first aspect of the functional approach to be evaluated is its ability, indeed encouragement, to work within the emerging understanding of labour law as consisting of a range of different regulatory domains. In designing the evaluation criteria at the end of Part II, a second, parallel, tension underpinning the existing concept of the employer was noted, in the form of an assumption of homogeneity, viz that the employer must always be the same, substantively identical, singular entity across a unified body of employment law. The functional approach, on the other hand, permits a perception of the subject as constituted by a range of different domains. It even goes further in this regard, by allowing for an additional analytical subdivision of these domains, and an analysis of at least three relevant sub-aspects: different areas will frequently have different aims, rely on a combination of different regulatory techniques to achieve them, and, crucially, the role of the employer will differ accordingly.

Before exploring this point further, it must be acknowledged that such a multi-domain analysis of employment law is far from being analytically settled or uncontroversial. It is therefore important to emphasize that an analysis of labour law as consisting of different domains is not at odds with the account by Deakin and Morris that labour law today can be seen 'as a unified discipline which has outgrown its diverse origins in the law of obligations and in the regulatory intervention of the state [to become] a subject with its own doctrinal unity and structure'.[154] The emphasis on external coherence there is not to be mistaken for a suggestion of internal homogeneity. The latter view may lead to mistaken criticism of the functional approach, as seen for example in Wynn and Leighton's concerns in response to the doctrine of implied contracts, when they suggest that the result of the functional approach in cases such as '*Muscat* is to impose liability on the party who is perhaps least suited to shoulder responsibility for temporary agency workers, i.e. the client of the agency'.[155] With respect, such thinking is underpinned by the fallacious assumption that the unity referred to above equals homogeneity, ie that once identified as an employer, that entity must be fully liable for all employment law claims.

Fudge identifies the 'plurality of different legal contexts and legal norms that make up the broad field of employment and labour law' as one of the main sources of complexity in regulating multilateral factual scenarios.[156] What, then, is the precise meaning of this idea of different legal contexts, or domains or areas of labour law? The concept is different from the idea of sources of labour law, in that it does not suggest the drawing of stark lines between different regulatory modes such as statute and common law, or contract and collective bargaining,[157] fully subscribing to the analysis of 'the Rules of Employment [as] . . . a complex amalgam'[158] of different sources. It is in that sense also different from the more sophisticated analysis of the heterogeneous composition of labour market regulation developed in Freedland and Kountouris's notion of layered regulation.[159]

'Labour regulation occurs at different levels and is multi-dimensional, serving a variety of instrumental goals and responding to different normative concerns.'[160] For present purposes, the domains can best be understood as concrete areas of labour law regulation, without suggesting mutual exclusivity or that a definite list should be drawn up. Examples of domains that have been directly touched upon

---

[154] Deakin and Morris, *Labour Law* (n 86) 1.

[155] Wynn and Leighton, 'Will the Real Employer Please Stand Up?' (n 74) 302.

[156] Fudge, 'The Legal Boundaries of the Employer, Precarious Workers, and Labour Protection' (n 12) 304.

[157] Though there is some utility in exposition: Deakin and Morris, *Labour Law* (n 86) 57.

[158] M Freedland and P Davies, *Kahn-Freund's Labour and the Law* (Stevens 1983) 51.

[159] Freedland and Kountouris, *The Legal Construction of Personal Work Relations* (n 2) 96.

[160] Fudge, 'The Legal Boundaries of the Employer, Precarious Workers, and Labour Protection' (n 12) 304.

over the course of this and previous chapters include non-discrimination, employment protection, and health and safety. Each area is made up of different layers: in the domain regulating employees' remuneration, for example, these will include the parties' contractual agreement, statutory provisions in a range of areas such as tax, equal pay, and minimum wage provisions, and potentially even further layers such as the regulation of occupational pension schemes.

The key reason why a functional approach needs to be able to respond to this model of different domains is that each area is also a blend of distinct aims and regulatory techniques, leading to a further set of complex permutations in the role of the concept of the employer. Within the broad mantle of employment law, a range of different aims is pursued: whilst all areas tie in with the larger purpose of redressing inequality of bargaining power or regulating the labour market, the regulation of equal pay is, in that sense, very different from minimum wage provisions: crudely speaking, the former may be said to be about ensuring equality between workers, the latter concerned with ensuring minimum economic provision. Similarly with the law of unfair dismissal, the aims of which can be seen as rather different from provisions on the information and consultation of employees: one is about balancing the employer's interest in having a flexible workforce and the employee's ongoing interest in a stable relationship; the other about giving workers a voice in corporate decision-making that may influence the ongoing existence of certain jobs. The broad range of regulatory sources and technique has already been seen. As each domain is made up of several layers, it will combine several regulatory techniques, from implied terms of contract and statutory provisions linked to the existence of particular forms of contracts to imposing obligations or levying penalties and fines.

As a logical consequence of these variations, the concept of the employer will have very different instantiations in different contexts, 'depending on the purpose of the specific regulation in question' and possibly even the regulatory devices used.[161] Put differently, the role of the employer will be different as a result of these factors, and the concept of the employer needs to be able to respond to that fact.[162] It will only be able to do so successfully when conceived as a functional one: the same flexibility that was analysed in the preceding section to show how the functional concept *recognizes* employers applies when it comes to accurately *responding* to that status.

In conclusion, therefore, the attempted reconceptualization of the first strand has come to preliminary completion: in explaining the conceptual basis for a functional approach and developing detailed examples to demonstrate how it may be put into practice, the groundwork is laid for the next, and final, task of this work: to reconceptualize the second, unitary strand of the concept of the employer.

---

[161] Davidov, 'Joint Employer Status in Triangular Employment Relationships' (n 27) 738.
[162] Fudge, 'Fragmenting Work and Fragmenting Organizations: the Contract of Employment and the Scope of Labour Regulation' (n 3) 636.

Resilient Coverage

The second lesson that emerged from earlier parts was that both the unitary and the functional strands of the concept were in need of reform, but to different degrees, and indeed in different directions: as the unitary aspect is not flexible enough to respond to complex and changing fact patterns, it has to recede to a higher, conceptual level. The functional approach, on the other hand, needs to be brought to the fore—if, that is, the proposed concept can make employment law coverage resilient to a plethora of economic organizational models.

At a conceptual level, the core problem of a missing 'fit'[163] between labour law and changed employment circumstances can be traced back to the very way in which the law conceives of the concept of the employer. Nogler's work clearly demonstrated this deep link between the particular analytical method used today and employment law's lack of flexibility and adaptability.[164] The current formalistic approach cannot achieve this because of its very structure: it is either too rigid (in accepting only pre-specified models, notably, the employer as the counterparty to the contract of employment), or it is too unclear and capricious, for example where several overlapping tests are used to determine the same question. In regard to these inherent negative consequences, the functional approach proposed is the very opposite of the prevailing contractual analysis. The only answer to the increasingly complex factual matrix in which the employment relationship is embedded is to take as many factors as possible into account, including different kinds of linkage between multiple entities and different modes of sharing. As the possible permutations are seemingly endless, however, this needs to be done in a structured way. The functional concept provides such a tool: it analyses the different factors in the round, synthesizing them as particular instantiations of the general criterion. The moment when it is not the presence or absence of a particular element in and of itself that matters, but rather the *function* which that element performs in the relation in question, employment coverage becomes flexible, and thus resilient to external change.

This proposition can be put to the test in the context of some of the actual scenarios that have been encountered. As discussed, Collins identified three forms of 'bonding between productive organisations': ownership, contract, and authority.[165] These can be translated, broadly speaking, into three scenarios: several distinct entities exercising joint control; control diversified across independently managed entities; and more diffuse areas such as multi-employer labour outsourcing or franchising.[166] Once multiplied by the number of modes in which employer functions can be jointly exercised across these different scenarios, a large number of possible permutations emerges. Yet, on a conceptual level they can quickly be

---

[163] L Dickens, 'Problems of Fit: Changing Employment and Labour Regulation' (2004) 42 BJIR 595, 604.

[164] Nogler, 'Die Typologisch-Funktionale Methode' (n 15) 462.

[165] Collins, 'Ascription of Legal Responsibility to Groups in Complex Patterns of Economic Integration' (n 30) 733.

[166] J Fudge, E Ticker, and L Vosko, 'Changing Boundaries in Employment: Developing A New Platform for Labour Law' (2003) 10 CLELJ 329, 361.

processed by a functional definition. The key difference in the various scenarios is as to *how* the relationship between different entities is organized: it may be through shareholdings, it may be a labour supply contract, or even a franchise contract. The legal form which the relationship takes, however, serves only as one of several possible indicators of its function, ie whether it puts the relevant entity into a position of decisive influence in the exercise of employer functions.

As a result, the functional approach can accept multi-polarity and bring the full set of possible combinations back into the scope of employment law. At the same time it also keeps inappropriate parties out of the picture: a worker could have a contract of employment with an agency, for example, but that would not be determinative for health and safety purposes if the agency had no relationship with the end-user's activity that causes injury. On a practical level, this translates into an ability both to identify relevant entities, and to fasten the appropriate employment law obligations on them, as illustrations in contexts such as health and safety and equality legislation have shown. A focus on activities over structures in the Health and Safety at Work Act 1974, for example, shows how courts can rely on the functional strand to grapple with multipolar structures, whereas various models of joint and several or primary and secondary liability discussed in section 2 ensure that responsibility can be allocated appropriately. The functional approach thus lives up to the 'need to be able to envisage and accept multipolar and multi-agency employment relations and contracts as falling within the realm of employment law'.[167]

A perhaps less obvious way in which the functional concept makes employment law coverage more resilient to market-driven structural changes, finally, is by removing the current incentives for rational employers to exploit overly formalistic structures: changes in enterprise organization will no longer be driven by a desire to avoid the application of particular norms. In Fudge's analysis, the existing bilateral and unitary setup may actually invite rational firms to externalize employment responsibility.[168] If the use of complex legal structures allows an entity to receive the benefit of labour without having to bear its risk, it will make sense to incur the additional transaction cost involved in setting up various subsidiary service companies, or paying labour agencies. Under a functional approach this incentive falls away. It could thus even be seen as restoring parties' contractual freedom, returning to a position where a 'person conducting his own undertaking is free to decide how he will do so'.[169]

Relationship with the Current Approach

The methodological tension underpinning the reconceptualization project was briefly addressed in the introduction to Part III in justifying the move from an

---

[167] Davies and Freedland, 'The Complexities of the Employing Enterprise' (n 38) 284.
[168] Fudge, 'The Legal Boundaries of the Employer, Precarious Workers, and Labour Protection' (n 12) 301.
[169] *Octel* (n 34) 850.

analytical-descriptive account of the concept of the employer to an openly normative suggestion of what it should (and could) become. In order to function successfully, the concept needs to leave sufficient material behind in order to break
free of existing assumptions that are the cause of its conceptual limitations. At the
same time, however, it cannot roam too freely, as respect for the broader framework is essential to ensure the solution's eventual 'fit', in the sense of being able to
be superimposed onto existing law.

The functional concept of the employer achieves this balancing act in two ways.
First, on a conceptual level, by building in its approach on the existing multi-
functional concept of the employment relationship as embodied in the different
tests for employee status: the common law is conceptually capable of identifying
particular employer functions, both in order to regulate them and to determine
who should be the subject of that regulation. The reconceptualization will, of
course, also have to involve significant modification; primarily of the second, unitary, strand. Even as regards the functional strand, however, some of the practical results that emerged from this chapter may initially look like bold moves:
the array of potential counterparties is significantly widened; different employers
can be picked depending on the context; and liability may be ascribed to more
than one employer within a particular domain. By relying on the pre-existing
functional strand, however, the underlying conceptual shift does not constitute
a radical change in conceptual terms, despite the potentially considerable differences in its practical emanations. This assertion can be further substantiated when
recalling the avenues through which the functional concept could be put into
practice. Again, the central proposition in practical terms—that the contract of
employment moves from being the end-point of the enquiry into the nature of the
employer to its beginning—might be seen as a drastic departure from the status
quo. This is countered by the fact that there is no need to conjure up new, special
technical avenues to give effect to the functional concept. It is of course true that
the various contractual and statutory extensions discussed are not used in that
particular way at the moment. They are, however, close enough to the proposed
approach that the reconceptualization, if adopted, could work within the existing
framework of employment law. Indeed, as a survey of different methods showed,
many of the existing extensions already contain traces of an openly functional
approach. The fact that the extension sought is thus a careful and gradual one
should not be mistaken as a suggestion that the present chapters, and indeed the
entire work, are not underpinned by a clear normative goal: to restore congruence
between employment law coverage and businesses' economic activity. The respect
expressed for the existing framework primarily serves the purpose of ensuring that
the reconceptualized definition can be superimposed onto existing law, whilst at
the same time remaining flexible enough to operate in other frameworks, such
as the reconsideration of employment relationships as Personal Employment
Contracts.[170]

---

[170] Freedland, *The Personal Employment Contract* (n 62).

6

A Single Concept in Different Contexts

Part I of this work identified the key reason why employment law regulation fails to impose obligations consistently on whichever entity or combination of entities is exercising, or has a decisive role in the exercise of, employer functions: there is a deep underlying tension between a unitary and a multi-functional conceptualization of the employer. Part III set out to address the problem, by working on a reconceptualization of both strands. Its first step, in Chapter 5, was to look at the multi-functional conceptualization of the employer, and show how it could be shaped into a fully-fledged functional approach, with surprisingly little need to depart from existing structures. As a result of these relatively small adjustments, it was implicit that the other, unitary, strand (in the sense of only ever designating a single, substantively identical, entity, the immediate counterparty to the bilateral contract of employment, as the employer across all domains of employment law) would have to give way to a much larger extent. This should not be taken to suggest, however, that the price to pay for a move towards a functional concept is a complete lack of principled approaches, with the concept simply adjusting to the factual realities of each case. As the discussion in the present, final, chapter will show, reform of the unitary concept is possible without sacrificing a coherent underlying conceptualization.

Introduction

Two steps need to be taken towards that goal. Recalling the earlier lesson that any change in approach needs to stay within existing frameworks, an initial question to be addressed is whether the unitary strand can be refashioned without coming into conflict with other areas of the law. In analysing the original concept, Chapter 1 identified three external factors that shaped its unitary strand. The first section of this chapter is designed to demonstrate how the law has developed in these areas, leaving the strict unitary approach of employment law out of step with its broader context; what appears to be quite radical change and a departure from the traditional unitary conception could therefore also be seen as bringing employment law back into line. Discussion then turns to the question why a unitary concept of some form is necessary in the first place: there needs to be a deep, underlying concept of the employer to ensure coherence in employment law overall. As Section 2 will show, the assumption that the current version of the unitary concept provides such coherence is deeply flawed on a number of accounts. The proposed functional reconceptualization, on the other hand, provides both the necessary factual flexibility and doctrinal clarity to ensure congruent employment law coverage.

Section 1: Moving Beyond the Received Unitary Concept

At first glance, the practical implications of the current concept as explored in Chapter 3 may lead one to agree with the suggestion that the law's 'traditional focus on regulation within the confines of a single organization remains largely untouched',[1] and that the functional approach proposed would therefore lead to significant upheaval in existing structures: different entities may, after all, now be held to be responsible employers, in line with different modes of joint exercise of employer functions in different contexts and combinations. Its substantive instantiations will therefore frequently appear to go against the three factors identified as crucial in shaping the original unitary concept of the employer.

First, under the wide variety of possible combinations there will be situations with more than one employer, or even different employers, depending on the domain in question: how does this work with the meaning of 'the employer' in ordinary language and the historic evolution of fact patterns? A second implication of the functional concept is that a search for a contractual link will no longer be the sole method in selecting the responsible party from an array of potential employers, which seems to go against the idea of privity, a crucial doctrine in the analysis of bilateral contracts. Third, in the context of complex corporate group 'employers', the idea of holding an entity that is not an immediate contractual counterparty liable could also be seen as a violation of each company's distinct legal personality. The following subsections consider each of these three factors in order to demonstrate the absence of the perceived conflicts. Indeed, the opposite will emerge: in many respects, the unitary concept of the employer is drawn much more strictly than modern language and fact patterns or legal doctrine require. A brief conclusion to this section, finally, will examine why this may have come to be the case.

A. Language and Fact Patterns

As regards the first aspect, Chapter 1 identified two factors that laid the foundations for a unitary concept: the singular, traditionally male, language used to describe '*the* employer', and the unitary fact patterns of early cases on the existence of a contract of service, which were soon applied as a fixed scheme to analyse

---

[1] J Rubery, J Earnshaw, and M Marchington, 'Blurring the Boundaries to the Employment Relationship: From Single to Multi-employer Relationships' in Marchington et al (eds), *Fragmenting Work: Blurring Organizational Boundaries and Disordering Hierarchies* (OUP 2005) 73.

more complex scenarios, even where that led to highly artificial outcomes. Neither of these aspects, however, is conceptually as narrow as traditionally assumed, or could warrant caution as regards the proposed reconceptualization.

The potential difficulty of discussing the 'ordinary' meaning of the 'employer' today has already been alluded to in the introduction to Part III: the results of a functional approach may on occasion depart from its general usage in particular factual scenarios. The present context is however a narrower one, reflecting the specific point made initially about the role of language in shaping a concept. The historic starting point from which the concept of the employer developed is the notion of the master, a single male individual in exclusive exercise of the control right over the servant: '[n]o man can serve two masters'.[2] Indeed, under the Master and Servant Acts the test of 'exclusive service' firmly entrenched that approach.[3] Even linguistically, the concept of the employer has, however, moved on, and can no longer be seen as admitting only the current unitary interpretation of 'the *one* employer in all circumstances'.

Whilst it is not suggested that all instantiations of the functional concept will map neatly onto everyday usage, there are two reasons why the gap between the legal concept and the general understanding will not be particularly large: as a result of the earlier rejection of a form of group or collective liability, the proposed approach does not imply that all entities should be seen as together forming *one* employer: the exercise of a particular employer function will only make the relevant entity the employer for the purposes of that specific area of employment law. Given this domain-specificity, different employers may therefore be identified in different contexts. This analysis is made slightly more complex where the exercise of a particular function is not cleanly parcelled out between different entities, but shared: there, the test might lead to two employers' being held responsible in the same domain. Despite long-established assumptions, however,[4] there is no clear-cut law rule at common law today 'that an employee cannot be the servant of two masters'.[5] As the discussion of *Viasystems*, above, showed, duality of employers is legally possible without creating much linguistic difficulty. Rix LJ, for example, embraced this 'possibility of dual responsibility' where '*[b]oth employers* are using the employee for the purposes of their business'.[6]

A second potential objection to address is the contention that the leading statutory definition of the employer in section 230 of the Employment Rights Act 1996 is firmly limited to single entities. The relevant subsections stipulate that:

(4)   In this Act 'employer', in relation to an employee or a worker, means the person by whom the employee or worker is (or, where the employment has ceased, was) employed.

---

[2] *Yewens v Noakes* (1880–81) LR 6 QBD 530 (CA); *Sadler v Henlock* 119 ER 209, (1855) 4 El&Bl 570 (HC).

[3] Notably the Master and Servant Act 1867: S Deakin and F Wilkinson, *The Law of the Labour Market* (Oxford Monographs on Labour Law, OUP 2005) 90.

[4] *Viasystems Ltd v Thermal Transfer Ltd* [2005] EWCA Civ 1151, [2006] QB 510 [76].

[5] *Viasystems* (n 4) [40], citing *Oceanic Crest Shipping Co v Pilbara Harbour Services Pty Ltd* (1986) 160 CLR 626 (HCA) [32].

[6] *Viasystems* (n 4) [77] (emphasis supplied).

(5)　In this Act 'employment'—

  (a)　in relation to an employee, means (except for the purposes of section 171) employment under a contract of employment, and

  (b)　in relation to a worker, means employment under his contract;

and 'employed' shall be construed accordingly.

Upon closer inspection, this is not a direct, but an indirect definition of the concept, *via* the contract of employment. As has already been seen, that contractual model is more flexible than traditional analyses might suggest: there is nothing in principle to suggest that a contract of employment could not be a multilateral arrangement, therefore involving more than one party on the employer side.[7] The variety of different definitions offered in specific regulatory contexts, such as the extension in various discrimination statutes, is further evidence that even in its statutory definition, the concept is a flexible and context-sensitive one.

Seen from the perspective of the rules of statutory interpretation, 'the employer' is of course a technical term, as it is defined in various Acts of Parliament.[8] A lack of congruence between a term's technical and ordinary meanings is not uncommon. Blackstone noted that, whilst lawyers normally ought to see words in their 'usual and most known signification', technical terms should be 'taken according to the acceptation of the learned in each art, trade and science'.[9] In discussing this choice between ordinary and technical meaning, Lord Esher suggested that;

[i]f the Act is one passed with reference to a particular trade, business, or transaction, and words are used which everybody conversant with that trade, business or transaction knows and understands to have a particular meaning in it then the words are to be construed as having that particular meaning, though it may differ from the common or ordinary meaning of the words.[10]

Even if one were to disagree with what the words 'the employer' are capable of expressing in ordinary language, the focus for present purposes is on their specific meaning in employment law. Indeed, there is a clear presumption in favour of the technical meaning as long as the concept is deployed within the intended context.[11]

The mere fact that a term has been defined in statute for some time, finally, does not suggest that its meaning cannot evolve:[12] '[t]here is . . . no inconsistency between the rule that statutory language retains the meaning it had when Parliament used it and the rule that a statute is always speaking'.[13] This point can be illustrated

---

[7]　*James v Greenwich LBC* [2008] EWCA Civ 35, [2008] ICR 545 [20].

[8]　It is important to note that s 6(c) of the Interpretation Act 1978 stipulates that in 'any Act, unless the contrary intention appears . . . words in the singular include the plural and words in the plural include the singular'.

[9]　J Bell and G Engle, *Cross on Statutory Interpretation* (3rd edn Butterworths 1995) 72, citing Blackstone's Commentaries, vol 1, 59.

[10]　*Unwin v Hanson* [1891] 2 QB 115 (CA) 119.

[11]　F Bennion, *Bennion on Statutory Interpretation: A Code* (5th edn Lexis Nexis 2008) 1206.

[12]　D Greenberg, *Craies on Legislation* (9th edn Sweet & Maxwell 2008) 702ff is the source of most of the following examples.

[13]　*R (Quintavalle) v Secretary of State for Health* [2003] 2 WLR 692 (HL) [9].

briefly with reference to a concept taken from another area of the law, the notion of 'the family': even though its context and technical details are different, the notion similarly plays an important role in a specialist body of law, without however being exhaustively defined in statute, leaving the judiciary with an important interpretative role. Indeed, the term 'family' can be a good example of the proposed functional approach in the larger sense: even though in historic parlance it would have clearly been understood as referring to a married man, his wife, and their child or children,[14] it could today also be seen as including everything from large families and single parents to a homosexual couple and their adopted children.

As the House of Lord's decision in *Fitzpatrick* shows,[15] the courts' approach to the notion of the family has not been a static one. In that case, questions arose as to the transfer of a protected tenancy upon the death of the claimant's long-term homosexual partner. One of the questions that fell to be determined was whether the homosexual partner could count 'as a member of the original tenant's family'.[16] As the term was not exhaustively defined in statute, the House of Lords felt able to apply its definition in the modern context.[17] Lord Slynn, having noted that social conventions had moved on considerably from when the term first became used in 1920,[18] applied an openly functional-relational approach in updating its meaning. His Lordship looked at the 'hall marks of the relationship' such as stability and mutual commitment,[19] and found that the claimant's relationship clearly met them on the facts, thus bringing him within the scope of the relevant statutory provisions.

The importance of fact patterns in shaping a unitary concept has similarly declined. Even if Master and Servant were historically an appropriate paradigm employment situation,[20] not all cases before the courts dealt with simple bilateral scenarios. As a result of the increasing vertical disintegration of enterprise,[21] even the concept of a single company employer is no longer entirely accurate. Chapter 2 showed how the reality of employment today has evolved drastically, to the extent that even relatively new models such as agency work can no longer be considered as atypical. As academia and the judiciary take cognisance of these developments,[22] there is an increasing expression of unease as regards the 'morally. . . unattractive proposition[s]'[23] that may result from a strict unitary analysis.

---

[14] This can be seen in early family law textbooks, eg P Bromley, *Family Law* (Butterworth, London 1957). The author is grateful to Dr Rob George for advice on this point.

[15] *Fitzpatrick v Sterling Housing Association Ltd* [1993] 3 WLR 1113 (HL). Though today see also *Ghaidan v Godin-Mendoza* [2004] 2 AC 557 (HL).

[16] The term used in the (then) Rent Act 1977, Sch 1, para 3(1).

[17] *Fitzpatrick* (n 15); Lord Hutton and Lord Hobhouse dissenting.

[18] *Fitzpatrick* (n 15) 35.   [19] *Fitzpatrick* (n 15) 38.

[20] Deakin and Wilkinson, *The Law of the Labour Market* (n 3).

[21] H Collins, 'Independent Contractors and the Challenge of Vertical Disintegration to Employment Protection Laws' (1990) 10 OJLS 353.

[22] *JGE v Portsmouth Roman Catholic Diocesan Trust* [2012] EWCA Civ 938, [2012] IRLR 846 [58]; E McKendrick, 'Vicarious Liability and Independent Contractors: A Re-Examination' (1990) 53 MLR 770; R Kidner, 'Vicarious Liability: for whom should the "Employer" be liable?' (1995) 15 LS 47.

[23] *McDermid v Nash Dredging & Reclamation Co Ltd* [1987] AC 906 (HL) 912A.

The practical impact of these changes can be illustrated by reference to *Vamplew v Parkgate*.[24] As discussed in Chapter 1, the court there held that a worker killed in the pits had been an independent contractor, rather than a servant, emphasizing in particular his exercise of employer functions vis-à-vis a group of men and boys engaged to work below him. The unitary conception as shaped by master-servant work patterns meant that by acting, in part, as an employer, Mr Vamplew could not at the same time also be an employee. Today, a similar analysis would not be followed, for example in the context of managerial employees. Whilst it is conceptually difficult to analyse the scenario with satisfactory analytical clarity,[25] there is no suggestion that a departmental manager in a large corporation, with the right to exercise a range of employer functions over his subordinates, would not *as a result thereof* qualify as an employee.

In summary, therefore, even though language and fact patterns were earlier noted as important historical drivers of a unitary concept of the employer, these factors no longer necessarily play that role today. Indeed, they could today be seen as arguments in the opposite direction: employment law's concept of the employer is too narrow to capture the full spectrum of the economic and social reality of modern work relations.

B. Privity of Contract

The second factor identified as driving the unitary concept of the employer was the casting of employment relationships in contractual terms, with contract once described as the 'fundamental legal institution' of employment law.[26] The unitary view emerges as the result of analysing the employment relationship as a bilateral contractual exchange of wages and work, with a single party at either end. This is supported by the strict assumption that a bilateral contractual arrangement may have no impact on other parties: as a result of the strict rules of privity, the idea(l) of freedom of contract in this context is equated to freedom from contract.

In returning to an analysis of the role of contract law doctrine in shaping the concept of the employer, it should be kept in mind that the accuracy of Lord Wedderburn's characterization of the pre-eminence of contract in the preceding paragraph is more limited than may at first be thought, both in its historical and potentially future significance.[27] That said, it is nonetheless important to engage with the underlying doctrine directly in order to show how it does not necessarily condition the current singular concept of the employer. Put at its most concise, the doctrine of privity in English law confines the effect of a bilateral contractual relationship to its two parties, who cannot impose a benefit or a burden on a third party.[28] As the

---

[24] *Vamplew v Parkgate Iron & Steel Co Ltd* [1903] 1 KB 851 (CA).

[25] P Davies and M Freedland, 'The Complexities of the Employing Enterprise' in G Davidov and B Langile (eds), *Boundaries and Frontiers of Labour Law* (Hart 2006).

[26] K Wedderburn, *Cases and Materials on Labour Law* (CUP 1967) 1.

[27] L Barmes, H Collins, and C Kilpatrick, 'Reconstructing Employment Contracts' (2007) 36 ILJ 1, and subsequent articles in that special issue.

[28] But cf the Contracts (Rights of Third Parties) Act 1999.

following discussion shows, however, an exclusive emphasis on privity in contract law may frequently obscure the importance of other sources of multilateral obligations.

Whereas several continental jurisdictions have flirted with multilateral ideas such as network contracts to regulate the economic reality of multi-entity inter-dependency,[29] English law has eschewed these models for two reasons: privity, as just outlined, and a seemingly strong commitment to the principle of freedom of contract, in the sense of respecting group entities' choice not to contract with employees or each other. Other ways of dealing with the issues raised by 'complex commercial and economic relations' can nonetheless be found.[30] Even before the introduction of a statutory avenue for the creation of third party rights in 1999,[31] the courts had started to develop a series of 'juristic subterfuges'[32] in order to achieve the recognized need for flexibility. A notable example of this can be seen in the law of tort, and the tort of negligence in particular, allowing recovery for loss caused as the result of a contract, but not under the contract itself. Whilst a detailed discussion of the tort law exceptions and their particular problems (such as regards the recovery of pure economic loss, for example) is beyond the scope of the present discussion, several crucial lessons can nonetheless be learned from the fact that even a contractual framing of a set of facts does not limit their legal analysis to a bilateral and unitary view.

Whittaker has convincingly argued that 'true exceptions' to privity can, and already have been, developed by the courts. Whilst:

> parties are free in principle to agree what contracts they wish, in most situations the law's response to this agreement is to classify it and regulate its consequences . . . [W]here the consequences of a (voluntary) creation of a particular relationship fall to be determined by the law, there is no logical or conceptual reason why the law should not draw consequences for third parties from its creation not merely where this can be justified by the existence of an intention in the parties to do so, but also from the nature of the contract which the parties have entered.[33]

As a broader analysis of situations is thus both within the abilities and proper constitutional role of the courts, the question arises as to how and where such policy-driven exceptions should be identified. There are two crucial limitations: context-specificity, and the need for clear-cut additional criteria. As regards the former, exceptions cannot become freely available, lest they subvert the doctrine of privity completely:[34] they can only be found in limited areas (such as employment law) in line with the demands of specific policy objectives.

---

[29] G Teubner and H Collins, *Networks as Connected Contracts* (Hart 2011); J Morgan, 'Publication Review: Networks as Connected Contracts' (2012) 128 LQR 472.

[30] S Whittaker, 'Reciprocity Beyond Privity' in P Kincaid (ed), *Privity: Private Justice or Public Regulation* (Ashgate 2001) 180.

[31] Contracts (Rights of Third Parties) Act 1999.

[32] *Swan v Law Society* [1983] 1 AC 598 (HL) 611 (Lord Diplock); as quoted by Whittaker, 'Reciprocity Beyond Privity' (n 30) 190.

[33] S Whittaker, 'Privity of Contract and the Tort of Negligence: Future Directions' (1996) 16 OJLS 191, 193.

[34] S Whittaker, 'Contract Networks, Freedom of Contract and the Restructuring of Privity of Contract' in F Cafaggi (ed), *Contractual Networks, Inter-Firm Cooperation and Economic Growth*

The need for clear-cut criteria is expressed in the idea of *reciprocity*: 'qui sentit commodum sentire debet et onus; a person who enjoys the benefit must also bear the burden'.[35] Whittaker relies on the provisions of the Acquired Rights Directive[36] as an illustration of this principle: with the acquisition of a business comes the acquisition of employment law obligations. Despite some remaining questions in domestic contract law doctrine as to its precise terminology or mechanism, the principle underpinning the ARD and TUPE Regulations is a simultaneous transfer of benefit *and* burden. This is significant in two ways: the new employer, first, cannot take the benefit of an existing business without being subjected to the relevant 'burden', or employment law obligations. Second, 'it makes clear that for the future the employees' work for the new employer must be reciprocated by performance of an employer's obligations'.[37]

A strict bilateral conception of the employer is therefore not inherent in a contractual analysis of employment relationships. This is not to downplay the general role of privity in English law: it should be noted that neither a particular context nor reciprocity between parties are in and of themselves enough to construe relationships beyond the contractual scope: reciprocity, for example, is *not* the justification for extending the relationship's scope; that element is primarily policy-driven. Taken together, on the other hand, these factors become very potent.[38] Their effect includes the imposition of clear outer limits in putting into effect these purposes: the reciprocity of rights and duties was at the core of the original relationship, so it should also form part of the additional benefits and obligations recognized by law as existing between contractual non-parties.[39] This model is very close indeed to the functional approach as advocated, in looking at the exercise of employer functions in particular relationships to attach regulatory obligations. It is equally context-specific, and functions exercised as a result of a reciprocal relationship are not only the trigger, but also the limitation of liability.

Even if contract continues to play a central role in shaping the employment relationship, therefore, it does not have to play the limiting unitary effect frequently ascribed to it: indeed, the courts are happy to move beyond it in a wide range of contexts. Chapter 5 explored several significant examples resulting from statutory intervention to impose duties on the employer in the absence of a contractual relationship. Recent decisions have taken this point even further, relying on (and extending) tortious principles in the absence of contractual relationships and specific statutory regulation.

(Edward Elgar 2011) 278; citing *Law Debenture Trust Corp v Ural Caspian Oil Corp Ltd* [1995] 1 All ER 157 (CA) 364 (Hoffmann J).

[35] Whittaker, 'Contract Networks' (n 34) 261; quoting Coke, 1 Inst 230b.

[36] Council Directive (EC) 23/2001 on the approximation of the laws of the Member States relating to the safeguarding of employees' rights in the event of transfers of undertakings, businesses or parts of undertakings or businesses [2001] OJ L 082/16 ('ARD').

[37] Whittaker, 'Contract Networks' (n 34) 268.

[38] Whittaker, 'Contract Networks' (n 34) 283.

[39] Whittaker, 'Contract Networks' (n 34) 270.

In *JGE*,[40] a victim who had been sexually abused by a priest whilst in a religious care home brought an action for tortious compensation. As the alleged abuser was no longer alive, the preliminary question arose whether the Diocese of Portsmouth (the Trustees of the Diocesan Trust being sued for that purpose[41]) could be held liable vicariously. After an extensive review of the authorities,[42] Ward LJ unambiguously found that there was no contract of service between the bishop and the priest. His Lordship thus noted that '[b]ecause there [was] no relationship of employer/employee between them, then, if one [were] judging the question on conventional lines, the bishop is not vicariously liable for the tortious acts of the priest'. He nonetheless went on to enquire whether the bishop could 'be vicariously liable if the *relationship [was] akin to employment*? [Could] the law be extended that far?'[43]

In answering this question considerable reliance was placed on the decision of *Viasystems*, discussed above, as clear evidence of the significance of the *role*, or function, of the employer in any particular area.[44] Indeed, '[t]he actual contract of employment [there] was treated as no more than an irrelevant distraction. Function triumphed over form'.[45] Ward LJ next recalled recent extensions of the second crucial ingredient in vicarious liability, actions within the 'scope of employment',[46] before turning to the policy considerations underpinning vicarious liability to emphasize the context-specificity of the concept of the employer: 'the time has come to recognise that the context in which the question arises cannot be ignored'.[47]

In order to determine whether the present facts constituted a 'relationship akin to employment' for the purposes of vicarious liability, his Lordship extensively analysed how close the tortfeasor's relationship with the bishop was to one of contractual employment. Sufficient proximity was found, as the church could be equated to a multinational organization, 'with the Pope in the head office, with its "regional offices" with their appointed bishops and with "local branches", the parishes with their appointed priests. This looks like a business and operates like a business. Its objective is to spread the word of God. The priest has a central role in meeting that target.'[48] The 'relationship with his bishop [was therefore] close enough and so akin to employer/employee as to make it just and fair to impose vicarious liability'.[49] In the Supreme Court's subsequent decision in another child abuse case with multiple potential defendants, *The Catholic Child Welfare Society v The Institute of the Brothers of the Christian Schools*,[50] Ward LJ's 'impressive leading

---

[40] *JGE* (n 22).

[41] As the Roman Catholic Church in England has no legal personality as such, the judgment was framed in terms of the relationship between the clergyman and his bishop: *JGE* (n 22) [18].

[42] Including *President of the Methodist Conference v Parfitt* [1984] QB 368 (CA); *Percy v Church of Scotland Board of National Mission* [2005] UKHL 73, [2006] AC 28.

[43] *JGE* (n 22) [31] (emphasis supplied).

[44] *JGE* (n 22) [39]; quoting *Viasystems* (n 4) [55] (Rix LJ).   [45] *JGE* (n 22) [60].

[46] *Lister v Hesley Hall Ltd* [2001] UKHL 22, [2002] 1 AC 215.   [47] *JGE* (n 22) [59].

[48] *JGE* (n 22) [77].   [49] *JGE* (n 22) [81].

[50] *Catholic Child Welfare Society v Institute of the Brothers of the Christian Schools* [2012] UKSC 56, [2013] 2 AC 1.

judgment'[51] was explicitly approved by Lord Phillips.[52] After an extensive review of the authorities, his Lordship applied a similar test of whether 'the relationship between [abuser and defendant] was sufficiently akin to that of employer and employees'.[53]

It is important to note that whilst these decisions were technically of course not in situations where an exception to privity had to be applied, they were nonetheless equally driven by the factors underpinning the proposed functional approach: context-specificity, and a focus on the nature of a relationship rather than its form. Indeed, in that sense Whittaker's conclusion rings true in both scenarios: 'concentration on one contract as the basis of liability in multi-contractual situations obscures the possibility of the creation of a bilateral entitlement between the parties beyond privity'.[54] Whereas earlier paragraphs showed how the *presence* of contract is not an obstacle to multilateral imposition of liability; the decisions in *JGE* and *Catholic Child Welfare Society* demonstrate how the courts have come to view that its *absence* is not necessarily a problem, either.

C. Company Law

In Chapter 1, discussion of language, fact patterns, and contract as general factors shaping the unitary concept was followed by a set of factors specific to the subset of limited liability companies as corporate employers, where the crucial interrelationship between different entities is primarily driven by equity ownership. It was suggested that despite a multitude of actors, from employees and management to a board of directors and shareholders, the company has become a singular focal point for a unitary conception of the corporate entity, with powers and responsibilities perceived in anthropomorphic terms; an entity to which employment relationships then fasten.

Analysis focused on the split between the three classic functions of enterprise: 'having interests in an enterprise, . . . having power over it, and . . . acting with respect to it'.[55] It explained how the corporate form led to their separation, in particular by breaking the link between the first pair. Once the interest in an enterprise and the power over it are no longer in the same hands, particularly in companies whose shares are publicly traded and widely held, two distinct groups emerge: 'the owners without appreciable control and the control without appreciable ownership'.[56] These developments are the background for the operation of the doctrine of separate legal personality and, as one of the consequences flowing from it, the idea of limited liability, that is to say that shareholders can limit their

---

[51] *Catholic Child Welfare Society* (n 50) [19].
[52] Though cf (writing extra-judicially) Lord Hope of Craighead, 'Tailoring the Law on Vicarious Liability' (2013) 129 LQR 514, 523ff.
[53] *Catholic Child Welfare Society* (n 50) [60].
[54] Whittaker, 'Privity of Contract and the Tort of Negligence: Future Directions' (n 33) 198.
[55] A Berle and G Means, *The Modern Corporation and Private Property* (Macmillan 1939) 119.
[56] Berle and Means, *The Modern Corporation and Private Property* (n 55) 121.

economic and legal risk exposure to the value of their shares, and that claims can only be brought directly against the company itself.[57]

Exceptions to this rule were characterized as the piercing or lifting of the corporate veil,[58] noting the common law's traditional hostility to the imposition of liability for a distinct legal entity's acts on the shareholders standing behind it: the veil may only be lifted (in the sense just outlined) in cases of fraud,[59] evasion,[60] or certain statutory provisions.[61] Whilst critics have noted the potential for abuse and artificial technicalities resulting from this approach,[62] a range of policy explanations have been adopted to support this strict line—most notably the idea that limited liability is necessary for the efficient functioning of public securities markets,[63] and the assignment of creditors to relevant economic units.[64]

The present context is a more specific one, however, as the shareholder is itself a legal person, ie a different company.[65] Such arrangements were not the paradigm situation at the origins of company law, with its emphasis on arm's-length dealing.[66] As Strasser notes, 'parent companies in fact present different policy issues and their limited liability should be determined by a different analysis'.[67] 'Changes to the profile of shareholders through the emergence of corporate groups and increased participation of institutional investors in the market for shares[68] provide a principled case for corporate shareholders to be treated differently from individual shareholders.'[69] This is compounded by the fact that employees (other

---

[57] P Davies and S Worthington, *Gower and Davies' Principles of Modern Company Law* (9th edn Sweet & Maxwell 2012) 207.

[58] S Ottolenghi, 'From Peeping Behind the Corporate Veil, to Ignoring It Completely' (1990) 53 MLR 338.

[59] The bar for which is set high: *Adams v Cape Industries Plc* [1990] Ch 433 (CA).

[60] *Petrodel Resources Ltd v Prest* [2013] UKSC 34, [2013] 2 AC 415 [28] (Lord Sumption).

[61] For example in the Insolvency Act 1986, s 213 and s 214 (fraudulent and wrongful trading).

[62] O Kahn-Freund, 'Some Reflections on Company Law Reform' (1944) 7 MLR 54, 56; K Wedderburn, 'Multinationals and the Antiquities of Company Law' (1984) 47 MLR 87, 90.

[63] P Halpern, M Trebilcock, and S Turnbull, 'An Economic Analysis of Limited Liability' (1980) 30 University of Toronto Law Journal 117 (as cited in Davies and Worthington, *Gower and Davies' Principles of Modern Company Law* (n 57)).

[64] The 'asset partitioning rationale' set out in H Hansmann and R Kraakman, 'The Essential Role of Organizational Law' (2000) 110 Yale Law Journal 387 (as cited in Davies and Worthington, *Gower and Davies' Principles of Modern Company Law* (n 57)).

[65] P Blumberg, 'The Corporate Entity in an Era of Multinational Corporations' (1990) 15 Delaware Journal of Corporate Law 283, 285.

[66] K Hofstetter, 'Parent Responsibility for Subsidiary Corporations: Evaluating European Trends' (1990) 39 International and Comparative Law Quarterly 576, 576; J Borg-Barthet, *The Governing Law of Companies in EU Law* (Hart 2012) 58, on which citations and structure of this passage build.

[67] K Strasser, 'Piercing the Veil in Corporate Groups' [2005] 37 Connecticut Law Review 637, 638; citing P Blumberg, 'Limited Liability and Corporate Groups' (1986) 11 Delaware Journal of Corporate Law 573, 575. The author is grateful to Professor Jane Stapleton for drawing these articles, as well as further cases and materials on 'veil piercing' in the US context, to his attention: T Heiden, 'The New Limits of Limited Liability: Differing Standards and Theories for Measuring a Parent/Shareholder's Responsibility for the Operations of Its Subsidiaries' in Practising Law Institute (eds), *Protecting the Corporate Parent: Avoiding Liability for Acts of the Subsidiary* (PLI 1993).

[68] C Bruner, 'The Enduring Ambivalence of Corporate Law' (2008) 59 Alabama Law Review 1385, 1432–3.

[69] Borg-Barthet, *The Governing Law of Companies in EU Law* (n 66) 58.

than as wage creditors in insolvency) are a very specific group of claimants, who may appear to be voluntary creditors of the company, but do not in reality enjoy the freedom to bargain for their protection as perceived in most economics literature.[70] The standard rationales become difficult to defend in situations where there is a clear economic unit across legally distinct entities, and the claimants in question cannot contractually adjust to this risk distribution. After some initial equivocation, however, the English courts saw no reason to hesitate in extending the orthodox position to corporate groups.[71] It is therefore perhaps unsurprising that leading authors have repeatedly concluded that 'ignoring the group structure will rarely be a policy available to the courts'.[72]

Upon closer investigation in line with the purpose of the earlier two subsections, however, that question may not be as clear-cut as it initially appears. In discussing exceptions to the doctrine of separate legal personality, Davies notes that there is only a narrow set of situations where such piercing may take place, in the sense of holding shareholders responsible for the debts or other liabilities of the company. While the rule in *Salomon v Salomon*[73] was intended to apply across the board, an 'impressively long' list of situations where the courts have felt able to ignore separate legal personality has developed.[74] It is not surprising, then, that Easterbrook and Fischel find that '"Piercing" seems to happen freakishly. Like lightning it is rare, severe, and unprincipled'.[75] The problem is particularly acute in groups of companies. Writing in the US context, Cardozo J noted that '[t]he whole problem of the relation between parent and subsidiary corporations is one that is still enveloped in the mists of metaphor [which] starting as devices to liberate thought . . . end often by enslaving it.'[76]

Davies notes a potential path to resolving many of these puzzles, in making the 'apparently radical suggestion' that:

no single explanation for these cases will be found . . . on the basis that it is possible to decide whether to ignore the separate legal personality of the company in this class of case only on the basis of an understanding of the purpose of the rule which is alleged to require this step to be taken. This is true whether the rule in question is statutory, common law, or contained in a contract.[77]

---

[70] cf the position of tort victims: H Hansmann and R Kraakman, 'Towards Unlimited Shareholder Liability for Corporate Torts' (1991) 100 Yale Law Journal 1879.

[71] P Blumberg, 'The Transformation of Modern Corporation Law: The Law of Corporate Groups' (2005) 37 Connecticut Law Review 605, 607–8.

[72] P Davies and M Freedland, 'The Employment Relationship in British Labour Law' in C Barnard, S Deakin, and G Morris (eds), *The Future of Labour Law: Liber Amicorum for Sir Bob Hepple QC* (Hart 2004) 137.

[73] *Salomon v Salomon & Co Ltd* [1897] AC 22 (HL).

[74] P Davies, *Introduction to Company Law* (2nd edn Clarendon Law Series, OUP 2010) 32.

[75] F Easterbrook and D Fischel, 'Limited Liability and the Corporation' (1985) 52 University of Chicago Law Review 89, 89.

[76] *Berkey v Third Ave Ry* 155 NE 58 (NY 1926), 61 as cited in A Crawley, 'Environmental Auditing and the *Good Samaritan* Doctrine: Implications for Parent Corporations' (1993) 28 Georgia Law Review 223, 223.

[77] Davies, *Introduction to Company Law* (n 74) 33.

This context-specific approach means that, for example, the resolution of a particular point will be 'a matter for employment lawyers and the vital interests of company law are not implicated, whichever way the decision turns out'.[78] Turning to specific examples of that in the group context, the starting position is nonetheless the applicability of *Salomon v Salomon*.[79] There is no 'routine liability [of corporate group entities for each other], flowing simply from the fact of the existence of a parent and subsidiary relationship'.[80] This is not, however, because English law lacks the necessary conceptual apparatus: there are specific exceptions in both statute and at common law, marked out by a particular domain and additional requirements that are closely related to the purpose of the rules regulating that context.[81]

As regards statute, the Companies Act 2006, for example, imposes a range of obligations on shadow directors, defined in section 251 as persons 'in accordance with whose directions or instructions the directors of a company are accustomed to act'. This provision has been held to encompass corporate shareholders.[82] One context in which the provisions play an important role is wrongful trading,[83] the additional features to trigger parent liability being closely in line with the purpose of protecting creditors in the run-up to insolvency: 'the failure of the parent company to treat the management of the subsidiary as having an independent existence, plus negligent disregard by the parent of the interests of the subsidiary's creditors in the period before insolvency'.[84] This limited, context-specific approach does not compromise the default position in company law: while a particular relationship in and of itself will not be enough to trigger liability, additional features in line with the purpose of a particular area justify the exception. Applying a single doctrine across all areas on the other hand would have asked the wrong questions, focusing on 'abstract, generalized ideas of entity separateness, and of "wrongful" conduct'.[85] Despite initial appearances, no significant doctrinal change is involved in achieving this result.[86]

The approach at common law is not dissimilar, as recent developments in the law of torts illustrate. The ordinary requirements for ignoring the corporate veil have already been seen in Chapter 1; the threshold is very high indeed.[87] That, however, is the *general* case; in the specific context of employer obligations different requirements may be in operation, as the most recent decision resulting from Cape Industries' asbestos manufacturing activities shows. In *Chandler v Cape*,[88]

---

[78] Davies, *Introduction to Company Law* (n 74) 33.

[79] For a short-lived exception, see Lord Denning in *DHN Food Distributors v Tower Hamlets LBC* [1976] 1 WLR 852 (CA).

[80] Davies, *Introduction to Company Law* (n 74) 97.

[81] Davies, *Introduction to Company Law* (n 74) 96–9, on which the following discussion builds.

[82] *Re Hydrodan (Corby Ltd)* [1994] 2 BCLC 180 (HC); *Re Paycheck Services 3 Ltd* [2009] 2 BCLC 309 (CA).

[83] Insolvency Act 1986, s 214(7).

[84] Davies, *Introduction to Company Law* (n 74) 97.

[85] Strasser, 'Piercing the Veil in Corporate Groups' (n 67) 657, 660–1.

[86] Strasser, 'Piercing the Veil in Corporate Groups' (n 67) 662.

[87] *Adams v Cape Industries Plc* [1990] Ch 433 (CA).

[88] *Chandler v Cape Plc* [2011] EWHC 951, (2011) 108(19) LSG 20; upheld [2012] EWCA Civ 525, [2012] 3 All ER 640. See also *Thompson v Renwick Group plc* [2014] EWCA Civ 635, [2014] 2

the claimant had contracted mesothelioma whilst working for a subsidiary of Cape plc; that contractual employer had ceased to exist by the time of the claim. The question therefore arose whether Mr Chandler could bring a direct claim against the parent company. Whilst a separate legal entity, the subsidiary had been managed as a 'branch of the defendant'[89] within the larger group of companies, the core business of which was the manufacture of asbestos-based products.[90] The court took the existence of a Group Medical Advisor and a long course of dealings between the entities as 'clear evidence that the Defendant was taking an active part in discussions relating to the health and safety of an employee of one of its subsidiaries'. There was no need to demonstrate full control over all activities of the subsidiary, a focus on a particular employer function sufficed. 'It is enough . . . [to] establish that the Defendant either controlled or took overall responsibility for the measures adopted by Cape Products to protect its employees against harm from asbestos exposure'.[91] When it came to an application of the three-stage *Caparo* test to determine whether the parent company owed a duty of care to the employee of its subsidiary,[92] the court found that it had assumed such responsibilities.

In concluding his judgment, Wyn Williams J added a crucial note to 'dispel certain possible misunderstandings'.[93] Each of the three points listed there merits brief further elaboration.

First, the fact that the Claimant was owed a duty of care by Cape Products does not prevent such a duty arising between the Claimant and other parties.

As has already been seen in the last chapter, the functional approach evident in this judgment easily overcomes the involvement of multiple entities in the employment relationship. The fact that the subsidiary had operated its own health committee was irrelevant:[94] the employer function could be jointly exercised.

Second, the fact that Cape Products was a subsidiary of the Defendant or part of a group of companies of which the Defendant was the parent cannot mean by itself that the Defendant owes a duty to the employees of Cape Products . . . Equally, the fact that Cape Products was a separate legal entity from the Defendant cannot preclude the duty arising.

This observation confirms the important safeguard built into the proposed approach: in order to trigger liability, both the particular context of a claim and the specific functions individual factors exercise in relation to it need to be present: the mere existence of a corporate group is not enough unless it provides the context for further factors, in line with the relevant domain, such as health and safety on the facts of *Chandler*. The reverse implication, a further aspect of the

---

BCLC 97. These developments were arguably foreshadowed in US law by *Johnson v Abbe Engineering Co* 749 F.2d 1131 (5th Circuit, 1984), as noted by Strasser, 'Piercing the Veil in Corporate Groups' (n 67) 648.

[89] *Chandler* (n 88) [14].   [90] *Chandler* (n 88) [23], [24].   [91] *Chandler* (n 88) [49].
[92] *Chandler* (n 88) [72], [77]; *Caparo Industries plc v Dickman* [1992] 2 AC 605 (HL).
[93] *Chandler* (n 88) [66].   [94] *Chandler* (n 88) [59].

functional approach, is equally important: formalistic distinctions will not defeat the applicability of employment law norms.

Third, this case has not been presented on the basis that Cape Products was a sham—nothing more than a veil for the activities of the Defendant. Accordingly, this is not a case in which it would be appropriate to 'pierce the corporate veil'.

The outcome on the facts of the case was not one of holding the parent entity liable for its subsidiary's obligations; strictly speaking it was found to have assumed a direct duty of care itself. Functionally speaking, this is nonetheless equivalent to the ideas developed in this subsection in general,[95] and the shadow director/wrongful trading scenario under section 214(7) of the Insolvency Act 1986 in particular.[96] The judge's final observation thus returns to the fact that the existence of separate legal entities, shielded against creditor claims by a corporate veil, is not logically tied to the present unitary conceptualization of the employer. Domain-specific 'exceptions' to the corporate veil exist in a range of areas; their operation is closely aligned with the functional approach proposed.

This increasingly flexible approach to the purposive pursuit of particular regulatory aims is by no means limited to the examples discussed above. In EU competition law, for example, the CJEU has adopted a 'single economic entity doctrine' in dealing with infringements in corporate groups;[97] there is at least one documented instance where a Private Equity investor (Goldman Sachs PE) was served with a notice on the basis of alleged infringements of Article 101 TFEU.[98]

As a result of the full development of the functional aspects of the concept of the employer in the preceding chapter, a fundamental reconceptualization of its unitary strand has become necessary. The purpose of the first section of this chapter was to show that such a development would not be incongruent with developments in the broader areas surrounding the legal concept of the employer. In returning to the three factors identified at the beginning of this work as key influences in shaping the concept of the employer as a substantively identical, singular entity across all domains of employment law, it demonstrated how each of these areas has developed beyond the original features. Indeed, the case could be made out that these external developments alone exert a positive pressure for reform.

It furthermore leads to an interesting side-question as to how and why the unitary concept of the employer has continued to exert its influence over time. Freedland and Davies suggest that 'much of the sustaining ideology for the unity of the employer and the bipolarity of the employment relation comes from within

---

[95] Strasser, 'Piercing the Veil in Corporate Groups' (n 67) 648.

[96] Davies, *Introduction to Company Law* (n 74) 99. Written before *Chandler* (n 88), the relevant passage cites several cases, including that of a Cape subsidiary in South Africa, as examples: *Lubbe v Cape Plc* [2001] 1 WLR 1545 (HL).

[97] R Whish and D Bailey, *Competition Law* (12th edn OUP 2012) 92ff.

[98] L Crofts, 'Buyout Firms should heed EC Action over Cartel Liability' (mLex Market Intelligence, 25 July 2011); Slaughter & May, 'Private Equity and Competition Law: Liability for Infringements by Portfolio Companies' (Client Briefing 2011). The author is grateful to Dr Okeoghene Odudu for this point.

employment law'.[99] The unitary concept may thus be linked, at a subconscious level at least, to a particular normative underpinning of the discipline of labour law in general, seeing its primary purpose as the recalibration of a power inequality inherent in the relationship between 'the employer' and 'his' employees; between the master and his servants. With a shift in the normativity of employment law to include the idea of labour market regulation,[100] that influence (and any consequent subject-internal resistance to a reconceptualization of the employer as a functional one) may weaken over time: indeed, it may constitute a further reason in favour of reconceptualizing the unitary strand. Space limitations prohibit further development of this point; it should in any instance not be taken as a suggestion that there are no other good reasons for having a single, coherent, concept of the employer. It is this point to which discussion in the following section now turns.

Section 2: The Different Meanings of a Unitary Concept

The material discussed in the previous section provided further evidence in favour of reforming the existing unitary concept of the employer. The crucial question left unanswered there, however, was as to the precise nature of such a reconceptualization: what goals should it pursue? On one level, it may be tempting to suggest that any search for a unitary concept can simply be abandoned, with individual solutions to be developed in each regulatory domain instead. This is not a safe conclusion to draw from the analysis of the three factors shaping the received concept above, however: the purpose there was limited to demonstrating how the current approach is unnecessarily restrictive and inflexible.

The final section of this chapter therefore turns to the very nature of the unitary concept, exploring the importance of an underlying concept generally and linking this to the precise criteria against which any such approach must be evaluated. Put differently, in order to complete the final steps in the reconceptualization of the employer, two crucial questions remain to be addressed: why, first, is there a need to have a single, coherent concept of the employer? Second, and intimately related to the first point, what should the nature of that singular concept be? It is suggested that the answers to both questions are driven by the historical evolution of labour market regulation, and can therefore be illuminated by drawing on the work of Deakin and Wilkinson in this area.[101]

A. The Requirement of a Single Concept

For present purposes, this will be broken down into four parts: an examination of the regulatory function of a single underlying concept, first, will explain on which

---

[99] Davies and Freedland, 'The Complexities of the Employing Enterprise' (n 25) 276.
[100] See eg the essays in H Collins, P Davies, and R Rideout, *Legal Regulation of the Employment Relation* (Kluwer 2000).
[101] Deakin and Wilkinson, *The Law of the Labour Market* (n 3).

level the reconceptualized definition needs to be a unitary one: in its *conceptual* definition of the employer. A second part then explores to what end the concept needs to provide this conceptual unity, recalling its crucial substantive task in balancing employers' control rights and risk-absorption obligations. Having explored how the traditional approaches, focused on the contract of employment as the key 'public-regulatory' device, fail to achieve this, the third part explains why a specific focus on the concept of the employer may overcome the challenges faced by the broader analysis of contracts of employment, or indeed the concept of the employee. The fourth part brings these arguments together in developing a concise two-pronged test against which both existing and proposed concepts of the employer will then be evaluated.

'Public-Regulatory' Functions

The need for coherent underlying norms in employment law cannot be understated. 'It is no exaggeration to think of the classification of work relationships as the central, defining operation of any labour law system.'[102] Deakin and Wilkinson have shown how this need emerged as a result of the increasing regulation of the employment sphere, in particular through the 'gradual spread of social legislation in the field of workmen's compensation, social insurance and employment protection'.[103] In order to regulate effectively the wide spectrum of different factual patterns across a range of different contexts, from national insurance and taxation to employment protective legislation, a central unified model was required:[104] that model became the contract of employment. Without coherence in its underlying concepts,[105] however, the contract of employment could not live up to this 'public-regulatory character'.[106] The broader implications of the need for a unitary concept are significant: the search for a singular regulatory device is, 'in the final analysis, an argument in favour of an integrative mechanism, or set of mechanisms, which makes it possible for a market economy and a social state to co-exist'.[107]

Translated into the present context, these observations suggest a need for conceptually unified categories which are able to transcend a wide range of factual situations. The way in which the concept of the employer is traditionally seen as being unitary overshoots this requirement and therefore fails to perform its task properly, as the following subsection will demonstrate. Its singular substantive definition (in the sense of the employer being a single legal entity, the counterparty to a bilateral contract of employment) is radically different from the *conceptual unity* that is actually required.

---

[102] Deakin and Wilkinson, *The Law of the Labour Market* (n 3) 4.
[103] Deakin and Wilkinson, *The Law of the Labour Market* (n 3) 15.
[104] National Insurance Act 1946; Contracts of Employment Act 1963; Deakin and Wilkinson, *The Law of the Labour Market* (n 3) 94–5, 36.
[105] Including, not least, the concept of the employer, as discussed in the Introduction.
[106] Deakin and Wilkinson, *The Law of the Labour Market* (n 3) 16.
[107] Deakin and Wilkinson, *The Law of the Labour Market* (n 3) 109.

The Trade-Off Between Employer Control and Employer Duties

Given this need for unitary concepts in labour market regulation, the question as to what the precise task of such concepts should be immediately arises. From an historical perspective, the contractualization of the employment relationship united two previously distinct aspects in order to establish its central role: the 'placing of limits on the employer's legal powers of command' and 'the use of the employment relationship as a vehicle for channelling and redistributing social and economic risks, through the imposition on employers of obligations of revenue collection, and compensation for interruptions to earnings'.[108] Having gained a foothold in the liability of employers for injuries caused by managerial or superior staff,[109] this latter 'principle that the employer should assume responsibility for social and economic risks arising from the employment relationship began to take shape'.[110] Whilst the traditionally assumed stability and regularity of employment relationships may have become significantly weakened today, the idea of a fundamental trade-off continues to exert considerable force. The modern idea of a unitary concept should continue to be driven by the balance of a ' "coordination function", which expresses the worker's subordination to the managerial power of the employer within the enterprise, and a "risk function", [which] channels the risks of economic insecurity in such a way as to protect the individual worker against the consequences of that very same dependence on, and subordination to, the employer's superior resources'.[111]

This role of the underlying concept is by no means limited to English law. As Supiot has noted in the pan-European context:

Under the model of the welfare state, the work relationship became the site on which a fundamental trade-off between economic dependence and social protection took place. While it was of course the case that the employee was subjected to the power of another, it was understood that, in return, there was a guarantee of the basic conditions for participation in society.[112]

In the evolution of regulation as outlined thus far, the regulatory focus was undoubtedly on the employment *relationship*, as embodied in the idea of the contract of employment. Judicial interpretation of this underlying concept, on the other hand, focused on the classification of employees in order to determine the existence of a relevant relationship.[113] In its 'public-regulatory character', the contract of employment as the underlying unitary concept was therefore called upon to perform a multiplicity of tasks, including 'classification, regulation and redistribution'.[114] It was not necessarily successful in this range of endeavours: 'the employment model

---

[108] Deakin and Wilkinson, *The Law of the Labour Market* (n 3) 15.
[109] Employers Liability Act 1880.
[110] Deakin and Wilkinson, *The Law of the Labour Market* (n 3) 86–7.
[111] Deakin and Wilkinson, *The Law of the Labour Market* (n 3) 109.
[112] A Supiot, *Beyond Employment: Changes in Work and the Future of Labour Law in Europe* (OUP 2001) 10, as cited in Deakin and Wilkinson, *The Law of the Labour Market* (n 3) 14.
[113] M Freedland and N Kountouris, *The Legal Construction of Personal Work Relations* (OUP 2011).
[114] Deakin and Wilkinson, *The Law of the Labour Market* (n 3) 16.

can . . . be seen as a construction which was imposed upon a number of different types of work relationship at the cost of varying degrees of artificiality, and which was bound, eventually, to unravel'.[115] It is submitted that the key reason for this failure was the immense rigidity as regards substantive manifestations, resulting perhaps from an overzealous quest for conceptual unity. As advocated in the Introduction, a focus on and thorough conceptualization of the 'other party' to the employment relationship, the employer, might be a promising response to this impasse.

The Concept of the Employer as a 'Public-Regulatory' Device?

The contract of employment, chosen as the fundamental regulatory concept in English labour law, is thus characterized by a tension between the 'functions of economic coordination on the one hand and risk redistribution on the other'.[116] In searching for a better answer to the need for a central 'public-regulatory' device or concept, this trade-off must remain central: as discussed earlier, any potential reform must be closely tied to the original motivation of the unitary conception.

Upon further reflection, both of the required aspects (micro-economic coordination powers, and macro-economic risk distribution) could be viewed through the perspective of the employer; indeed, they may best be understood as centred on it. In the traditional analysis, the employer is the party that exercises the coordination function and reaps the benefits thereof; it is also the party that bears the majority of the burden resulting from the risk redistribution function. A coherent conceptualization of the employer could therefore be the starting point for a resolution of the often circular reasoning that characterizes existing problems with the larger notion of the employment relationship, the contract of service and the notion of the employee—without a danger of abandoning those existing frameworks in their entirety. The potential of this different perspective is echoed by Davies and Freedland in their already quoted suggestion that the debate as to the appropriate scope of employment law coverage might 'best be understood from an unfamiliar perspective, indeed initially a counterintuitive one, [where the] problem lies not in the binary analysis of the worker, but in the unitary analysis of the employer'.[117]

The Crucial Elements of the Concept of the Employer

Writing in the much broader context of reconceptualizing personal work relations generally, Freedland and Kountouris formulate two criteria of which an adequate re-conceptualization needs to take account. They suggest two different levels, each with its own particular kind of conceptualization:

One of those two levels— . . . the macroscopic or 'macro' one—is a taxonomical level in which all personal work relations are mapped out and classified into categories.

---

[115] Deakin and Wilkinson, *The Law of the Labour Market* (n 3) 105.
[116] Deakin and Wilkinson, *The Law of the Labour Market* (n 3) 19.
[117] Davies and Freedland, 'The Complexities of the Employing Enterprise' (n 25) 273.

The other of those two levels— . . . the microscopic or 'micro' one—is a structural level in which the structural features of particular personal work relations are identified or assigned.[118]

The direct applicability of this model is limited to a fairly general level, given the different purpose and context of the authors' much larger endeavour of looking at and reconceptualizing personal work relations from a comparative perspective. The crucial idea that can be adopted for the present context, however, is that scrutiny of the concept of the employer needs to happen at 'two focus-levels—a broad and distant focus-level on the macro map of personal work relations in general and a narrow and close-up focus-level on the micro-map of particular personal work relations'.[119] Recognizing the potential for analytical duality is useful first guidance for present purposes, as is the reminder to consider the close interdependence of both levels.

Seen from the perspective developed in the preceding paragraphs and the broader context of the historical evolution of employment regulation, the concept of the employer thus needs to achieve two aims in order to restore coherence to the larger regulatory regime:

- It must be a unitary concept, in the limited formal sense of being able to identify 'the employer' according to the same clear singular set of criteria in all circumstances.

- It must furthermore, in a substantive sense, ensure that the entity or combination of entities thus identified will be the one best placed to facilitate the risk/control trade-off at the heart of labour market regulation.

This, therefore, is the test to be developed and applied in the final two subsections: on the macro-level, does the particular conception under scrutiny offer a singular set of identification principles? On the micro-level, do they ensure that the party who can best effect the relevant trade-off is selected in all circumstances? It will be seen that when this two-pronged, or dual focus, test is applied to the traditional interpretation of the unitary concept, its shortcomings quickly become apparent. Using a functional perspective, on the other hand, means that the unitary strand of the concept of the employer can be reconceptualized to meet both criteria successfully.

Before embarking on this analysis, two linguistic points should be re-emphasized. The sense in which the concept is expected to be *unitary* in the first limb may appear as a rather unfamiliar idea of a unitary category, different in particular from the 'unitary' bilateral contractual paradigm being reconceptualized in this chapter. As the preceding pages have shown, this is due to the need for unity being a *conceptual*, rather than substantive one; in line with the larger structure of labour market regulation in the United Kingdom. The second observation relates to the very different senses in which the test's two limbs could be said to reflect the move towards a functional concept of the employer. It will be recalled from the discussion in Chapter 5 that there are at least two ways in which that term can be deployed: the first limb is functional in the sense of *defining* the employer via the exercise of one or a combination of the five particular

---

[118] Freedland and Kountouris, *The Legal Construction of Personal Work Relations* (n 113) 313.
[119] Freedland and Kountouris, *The Legal Construction of Personal Work Relations* (n 113) 313–4.

functions identified. The second limb, on the other hand, is functional in the sense of providing for an *ex post facto* analysis of the socio-economic consequences of adopting the new concept: is the entity, or combination of entities, selected on the basis of the underlying concept the one best placed to perform the risk/control trade-off in the layer of employment under scrutiny?

B. The Traditional 'Unitary' Concept

The traditional conceptualization of the unitary strand of the concept of the employer is a very narrow one, defining it exclusively as a singular counterparty to the contract of employment, substantively identical across all regulatory domains of employment law. In a formal sense, it could therefore be analysed as meeting the first criterion set out, above: it is able to identify the employer according to a single clear set of principles in all circumstances. As the discussion in Part II has shown, however, the received concept is at the same time vastly under-determinative, failing to identify an employer in most multi-entity employment scenarios. As its operation is limited to a narrow set of paradigm cases, therefore, that analysis is at least open to serious doubt. In the second, *substantive* sense, it is clear that the current concept cannot ensure that the party thus identified will be the one best placed to perform the necessary balancing exercise between controlling employer's direction rights and imposing protective obligations on them. Factual complexity quickly destroys conceptual unity, with immediate consequences as illustrated in Chapter 3: employment law coverage becomes incongruent, and may even break down completely where no responsible employer can be identified.

One possible response to this analysis would be to point to the specific exceptions that have sprung up to extend regulatory coverage in particular circumstances, fixing regulatory obligations on entities other than those identified by the traditional unitary approach. Such piecemeal responses to the identified shortcomings of the existing concept cannot, however, remedy the underlying problem. Indeed, they may exacerbate it by perpetuating the existence of a flawed concept, masked with exceptions that 'lack . . . precision that is conceptual, as well as operational'.[120] Fudge notes this point in criticizing 'rehabilitative' efforts to address the incongruent scope of employment protection: partial responses not only accept, but indirectly affirm, the status quo.[121]

The notion of the associated employer provides a good illustration of this point. It can be found in a series of materially identical statutory provisions in different contexts,[122] decreeing that:

any two employers shall be treated as associated if—
   (a) one is a company of which the other (directly or indirectly) has control, or
   (b) both are companies of which a third person (directly or indirectly) has control;
and 'associated employer' shall be construed accordingly.

---

[120] J Fudge, 'Fragmenting Work and Fragmenting Organizations: the Contract of Employment and the Scope of Labour Regulation' (2006) 44 Osgoode Hall Law Journal 609, 632.
[121] Fudge, 'Fragmenting Work and Fragmenting Organizations' (n 120) 631.
[122] Employment Rights Act 1996 ('ERA 1996'), s 231; Trade Union and Labour Relations (Consolidation) Act 1992, s 297; Equality Act 2010, s 79(9).

Employees may rely upon these provisions in an eclectic mix of circumstances.[123] The most frequent application in practice is in the context of employment rights that are subject to statutory minimum periods. Time spent working for associated employers will be added up towards the qualification threshold, despite the separate legal identity of the associated employers.[124] Another example where the associated employer provisions will be helpful can be found in the discrimination context. In pursuing an equal pay claim, the claimant can choose to rely on an employee of an associated employer as the relevant comparator, as long as all other conditions have been met.[125] At a quick glance, the route thus looks promising, especially now that it has potentially overcome some of the older criticisms of excessive formality in determining whether 'control' has been exercised.[126] However, as Deakin and Morris conclude, whilst 'the notion of associated employers provides a useful means of closing off some of the more obvious routes by which the application of statutory rights could be avoided by the adoption of separate corporate personality . . . [b]y no means all the possible escape routes are covered'.[127]

From the perspective of the double criterion developed earlier, therefore, the use of such exceptions falls already at the first hurdle: no consistent explanation for the presence of different exceptions is offered. The associated employer notion could be characterized as positively capricious, with extensions added and even withdrawn without coherent justification.[128] Indeed, it may make matters worse in specific circumstances, as the House of Lords' decision in *Dimbleby v NUJ* illustrates.[129] In granting an anti-strike injunction in a multi-entity industrial dispute, their Lordships found that whilst a purposive interpretation of the relevant statutory provisions (whether the relevant employer was a party to an industrial dispute[130]) would have generally been within their remit, the fact that Parliament had explicitly provided for an extension of the immediately following subsections to associated employers meant that a strict literal approach was to be followed on the issue before the court.[131]

---

[123] For a full account of the concept and its operation, see S Deakin and G Morris, *Labour Law* (6th edn Hart 2012) 231.

[124] ERA 1996 (n 122), s 218(6).   [125] Equality Act 2010, s 79(3), (4).

[126] H Collins, 'Ascription of Legal Responsibility to Groups in Complex Patterns of Economic Integration' (1990) 53 MLR 731, 740. Deakin and Morris partially disagree with this assessment, relying, inter alia, on *Pinkney v Sandpiper Drilling Co* [1989] IRLR 425 (EAT) as evidence; at the same time acknowledging that it is an 'unusual case' and that the outcome could be changed by deploying more complex corporate structures: *Labour Law* (n 123) 232.

[127] Deakin and Morris, *Labour Law* (n 123) 232.

[128] eg Employment Act 1989, s 14: union representatives' right to remunerated time off restricted to work done for the employer only (cf Employment Protection (Consolidation) Act 1978, s 27, which included associated employers' industrial relations).

[129] *Dimbleby & Sons Ltd v National Union of Journalists* [1984] ICR 386 (HL). See also *Hardie v CD Northern* [2000] ICR 207 (EAT): 'employer' in the Disability Discrimination Act 1995 cannot be purposively extended to include associated employers.

[130] Employment Act 1980, s 17(3).

[131] Though this may now be attenuating: *British Airways Plc v Unite the Union (No 2)* [2010] EWCA Civ 669, [2010] ICR 1316 (CA).

As Whittaker has noted, a powerful consequence of the 'reliance on the idea of an exception to an existing principle is that it recognizes the force of the principle itself'.[132] It is therefore unsurprising that Davies and Freedland have suggested that, while there have been some responses to the multipolar dynamics of complex employment relationships, these efforts 'still [fall] very short of the kind of rethinking of the concept of "the employer" which [is] functionally required'.[133] In the absence of a significant reconceptualization of its unitary limb, neither the original concept of the employer nor its combination with specific statutory or common law extensions can fulfil the required unifying role. When measured against the criteria developed in subsection 1, both fall at the first hurdle: the former as it is conceptually too narrow to identify an employer in situations beyond a small set of paradigm cases; the latter as it does not even aspire to any conceptual unity at all.

C. The Unitary Employer Reconceptualized

The central argument of this chapter has focused on the suggestion that the unitary strand of the employer concept can be reconceptualized to successfully resolve the underlying tension with an openly functional approach. Its new formulation therefore comes as a logical consequence of the stronger position of the concept's functional strand. As has been seen, the employer no longer has to be a substantially identical entity or combination of entities in all domains of labour market regulation. In consequence, the traditional *singular* way of understanding the unitary concept is no longer tenable. That does not mean that the search for a coherent underlying concept is simply abandoned, however. The necessary conceptual unity is provided by redefining the unitary strand of the concept as identifying:

the entity, or combination of entities, playing a decisive role in the exercise of relational employing functions, as regulated or controlled in each particular domain of employment law.

In embracing the potentially multi-contextual and multi-entity scenarios arising from the modern organization of employment relationships, this definition ensures conceptual unity irrespective of factual complexity. The concept of the employer is seen as an aggregate of employer functions as exercised in different domains; it admits of variation between regulatory contexts and different entity patterns.

As in the previous subsection, this conceptualization must be tested against the context of the organization of employment regulation as it has historically evolved. It must be able to meet the requirements of dual criteria; both limbs must in fact be closely tied in with the developments seen in the introduction to the present section. The concept must, first, be unitary, in the *formal* or *macro*

---

[132] Whittaker, 'Privity of Contract and the Tort of Negligence: Future Directions' (n 33) 216.
[133] Davies and Freedland, 'The Complexities of the Employing Enterprise' (n 25) 289.

sense of being able to identify the employer according to the same, clear set of principles in all circumstances. This test is met by the criterion of the exercise, or decisive role in the exercise, of an employer function regulated in a particular legal domain. The potential variety of instantiations does not distract from the fact that every entity or combination of entities will always have been identified according to a singular criterion: in this limited sense the concept continues to be firmly unitary. Whilst this emphasis on conceptual unity instead of substantive unity may be an unfamiliar departure from the current approach, its provision of a conceptually unified transcendent meets the criterion as established above; indeed it succeeds in this regard where the previous concept failed due to its too narrow remit.

On a *substantive* or micro-level, the concept must ensure that the party or parties thus identified will be the one(s) best placed to perform the relevant risk/control trade-off in each domain: this was the feature identified as the original reason for stipulating a unitary concept. The reconceptualized unitary strand can equally meet this requirement, as obligations will be imposed, by definition, on the entity that takes the actions employment law seeks to regulate. From a broader normative perspective, this argument that each entity should bear the obligations attached to the exercise of relevant employer functions can be supported both on the basis of the idea of fairness, or reciprocity more specifically, and economic efficiency: employers' incentives will be optimized once 'costs [are] borne by the activity which causes them'.[134]

This point reflects the broader functional perspective, in the sense differentiated at the beginning of Chapter 5: the role or economic function the particular institution of the employer plays in different contexts.[135] This analysis starts from the observation that the reconceptualized definition alleges that there can be a singular underlying conceptualization despite the nearly limitless possible permutations of practical outcomes. It formalizes the two observations to determine whether they can be integrated coherently, relying on the account of different domains, or layers, of employment law regulation as developed above.

The initial claim, then, is one of *functional commonality across different layers*. It is furthermore suggested that that functional role of the concept of the employer (in the current sense) is in a certain sense identical across all regulatory domains: it is the regulatory focal point for employers' control rights and risk absorption obligations. This is met by the observation of *substantive differences in each layer*. Different entities or combinations of entities can be found to be employers, depending on each context. The solution to this apparent impasse lies

---

[134] G Calabresi, 'Some thoughts on Risk Distribution and the Law of Torts' (1961) 70 Yale Law Journal 499, 533 (writing in the context of 'tort costs'). The Coasian counter-argument that this would lead to difficult allocation questions in the tort context is not applicable in the present context of employer functions: the 'activity' and the 'cheapest cost avoider' overlap under the functional approach proposed: G Calabresi and J Hirschoff, 'Towards a Test for Strict Liability in Torts' (1972) 81 Yale Law Journal 1054, 1060; both as discussed extensively in J Stapleton, *Product Liability* (Butterworths 1994) 99–105.

[135] This is not to be confused with the functional account applied hitherto, ie the definition of a concept *via* the exercise of particular operational functions.

in the recognition that whilst employment regulation overall will always be about the risk/control trade-off identified by Deakin and Wilkinson, the specific functionality of each layer in question is different (eg to ensure equal pay, or ensure stable long-term provision of work), as is therefore the operational or substantive role of the employer (eg to serve as a comparator boundary, or to consult with employees to avoid mass redundancies).

Thinking back to the practical examples developed in Chapter 5, a single entity could be identified as the employer, as could be different entities for different contexts, or even multiple entities for a particular function. Seen on its own, this may lead to the allegation that the different substantive employer concepts cannot be linked by a coherent underlying concept. The solution to this lies in an analysis of the broader picture. The first step is to note how each different layer represents a unique amalgamation of specific goals and the variety of regulatory techniques deployed to achieve them. The second step is then to recall the idea that a single test is being applied equally across all different areas: the reason that the practical manifestations are different is *not* the result of a lacking underlying conception, rather it is simply the recognition of the reality that the single test (the function of the employer) is applied in different contexts, and will therefore lead to different practical outcomes. From a functional *ex post* analysis, this ensures that the entity or entities identified as the employer will be the one(s) best placed to fulfil the overall purpose of the employer (the balance of the control and risk functions) as required in that particular layer, regardless of the formal structures shaping the employment relationship.

Conclusion

The second section of this chapter started with a brief summary of the historical development of the labour market and its regulation to understand the need for a single concept, as well as its precise nature. It then applied these findings as a two-limbed test to the competing unitary concepts of the employer. In looking at the traditional approach, it was shown how that conceptualization fails at the second stage, and how piecemeal reform attempts cannot improve the situation. The functional approach proposed, on the other hand, brings a different unitary concept with it, in the sense that the single criterion is defined as the exercise of a relevant regulated function. This conceptualization lives up to the test. Indeed, it even stands up to further scrutiny from a functional perspective: while its novel approach will lead to substantively different outcomes in varying factual scenarios, it is nonetheless underpinned by a consistent theoretical framework.

The functional reconceptualization proposed is thus successful because it presents a unitary concept of the employer, in the *dual sense* as historically required: it offers a single organizing device, capable of identifying the *locus* where the key trade-off that underpins the regulation of the modern labour market should take place.

Conclusion

The Broader Implications of a Tension Resolved

This work set out to explore the legal concept of the employer, with a particular emphasis on its operation in complex multilateral structures. The present conclusion draws together the main lines of argument developed in the course of previous chapters, and returns to an illustration of the functional concept in the context of two multilateral situations first encountered in Chapter 3: the division of employer functions in triangular work settings, and the information and consultation of worker representatives in corporate groups. It then applies a final, overarching test to the suggested modifications—can the reconceptualized definition of the employer directly address the fundamental conceptual tensions underpinning the current approach?—before sketching out the broader implications of a functional concept in the context of the personal scope of employment law.

Summary of the Argument

The first part of the work set out to identify the concept of the employer in English law. Moving beyond a series of frequently unspoken and unchallenged assumptions, it discovered two competing conceptual strands in the existing case law: the concept was shaped as a unitary one, first, by a range of external factors. The perception of the employer as the same, singular entity serving as the immediate counterparty to a contract of employment started from traditional assumptions surrounding the singular, male Master; developing complex fact patterns continued to be analysed through that unitary prism. This was exacerbated by the subsequent rise of contract as the main conceptual device in the organization and the growing regulation of employment relationships, with limited liability companies soon taking over the mantle of the unitary employer.

At the same time, there is little evidence in the traditional tests to suggest an inherent need for the employer always to be a singular entity. Indeed, the common law frequently betrays a strongly multi-functional conception of the employer. Five different groups of such functions were identified, and traced through a wide range of examples. The first chapter concluded by suggesting that, whilst in the paradigm bilateral situation of a single entity exercising all employer functions these different strands are no immediate cause for concern, there is an inherent tension which can quickly come to the fore once more than one entity becomes involved in the direct management of employment relationships.

Chapter 2 then illustrated how developments in modern enterprise organization, from agency work to corporate groups and activist investors such as Private Equity funds, are increasingly building on complex multilateral arrangements, thus rapidly moving the majority of employment relationships outside the narrow traditional paradigm. Whilst the different structures surveyed vary considerably in their technical setup and day-to-day operation, they are united in a nearly limitless variety in the shared or parcelled-out management of work. As soon as employer functions are exercised from more than one *locus* of management power and dispersed between several legal entities instead, the tension inherent in the traditional conceptualization becomes a challenge to the coherence of employment law coverage.

Depending on the mode of joint employer function exercise, workers may find themselves beyond the scope of most protective legislation, in the sense that they cannot identify any employer at all, or obligations may be placed on entities other than those best placed to fulfil them. In the employment agency scenario, for example, the courts have increasingly been motivated to deny the existence of a contract of employment with either party exercising some of the traditional employer functions, thus leaving the worker without recourse against either the agency or its end-user clients in the case of many fundamental employment norms. In complex corporate setups, on the other hand, it is becoming increasingly difficult to identify the relevant employer for purposes of statutory obligations, such as the consultation and information of employees. As relevant decision-making is rarely limited to the management of the subsidiary serving as the immediate contractual counterparty to an employee's contract of service, protective obligations may be placed on inappropriate entities or become entirely fictional.

In setting out these examples, several previous attempts at addressing the problems under discussion were analysed to demonstrate their potential flaws: instead of addressing the underlying tension in the concept of the employer, judicial, legislative, and policy-based responses have historically been limited in their focus to a particular subset of issues. The difficulty with this approach lies in its focus on the consequences, rather than the cause of the incongruent application of employment law: partial on-the-spot fixes, even if undertaken with clear worker-protective intentions, can cause problems in other areas of the regulatory framework. Attempts at partial reform are furthermore difficult insofar as they tend to perpetuate received concepts and thus the very problem itself.

Chapter 4 turned to a comparative exploration of the scope of employment regulation in multilateral structures under German law, particularly as regards the situation in corporate groups (the *Konzern*). The evidence there confirmed the tentative guidelines for a possible reconceptualization drawn up in earlier sections. Any successful attempt must not only address the deep underlying tension identified in Part I, but also grapple with the assumption of excessive homogeneity which underpins the current regulatory approach: the concept of the employer does not necessarily need to be identical in different domains of labour law, or always be constituted by the same singular entity. Second, as regards reform of each of the two conceptual strands, the unitary one is particularly problematic insofar as it leads to rigidly formalistic outcomes. The reconceptualization project, finally, needs to strive for a careful balance between overall coherence and flexibility, avoiding a radical departure from existing frameworks whilst at the same time remaining adaptable to future doctrinal development.

With these guidelines in mind, the third part shifted from the previous analytical-descriptive approach to an openly normative attempt fundamentally to reconceptualize the employer. Keeping in mind the previous chapter's conclusions, its steps were carefully structured around the functional and unitary strands of the concept of the employer as identified at the outset, with a chapter broadly dedicated to exploring the necessary changes to each limb. Overall, this resulted in very different modifications being proposed: the functional strand was to be strengthened, in particular by the development of a robust theoretical framework, and an extensive demonstration of how existing structures could be deployed to that end. In the unitary strand, on the other hand, the proposed changes were more significant, designed to leave behind its current analytical straitjacket without, however, abandoning a commitment to an overarching concept of the employer.

Chapter 5 thus built on the existing multi-functional limb to show how a careful extension to a fully functional concept could be achieved. A first section developed a detailed theoretical account of the proposed functional typology, noting in particular its roots in the existing approach and testing its ability to draw clear outer boundaries of the application of employment law norms. Different avenues for the practical operation of such a functional concept were explored in the following section, drawing on a range of existing examples from both common law and different models of statutory regulation, before concluding with a positive evaluation of the proposed modifications of the multi-functional strand against the previously developed criteria.

The final chapter then turned to addressing the unitary strand to show that, while some clear breaks have to be made from the existing setup, a unifying conceptual definition of the employer can be maintained. The initial section returned to the three main factors identified as driving the unitary strand in Chapter 1, re-examining each one to demonstrate a growing incongruence between developments in the relevant areas and labour law's rigid attachment to perceived historical approaches. This was demonstrated in particular in the areas of privity of contract, and the implications of the 'corporate veil', resulting from the operation of the doctrines of corporate personality and limited liability. Discussion finally moved on to exploring the need for an overarching concept of the employer, developing the formal and substantive expectations against which the existing and proposed approaches could be measured. Analysed thus, the received concept fails to achieve its basic tasks in nearly all situations beyond a narrow factual paradigm, whereas the reconceptualized strands ensure that there is a clear overarching concept of the employer, which can unify even complex multilateral manifestations of shared employer functions.

Translating the Functional Concept into Practice

A brief return to the examples first seen in Chapter 3 can helpfully illustrate the implications of the proposed development in practice. In exploring how the received concept of the employer leaves the scope of employment protective legislation fragile and incoherent, discussion there showed how employment law coverage could break down completely in triangular agency employment settings, or identify inappropriate entities as the bearer of employment law obligations in complex group structures.

In the agency work setting, first, the key problem with the received unitary concept was its emphasis on identifying a single employer, even though the relevant functions were parcelled out between an employment agency and a client or end-user. As a result, workers are often left without a contract of employment with either party. Under a functional concept of the employer, on the other hand, this would not be the case: the multilateral dimension of that work arrangement no longer stands in the way of identifying responsible employers.[1]

Take the Court of Appeal's decision in *Bunce v Postworth* as an example.[2] As explained in Chapter 3, the applicant there was a welder on the books of an employment agency, Skyblue, which in turn was an 'associated company' of Carillion Rail, a railway maintenance and civil engineering firm.[3] Over the course of Mr Bunce's employment, the agency exercised a range of employer functions, including payment, training, and the provision of certification materials and tools.[4] Once at the actual job sites, however, the welder worked directly under the control of Carillion. Under a unitary concept of the employer, that division of functions was 'really fatal to [the claimant's] case'.[5]

When using the functional concept of the employer proposed, on the other hand, the complex fact pattern is no longer automatically excluded from the personal scope of employment law. Depending on the exercise of particular functions, responsible entities can quickly be identified. If the worker's claim was one for purposes of minimum wage protection, the relevant employer would be the agency, as it was in charge of monthly payments. If, on the other hand, the issue at stake was an onsite health and safety violation, the railway company would be the relevant employer, as its employees directed the work and inspected its results.[6] In case of an unfair dismissal claim (the underlying question at stake in *Bunce* itself), the employment tribunal's finding of fact as to who exercised the relevant function would determine responsibility: if, as on the facts of *Bunce*, the termination was the result of action taken jointly by the end-user and the agency,[7] both entities would fall within the provisions of section 94 ERA 1996.

---

[1] D McCann, *Regulating Flexible Work* (OUP 2008) 147.
[2] *Bunce v Postworth Limited t/a Skyblue* [2005] EWCA Civ 490, [2005] IRLR 557.
[3] *Bunce v Postworth* (n 2) [3].   [4] *Bunce v Postworth* (n 2) [9].
[5] *Bunce v Postworth* (n 2) [29]–[30].   [6] *Bunce v Postworth* (n 2) [10].
[7] *Bunce v Postworth* (n 2) [12].

In giving effect to this broader scope of employment law, the courts could draw on a range of techniques discussed in the third part: a contractual relationship could be implied despite (or indeed because of) *James v Greenwich LBC*, as the functional concept of the employer meets the necessity criterion so firmly adopted there: as suggested in Chapter 5, that very enquiry (as to which contractual structures are necessary 'in order to give business reality to a transaction and to create enforceable obligations between parties'[8]) is a functional one in the sense of the proposed reconceptualization, insofar as it looks at the reality of the parties' actions, rather than the formal structure of their relationships.

A second example set out in Chapter 3 concerned the identification of a relevant employer in corporate group settings, as seen in the case of *Fujitsu Siemens*.[9] There, the fundamental issue at stake was which entity in a cross-European group should be responsible to comply with the obligation to inform and consult with employee representatives in the case of collective redundancies:[10] the local plant management in Finland, or the group board in the Netherlands. Whilst the Court of Justice noted that 'in the context of a group of undertakings . . . [the] decision by the parent company which has the direct effect of compelling one of its subsidiaries to terminate the contracts of employees . . . [could] be taken only on the conclusion of the consultation procedure within that subsidiary',[11] it nonetheless concluded that the Directive's obligations were squarely based on the Finnish plant management as the 'employer, in other words a natural or legal person who stands in an employment relationship with the workers who may be made redundant'.[12] An undertaking, even if capable of controlling the employer through binding decisions, was said not to have that status: a unitary concept of the employer, which looks merely at the presence of a single factor (viz, the presence of a contract of employment), thus placed the obligation on an unsuitable entity. As the local company's management had no option but to implement the decisions taken by the Dutch holding company, little if any meaningful dialogue between worker representatives and the actual decision-maker could take place.

The functional concept of the employer, on the other hand, would have identified the parent company as the relevant employer for purposes of the redundancy decision, as well as involving the local entity if its management had scope to affect the outcome: taking the actual decision as to the future employment of a large group of workers is the key function regulated by Directive 59/1998. In different contexts, the same concept may of course lead to different outcomes, given its focus on the exercise of relevant functions. If local management had decided to use collective redundancies for part of its workforce as a pretext to fire protected

---

[8] *James v Greenwich LBC* [2008] EWCA Civ 35, [2008] ICR 545 [23], [42]; citing *The Aramis* [1989] 1 Lloyd's Rep 213 (CA) 224.

[9] Case C-44/2008 *Akavan Erityisalojen Keskusliitto AEK ry and Others v Fujitsu Siemens Computers Oy* [2009] ECR I-8163.

[10] Council Directive (EC) 59/1998 on the approximation of the laws of the Member States relating to collective redundancies [1998] OJ L225/16, art 2.

[11] *Fujitsu Siemens* (n 9) [71].   [12] *Fujitsu Siemens* (n 9) [57]–[58].

employees, such as trade union representatives, for example, the relevant sanctions would apply to the daughter undertaking alone.

Even a brief re-analysis of two problematic cases from earlier chapters has thus demonstrated that a functional concept of the employer would have had a significant impact in both areas, avoiding the breakdown of employment law coverage and the identification of inappropriate counterparties, respectively. The operation of both strands is clearly visible: as regard the functional strand, employment law obligations are placed on the entity or entities exercising the relevant function: a question of fact, to be determined by employment tribunals acting as an expert 'industrial jury'.[13] The personal scope of employment law becomes responsive to the individual regulatory goals of each layer or domain, and thus resilient to complex organizational settings.

As regards the unitary strand, the previous chapter suggested that any reconceptualization could only be successful if the concept of the employer remained a unitary one, in the limited formal sense of being able to identify 'the employer' according to the same clear singular set of criteria in all circumstances. Whilst the substantive outcomes in the above examples are indeed very different, the application of a single underlying concept ensures that conceptual unity is retained. A functional concept of the employer is therefore able to grapple with both sources of complexity in identifying responsible counterparties as highlighted by Fudge: it does not interfere with 'the freedom of entrepreneurs to structure their business enterprise as they see fit' and recognizes 'the plurality of different legal contexts and legal norms that make up the broad field of employment law and labour law'.[14]

In concluding these practical illustrations, it is important to keep in the mind the important caveat set out throughout Part III, viz that whilst there are a series of potential avenues to translate the functional concept of the employer into practice, such an approach has not yet been embraced coherently by the English courts. As Chapter 6 in particular was at pains to show, however, many of the factors which originally shaped the unitary concept of the employer—from a strict bilateral contractual analysis to the separate legal personality of different entities within a group—have today given way to broader, context-specific approaches

Restoring the Personal Scope of Employment Law

Previous chapters noted three important criteria in reconceptualizing the definition of the employer in English law: any solution proposed was to recognize both the heterogeneity of modern-day work arrangements and the multiplicity of contexts within which employment protective norms operate; to recognize a clearly functional approach in order to overcome the received formalistic attachment

---

[13] *Williams v Compair Maxam Ltd* [1982] ICR 156 (EAT) 160; though cf now B Hepple, 'Back to the Future: Employment Law under the Coalition Government' (2013) 42 ILJ 203, 212.

[14] J Fudge, 'The Legal Boundaries of the Employer, Precarious Workers, and Labour Protection' in G Davidov and B Langile (eds), *Boundaries and Frontiers of Labour Law* (Hart 2006) 304.

to enterprise structures; and at the same time to remain practically feasible within the established understanding of the legal construction of employment relationships. These criteria were developed and applied throughout, while suggesting that a final hurdle was still to be overcome: could the functional concept of the employer proposed successfully resolve the fundamental problem identified at the outset, viz the tension between a unitary and a multi-functional perception of the employer?

Preceding chapters hope to have demonstrated that the only way the reconceptualization of a definition as fundamental as that of the employer can be successful is by directly addressing the inherent tension identified at the outset. It is not possible simply to ignore either the unitary or the multi-functional strand by radically departing from the existing case law. Partial statutory or judicial interventions are similarly bound to unravel, as they look to the symptoms rather than the cause of existing problems, and further perpetuate the received approach. Indeed, it is in this regard that most previous attempts at grappling with the question at hand have struggled.

The proposed reconceptualization, on the other hand, responds directly to the specific problems identified in earlier parts, both as regards the theoretical setup and its practical implications. It addresses the two strands to build on their respective strengths and to remedy specific weaknesses in a careful modification that takes account of the interdependence of the concept's functional and unitary aspects. The resulting concept of the employer continues to rely on a single definition, whilst recognizing the potential exercise of employer functions across a range of entities: the unitary concept has become functional.

By resolving the tension at the heart of the received concept, the reconceptualization allows for conceptual unity in the face of factual complexity. What, however, are the broader (normative) implications of this resolution? The underlying purpose of this work was of course not just the technical analysis and development of a theoretical construct. Once slotted into the broader edifice of the contract of employment as the key regulatory device in employment law, the functional concept of the employer has the potential to restore coherence to the personal scope of employment law, bringing complex multilateral relationships back within the coverage of the contract of service. This conceptual restoration of personal scope will on occasion go hand in hand with an extension of the application of existing employment law norms beyond their current reach. This is the main practical outcome of the proposed reconceptualization: entities exercising employer functions beyond the reach of the current, unitary concept will come to be recognized, and thus regulated, as such. By correctly identifying a broad range of potential counterparties, the functional concept of the employer therefore allows the contract of employment to regain its proper functionality in complex employment settings.[15]

As discussion of the contract conundrum in Part I showed, the concept of the employer is intimately linked to the structure of the contract of employment

---

[15] In the *ex post facto* sense as developed in Chapter 5.

in English law. Historically, that meant that a unitary concept of the employer was driven not least by English law's 'adherence to the contract of employment as a normative category [which] gives rise to a legal analysis of personal work relations in essentially binary terms with which theorists and practitioners of employment have constantly to struggle, because of its constant and increasing counter-factuality'.[16] Given the close link between the structural analysis of the employment relationship as a contractual one and the nature of the parties privy to it, however, a functional concept of the employer has the potential to restore the scope of employment law by opening up ways to bring complex multilateral scenarios back within the scope of employment protective norms.

A differentiated understanding of the employer allows the contract of employment to encompass many more work arrangements than the current, narrow approach. It is for that reason that the functional concept proposed eschews any clean break from the underlying contractual model, and advocates careful development instead. The work, in that sense, subscribes to a view of developing 'employment law within a framework which remains an essentially contractual one',[17] especially as 'both in theoretical terms and in terms of positive law, general contract law is evolving from an apparatus primarily for the construction and enforcement of voluntary agreements into a body of law for the regulating of contracting in a wider sense'.[18] As Deakin has recently argued, the 'initial conditions of [the standard employment relationship's] origins—the vertically integrated industrial enterprise and the male breadwinner family—do not exhaust the conditions of its application. The SER continues to evolve and to adjust to its changing economic context'.[19]

A functional concept of the employer provides one important element in the necessary theoretical underpinning to allow the contract of employment to develop so as to bring complex multilateral relationships back within its scope: situations such as triangular agency employment or Private Equity-owned corporate groups fell outside regulatory reach precisely because of the tensions identified. 'Protection for employees in the workplace is being compromised by a number of ambiguities in the employment relationship';[20] with the fundamental tension in the concept of the employer resolved, a more inclusive evolution of that relationship becomes possible.

A final potential objection remains to be addressed. It might be suggested that the proposed ascription of employer responsibility to a wide range of entities might in reality constitute a more significant practical step than the measured

---

[16] P Davies and M Freedland, 'The Complexities of the Employing Enterprise' in G Davidov and B Langile (eds), *Boundaries and Frontiers of Labour Law* (Hart 2006) 274.

[17] M Freedland, *The Personal Employment Contract* (OUP 2003) 520.

[18] Freedland, *The Personal Employment Contract* (n 17) 522.

[19] S Deakin, 'The Standard Employment Relationship in Europe—Recent Developments and Future Prognosis' (2014) 5 Soziales Recht 89, 96.

[20] D Grimshaw, M Marchington, J Rubery, and H Willmott, 'Conclusion: Redrawing Boundaries, Reflecting on Practice and Policy' in M Marchington, D Grimshaw, J Rubery, and H Willmott (eds) *Fragmenting Work—Blurring Organizational Boundaries and Disordering Hierarchies* (OUP 2005) 281.

development envisaged by discussion in the preceding paragraphs: the restoration of the personal scope can also be seen as an extension of liability, placing obligations on a wider range of actors than those hitherto identified as 'the employer'. Such an extension of liability beyond 'capital boundaries'[21] could be said to run counter to the allocations of property and contractual rights made by the controllers of an enterprise,[22] which would, at least initially, test 'the limits of a contractual analysis of employment'.[23]

Upon closer inspection, however, these arguments have been shown to be much less clear-cut. Where several entities share a close economic connection, for example, 'the case for discovering routes which circumvent privity in order to give the notional third party rights appears particularly pressing'.[24] Indeed, even corporate law scholarship has long recognized that the boundaries drawn by a company's separate legal personality are less absolute than often assumed,[25] with individual contexts warranting departures from a formalistic attachment to the corporate veil.[26] The functional identification of the most appropriate party, or combination of parties, to bear different employer obligations might even lead to increased economic efficiency and a decline in avoidance efforts: employers' incentives will be optimized once 'costs [are] borne by the activity which causes them'.[27]

In the final analysis, any *practical* increase in employer responsibility can ultimately be justified as no more than a restoration of coherence in the personal scope of employment law: only a functional concept of the employer will ensure that the contract of employment continues to encapsulate a wide range of different employment models, and that it will therefore be able to continue in the performance of its 'crucial functions in a market-based economy even in an era of deregulation and liberalization: . . . to serve as a device for shifting and controlling for the social risks of a loss of income through sickness, unemployment and old age'.[28]

Chapter 6 demonstrated how the concept of the employer plays a crucial role in this larger redistributive functionality of the contract of employment: it serves as the attachment point for regulation which ensures the trade-off between economic dependence and social protection. As long as the conceptualization of that key element in the contractual structure is riddled with internal contradictions, its overall role will only be fulfilled in an increasingly narrow set of single-entity

---

[21] H Collins, 'Ascription of Legal Responsibility to Groups in Complex Patterns of Economic Integration' (1990) 53 MLR 731.

[22] S Deakin, ' "Enterprise Risk": The Juridical Nature of the Firm Revisited' (2003) 32 ILJ 97, 97ff.

[23] Fudge, 'Legal Boundaries of the Employer' (n 14) 31.

[24] Collins, 'Ascription of Legal Responsibility to Groups' (n 21) 735.

[25] H Hansmann and R Kraakman, 'Towards Unlimited Shareholder Liability for Corporate Torts' (1991) 100 Yale Law Journal 1879.

[26] P Davies, *Introduction to Company Law* (2nd edn Clarendon Law Series, OUP 2010) 33.

[27] G Calabresi 'Some Thoughts on Risk Distribution and the Law of Torts' (1961) 70 Yale Law Journal 499, 533.

[28] S Deakin, 'The Comparative Evolution of the Employment Relationship' in G Davidov and B Langile (eds), *Boundaries and Frontiers of Labour Law* (Hart 2006) 104.

employment settings. In an economy marked by complex multilateral work arrangements and a multiplicity of regulatory contexts, on the other hand, the concept of the employer (and thus the contract of employment) can only discharge its broader regulatory role if it can encapsulate complex structures of management and control, recognizing inputs both from within and beyond (legal) organizational boundaries.

By resolving the tension between the unitary and the functional strand, the concept of the employer (and thus the contract of employment at large) can once more focus on its integral risk-distributive function. In practice, the range of entities which will become subject to employment law obligations may well be extended beyond its current level. As preceding chapters hope to have demonstrated, however, this is done in a principled and coherent way; indeed, from a broader normative perspective that extension is a necessary step to restore the coherent operation of the contract of employment, and thus employment law at large. The overarching normative argument is perhaps put most clearly by Weil in noting that:

Realigning the incentives driving businesses at the lead of industries in our economy could move the standards upward once again, making the network of workplaces that underlie many industries better places for workers at all levels of skill and education even while enjoying the advantages that arise from harnessing new ways of organizing production.[29]

Fudge, drawing on Woodiwiss,[30] has suggested that one factor that has historically kept courts from embracing an openly functional concept of the employer was the fear that this would lead to a lack of consistency and coherence across different domains.[31] As this work has demonstrated, however, the opposite is in fact the case: it is the current approach that leads to inconsistency and incoherence in employment law coverage. Indeed, only a functional concept of the employer may overcome these problems by addressing the tension at the very core of the received approach: the proposed reconceptualization seeks to restore conceptual coherence by re-establishing an underlying unitary concept, straddling the different legal domains in which the problem arises. Once this tension at the conceptual level is resolved, the concept of the employer can once more play an important role in ensuring that the scope of employee-protective norms will become resilient to domain-, entity-, and function-specific variations.

In his exploration of complex employment settings, Collins concluded that any potential solution required:

extremely subtle legal principles . . . [which] . . . continue to respect the general principle that one person should not be held responsible for the actions of another, whilst recognising that the formal separation of legal identities in complex economic organisations may

---

[29] D Weil, *The Fissured Workplace—Why Work Became so Bad for so Many, and What Can be Done to Improve It* (Harvard University Press 2014) 289.

[30] A Woodiwiss, *Social Theory after Post-Modernism: Rethinking Production, Law and Class* (London, Pluto Press, 1990).

[31] Fudge, 'Legal Boundaries of the Employer' (n 14) 310–11.

conceal what in reality constitutes a single set of productive relations . . . for the purpose of the ascription of legal responsibility.[32]

It is hoped that the functional concept of the employer developed in this work will provide employment law with just such a model for ascribing responsibility in a clear, yet nuanced way, and that the preceding chapters have presented some initial pointers towards the paths which might be followed in its adoption.

---

[32] Collins, 'Ascription of Legal Responsibility to Groups' (n 21) 744.

Bibliography

Achleitner A-K and Kloeckner O, 'Employment Contribution of Private Equity and Venture Capital in Europe' (EVCA Research Paper 2005).

Akerlof G, 'The Market for "Lemons": Qualitative Uncertainty and the Market Mechanism' (1970) 84 Quarterly Journal of Economics 488.

Albin E, 'A Worker–Employer–Customer Triangle: The Case of Tips' (2011) 40 ILJ 181.

Albin E, 'The Case of Quashie: Between the Legalisation of Sex Work and the Precariousness of Personal Service Work' (2013) 42 ILJ 80.

Alchian A and H Demsetz, 'Production, Information Costs, and Economic Organization' (1972) 62 The American Economic Review 777.

Allan P, 'The Contingent Workforce; Challenges and New Directions' (2002) American Business Review 103.

Allen & Overy, 'ECJ Confirms its Broad Interpretation of the Scope of Transfer of Undertakings Protection' (London 2010).

Allen W, Kraakman R, and Subramanian G, *Commentaries and Cases on the Law of Business Organization* (2nd edn Wolters Kluwer, New York 2007).

Amess K, Brown S, and Thompson S, 'Management Buy-Outs, Supervision and Employee Discretion' (2007) 54 Scottish Journal of Political Economy 447.

Amess K and Wright M, 'The Wage and Employment Effects of Leverage Buyouts in the UK' (2007) 14 International Journal of the Economics of Business 179.

Ancel M, *Utilité et Méthodes du Droit Comparé: Eléments d'Introduction Générale à l'étude Comparative des Droits* (Ides et Calendes, Neuchâtel 1971).

Annus T, 'Comparative Constitutional Reasoning: The Law And Strategy Of Selecting The Right Arguments' (2004) 14 Duke Journal of Comparative and International Law 301.

Annuß G, 'Die rechtsmissbräuchliche Unternehmerentscheidung im Konzern (2003) 20 NZA 783.

Anon, 'Locust, pocus—German Capitalism' (*The Economist*, 7 May 2005).

Anon, 'TUPE: When is a Share Sale Not a Share Sale?' (Linklaters 2007).

Appelbaum E and Batt R, *Private Equity at Work—When Wall Street Manages Main Street* (Russel Sage Foundation, New York 2014).

Archarya V, Kehoe C, and Reyner M, 'Private Equity vs PLC Boards: A Comparison of Practices and Effectiveness' (2009) 21 Journal of Applied Corporate Finance 45.

Armour J, Mayer C, and Polo A, 'Regulatory Sanctions and Reputational Damage in Financial Markets' CELF conference paper, Oxford 13 April 2011.

Arrowsmith J, 'Temporary Agency Work in an Enlarged European Union' (Office for Official Publications of the European Communities, Luxembourg 2006).

AS Associates, *The Impact of Private Equity as a UK Financial Service* (BVCA, London 2008).

Aziz M, Barber B, Beeston K, Bennett F, Bunting M, Cartmail G, Coulter D, Dromey J, Earl B, Hannett J, Manasseh L, Myner P, O'Grady F, Prentis D, Ritchie A, and Verne J, 'Hard Work, Hidden Lives: The Full Report' (TUC Commission on Vulnerable Employment, London 2008).

Bäck U and Winzer T, 'BAG Konzernbetriebsrat—Möglichkeit eines Sparten-konzernbetriebsrats?' (2011) 38 NZG 944.

Bacon N, Wright M, and Demina N, 'Management Buy-Outs and Human Resource Management' (2004) 42 BJIR 325.

Bacon N, Meuleman M, Scholes L, and Wright M, 'Assessing the Impact of Private Equity on Industrial Relations in Europe' (2010) 63 Human Relations 1343.

Bamforth N, Malik M, and O'Cinneide C, *Discrimination Law: Theory and Context* (Thomson Sweet & Maxwell, London 2008).

Barmes L, 'Learning from Case Law Accounts of Marginalised Working' in J Fudge, S McCrystal, and K Sankaran (eds), *Challenging the Legal Boundaries of Work Regulation* (Oñati International Series in Law and Society Hart, Oxford 2012).

Barmes L, Collins H, and Kilpatrick C, 'Reconstructing Employment Contracts' (2007) 36 ILJ 1.

Barrett B, 'Commentary: Employers' Criminal Liability Under HSWA 1974' (1997) 26 ILJ 149.

Bauer J and Herzberg D, 'Arbeitsrechtliche Probleme in Konzernen mit Matrixstrukturen' (2011) 28 NZA 713.

Bell J and Engle G, *Cross on Statutory Interpretation* (3rd edn Butterworths, London 1995).

Bennion F, *Bennion on Statutory Interpretation: A Code* (5th edn Lexis Nexis, London 2008).

Bercusson B, *European Labour Law* (2nd edn CUP, Cambridge 2009).

Berglöf E, 'Reforming Corporate Governance: Redirecting the European Agenda' (1997) 12 Economic Policy 91.

Berkhout E, Dustmann C, and Emmder P, 'Mind the Gap' (International Database on Employment and Adaptable Labour, Amsterdam 2007).

Berle A and Means G, *The Modern Corporation and Private Property* (The Macmillan Company, New York 1939).

Bevilacqua J, 'Convergence and Divergence: Blurring the Lines between Hedge Funds and Private Equity Funds' (2006) 54 Buffalo Law Review 251.

Biedenkopf K, 'Konzernbetriebsrat und Konzernbegriff' in P Zonderland (ed), *Liber amicorum Sanders* (Kluwer, Deventer 1973).

Bloom N, van Reenen J, and Sadun R, 'Do Private Equity-Owned Firms Have Better Management Practices?' in J Lerner and A Gurung (eds), *The Global Impact of Private Equity Report* 2008 (World Economic Forum, Davos 2008).

Blumberg P, 'Limited Liability and Corporate Groups' (1986) 11 Delaware Journal of Corporate Law 573.

Blumberg P, 'The Corporate Entity in an Era of Multinational Corporations' (1990) 15 Delaware Journal of Corporate Law 283.

Blumberg P, 'The Transformation of Modern Corporation Law: The Law of Corporate Groups' (2005) 37 Connecticut Law Review 605.

Boehm W and Pawlowski H, 'Konzernweite Beschäftigungsgarantien bei Umstrukturierung—aber was, wenn die "Heuschrecken" kommen?' (2005) 22 NZA 1377.

Bogg A, 'Sham Self-Employment in the Supreme Court' (2012) 41 ILJ 328.

Bogg A and Ewing K, 'The Implications of the *RMT* Case' (2014) 43 ILJ 221.

Borg-Barthet J, *The Governing Law of Companies in EU Law* (Hart, Oxford 2012).

Bradley A and Ewing K, *Constitutional and Administrative Law* (15th edn Pearson, Harlow 2010).

Brafman G and Wheeler J, 'Due Diligence—Management/Employees' in M Soundy, T Spangler, and A Hampton (eds), *A Practitioner's Guide to Private Equity* (City & Financial Publishing, Surrey 2009).

Brodie D, 'The Enterprise and the Borrowed Worker' (2006) 35 ILJ 87.

Brodie D, *Enterprise Liability and the Common Law* (CUP, Cambridge 2010).

Brodie D, 'Voice and the Employment Contract' in A Bogg and T Novitz, *Voices At Work—Continuity and Change in the Common Law World* (OUP, Oxford 2014).

Bromley P, *Family Law* (Butterworth, London 1957).

Brown E, 'Protecting Agency Workers: Implied Contract or Legislation?' (2008) 37 ILJ 178.

Bruner C, 'The Enduring Ambivalence of Corporate Law' (2008) 59 Alabama Law Review 1385.

Buchner H, 'Konzernbetriebsratsbildung trotz Auslandssitz der Obergesellschaft' in H Konzen, Krebber S, Veit B, and Waas B (eds), *Festschrift für Rolf Birk* (Mohr Siebeck, Tübingen 2008).

Burchell B, Deakin S, and Honey S, *The Employment Status of Individuals in Non-Standard Employment* (DTI, London 1999).

Burrows A, 'The Relationship between Common Law and Statute in the Law of Obligations' (2012) 128 LQR 232.

BVCA, 'February Briefing' (London 2010) 26.

BVCA, 'TUPE Briefing Note' (London 2008).

Cairns J, 'Development of Comparative Law in Great Britain' in M Reiman and R Zimmermann (eds), *The Oxford Handbook of Comparative Law* (OUP, Oxford 2007).

Calabresi G, 'Some Thoughts on Risk Distribution and the Law of Torts' (1961) 70 Yale Law Journal 499.

Calabresi G and Hirschoff J, 'Towards a Test for Strict Liability in Torts' (1972) 81 Yale Law Journal 1054.

Chacartegui C, 'Resocialising Temporary Agency Work Through a Theory of "Reinforced" Employers' Liability' in N Countouris and M Freedland, *Resocialising Europe in a Time of Crisis* (CUP, Cambridge 2013).

Cheffins B, 'Corporate Law and Ownership Structure: A Darwinian Link?' (2002) 25 University of New South Wales Law Journal 346.

Cheffins B and Armour J, 'The Eclipse of Private Equity' (2008) 33 The Delaware Journal of Corporate Law 1.

Clark I, 'The Private Equity Business Model and Associated Strategies for HRM: Evidence and Implications?' (2009) 20 The International Journal of Human Resource Management 2030.

Clifford Chance, 'AIFM Directive and Private Equity' (Client Briefing, London January 2011).

Coase R, 'The Nature of the Firm' (1937) 4 Economica 386.

Cohen F, 'Transcendental Nonsense and the Functional Approach' (1935) 35 Columbia Law Review 809.

Collins H, 'Labour Law as a Vocation' (1989) 105 LQR 468.

Collins H, 'Methods and Aims of Comparative Contract Law' (1989) 11 OJLS 396.

Collins H, 'Ascription of Legal Responsibility to Groups in Complex Patterns of Economic Integration' (1990) 53 MLR 731.

Collins H, 'Independent Contractors and the Challenge of Vertical Disintegration to Employment Protection Laws' (1990) 10 OJLS 353.

Collins H, 'Book Review: D McCann *Regulating Flexible Work* (OUP, Oxford 2008)' (200972 MLR 141.

Collins H, Davies P, and Rideout R, *Legal Regulation of the Employment Relation* (Kluwer Law International, London 2000).

Commission (EC), 'Proposal for a Directive of the European Parliament and of the Council on Alternative Investment Fund Managers and amending Directives 2004/39/EC and 2009/.../EC' COM(2009) 207 final, 30 April 2009.

Commission Report on Council Directive 2001/23/EC of 12 March 2001 on the approximation of the laws of the Member States relating to the safeguarding of employees' rights in the event of transfers of undertakings, businesses or parts of undertakings or businesses (Brussels, 18 June 2007) COM(2007) 334 final.

Cornelli F and Karakas O, 'Private Equity and Corporate Governance: Do LBOs Have More Effective Boards?' in J Lerner and A Gurung (eds), *The Global Impact of Private Equity Report* 2008 (World Economic Forum, Davos 2008).

Countouris N, *The Changing Law of the Employment Relationship: Comparative Analyses in the European Context* (Ashgate, Farnham 2007).

Countouris N and Horton R 'The Temporary Agency Work Directive: Another Broken Promise?' (2009) 38 ILJ 329.

Craig P and de Búrca G, *EU Law* (5th edn OUP, Oxford 2011).

Crawley R, 'Environmental Auditing and the *Good Samaritan* Doctrine: Implications for Parent Corporations' (1993) 28 Georgia Law Review 223.

Cressy R, Munari F, and Malipiero A, 'Creative Destruction? Evidence that Buyouts Shed Jobs to Raise Returns' (2011) 13 Venture Capital: An International Journal of Entrepreneurial Finance 1.

Crofts L, 'Buyout Firms should heed EC Action over Cartel Liability' (mLex Market Intelligence, London 25 July 2011).

de Cruz P, *Comparative Law in a Changing World* (3rd edn Routledge-Cavendish, Abingdon 2007).

Dannemann G, 'Comparative Law: Study of Similarities or Differences?' in M Reiman and R Zimmermann (eds), *The Oxford Handbook of Comparative Law* (OUP, Oxford 2007) 403.

Däubler W, 'Working People in Germany' (1999-2000) 21 CLLPJ 77.

Däubler W, 'Ausklammerung sozialer und personeller Angelegenheiten aus einem Beherrschungsvertrag' (2005) 32 NZG 617.

Davidov G, 'Joint Employer Status in Triangular Employment Relationships' (2004) 42 BJIR 727.

Davidov G, 'Who is a Worker?' (2005) 34 ILJ 57.

Davies P, 'Transfers—The UK Will Have to Make Up Its Own Mind' (2001) 30 ILJ 231.

Davies P, *Introduction to Company Law* (2nd edn Clarendon Law Series, OUP, Oxford 2010) 32.

Davies P and Freedland M, 'The Effects of Receivership upon Employees of Companies' (1980) 9 ILJ 95.

Davies P and Freedland M (eds), *Kahn-Freund's Labour and the Law* (3rd edn Stevens London 1983).

Davies P and Freedland M, *Labour Legislation and Public Policy* (OUP, Oxford 1993).

Davies P and Freedland M, 'The Employment Relationship in British Labour Law' in C Barnard, S Deakin, and G Morris (eds), *The Future of Labour Law: Liber Amicorum for Sir Bob Hepple QC* (Hart, Oxford 2004).

Davies P and Freedland M, 'The Complexities of the Employing Enterprise' in G Davidov and B Langile (eds), *Boundaries and Frontiers of Labour Law* (Hart Publishing, Oxford 2006).

Davies P and Freedland M, *Towards a Flexible Labour Market: Labour Legislation and Regulation since the 1990s* (Oxford Monographs on Labour Law, OUP, Oxford 2007).

Davies P and Worthington S, *Gower and Davies' Principles of Modern Company Law* (9th edn Sweet & Maxwell Ltd, London 2012).

Deakin S, 'The Evolution of the Contract of Employment, 1900 to 1950—the Influence of the Welfare State' in N Whiteside and R Salais (eds), *Governance, Industry and Labour Markets in Britain and France—The Modernising State in the Mid-Twentieth Century* (Routledge, London 1998).

Deakin S, 'Commentary. The Changing Concept of the "Employer" in Labour Law' (2001) 30 ILJ 72.

Deakin S, '"Enterprise Risk": The Juridical Nature of the Firm Revisited' (2003) 32 ILJ 97.

Deakin S, 'The Standard Employment Relationship in Europe—Recent Developments and Future Prognosis' (2014) 5 Soziales Recht 89.

Deakin S, 'The Comparative Evolution of the Employment Relationship' in G Davidov and B Langile (eds), *Boundaries and Frontiers of Labour Law* (Hart Publishing, Oxford 2006).

Deakin S and Morris G, *Labour Law* (6th edn Hart Publishing, Oxford 2012).

Deakin S and Wilkinson F, *The Law of the Labour Market* (Oxford Monographs on Labour Law, OUP, Oxford 2005) 90.

Dicey A, *Introduction to the Study of the Law of the Constitution* (Macmillan, London 1885).

Dickens L, 'Exploring the Atypical: Zero Hours Contracts' (1997) 26 ILJ 262.

Dickens L, 'Problems of Fit: Changing Employment and Labour Regulation' (2004) 42 BJIR 595.

DLA Piper, 'TUPE: *Albron Catering BV v FNV Bondgenoten*' (London 2010).

Douglas W, 'A Functional Approach to the Law of Business Associations' (1928-29) 23 Illinois Law Review 673.

Dromey J, 'Protect Workers from Private Equiteers' (*Financial Times*, London 3 July 2007).

Dugdale A and Jones M, *Clerk & Lindsell on Torts* (20th edn Sweet & Maxwell, London 2010).

Easterbrook F and Fischel D, 'Limited Liability and the Corporation' (1985) 52 University of Chicago Law Review 89.

Elias P and Bowers J, *Intelligence Report. Transfer of Undertakings: The Legal Pitfalls* (6th edn FT Law & Tax, London 1997).

EMAR, 'Agency Working in the UK: A Review of the Evidence' (Employment Relations Research Series No 93, BERR, London 2008).

Emmerich V and Habersack M, *Konzernrecht* (9th edn Beck, Munich 2008).

Employment Relations Directorate, 'Transfer of Undertakings (Protection of Employment Regulations 1981: Government Proposals for Reform. Detailed Background Paper' (DTI, London 2001).

Equality and Human Rights Commission (EHRC), 'Inquiry into Recruitment and Employment in the Meat and Poultry Processing Sector' (EHRC, London 2010).

Ernst & Young, 'How Do Private Equity Investors Create Value? A Study of 2006 Exits in the US and Western Europe' (London 2006).

European Commission, Explanatory Memorandum to the Proposal for a Council Directive amending Directive 75/129 COM(91) 292 Final; OJ 1991 C310.

Eversheds LLP, 'Terms and Conditions for the Supply of Services from an Employment Business to an End-User Client' (PLC Employment and PLC Commercial, Practical Law Company, London 2012).

Fabricius F, *Rechtsprobleme gespaltener Arbeitsverhältnisse im Konzern: Dargestellt am Rechtsverhältnis der Ruhrkohle Aktiengesellschaft zu ihren Betriebsführungsgesellschaften* (Luchterhand, Cologne 1982).

Fahlbeck R, 'Comparative Law—Quo Vadis?' (2003-2004) 25 CLLPJ 7.

Fedtke J, 'Legal Transplants' in J Smits (ed), *Elgar Encyclopedia of Comparative Law* (Edward Elgar, Cheltenham 2006).

Financial Services Authority, 'Private Equity: a Discussion of Risk and Regulatory Engagement' (Discussion Paper 06/6, London 2006).

Finkin M, 'Comparative Labour Law' in M Reiman and R Zimmermann (eds), *The Oxford Handbook of Comparative Law* (OUP, Oxford 2007).

Firth S and Watkins O, 'The Regulatory Environment for Funds and Private Equity Houses' in M Soundy, T Spangler, and A Hampton (eds), *A Practitioner's Guide to Private Equity* (City & Financial Publishing, Surrey 2009).

Forde C, ' "You know we are not an employment agency": Manpower, Government and the Development of the Temporary Employment Agency Industry in Britain' (2008) 9 Enterprise and Society 337.

Forde C, Slater G, and Green F, 'Agency Working in Britain: What Do We Know?' (Centre for Employment Relations Innovation and Change Policy Report Number 2, CERIC, Leeds 2008).

Forde C and Slater G, 'A Survey of Non Regular Work in the UK' (Report prepared for the Japan Institute of Labour Policy and Training, Tokyo 2010).

Forde C and Slater G, 'The Role of Employment Agencies in Pay Setting' (ACAS Research Paper 05/11, London 2011).

Franklin T, 'What Private Equity Investors Look For: Investments, Managers, Advisers and Professionals' in M Soundy, T Spangler, and A Hampton (eds), *A Practitioner's Guide to Private Equity* (City & Financial Publishing, Surrey 2009).

Franks J and Mayer C, 'Governance as a Source of Managerial Discipline' (2002) National Bank of Belgium Working Paper 31.

Franzen M, *Gemeinschaftskommentar zum Betriebsverfassungsgesetz: GK-BetrVG* (9th edn Beck, Munich 2010).

Freedland M, *The Personal Employment Contract* (OUP, Oxford 2003).

Freedland M, 'Otto Kahn-Freund (1900-1979)' in J Beatson and R Zimmermann (eds), *Jurists Uprooted—German Speaking Émigré Lawyers in Twentieth-century Britain* (OUP, Oxford 2004).

Freedland M, 'Developing the European Comparative Law of Personal Work Contracts' (2006-2007) 28 CLLPJ 487.

Freedland M and Davies P, 'National Styles in Labor Law Scholarship: the United Kingdom' (2001-2002) 23 CLLPJ 765.

Freedland M and Kountouris N, *The Legal Construction of Personal Work Relations* (OUP, Oxford 2011).

Freedland M and Kountouris N, 'Common Law and Voice' in A Bogg and T Novitz, *Voices At Work—Continuity and Change in the Common Law World* (OUP, Oxford 2014).

Freedland M and Kountouris N, 'Employment Equality and Personal Work Relations—A Critique of *Jivraj v Hashwani*' (2012) 41 ILJ 30.

Freedland M and Prassl J, 'Resolving Ownership Invention Disputes: Limitations of the Contract of Employment' in M Pittard (ed), *Business Innovation—A Legal Balancing Act* (Edward Elgar, Cheltenham 2012).

Freedland M and Prassl J (eds), *EU Law in the Member States: Viking, Laval and Beyond* (Hart, Oxford 2014).

Freshfields Bruckhaus Deringer, 'Simplifying the Application of the Acquired Rights Directive to Complex Corporate Structures?' (London 2010).

Froud J and Williams K, 'Private Equity and the Culture of Value Extraction' (2007) 12 New Political Economy 405.

Fudge J, 'Fragmenting Work and Fragmenting Organizations: the Contract of Employment and the Scope of Labour Regulation' (2006) 44 Osgoode Hall Law Journal 609.

Fudge J, 'The Legal Boundaries of the Employer, Precarious Workers, and Labour Protection' in G Davidov and B Langile (eds), *Boundaries and Frontiers of Labour Law* (Hart Publishing, Oxford 2006).

Fudge J, McCrystal S, and Sankaran K, *Challenging the Legal Boundaries of Work Regulation* (Oñati International Series in Law and Society, Hart, Oxford 2012).

Fudge J, Ticker E, and Vosko L, 'Changing Boundaries in Employment: Developing A New Platform for Labour Law' (2003) 10 CLELJ 329.

Gardner J, 'Liberals and Unlawful Discrimination' (1989) 9 OJLS 1.

Gardner J, 'On the Ground of Her Sex(uality)' (1998) 18 OJLS 167.

Gentz M, 'Das Arbeitsrecht im Internationalen Konzern' (2000) 17 NZA 3.

George R, 'The Veil of Incorporation and Post-Divorce Financial Remedies' (2014) 130 LQR 373.

Getzler J, 'The Role of Security over Future and Circulating Capital: Evidence from the British Economy circa 1850-1920' in J Getzler and J Payne (eds), *Company Charges: Spectrum and Beyond* (OUP, Oxford 2006).

Getzler J and Macnair M, 'The Firm as an Entity Before the Companies Acts' in P Brand, K Costello, and W Osborough (eds), *Adventures of the Law* (Four Courts Press, Dublin 2005) 267.

Gillen C and O Vahle, 'Personalabbau und Betriebsänderung' (2005) 22 NZA 1385.

Gilligan J and Wright M, *Private Equity Demystified: An Explanatory Guide* (2nd edn ICAEW Corporate Finance Faculty, London 2010).

Gompers P and Lerner J, *The Venture Capital Cycle* (MIT Press, Cambridge 2004).

Gospel H and Pendleton A, 'Corporate Governance and Labour Management: An International Comparison' in H Gospel and A Pendleton (eds), *Corporate Governance and Labour Management: An International Comparison* (OUP, Oxford 2005).

Gospel H and Pendleton A, 'Markets and Relationships: Finance, Governance, and Labour in the United Kingdom' in H Gospel and A Pendleton (eds), *Corporate Governance and Labour Management: An International Comparison* (OUP, Oxford 2005).

Gospel H and Pendleton A, 'Financialization, New Investment Funds, and Labour' in Gospel H, Pendleton A, and Vitols S (eds), *Financialization, New Investment Funds, and Labour—An International Comparison* (OUP 2014).

Gourevitch P and Shinn J, *Political Power and Corporate Control: The New Global Politics of Corporate Governance* (Princeton University Press, Princeton NJ 2005).

Gramm L and Schnell J, 'The Use of Flexible Staffing Arrangements in Core Production Jobs' (2001) 54 Industrial and Labour Relations Review 245.

Graziadei M, 'Comparative Law as the Study of Transplants and Receptions' in M Reiman and R Zimmermann (eds), *The Oxford Handbook of Comparative Law* (OUP, Oxford 2007).

Green S, 'The Impact of Ownership and Capital Structure on Managerial Motivation and Strategy in Management Buy-Outs: A Cultural Analysis' (1992) 29 Journal of Management Studies 513.

Greenberg D, *Craies on Legislation* (9th edn Sweet & Maxwell, London 2008).

Grimshaw D, Marchington M, Rubery J, and Willmott H, 'Conclusion: Redrawing Boundaries, Reflecting on Practice and Policy' in M Marchington, D Grimshaw, J Rubery, and H Willmott (eds), *Fragmenting Work: Blurring Organizational Boundaries and Disordering Hierarchies* (OUP, Oxford 2005).

Guardini, *Der Gegensatz. Versuch zu einer Philosophie des Lebendig-Konkreten* (4th edn Schoningh, Paderborn 1998).

Gullifer L and Payne J, *Corporate Finance Law: Principles and Policy* (Hart, Oxford 2011).

Gutteridge H, *Comparative Law: An Introduction to the Comparative Method of Legal Study & Research* (Cambridge Studies in International and Comparative Law, Cambridge University Press, Cambridge 1946).

Hacker J, *The Great Risk Shift: the New Economic Insecurity and the Decline of the American Dream* (OUP, New York 2008).

Hakansson K and Isidorsson T, 'Flexibility, Stability and Agency Work: A Comparison of the Use of Agency Work in Sweden and the UK' in B Furaker, K Hakansson, and J Karlsson, *Flexibility and Stability in Working Life* (Palgrave Macmillan, New York 2007).

Hall D, 'Methodological Issues in Estimating the Impact of Private Equity Buyouts on Employment' (Public Services International Research Unit, UNITE, London 2007).

Halpern P, Trebilcock M, and Turnbull S, 'An Economic Analysis of Limited Liability' (1980) 30 University of Toronto Law Journal 117.

Hampton A, 'Corporate Governance/Risk Management' in M Soundy, T Spangler, and A Hampton (eds), *A Practitioner's Guide to Private Equity* (City & Financial Publishing, Surrey 2009).

Hansmann H and Kraakman R, 'Towards Unlimited Shareholder Liability for Corporate Torts' (1991) 100 Yale Law Journal 1879.

Hansmann H and Kraakman R, 'The Essential Role of Organizational Law' (2000) 110 Yale Law Journal 387.

Hardy S, *Understanding TUPE—A Legal Guide* (Chandos Publishing Ltd, Oxford 2001).

Hardy S and Painter R, 'Revising the Acquired Rights Directive' (1996) 25 ILJ 160.

Harris R, Siegel D, and Wright M, 'Assessing the Impact of Management Buy-Outs on Economic Efficiency: Plant-Level Evidence from the United Kingdom' (2005) 87 The Review of Economics and Statistics 148.

Harlow C, 'Changing the Mindset: The Place of Theory in English Administrative Law' (1994) 14 OJLS 419.

Haves J, Vitols S, and Wilke P, 'Financialization and Ownership Change: Challenges for the German Model of Labour Relations' in H Gospel, A Pendleton, and S Vitols, *Financialization, New Investment Funds, and Labour* (OUP, Oxford 2014).

Heiden T, 'The New Limits of Limited Liability: Differing Standards and Theories for Measuring a Parent/Shareholder's Responsibility for the Operations of Its Subsidiaries' in Practising Law Institute (eds), *Protecting the Corporate Parent: Avoiding Liability for Acts of the Subsidiary* (Corporate Law and Practice Course Handbook Series, PLI 1993).

Heinsius J, 'Commentary on the EU Court's Decision in *Fujitsu*' (2010) 7 European Company Law 165.

Heinze M, 'Rechtsprobleme des sog. echten Leiharbeitsverhältnisses' (1976) 7 ZfA 183.

Heinze M and Söllner A, *Arbeitsrecht in der Bewährung: Festschrift für Otto Rudolf Kissel* (Beck, Munich 1994).

Hempel C, 'Typological Methods in the Social Sciences' in M Nathanson (ed), *Philosophy of the Social Sciences* (Random House, New York 1952).

Henssler M, *Der Arbeitsvertrag im Konzern* (Schriften zum Sozial- und Arbeitsrecht, Duncker & Humblot, Berlin 1983).

Henssler M, *Münchener Kommentar zum Bürgerlichen Gesetzbuch: BGB. Band 4: Schuldrecht* (6th edn Beck, Munich 2012).

Hepple B, 'Workers' Rights in Mergers and Takeovers: The EEC Proposals' (1976) 5 ILJ 197.

Hepple B, 'Recent Legislation: European Economic Community' (1977) 6 ILJ 106.

Hepple B, 'The Transfer of Undertakings (Protection of Employment) Regulations (1982)' 11 ILJ 29.

Hepple B, 'Back to the Future: Employment Law under the Coalition Government' (2013) 42 ILJ 203.

HgCapital Trust plc, *Annual Report and Accounts* (London 2009).

HMRC, *Employment Status Manual*, ESM2002: <http://www.hmrc.gov.uk/manuals/esmmanual/ESM2002.htm> accessed 1 October 2014.

Hofstetter K, 'Parent Responsibility for Subsidiary Corporations: Evaluating European Trends' (1990) 39 International and Comparative Law Quarterly 576.

Holland J, 'The Corporate Governance Role of Financial Institutions in Their Investee Companies' (Research Report No. 46, Chartered Association of Certified Accountants, London 1995).

Hope of Craighead L, 'Tailoring the Law on Vicarious Liability' (2013) 129 LQR 514.

Hopt K and Wiedemann H, *Großkommentar Aktiengesetz* (4th edn De Gruyter, Berlin 1999).

Hoque K, Kirkpatrick I, De Ruyter A, and Lonsdale C, 'New Contractual Relationships in the Agency Worker Market: the Case of the UK's National Health Service' (2008) 46 BJIR 389.

House of Commons, Private Equity (Transfer of Undertakings and Protection of Employment) Bill, Bill 28/07-08.

House of Commons Treasury Committee, *Interim Report on Private Equity* (10-I, 2006-07).

House of Lords Select Committee on the European Communities, Fifth Report, Session 1995-96: *Transfer of Undertakings: Acquired Rights* (HL Paper (1995-96) No 38).

Howes V, 'Commentary: Duties and Liabilities under the Health and Safety at Work Act 1974: A Step Forward?' (2009) 38 ILJ 306.

Hüffer U, *Aktiengesetz* (8th ed Beck, Munich 2008).

IE Consulting, 'The Economic Impact of Private Equity in the UK' (BVCA, London 2008).

James P, Johnstone R, Quinlan M, and Walters D, 'Regulating Supply Chains to Improve Health and Safety' (2007) 36 ILJ 163.

Jenkinson T, 'Private Equity' in European Economic Advisory Group (ed), *Report on the European Economy* (CESifo, Munich 2009) 124.

Jensen M, 'The Eclipse of the Public Corporation' (1989) 67 HBR 61; 1997 revision.

Johnson H, 'Contract Workers—Disability Discrimination and Reasonable Adjustments' (2009) 90 Employment Law Bulletin 6.

Jones C, 'Accounting and Organizational Change: An Empirical Study of Management Buy-Outs' (1992) 17 Accounting, Organizations and Society 151.

Joost D, *Betrieb und Unternehmen als Grundbegriffe im Arbeitsrecht* (Beck, Munich 1988).

Kahn-Freund O, 'Some Reflections on Company Law Reform' (1944) 7 MLR 54.

Kahn-Freund O, 'Comparative Law as an Academic Subject' (1966) 82 LQR 40.

Kahn-Freund O, 'On Uses and Misuses of Comparative Law' (1974) 37 MLR 120.

Kersley B, Alpin C, Forth J, Dix G, Oxenbridge S, Bryson A, and Bewley H, *Inside the Workplace: First Findings from the 2004 Workplace Employment Relations Survey* (Routledge, London 2005).

Keter V, 'Private Equity (Transfer of Undertakings and Protection of Employment) Bill 2007-08: Research Paper 08/23' (House of Commons Library, London 2008).

Kidner R, 'Vicarious Liability: for whom should the "Employer" be liable?' (1995) 15 LS 47.

Kirchner J, Kremp P, and Magotsch M (eds), *Key Aspects of German Employment and Labour Law* (Springer Verlag, Berlin 2010).

Kirkpatrick I, Hoque K, Lonsdale C, and De Ruyter A, 'Professional Agency Working in Health and Social Services: Implications for Management' (CERIC Policy Report Number 3, CERIC, Leeds 2009).

Kliemt M, *Formerfordernisse im Arbeitsverhältnis* (Müller, Heidelberg 1998).

Koberski W, Kleinsorge G, Wlotzke O, and Wißmann H, *Kommentar: Mitbestimmungsrecht* (4th edn Beck, Munich 2011).

Kohlbacher E, *Streikrecht und Europarecht* (Linde, Vienna 2014).

Konzen H, 'Arbeitnehmerschutz im Konzern' (1984) 36 RdA 65, 66.

Konzen H, 'Arbeitsrechtliche Drittbeziehungen: Gedanken über Grundlagen und Wirkungen der "Gespaltenen Arbeitgeberstellung"' (1982) 13 ZfA 259.

Konzen H, 'Arbeitsverhältnisse im Konzern' (1987) 151 ZHR 566.

Kort M, 'Bildung und Stellung des Konzernbetriebsrats bei nationalen und internationalen Unternehmensverbindungen' (2009) 26 NZA 464.

Kort M, 'Der Konzernbegriff i.S. von §5 MitbestG' (2009) 36 NZG 81.

Kraakman R and others, *The Anatomy of Corporate Law* (OUP, Oxford 2009).

Lawson F, 'The Field of Comparative Law' (1949) 61 Juridical Review 16.

Leighton P and Wynn M, 'Temporary Agency Working: is the Law on the Turn?' (2008) 29(1) Company Lawyer 7.

Leighton P and Wynn M, 'Classifying Employment Relationships—More Sliding Doors or a Better Regulatory Framework?' (2011) 40 ILJ 5.

Lembke M, 'Neue Rechte von Leiharbeitnehmern gegenüber Entleihern' (2011) 28 NZA 319.

Liebscher T, *Münchener Kommentar zum Gesetz betreffend die Gesellschaften mit beschränkter Haftung 2015 GmbHG* (Beck, Munich 2010).

Linklaters, 'Hot Topic: Duke Street Capital's £8m Pension "Hit"' (London 2008).

Lukes S, *Power: A Radical View* (Palgrave MacMillan, London 2005).

Lyon-Caen G, 'Arbeitsrecht und Unternehmenskonzentration' (1984) 36 RdA 285.

Markesinis B, *Comparative Law in the Courtroom and Classroom: The Story of the Last Thirty-Five Years* (Hart, Oxford 2003).

Markesinis B and Fedtke J, *Engaging With Foreign Law* (Hart, Oxford 2009).

Markova E and McKay S, 'Agency and Migrant Workers: Literature Review' (TUC Commission on Vulnerable Employment, London 2008).

Markova E and McKay S, 'Understanding the Operation and Management of Employment Agencies in the UK Labour Market' (TUC Commission on Vulnerable Employment, London 2008).

Marsden D, '"The Network Economy" and Models of the Employment Contract' (2004) 42 BJIR 659.

Martens K, 'Grundlagen des Konzernarbeitsrechts' (1984) 12 ZGR 417.

McCahill D and Willcock S, 'Restructuring Issues for Private Equity Houses' in M Soundy, T Spangler, and A Hampton (eds), *A Practitioner's Guide to Private Equity* (City & Financial Publishing, Surrey 2009).

McCann D, *Regulating Flexible Work* (OUP, Oxford 2008).

McGaughey E, 'Should Agency Workers be Treated Differently?' (LSE Working Papers 07/10, London 2010).

McKay S, 'Employer Motivations for Using Agency Labour' (2008) 37 ILJ 296.

McKendrick E, 'Vicarious Liability and Independent Contractors: A Re-Examination' (1990) 53 MLR 770.

McMullen J, 'An Analysis of the Transfer of Undertakings (Protection of Employment) Regulations 2006' (2006) 35 ILJ 113.

Meckling W and Jensen M, 'A Theory of the Firm: Managerial Behavior, Agency Costs and Ownership Structure' (1976) 3 Journal of Financial Economics 4.

Mehrhoff F, *Die Veränderung des Arbeitgeberbegriffs* (Schriften zum Sozial- und Arbeitsrecht Band 75, Duncker & Humblot, Berlin 1984).

Memorandum of Understanding between the BVCA and Inland Revenue on the Income Tax Treatment of Venture Capital and Private Equity Limited Partnerships and Carried Interest (London, 2003).

Merritt A, 'Control v Economic Reality: Defining the Contract of Employment' (1982) 10 Australian Business Law Review 105.

Merryman J, 'Comparative Law and Scientific Explanation' (Reports to the Academie Internationale du Droit Comparé, New York 1974).

Michaels R, 'The Functional Method of Comparative Law' in M Reiman and R Zimmermann (eds), *The Oxford Handbook of Comparative Law* (OUP, Oxford 2007).

Mitlacher L and Burgess J, 'Temporary Agency Work in Germany and Australia: Contrasting Regulatory Regimes and Policy Challenges' (2007) 23 International Journal of Comparative Labour Law and Industrial Relations 401.

Molitor E, *Das Wesen des Arbeitsvertrages: eine Untersuchung über die Begriffe des Dienst- und Werkvertrags, sowie des Vertrags über abhängige Arbeit* (Deichert, Leipzig 1925).

Morgan J, 'Publication Review: Networks as Connected Contracts' (2012) 128 LQR 472.

Morgenroth S, 'Employment Contracts and Further Legal Sources' in J Kirchner, P Kremp, and M Magotsch (eds), *Key Aspects of German Employment and Labour Law* (Springer Verlag, Berlin 2010).

Morin M, 'Labour Law and New Forms of Corporate Organization' (2005) 144 International Labour Review 5.

Muchlinski P, *Multinational Enterprise and the Law* (2nd edn OUP, Oxford 2007).

Müllner W, *Aufgespaltene Arbeitgeberstellung und Betriebsverfassungsrecht* (Schriften zum Sozial- und Arbeitsrecht, Duncker & Humblot, Berlin 1978).

Myners P, *Institutional Investment in the United Kingdom: A Review* (HM Treasury, London 2001).

Nogler L, 'Die Typologisch-Funktionale Methode am Beispiel des Arbeitnehmerbegriffs' (2009) 10 ZESAR 459.

Örücü AE, 'Methodology of Comparative Law' in J Smits (ed), *Elgar Encyclopedia of Comparative Law* (Edward Elgar, Cheltenham 2006).

Ottolenghi S, 'From Peeping Behind the Corporate Veil, to Ignoring It Completely' (1990) 53 MLR 338.

Payne J, 'Book Review: the Anatomy of Corporate Law' (2010) 11 EBOR 477.

Peacock L, 'MP Vows to Carry on Fighting for TUPE' Private Equity Deals' (Personnel today, London 10 March 2008).

Pendleton A and Gospel H, 'Financialization, New Investment Funds, and Weakened Labour: The Case of the UK' in H Gospel, A Pendleton, and S Vitols (eds), *Financialization, New Investment Funds, and Labour—An International Comparison* (OUP, Oxford 2014).

Pila J, ' "Sewing the Fly Buttons on the Statute": Employee Inventions and the Employment Context' (2012) 32 OJLS 265.

Pollert A and Charlwood A, 'The Vulnerable Worker in Britain and Problems at Work' (2009) 23 Work, Employment and Society 343.

Powell W, 'The Capitalist Firm in the Twenty-First Century: Emerging Patterns in Western Enterprise' in P DiMaggio (ed), *The Twenty-First Century Firm: Changing Economic Organization in International Perspective* (Princeton, Princeton University Press 2003).

Prassl J, 'The Notion of the Employer' (2013) 129 LQR 380.

Prassl J, 'Die Suche nach dem Arbeitgeber im Englischen Recht' (2013) 4 Europäische Zeitschrift für Arbeitsrecht 472.

Prassl J, 'L'emploi multilatéral en droit anglais: à la recherche du patron perdu' (2014) 4 Revue de Droit du Travail 236.

Prassl J, 'Three Dimensions of Heterogeneity' in M Freedland and J Prassl (eds), *EU Law in the Member States:* Viking, Laval *and Beyond* (Hart, Oxford 2014).

Prassl J, 'Members, Partners, Employees, Workers? Partnership Law and Employment Status Revisited' (2014) 43 ILJ 495.

Preis U, 'Legitimation und Grenzen des Betriebsbegriffs im Arbeitsrecht' (2000) 52 RdA 257.

Preis U, *Erfurter Kommentar zum Arbeitsrecht* (11th edn Beck, Munich 2011).

Press Release, 'TUC Lodges Complaint Against Government For Failing To Give Equal Pay To Agency Workers' (TUC, London 2 September 2013).

PriceWaterhouseCoopers, 'PE and VC Performance Measurement Survey' (BVCA, London 2008).

PriceWaterhouseCoopers, 'Private Equity and Venture Capital Report on Investment Activity 2008' (BVCA, London 2008).

PriceWaterhouseCoopers, 'Private Equity and Venture Capital Report on Investment Activity 2012' (BVCA, London 2013).

Purcell K, Purcell J, and Tailby S, 'Temporary Work Agencies: Here Today, Gone Tomorrow?' (2004) 42 BJIR 705.

Raade K and Dantas Machado C, 'Recent Developments in the European Private Equity Markets' 319 European Commission Economic Papers 27.

Radbruch G, *Einführung in die Rechtswissenschaft* (12th edn Köhler, Stuttgart 1969).

Raiser T, 'Einleitung' in K Forster, Grunewald B, Lutter M, and Semler J (eds), *Festschrift für Bruno Kropff. Aktien- und Bilanzrecht* (IDW, Düsseldorf 1997).

Ramm T, 'Die Aufspaltung der Arbeitgeberfunktionen (Leiharbeitsverhältnis, mittelbares Arbeitsverhältnis, Arbeitnehmerüberlassung und Gesamthafenarbeitsverhältnis)' (1973) 4 ZfA 263.

Rasmussen P, Report of the European Parliament with Recommendations to the Commission on Hedge Funds and Private Equity (A6-0338, Brussels 2008).

REC, *Flex Appeal: Why Freelancers, Contractors and Agency Workers Choose to Work This Way* (Recruitment & Employment Confederation 2014).

Reynold F, 'The Status of Agency Workers: A Question of Legal Principle' (2006) 35 ILJ 320.

Richardi R, *Münchener Handbuch zum Arbeitsrecht* (Beck, Munich 2009).

Richardi R, 'Arbeitnehmer als Beschäftigte' (2010) 27 NZA 1101.

Richardi R, Thüsing G, and Annuß G, *Betriebsverfassungsgesetz: BetrVG* (10th edn Beck, Munich 2006).

Rigby E and Felsted A, 'Pessina to Boost Alliance Boots Skincare Brands' (*Financial Times*, 28 April 2010).

Rixon F, 'Lifting the Veil Between Holding and Subsidiary Companies' (1986) 102 LQR 415.

Robens A, 'Report of the Committee on Health and Safety at Work,' Cmnd 5043 (London, 1972).

Robbie K, Wright M, and Thompson S, 'Management Buyins in the UK' (1992) 20 Omega 445.

Robbie K and Wright M, 'Managerial and Owernship Succession and Corporate Restructuring: the Case of Management Buy-Ins' (1995) 32 Journal of Management Studies 527.

Rogers J and Streeck W (eds), *Works Councils: Consultation, Representation, and Cooperation in Industrial Relations* (University of Chicago Press, Chicago 1995).

de Roo A and Jagtenberg R, *Settling Labour Disputes in Europe* (Kluwer, Deventer 1994).

Royston T, 'Agency Workers and Discrimination Law; *Muschett v HM Prison Service*' (2011) 40 ILJ 92.

Rubery J, Earnshaw J, and Marchington M, 'Blurring the Boundaries to the Employment Relationship: From Single to Multi-Employer Relationships in M Marchington, D Grimshaw, J Rubery, and H Willmott (eds), *Fragmenting Work: Blurring Organizational Boundaries and Disordering Hierarchies* (OUP, Oxford 2005).

Ruckelshaus C, Smith R, Leberstein S, and Cho E, *Who's the Boss: Resoring Accountability for Labor Standardas in Outsourced Work* (NELP, New York 2014).

Salamon E, 'Die Konzernbetriebsvereinbarung beim Betriebsübergang' (2009) 26 NZA 471.

Scheiwe K, 'Was ist ein funktionales Äquivalent in der Rechtsvergleichung? Eine Diskussion an Hand von Beispielen aus dem Familien- und Sozialrecht' (2000) 83 Kritische Vierteljahresschrift für Gesetzgebung und Rechtswissenschaft 30.

Schmidt R, 'Das Mitbestimmungsgesetz auf dem verfassungsrechtlichen Prüfstand' (1980) 19 Der Staat 235.

Schmidt R, 'The Need for a Multi-Axial Method in Comparative Law' in H Bernstein, H Kötz and U Drobnig (eds), *Festschrift für Konrad Zweigert* (Mohr, Tübingen 1981).

Schmidt R and Spindler G, *Finanzinvestoren aus Ökonomischer und Juristischer Perspektive* (Nomos, Baden-Baden 2008).

Schwab B, 'Der Konzernbetriebsrat—Seine Rechtsstellung und Zuständigkeit' (2007) 24 NZA 337.

Sharp G, *Buyouts: A Guide for the Management Team* (Montagu Private Equity, London 2009).

Shleifer A and Summers L, 'Breach of Trust in Hostile Takeovers' (1987) NBER Working Paper 2342.

Simitis S, 'Juridification of Labor Relations' in G Teubner (ed), *Juridification of Social Spheres* (Walter de Gruyter, Berlin 1987).

Simpson B, 'A Not So Golden Formula: In Contemplation or Furtherance of a Trade Dispute After 1982' (1983) 46 MLR 463.

Slaughter & May, *Private Equity and Competition Law: Liability for Infringements by Portfolio Companies* (Client Briefing, London 2011).

Smits J, 'Comparative Law and its Influence on National Legal Systems' in M Reiman and R Zimmermann (eds), *The Oxford Handbook of Comparative Law* (OUP, Oxford 2007).

Smits J, 'Redefining Normative Legal Science: Towards an Argumentative Discipline' in F Coomans, F Grünfeld, and M Kamminga (eds), *Methods Of Human Rights Research* (Intersentia, Antwerpen-Oxford 2009).

Spangler T, 'Private Equity Fund Structures' in M Soundy, T Spangler, and A Hampton (eds), *A Practitioner's Guide to Private Equity* (City & Financial Publishing, Surrey 2009).

Staab H, 'Der Arbeitnehmer-Gesellschafter der GmbH im Spannungseld zwischen Arbeitnehmerschutz und gesellschaftsrechtlichem Gläubigerschutz' (1995) 12 NZA 608.

Stanworth C and Druker J, 'Human Resource Solutions? Dimensions of Employers' Use of Temporary Agency Labour in the UK' (2006) 35 Personnel Review 175.

Stapleton J, *Product Liability* (Law in Context, Butterworths, London 1994).

Stevens R, 'A Servant of Two Masters' (2006) 122 LQR 201.

Strasser K, 'Piercing the Veil in Corporate Groups' [2005] 37 Connecticut Law Review 637.

Supiot A, *Beyond Employment: Changes in Work and the Future of Labour Law in Europe* (OUP, Oxford 2001).

Teklè T, 'Labour Law and Worker Protection in the South: An Evolving Tension Between Models and Reality' in T Teklè (ed), *Labour Law and Worker Protection in Developing Countries* (Hart Publishing, Oxford 2010).

Teubner, G, 'Unitas Multiplex: Corporate Governance in Group Enterprises' in D Sugarman and G Teubner (eds), *Regulating Corporate Groups in Europe* (Baden-Baden. Nomos, 1990).

Teubner, G, 'Nouvelles formes d'organisation et droit' (1993) 96 Revue Française de Gestion 50.

Teubner G and Collins H, *Networks as Connected Contracts* (Hart, Oxford 2011).

Thompsons Solicitors, 'An Acquired Taste: *Albron Catering BV v FNV Bondegenoten*' (London 2010).

Thornton P, *Inside the Dark Box: Shedding Light on Private Equity* (The Work Foundation, London 2007).

Trittin W, Däubler W, Kittner M, and Klebe T, *BetrVG—Kommentar für die Praxis* (10th edn Bund, Frankfurt am Main 2006).

van Haasteren F, Muntz A and Pennel D, *Economic Report: 2014 Edition* (CIET, Brussels 2014).

Walker D, 'Guidelines for Disclosure and Transparency in Private Equity' (London 2007).

Ward K, 'Making Manchester "Flexible": Competition and Change in the Temporary Staffing Industry' (2005) 36 Geoforum 223.

Waas B, *Konzernarbeitsrecht in Großbritannien* (Nomos, Baden-Baden 1993).

Wedderburn K, *Cases and Materials on Labour Law* (CUP, Cambridge 1967).

Wedderburn K, 'Multinationals and the Antiquities of Company Law' (1984) 47 MLR 87.

Wedderburn K, Lewis R, and Clark J (eds), *Labour Law and Industrial Relations: Building on Kahn-Freund* (Clarendon Press, Oxford 1983).

Weil D, *The Fissure Workplace—Why Work Became so Bad for so Many, and What Can be Done to Improve It* (Harvard University Press, Cambridge MA 2014).

Weiss M, 'The Future of Comparative Labor Law as an Academic Discipline and as a Practical Tool' (2003-2004) 25 CLLPJ 169.

Whish R and Bailey D, *Competition Law* (12th edn OUP, Oxford 2012).

Whittaker S, 'Privity of Contract and the Tort of Negligence: Future Directions' (1996) 16 OJLS 191.

Whittaker S, 'Reciprocity Beyond Privity' in P Kincaid (ed) *Privity: Private Justice or Public Regulation* (Dartmouth Ashgate, Aldershot 2001).

Whittaker S, 'Contract Networks, Freedom of Contract and the Restructuring of Privity of Contract' in F Cafaggi (ed), *Contractual Networks, Inter-Firm Cooperation and Economic Growth* (Edward Elgar, Cheltenham 2011).

Wiedemann H, *Die Unternehmensgruppe im Privatrecht* (Mohr Siebeck, Tübingen 1988).

Willemsen H, 'Erosion des Arbeitgeberbegriffs nach der Albron-Entscheidung des EuGH? Betriebsübergang bei gespaltener Arbeitgeberfunktion' (2011) 22 NJW 1546.

Williamson O, *The Economic Institutions of Capitalism* (The Free Press, New York 1985).

Winchester D, 'Thematic Feature: Temporary Agency Work in the UK' (National Report 2007; available through the EIROnline database at <http://www.eurofound.europa.eu> (accessed 1 October 2014).

Windbichler C, *Arbeitsrecht im Konzern* (Beck, Munich 1989).

Windbichler C, 'Unternehmerisches Zusammenwirken von Arbeitgebern als arbeitsrechtliches Problem. Eine Skizze auch vor dem Hintergrund der EG-Richtlinie zum Europäischen Betriebsrat in Unternehmensgruppen' (1996) 27 ZfA 1.

Woodiwiss A, *Social Theory after Post-Modernism: Rethinking Production, Law and Class* (Pluto Press, London 1990).

Wright M and Coyne J, *Management Buy-Outs* (Croom Helm, London 1985).

Wright M, Coyne J, and Lockley H, 'Management Buy-Outs and Trade Unions: Dispelling the Myths' (1984) 15 Industrial Relations Journal 45.

Wright M, Chiplin B, Thompson S, and Robbie K 'Management Buy-Outs, Trade Unions and Employee Ownership' (1990) 21 Industrial Relations Journal 137.

Wright M, Burrows A, Ball R, Scholes L, Meuleman M, and Amess K, *The Implications of Alternative Investment Vehicles for Corporate Governance: a Survey of Empirical Research* (OECD, Paris 2007).

Wynn M, 'Regulating Rogues? Employment Agency Enforcement and Sections 15–18 of the Employment Act 2008' (2009) 38 ILJ 64.

Wynn M and Leighton P, 'Will the Real Employer Please Stand Up? Agencies, Client Companies and the Employment Status of the Temporary Agency Worker' (2006) 35 ILJ 301.

Wynn M and Leighton P, 'Agency Workers, Employment Rights and the Ebb and Flow of Freedom of Contract' (2009) 72 MLR 91.

Wynn-Evans C, 'TUPE or not TUPE?' 94 Dechert Comment: PE Europe 8.

Zöllner W, Loritz K, and Hergenröder C, *Arbeitsrecht* (Beck, Munich 2008).

Zweigert K and Kötz H, *Introduction to Comparative Law* (Tony Weir tr, 3rd edn Clarendon Press, Oxford 1998).

Index

Index

Printed and bound by CPI Group (UK) Ltd, Croydon, CR0 4YY